ENGLISH ASSOCIATION STUDIES

WRITING HOME

POETRY AND PLACE IN NORTHERN IRELAND
1968–2008

ENGLISH ASSOCIATION STUDIES

ISSN 1750–3892

Series Editor
Norman Vance

The English Association was founded in 1906 to further knowledge, understanding and enjoyment of the English language and its literatures. English Association Studies, inaugurated to mark the centenary, seeks to advance these aims by publishing distinctive original research in the various areas and periods of English studies.

Proposals for the series are welcomed, and should be sent in the first instance to the Chief Executive of the Association, the series editor, or the publisher, at the address below.

Helen Lucas, The English Association, University of Leicester, Leicester LE1 7RH

Professor Norman Vance, Department of English, University of Sussex, Brighton BN1 9QN

Boydell & Brewer Limited, PO Box 9, Woodbridge, Suffolk, IP12 3DF

WRITING HOME

POETRY AND PLACE IN NORTHERN IRELAND
1968–2008

Elmer Kennedy-Andrews

D. S. BREWER

First published 2008
D. S. Brewer, Cambridge

ISBN 978–1–84384–175–3

D. S. Brewer is an imprint of Boydell & Brewer Ltd
PO Box 9, Woodbridge, Suffolk IP12 3DF, UK
and of Boydell & Brewer Inc,
668 Mt Hope Avenue, Rochester, NY 14620, USA
website: www.boydellandbrewer.com

A CIP catalogue record for this book is available
from the British Library

The publisher has no responsibility for the persistence
or accuracy of URLs for external or third-party internet websites
referred to in this book, and does not guarantee that any content on such
websites is, or will remain, accurate or appropriate

This publication is printed on acid-free paper

Printed in Great Britain by
CPI Antony Rowe, Chippenham, Wiltshire

CONTENTS

PREFACE AND ACKNOWLEDGEMENTS

This exploration of poetry and place in Northern Ireland is chiefly concerned with the poetry written since the 1960s. Following on from the introductory first chapter which sets the scene, Chapter 2 focuses on precursor poets, John Hewitt, Louis MacNeice and Patrick Kavanagh. While this triumvirate seemed a natural starting-point, these poets of course pick up rather than originate the debate about poetry and place which is as old as Irish poetry itself. Kavanagh is included even though he hails from outside Northern Ireland (but from within one of the historic nine counties of Ulster – Co. Monaghan), because of the profound and pervasive influence which he has exerted on the poets from the six-county Northern Ireland who came after him, from Seamus Heaney to Sinéad Morrissey. There is no conventional 'Conclusion' to the book, a deliberate decision taken in the hope of keeping the idea of an open-ended process in play.

Two chapters in this book revise and expand three essays which have appeared previously. A version of 'John Montague: Global Regionalist?' appeared in *The Cambridge Quarterly*, 35, 1 (2006), and is here expanded to give more detailed discussion of the nature and extent of the American influence on Montague's writing (of) home. Parts of the chapter on Heaney and Muldoon were published earlier in a collection of essays on the work of Paul Muldoon which I edited, *Paul Muldoon. Poetry, Prose, Drama. A Collection of Critical Essays* (Gerrards Cross, Colin Smythe, 2005), and in my essay 'Bringing it all Back Home: Robert Frost, Seamus Heaney and Paul Muldoon', which appeared in *English: The Journal of the English Association* (Summer 2007).

I would like to express my gratitude to the English Association Higher Education Committee for commissioning this study as one of a new series of English Association monographs. I would also like to thank the University of Ulster and the Arts and Humanities Research Council (AHRC) for granting me study leave and funding to complete the project. A particular debt is owed to Professor Norman Vance for encouragement and guidance throughout the preparation of this book, and especially for taking the time and trouble to read and comment on the typescript. My thanks also go to Professor Stan Smith for reviewing early chapters of the book for the AHRC's peer review process. While the emphases, shortcomings and errors of this book are all entirely my responsibility, I have profited immensely from discussions with these and other interested parties, including Professor John Wilson Foster, Professor Michael Parker and Dr Robin Marsh. Like many other researchers in the field of Irish literature in English, I have profited hugely from the invaluable resources contained in the *Eirdata* and *Ricorso* web sites created and managed by Dr Bruce Stewart of the University of Ulster. Thanks, too, to Alan Gillis, who kindly let me see poems in draft form before they went to press, and whose correspondence with me about his work I found most engaging and illuminating. I am indebted to my research students at the University of Ulster, in particular Dan McAllister.

To the following, I am grateful for permission to quote copyright material: Blackstaff Press, for poems by John Hewitt, Padraic Fiacc and James Simmons; Faber & Faber, for poems by Louis MacNeice, Seamus Heaney and Tom Paulin; Faber & Faber, Wake Forest University Press, for poems by Paul Muldoon; Jonathan Cape, for poems by Michael Longley and Leontia Flynn; The Gallery Press, Loughcrew, for poems by John Montague, James Simmons, Derek Mahon, Paul Muldoon, Ciaran Carson, Medbh McGuckian and Alan Gillis; Carcanet Press, for poems by Peter McDonald and Sinéad Morrissey; Oxford University Press, for poems by Derek Mahon and Medbh McGuckian.

Elmer Kennedy-Andrews
Coleraine, September 2007

ABBREVIATIONS

The abbreviations are used locally, chapter by chapter; context should resolve any apparent ambiguities.

AV   *Ancestral Voices: The Selected Prose of John Hewitt*, ed. Tom Clyde (Belfast, Blackstaff Press, 1987)

BA   Medbh McGuckian, *The Book of the Angel* (Loughcrew, The Gallery Press, 2004)

BC   Ciaran Carson, *Belfast Confetti* (Loughcrew, The Gallery Press, 1989)

BHMSB   Ciaran Carson, *The Ballad of HMS Belfast* (Loughcrew, The Gallery Press, 1999)

BHT   Sinéad Morrissey, *Between Here and There* (Manchester, Carcanet Press, 2002)

BN   Ciaran Carson, *Breaking News* (Loughcrew, The Gallery Press, 2003)

C   John Montague, *Company: A Chosen Life* (London, Duckworth, 2001)

CC   James Simmons, *The Company of Children* (Cliffs of Moher, Salmon Publishing, 1999)

CL   Medbh McGuckian, *Captain Lavender* (Loughcrew, The Gallery Press, 1994)

CP   Frank Ormsby (ed.), *The Collected Poems of John Hewitt* (Belfast, Blackstaff Press, 1991)

CP   Michael Longley, *Collected Poems* (London, Jonathan Cape, 2006)

CP   Derek Mahon, *Collected Poems* (Loughcrew, The Gallery Press, 1999)

CP   John Montague, *Collected Poems* (Loughcrew, The Gallery Press, 2003)

CS   Tom Paulin, *Crusoe's Secret: The Aesthetics of Dissent* (London, Faber, 2005)

DB   Medbh McGuckian, *Drawing Ballerinas* (Loughcrew, The Gallery Press, 2001)

DC   Seamus Heaney, *District and Circle* (London, Faber, 2006)

DS   John Montague, *Drunken Sailor* (Loughcrew, The Gallery Press, 2004)

F   Tom Paulin, *Fivemiletown* (London, Faber, 1987)

FBPV   Tom Paulin (ed.), *The Faber Book of Political Verse* (London, Faber, 1986)

FBVV   Tom Paulin (ed.), *The Faber Book of Vernacular Verse* (London, Faber, 1990)

FC	John Montague, *The Figure in the Cave* (Dublin, Lilliput Press, 1989)
FE	Medbh McGuckian, *The Face of the Earth* (Loughcrew, The Gallery Press, 2002)
FM	Medbh McGuckian, *The Flower Master* (Loughcrew, The Gallery Press, 1993)
FV	Sinéad Morrissey, *There was Fire in Vancouver* (Manchester: Carcanet Press, 1996)
GT	Seamus Heaney, *The Government of the Tongue* (London, Faber, 1988)
HBN	Derek Mahon, *The Hunt By Night* (Oxford, Oxford University Press, 1982)
HD	Alan Gillis, *Hawks and Doves* (Loughcrew, The Gallery Press, 2007)
HL	Seamus Heaney, *The Haw Lantern* (London, Faber, 1987)
HL	Derek Mahon, *Harbour Lights* (Loughcrew, The Gallery Press, 2005)
HRF	Joseph Brodsky, Seamus Heaney and Derek Walcott, *Homage to Robert Frost* (London, Faber, 1997)
IRA	Irish Republican Army
JG	James Simmons, *Judy Garland and the Cold War* (Belfast, Blackstaff, 1975)
LSSTC	James Simmons, *The Long Summer Still to Come* (Belfast, Blackstaff Press, 1973)
LT	Tom Paulin, *Liberty Tree* (London, Faber, 1983)
M	James Simmons, *Mainstream* (Upper Fairhill, Galway, Salmon Publishing, 1995)
M	Tom Paulin, *Minotaur: Poetry and the Nation State* (London, Faber, 1991)
MC	Medbh McGuckian, *Marconi's Cottage* (Loughcrew, The Gallery Press, 1991)
MI	Peter McDonald, *Mistaken Identities: Poetry and Northern Ireland* (Oxford, Clarendon Press, 1997)
MSG	Paul Muldoon, *Moy Sand and Gravel* (London, Faber, 2002)
N	Seamus Heaney, *North* (London, Faber, 1975)
OBB	Medbh McGuckian, *On Ballycastle Beach* (Oxford, Oxford University Press, 1988)
OED	*Oxford English Dictionary*
OG	Seamus Heaney, *Opened Ground: Poems 1966–1996* (London, Faber, 1998)
P	Seamus Heaney, *Preoccupations: Selected Prose 1968–1978* (London, Faber, 1980)
P	Paul Muldoon, *Poems 1968–1998* (London, Faber, 2001)
P	James Simmons, *Poems 1965–1986* (Loughcrew, The Gallery Press, 1986)
P	Peter McDonald, *Pastorals* (Manchester, Carcanet, 2004)
RP	Seamus Heaney, *The Redress of Poetry: Oxford Lectures* (London, Faber, 1995)

RP	Padraic Fiacc, *Ruined Pages: Selected Poems*, ed. Gerald Dawe and Aodán MacPóilin (Belfast, Blackstaff, 1994)
RUC	Royal Ulster Constabulary
S	Medbh McGuckian, *Shelmalier* (Loughcrew, The Gallery Books, 1998)
SAF	Louis MacNeice, *The Strings are False: An Unfinished Autobiography* (London, Faber, 1965)
SJ	Tom Paulin, *A State of Justice* (London, Faber, 1977)
SL	Seamus Heaney, (London, Faber, 1996)
SM	Tom Paulin, *The Strange Museum* (London, Faber, 1980)
SP	Sinéad Morrissey, *The State of the Prisons* (Manchester, Carcanet Press, 2005)
SP	John Montague, *Smashing the Piano* (Loughcrew, The Gallery Press, 1999)
SS	Alan Gillis, *Somebody, Somewhere* (Loughcrew, The Gallery Press, 2004)
ST	Seamus Heaney, *Seeing Things* (London, Faber, 1991)
SV	Padraic Fiacc, *Semper Vacare* (Belfast, Lagan Press, 1999)
TD	Leontia Flynn, *These Days* (London, Jonathan Cape, 2004)
TII	Paul Muldoon, *To Ireland, I* (Oxford, Oxford University Press, 2000)
UDA	Ulster Defence Association
UFF	Ulster Freedom Fighters
UVF	Ulster Volunteer Force
VR	Medbh McGuckian, *Venus and the Rain* (Loughcrew, The Gallery Press, 1994)
WD	Tom Paulin, *The Wind Dog* (London, Faber, 1999)
WL	Tom Paulin, *Walking a Line* (London, Faber, 1994)
WM	Tom Paulin, *Writing to the Moment* (London, Faber, 1996)

EDITORIAL CONVENTIONS

For most of the poets considered here, the Troubles provide a constant ground-swell. In the interests of simplicity I have avoided placing speech marks around this euphemism that has come into common usage in reference to the civil unrest that dated from around 1969. 'North' and 'South' have been employed as convenient references to, respectively, Northern Ireland and the Republic of Ireland, even though Co. Donegal extends the Republic further north than any point in Northern Ireland. The 'west', like 'north' and 'south', is a geographical reference, and is distinguished from the 'West', which refers to the geographical west of Ireland in its cultural and mythical dimensions. More generally, 'Western' is used to refer to the developed Euro-American world.

Chapter 1

INTRODUCTION: THE LIE OF THE LAND

Space and place are crucial regulators of our being in the world. Geographically, place is differentiated from space: space is abstract, featureless, indefinite; place is lived space, and carries connotations of familiarity, stability, attachment, nostalgia and homeliness.[1] Place is, first of all, constructed materially, through processes of interconnection and interdependence. However, the meaning of place is an imaginative project involving the production of images and the creation of identities which epitomise the culture of a particular place. Place has always figured importantly in the work of Irish writers – Yeats's and Lady Gregory's Co. Galway, J.M. Synge's Aran Islands, Patrick Kavanagh's Co. Monaghan, John Hewitt's Glens of Antrim, Seamus Heaney's Co. Derry, John Montague's Co. Tyrone, Michael Longley's Co. Mayo – and the writers, in turn, have contributed powerfully to the mystique of particular landscape traditions. In Ireland, place, culture and identity are closely interconnected concepts. Cultural identity has often been interpreted as bound up with place, whether through notions of local culture (the parish or region, for example) or through the more abstract constructions of national identity, which often invoke a supporting imagery drawn from a particular landscape (the west of Ireland as a source of true 'Irishness'). In the literature of place, then, we might expect to find an account of the individual's relationship with a particular place, its landscape, history, culture and people. We might also expect such literature to provide a communal set of images to help a group towards ideological self-representation and foster a sense of social integration and identity. Place literature might even promote cultural or national revival. While this was indeed largely a function of literature in the period around the foundation of the independent Irish state in 1922, place in the Northern Irish context remains contested, the cultural landscape a palimpsest

---

[1] See Edward Soja, *Thirdspace: Journeys to Los Angeles and Other Real-and-Imagined Places* (Oxford, Blackwells, 1996), in which he distinguishes between 'Firstspace' which is the '"real" material world', 'Secondspace' which refers to 'imagined' and ideological space, and 'Thirdspace' which is the 'lived space' of everyday life; Yi-Fu Tuan, *Space and Place: The Perspective of Experience* (London, Arnold, 1977), where Tuan posits this distinction: '[I]f we think of space as that which allows movement, then place is pause; each pause in movement makes it possible for location to be transformed into place' (p. 6); David Jacobson, *Place and Belonging in America* (Baltimore, Johns Hopkins University Press, 2002), in which it is argued that 'place has a distinctly moral element, containing as it does notions of belonging, of one's rightful place in the world, locating individuals and people geographically and historically and orienting them in the cosmos' (p. 5).

1

capable of being read in different ways. In Northern Ireland, place is the site of division and dispute arising from conflicting claims to ownership and control. Meanings of place are tied up with questions of territoriality, belonging and social power. Places are invented – as the experience of Partition would demonstrate – and territorializing myths and tropes are used to legitimate identity and secure cultural hegemony. The history of Northern Ireland is bloody testimony to the trouble that arises when discourses of 'home', 'belonging' and 'nation' are linked to territory and bounded place. Individuals may identify with 'home-places' all the more strongly and exclusively if they are contested places, as in Northern Ireland. Place, as opposed to space, always implies borders, the boundaries that mark off one place as different from another. The question is, then, how secure or how porous should these borders be? Is it a case of 'Good fences make good neighbours', or a questioning of the need for walls: 'Before I built a wall I'd ask to know/ What I was walling in or walling out'.[2] In Northern Ireland, the discourses of both nationalism and unionism have favoured the former option, resulting in a typically reactionary, exclusivist sense of place. For nationalists, place is the essential ground of identity and a continuous, unified Irish culture. For unionists, Northern Ireland is their constitutionally established homeland founded to preserve their Protestant, British identity perceived to be constantly under siege from Catholic, Gaelic 'Irish Ireland'.

Seamus Heaney has sketched out the situation as follows:

> Each person in Ulster lives first in the Ulster of the actual present, and then in one or other Ulster of the mind ... The fountainhead of the Unionist's myth springs in the Crown of England but he has to hold his own in the island of Ireland. The fountainhead of the Nationalist's myth lies in the idea of an integral Ireland, but he too lives in an exile from his ideal place. Yet, while he has to concede that he is a citizen of the partitioned British state, the Nationalist can hold to the physical fact of his presence upon the Irish island just as the Unionist can affirm the reality of the political realm of the United Kingdom even as he recognises the geographical fact that Ireland is his insular home.[3]

Heaney's argument is that in dealing with such a situation, Northern Irish writers 'take the strain of being in two places at once, of needing to accommodate two opposing conditions of truthfulness simultaneously ... They belong to a place that is patently riven between notions of belonging to other places.' Such a situation, Heaney argues, has proved creatively productive, since 'the only reliable release for the poet was the appeasement of the achieved poem'.[4] Not all Northern Irish poets, as we shall see, would subscribe to Heaney's notion of poetry as 'appeasement' or 'symbolic resolution', but all of them would accept the premise of fractured belonging and uncertainty, and, in an era of rapidly accel-

---

2 Robert Frost, 'Mending Wall', in *Selected Poems*, edited by Ian Hamilton (London, Penguin, 1973) p. 43–4.
3 Seamus Heaney, 'Place and Displacement: Reflections on Some Recent Poetry from Northern Ireland', in Elmer Andrews (ed.), *Contemporary Irish Poetry: A Collection of Critical Essays* (Houndmills, Macmillan, 1992) pp. 124–44, 127.
4 Ibid.

erating globalisation, contemplate an even more extended sense of the multiple 'other places' secreted in the here and now than Heaney does.

This study sets out to explore Northern Irish poets' interrogation of inherited forms and received identities and concepts of place, especially the home place, concentrating on the period since the late 1960s, that is, since the latest outbreak of what has euphemistically become known as 'the Troubles'. A number of inter-related questions present themselves: What differences in the writing of place, particularly the home place, can be discerned among contemporary Northern Irish poets, taking account of generational, religious, geographical and gender factors? To what extent does their writing of place and identity represent a move away from concepts of rootedness and towards a poetics and politics of displace-ment, mobility, openness and pluralism? How has their writing of place, and our understanding of that writing, been affected by issues raised by contemporary developments in ecocriticism, postcolonialism, postmodernism, feminism and, most of all, by new theories of place and spatiality? How has the Northern Irish poets' writing of place been affected by international influences, such as those emanating from the U.S., from Russia and Eastern Europe, and elsewhere? What is the significance of the prevalence of classical Greek and Latin influences in Northern Irish place writing? What is the importance of translation as an aspect of cultural adaptation and transfer? My title, *Writing Home,* is deliber-ately ambiguous. It obviously indicates both a collection of writing *about* home reflecting in different ways on the meaning of home, and a cultural process whereby poems ascribe meaning to the concept of home, recording changes and working to encode new appreciations of home. Underlying the study is an assumption of the fundamental inextricability of the aesthetic and the ideolog-ical. This means that we need to concentrate not only on what is described – the 'home' being constructed – but on the ways in which the description is framed, the strategies employed by individual poets in order to engage with their imag-ined readers. The title *Writing Home* is also intended to raise questions about the position from which the poet is writing, and the readership he thinks he is addressing, questions of special moment in light of the fact that a substantial amount of the poetry considered in this study takes the form of home thoughts from abroad, sometimes even adopting an epistolary approach (Derek Mahon's 'Hudson Letter', for example). In these circumstances, 'home' can become even more of a shifting signifier, no longer simply equatable with birthplace, or family place, or even the place where one was reared and spent most of one's life. The crossing of boundaries and the experience of diaspora open up new under-standings of the relations between places, a new sense of the permeability and contingency of cultures, new concepts of identity and home.

As a starting-point we could take Yeats's celebration of rootedness in his 'A Prayer for my Daughter': 'O may she live like some green laurel/ Rooted in one dear perpetual place'.[5] Or in the later 'The Municipal Gallery Revisited', where he sings of how strong a man can grow from contact with ideal soil:

> John Synge, I and Augusta Gregory, thought
> All that we did, all that we said or sang

5   *W.B .Yeats: Selected Poetry*, ed. A. Norman Jeffares (London, Macmillan, 1974) p. 102.

Must come from contact with the soil, from that
Contact everything Antaeus-like grew strong.[6]

Yeats expresses the desire for fixity, continuity, tradition, for preservation of a conservative, hierarchical culture ('Dream of the noble and the beggar-man') in a time of upheaval and change. Cultural nationalism prescribed the embracement of essential Irishness as a means of distinguishing 'Ireland' from a modern, Anglo-Saxon, English 'other'. For Yeats, this was primarily an imaginative project, the challenge being to reflect, not the degenerate Ireland obsessed with 'Paudeen's pence', but a romantic Ireland of the imagination, 'an Ireland/ The poets have imagined, terrible and gay'. In this regard, Yeats's cultural nationalism exemplifies Benedict Anderson's idea of the nation as an 'imagined community' called into being largely through the agency of print culture. For Yeats, the recording of the folktales, legends and history of the peasantry, the celebration of Irish landscape and placenames in a national literature, and the founding of an Irish National Literary Society were aspects of a crusade to construct a spiritually and culturally defined nation. By these means he sought to develop a 'sense of place', of rootedness, especially for his own increasingly beleaguered Anglo-Irish class. Place becomes a way of life, a way of seeing and understanding, a way of being-in-the-world. Yeats echoes Martin Heidegger's notion of *dasein* or (roughly) 'dwelling' as the very essence of existence. Heidegger's description of a farmhouse in the Black Forest proposes a concept of home as a spiritual project rooted in place and a romantic mystique of the soil, the achievement of a transcendental unity of the human, the natural and the divine:

> Here the self-sufficiency of the power to let earth and heaven, divinities and mortals enter in simple oneness into things, ordered the house. It places the farm on the wind-sheltered slope looking south, among the meadows close to the spring. It gave it the wide overhanging shingle roof whose proper slope bears up under the burden of snow, and which, reaching deep down, shields the chambers against the storms of the long winter nights. It did not forget the altar corner behind the community table; it made room in its chamber for the hallowed places of childbed and the 'tree of the dead' – for that is what they called a coffin there; the Totenbaum – and in this way it designed for the different generations under one roof the character of their journey through time. A craft which itself sprung from dwelling, still uses its tools and frames as things, built the farmhouse.[7]

This sacramental, essentialist sense of place is discernible among the older generation of poets in this study. For poets such as Heaney and Montague from a Catholic, nationalist, rural background, culture and identity are immanent in place, and dislocation is the source of a profound anxiety. In *Being and Time*, Heidegger explained his view that man is no longer at home in an industrialised, modernist, capitalist world where the ancient experience of Being as a state of harmony with the cosmos has been irretrievably lost. Language, particularly poetry, he believed, was a way of reaching beyond the reality of not-being-at-home. Similarly, Montague and Heaney, preoccupied with a lost home, a lost

---

6   Ibid., p. 193.
7   Martin Heidegger, *Poetry, Language, Thought* (New York, Harper & Row, 1971) p. 160.

past, a lost language and way of life, seek to reclaim their inheritance and restore 'the culture to itself' through 'bedding the locale/ in the utterance',[8] through poetic excavations and place-name poems. Poetry becomes an act of imaginative repossession, the recreation of community as synonym or synecdoche for the nation.

Montague's and Heaney's poetics of home have proved controversial from several standpoints. These poets have, for example, been accused of failing to confront the reality of a divided society, indulging instead in myth-making and 'revivalist nostalgia'. Their poetry, it is alleged, tends to reproduce an established system of binary oppositions and, by enforcing an absolute difference between Planter and Gael, Protestant and Catholic, expresses native and nationalist resistance to alien occupation of Irish terrain. In the effort to maintain a coherent myth of identity, and thereby satisfy the longing for wholeness, unity and integrity, they stand accused of smoothing over historical anomalies and contradictions. David Lloyd, for example, dismisses Heaney's images of unity and historical continuity as unhelpful mystifications of Irish identity. Heaney, Lloyd argues, 'relocates an individual and racial identity through the reterritorialisation of language and culture ... enacted through linguistic and metaphoric usages which promise a healing of division simply by returning the subject to place'.[9] Heaney's language, Lloyd believes, 'performs the rituals of synthesis and identity'[10] in disregard of historical reality. Focusing on the 'place-name poems' and the 'bog poems', Lloyd charges Heaney with subordinating ethics, history and politics to aesthetics: by giving himself over to 'the establishment of myths' and the aesthetic ideal of the 'well-made poem',[11] Heaney, in Lloyd's view, is unable to critique traditional concepts of home and identity or interrogate the nature and function of acts of violence.

That Heaney is himself aware of the possibly illusory nature of his concept of home is indicated in the line from his poem 'Hercules and Antaeus' which Lloyd takes as title of his essay: 'pap for the dispossessed'. Lloyd seems perversely resistant to the pervasive note of critical self-reflection which complicates Heaney's expression of the standard sentiments of Romantic nationalism, and takes no account of the movement from 'reterritorialisation' to de-territorialisation ('the 'bright nowhere', 'the placeless heaven') which Heaney's poetry enacts in the interests of a more broadly human inclusiveness than that envisaged by cultural nationalism. Richard Kearney, keen to rescue Heaney from reactionary nationalism, further observes that, as with Heidegger, Heaney's poetic quest for a home 'presupposes the absence of a literally existing one'.[12] Kearney believes that it is through the comparison with Heidegger that we can understand 'the

---

8   Seamus Heaney, 'Gifts of Rain', in *Opened Ground: Poems 1966–1996* (London, Faber, 1998) p. 50.

9   David Lloyd, '"Pap for the dispossessed": Seamus Heaney and the Poetics of Identity', in Elmer Andrews (ed.), *Seamus Heaney: A Collection of Critical Essays* (Houndmills, Macmillan, 1992) pp. 87–116, 95.

10   Ibid., p. 98.

11   Ibid., p. 106.

12   Richard Kearney, *Transitions: Narratives in Modern Irish Culture* (Dublin, Wolfhound Press, 1988), p. 120.

trans-national and singularly modern nature'[13] of Heaney's literary concerns. Heaney's 'poetic project of "homecoming" is ... invariably accompanied by the literal awareness of "homelessness"':[14] his concern for the lost home 'is not some revivalist nostalgia for an ancient patria, but the anticipation of new possibilities of home hitherto unimagined'.[15] Without losing sight of this cultural revisionist Heaney, it is also possible to identify in his poetry a transcendent and metaphysical dimension which rewrites the religious vision of his early rural Catholic education, and increasingly provides the ground of meaning in his work.

The mythic home of Irish nationalism has also been questioned by feminist-oriented poets such as Eavan Boland and, in this study, Medbh McGuckian and Sinéad Morrissey. Both Montague and Heaney have been criticised for the way they seem to have unquestioningly taken over the traditional view of Ireland as a woman – Cathleen Ni Houlihan, the Shan Van Vocht or Mother Ireland – and failed to critique the repressive male discourse that defines both women and nation in terms of inferiority and subordination to colonial male power. Elizabeth Cullingford emphasises how the idealisation of Irish womanhood, far from conferring any real power upon women in Irish society, has in fact trapped them within a reductive stereotype of purity and passivity:

> The representation of the land as female is a function of the patriarchal opposi-tion between male Culture and female Nature, which defines women as the passive and silent embodiments of matter. Politically, the land is seen as an object to be possessed, or repossessed: to gender it as female, therefore, is to confirm and repro-duce the social arrangements which construct women as material possessions, not speaking subjects.[16]

Seeing how women have been objectified and denied agency within traditional masculine discourses of place, landscape and nation, how they have been identi-fied with exploited nature and confined within 'private' spaces, McGuckian and Morrissey have either asserted their freedom from place-based identity, or inter-rogated the public/private binary, shifting the focus from the 'public' landscape of country and nation that men have written about to other kinds of place that are more relevant to women's experience – internal spaces, the body, domestic spaces, rooms, houses, gardens.

Reacting against an insistently and damagingly gendered poetic tradition, McGuckian's re-writing of home ground gives a voice to autonomous female subjectivity, and articulates what Julia Kristeva calls the 'semiotic *chora*':

> We borrow the term *chora* from Plato's *Timaeus* to denote an essentially mobile and extremely provisional articulation constituted by movements and their ephemeral stases. We differentiate this uncertain and indeterminate *articulation* from a *dispo-sition* that already depends on representation, lends itself to phenomenological, spatial intuition and gives rise to geometry. Although our theoretical description of the *chora* is itself part of the discourse of representation that offers it as evidence,

---

13 Ibid., p. 122.
14 Ibid., p. 121.
15 Ibid.
16 Elizabeth Butler Cullingford, '"Thinking of Her ... as ... Ireland": Yeats, Pearse, and Heaney', *Textual Practice*, 4, 1 (Spring 1990).

the *chora*, as rupture and articulations (rhythm), precedes evidence, verisimilitude, spatiality and temporality. Our discourse – all discourse – moves with and against the *chora* in the sense that it simultaneously depends upon and refuses it.[17]

Kristeva suggests a radical feminist recuperation of the role of place in identity by rethinking male 'geometrical', fixed constructions of place in terms of 'mobility' and 'provisionality'. The concept of place no longer connotes fixity and security; women are no longer confined to a narrow range of paternally constructed identity positions – home-maker, mother, wife, symbol of the nation. The semiotic *chora*, characterised by indeterminacy and immanent productiveness, modifies linguistic structures, disturbs the symbolic order, and marks a female revolt against the male socio-symbolic contract. In creating a space for the articulation of the inherently feminine *chora*, McGuckian gives expression to that which has traditionally been denigrated 'as an abyss, as unfathomable, lacking, enigmatic, veiled, seductive, voracious, dangerous and disruptive'.[18] Yet her project is not simply a matter of seeking to insert 'women's experience' or 'the female subject' into the received modes of representation, but to make the very construction of experience and subjectivity a central point of inquiry. Rejecting the universalist and essentialist claims of mimetic representation, she assumes a situated point of view, a subject position that never resolves into a stable and coherent sense of self. As Teresa de Lauretis says, the feminist subject 'is most likely ideologically complicit with "the oppressor" whose position it may occupy in certain socio-sexual relations (if not in others)'.[19] Thus McGuckian, always conscious of her complicity with the patriarchal symbolic order that threatens to peripheralise distinctively female concerns and values, interrogates received modes of representation, disrupting their imposed coherence of space and subject. The question is how as a woman does she make a place for herself within the male discourses of place, from the most intimate discourses of subjectivity and the body, to the wider discursive fields of domestic, political, geopolitical, spiritual and metaphysical spaces? Writing in the interstices of masculine culture, she moves between use of the dominant (patriarchal and colonial) language, and specific versions of experience based on her marginality, imagining a fluid space that is fragmented, multidimensional, contradictory and provisional.

Confronted with the exclusivist, Gaelic, Catholic myth of home, explored by writers like Heaney and Montague, Protestant writers have sought to stake their own claim to an Ulster homeland. Ian Adamson, for example, has attempted to construct an answering myth of Ulster Protestant nationalism based on his notion of a pre-historic race, the Cruthin, who were, according to Adamson, displaced by the advancing Gaels and forced to re-settle in what is now Scotland.[20] The return of the Scots in succeeding centuries is thus seen as a repossession of ancestral Ulster territory. This view of Ulster history naturalises Partition since it sees the North-South border as the modern institutionalisation

---

17 Toril Moi (ed.), *The Kristeva Reader* (Oxford, Blackwell,1986) pp. 93–4.
18 E. Groscz, 'Women, Chora, Dwelling', in S. Watson and R. Gibson (eds.), *Postmodern Cities and Spaces* (London, Blackwell, 1994) pp. 47–68, 66.
19 Teresa de Lauretis, 'Feminist Studies/Critical Studies: Issues, Terms, Contexts,' in Teresa de Lauretis (ed.), *Feminist Studies/Critical Studies* (London: Macmillan, 1986) p. 137.
20 See Ian Adamson, *Cruthin: The Ancient Kindred* (Newtownards, Nosmada Books, 1974).

of primordial differences between the two parts of the island. The problem with Adamson's elaborate myth of Ulster Protestant nationalism is the stubborn fact that it doesn't have any historical basis.

An alternative theory of Protestant rootedness and belonging is that represented by John Hewitt's regionalism. Sharing Adamson's anxiety about Protestant legitimation in Ireland, Hewitt elaborates a vision of community, not as a matter of race or nation, but in terms of shared ground and feeling for landscape. While acknowledging difference, division and past wrong, Hewitt is determined to stake the 'Planter' claim to roots and belonging. For Hewitt, poetry is apologia, self-justification and the search for reconciliation. Ultimately, he fails to supply a coherent and unifying place-imagery for Northern Ireland, so deeply ingrained are the essentialist binary habits of mind which perpetuate exclusivist notions of place, identity and community.

An older generation of poets, both Catholic (Montague and Heaney) and Protestant (Hewitt), have tended to focus on rural images and places, on a familiar, stable world located safely in the past. But 'traditional' Ireland/Ulster has undergone rapid fundamental change in recent years, as evidenced by the unprecedented twentieth-century population shifts attendant upon increasing urbanisation, the mobility generated by new technology, the growth of travel and tourism, the influx of foreign investment, the influence of mass communications of TV, film and the internet. All these developments, in contributing to the creation of 'the global village', have had the effect of eroding traditional cultural values. Place is increasingly viewed as the product of global, interconnecting flows of peoples, cultures and meanings – of routes rather than roots. Concepts of place that are essentialist and exclusionary, based on notions of rooted authenticity, homogenous territory, single identities and internally generated history have become increasingly unsustainable in the (post)modern world. The processes of globalisation and migration are producing new senses of both placed and placeless identity, new relations between rootedness and mobility, centre and periphery, global and local. As the social geographer Doreen Massey remarks, 'The geography of social relations is changing. In many cases such relations are increasingly stretched out over space.'[21] Recent theories of culture and identity increasingly deploy spatial metaphors – 'location', 'territory', 'travel', 'positionality', 'centre', 'margin', 'ground', 'displacement', 'diaspora', 'migrancy', 'mapping', 'boundary'. According to Foucault, we are now living in 'the epoch of space':

> The great obsession of the nineteenth century was, as we know, history … The present epoch will perhaps be above all the epoch of space. We are in the epoch of simultaneity: we are in the epoch of juxtaposition, the epoch of the near and the far, of the side-by-side, of the dispersed. We are at a moment, I believe, when our experience of the world is less that of a long life developing through time [the temporal or historicist understanding of things] than that of a network that connects points.[22]

Reacting against the idea of 'total history', Foucault regards historical periods as characterised by difference and division. Neither periods nor places can be

---

[21] Doreen Massey, quoted in Tim Cresswell, *Places* (Oxford, Blackwell, 2004) p. 69.
[22] Michel Foucault 'Of Other Spaces', *Diacritics* (Spring 1986) pp. 22–7, 22.

said to have a 'central core': 'nothing is fundamental: that is what is interesting in the analysis of society'.[23] Rather, he sees history, in all its diversity, 'deploying the space of a dispersion'.[24] In Foucault's view, to understand the social world we must think spatially, and not in terms of fixed spaces, but in terms of 'series, divisions, limits, differences of level, shifts, chronological specificities, particular forms of rehandling, possible types of relation'.[25] Places are formed not only out of layers of history and tradition which become the bedrock of identity, but out of horizontal connections which are developed with surrounding places. Traditional notions of the continuity and historicity of place-identity come under pressure from newly evolving global cultural influences. Kevin Robins expresses an idea that, in the Irish context, is particularly associated with the drama of Brian Friel: 'The comforts of Tradition are fundamentally challenged by the imperative to forge a new self-interpretation based upon the responsibilities of cultural Translation.'[26] New theories of place and spatiality emphasise the social constructedness of places, and how these constructions have traditionally been founded on principles of exclusion. Place is seen as process rather than something to be understood in terms of rootedness, authenticity and ontological security. Manuel Castells, an urban theorist, argues that what we are witnessing is 'the historical emergence of the space of flows, superseding the meaning of the space of places'.[27] The interconnections that link places together have become not only increasingly stretched-out but also increasingly complex, with the result that we can no longer think of them as bounded, settled and coherent. Place can be marked by mobility, openness, change, hybridity and indeterminacy rather than boundedness and immutability. Places need not be thought to have single, unique, essential identities, but to be full of internal conflicts.

In the Preface to his book, *In Search of Ireland* (1997), the geographer Brian Graham confidently declares that contemporary interpretations of Ireland 'are far more likely to be inclusive and open-ended, stressing the diversity of Irish place and society and the fluidity of Irish identity'.[28] Richard Kearney argues for more flexible concepts of identity beyond the exclusive, monolithic ones on offer in the past: the Planter and the Gael, Catholic and Protestant, Republican and Loyalist, tribal and cosmopolitan. Irishness, he reminds us, 'is no longer co-terminous with the geographical outlines of an island',[29] but includes an international group of expatriates. And what the example of Northern Ireland teaches us, he says, is the need for 'more inclusive and pluralist forms of association' beyond that of the nation-state. The embrace of the other, Kearney argues, must be complemented by a renewed commitment to local belonging. Refurbishing

---

23 Michel Foucault, Interview with Michel Foucault on 'Space, Knowledge and Power', *Skyline* (March 1982) pp. 17–20, 18.
24 Michel Foucault, *The Archaeology of Knowledge* (London, Tavistock, 197) p. 10.
25 Ibid., p. 10.
26 Kevin Robins, 'Tradition and Translation: National Culture in its Global Context', in J. Corner and S. Harvey (eds.), *Enterprise and Heritage: Crosscurrents of National Culture* (London, Routledge, 1991) p. 41.
27 Manuel Castells, *The Informational City* (Oxford, Basil Blackwell, 1989) p. 348.
28 Brian Graham (ed.), *In Search of Ireland: A Cultural Geography* (London, Routledge, 1997) p. xii.
29 Richard Kearney, *Postnationalist Ireland: Politics, Culture, Philosophy* (London, Routledge, 1997) p. 99.

Hewitt's regionalism, Kearney proposes the ancient concept of the 'fifth province', 'where attachments to the local and the global find reciprocal articulation':

> This place, I submit, is not a fixed point or centralized power. It is not the source of some 'unitary and indivisible sovereignty'. If anything, it may be re-envisaged today as a network of relations extending from local communities at home to migrant communities abroad. The fifth province is to be found, if anywhere, at the swinging door which connects the 'parish' (in Kavanagh's sense) with the 'cosmos'.[30]

Kearney's emphasis redresses the extremism of Manuel Castells' view that 'social meaning evaporates from places, and therefore from society, and becomes diluted and diffused in the reconstructed logic of a space of flows whose profile, origin and ultimate purposes are unknown'.[31] Kearney holds on to a notion of the uniqueness of place, particularly of place as a source of identity. Similarly, Doreen Massey speaks of 'a global sense of place',[32] a sense of place, not as settled, enclosed and internally coherent, but as a meeting-point, the location of the intersection of multiple influences and interrelations, both internal and external, local and global. In this analysis, the uniqueness of a particular place is itself a construct, dependent on the nature of the combination of local character-istics with the wider complex webs of social relations that bind places together in global networks. The contemporary Northern Irish poet who has been exercised at a more conscious level than most by the tension between the local and the global is John Montague, and it is in terms of his self-description as a 'global regionalist' that his work will be of particular interest to this study.

Kearney's notion of the 'fifth province' is similar to Homi Bhabha's idea of 'the third space',[33] a contradictory and ambivalent 'space of enunciation' which makes the claim to a hierarchical 'purity' of cultures untenable. In horticul-ture, hybridity is the term used for the cross-breeding of two different species to produce a third 'hybrid' species. In post-colonial theory, hybridity refers to the creation of new transcultural forms within the 'contact zones' produced by colonisation. Hybridity thus represents an adulteration of the nationalist myth of origins and a complication of the unionist grand narrative of British imperialism and colonialism. However, 'contact zones' need not necessarily produce hybridity as Bhabha assumes, but rather entrenchment and further polarisation. Some of Northern Ireland's 'contact zones' have been particularly dangerous places – the 'Bandit Country' along the south Armagh border, or the Belfast interfaces where the Peace Wall was erected to protect the two communities from each other. There is no more depressing evidence of the difficulties of realising the ideal of common ground than the failure of John Hewitt's regionalist project, which was at least theoretically intended to produce an Ulster 'third space', neither nation-alist nor unionist, British nor Irish. Hewitt's regionalism proved in the end to be too conservative – not sufficiently radical – to negate the hierarchical nature of the colonial process and resolve cultural differences.

Two key factors to be considered in the evolving conceptualisation of Irish

---

30 Ibid., p. 100.
31 Castells, p. 349.
32 Doreen Massey, 'A Global Sense of Place', *Marxism Today* (June 1991) pp. 24–9.
33 Homi K. Bhabha, *The Location of Culture* (London, Routledge, 1994) p. 38.

place are, first, the shift in the centre of gravity from the country to the city, and, secondly, the move from 'rooted' to diasporic notions of culture and identity. Catholic nationalist representations of Ireland and Irishness have traditionally depended on a rural ethos and iconography. Derek Mahon, taking cognizance of this fetishisation of the rural in cultural nationalism, has alluded to the challenge posed by the urbanised and industrialised North to the Irish sense of place:

> The suburbs of Belfast have a peculiar relationship to the Irish cultural situation inasmuch as they're the final anathema for the traditional Irish imagination. A lot of people who are important in Irish poetry cannot accept that the Protestant suburbs in Belfast are a part of Ireland ... at an aesthetic level they can't accept that.[34]

In the city, the actual multifariousness and heterogeneity of Irish society are visibly concentrated. The city of flux and diversity is not the natural home of traditional religious, political or cultural pieties. The city, says Eamonn Hughes, quoting Roland Barthes, is 'the place of our meeting with the Other'.[35] Opposed to the idea of the rural 'which always has at its root an allegedly organicist social structure in which relationships are always familiar', Hughes argues, 'the city affronts the sense of the nation as homogenous'.[36] Joyce was the first to open up the literary potential of the Irish city. The city as a site of discontinuity and difference, of infinite 'pluralities', became the locus of an alternative vision to Yeats's totalising, rural-based cultural nationalism. Joyce's influence is clearly seen in succeeding poets such as Austin Clarke and Thomas Kinsella whose work reflects a distinctive Dublin poetic locale and engages with the emerging urban culture of the 1950s and 1960s that resulted from the opening of the South to the economics of modern international capitalism, the shift in the country's population from the country to the city, and the break with the values of an insular, rural, Gaelic past. In his lecture, 'The Irish Writer' (1967), Kinsella cites Joyce as the true 'father' of modern Irish poetry, specifically on account of Joyce's inscription of the city rather than the land as the central term in Irish literature, and his understanding of alienation, fragmentation and discontinuity as the essential features of the modern Irish condition.[37] In the North, as Edna Longley notes, Louis MacNeice, 'for whom Belfast was the first city', was 'in the vanguard of absorbing the city into English poetry generally',[38] though Padraic Fiacc has also been writing about Belfast as well as New York since the late 1940s. MacNeice's receptivity to the city is part and parcel of a vision of the world perceived as 'flux', as 'incorrigibly plural'.[39] His exile's *odi atque amo*[40] relationship with Belfast and Ireland more generally, and his poetic vantage point of the

[34] Derek Mahon, quoted in George Watson, 'Landscape in Ulster Poetry', in Gerald Dawe and John Wilson Foster (eds.), *The Poet's Place*, p. 11.

[35] Eamonn Hughes, '"What Itch of Contradiction?": Belfast in Poetry', in Nicholas Allen and Aaron Kelly (eds.), *The Cities of Belfast* (Dublin, Four Courts Press, 2003) p. 115.

[36] Ibid.

[37] Thomas Kinsella, 'The Irish Writer', *Eire-Ireland*, 2, 2 (1967) pp. 8–15.

[38] Edna Longley, *The Living Stream : Literature and Revisionism in Ireland* (Newcastle-upon-Tyne, Bloodaxe, 1994) p. 105.

[39] Louis MacNeice, 'Snow', *Collected Poems* (London, Faber, 1966) p. 30.

[40] Louis MacNeice, 'Autumn Journal XVI', *Collected Poems*, p. 134.

sceptical, cosmopolitan outsider in whom multiple strains criss-cross in productive tension, has made him an important example for succeeding poets who have also been interested in exploring hybrid, plural identity in a culture all too prone to fixity and fossilisation. Mahon, for example, follows MacNeice in conveying the fragmentation of urban modernity, while displaying a typically modernist nostalgia for authenticity and wholeness. This tension is just as pronounced in Mahon's more recent work, which shifts its urban focus from Belfast to New York and Dublin. Mahon shows an openness to the discontinuous culture of the postmodern city when it is New York ('The Hudson Letter'), but not at all when it is Dublin (*The Yellow Book*). Resisting the homogenising threat of globalisation and postmodern indifference, *The Yellow Book* is an elegy for a lost authenticity, for an imaginary past that has so often been dismissed as irrelevant. Contrasting with Mahon's stance of disaffected outsider, Longley identifies with the city, with its shopkeepers, civil servants and linen workers who represent the economic and civic life of the city. Where Heaney, coming from a close-knit rural background, memorialises casualties of the Troubles who were relatives (his second cousin Colum McCartney in 'The Strand at Lough Beg') or at least personal acquaintances (Louis O'Neal in 'Casualty'), Longley's elegies are tributes to anonymous urban strangers. Longley relates to Belfast not in terms of inherited familial, tribal or religious affiliation, but in terms of his own humane, 'baggage-free' sense of place, unencumbered by questions of identity. Carson's new urban poetics, emanating from the epicentre of the recent Troubles, unsettle the fixed versions of the city that we find in Heaney, Mahon and other poets who view Belfast in essentialist terms, as standing, unchanging and monolithic, in stark opposition to the pre- or anti-modern land. By experimenting with discontinuous, de-centred or ungrounded forms, Carson presents a city space that is unstable and unreliable yet always susceptible to re-construction and renewal. Exploring this new space leads to the creation of new maps, the formulation of new concepts of identity and place, and the relationships between them. Belfast is no longer merely the place which must be escaped (even if that was possible), but the location of post-national, encyclopaedic, labyrinthine, ever-shifting Northern scenarios.

Another way in which the new relationship between place, culture and identity has been re-imagined has been in terms of diaspora of which many contemporary Northern Irish poets have experience (Montague, Fiacc, Heaney, Mahon and Muldoon have all lived abroad for extended periods, or still do). Diaspora refers to a scattering that separates people from their original home, often for good. In becoming settlers elsewhere they are forced to come to some kind of accommodation with their new environment, whether oppressive or congenial, and forge a new cultural identity for themselves, drawing on the resources of different cultural repertoires. The diasporic dweller may of course resist foreign influence, and attempt to keep the links with the motherland and the past strong and pure. Others embrace the experience of difference and liminality, the opportunity to belong to more than one world, to have more than one home. They are the unmistakable products of their original culture, its history and traditions, but they are also involved in the process of translating between different cultures, continually re-making themselves. Heaney's image of the omphalos – a navel or centre – implies an originary point, both spatial and temporal, to which he is connected by the umbilical cord of tradition. This 'closed' version of Irishness assumes that the further you move from origins the more tenuous and unstable your identity becomes. It is a linear conception of culture. But in diasporic ideas of culture, the connections are circular rather than linear. As Paul Gilroy explains:

> The concept of space is itself transformed when it is seen in terms of the communicative circuitry that has enabled dispersed populations to converse, interact and more recently even to synchronize significant elements of their social lives.[41]

Thus, Muldoon's images of Irish-America (in *Madoc*, for instance) do not imply the dilution of an originary energy but its transformation in a constant process of circulation and exchange.

Edna Longley proposes the image of the web to describe the network of relations in which the Northern Irish poet may be seen to exist:

> The image of the web is female, feminist, connective – as contrasted with male polarisation. So is the ability to inhabit a range of relations rather than a single allegiance. The great advantage of living in Northern Ireland is that you can be in three places at once. However, the term 'identity' has been coarsened in Ulster politics to signify two ideological package-deals immemorially on offer. To admit to more varied, mixed, fluid and relational kinds of identity would advance nobody's territorial claim. It would undermine cultural defences. It would subvert the male pride that keeps up the double frontier-siege. It would dismantle the dangerous ratchet that locks Catholic advance into Protestant demoralisation and emigration. All this would be on the side of life ...[42]

Of course, the idea of the 'web of life', which Longley gestures towards here, extends far beyond conditions in Northern Ireland, and some contemporary poets, such as Michael Longley and Alan Gillis, have tended to see themselves ecologically, as part of the 'web of life' as understood by Fritjof Capra. For Capra, humanity cannot be separated from nature, but should be seen 'as just one strand in the web of life':

> The new paradigm may be called a holistic worldview, seeing the world as an integrated whole rather than as a dissociated collection of parts. It may also be called an ecological view, if the term 'ecological' is used in a much broader and deeper sense than usual. Deep ecological awareness recognizes the fundamental interdependence of all phenomena and the fact that, as individuals and societies, we are all embedded in (and ultimately dependent on) the cyclical processes of nature.[43]

The image of the ecological 'web of life' bears affinities with Deleuze and Guattari's rhizome. Because Deleuze and Guattari were opposed to essentialist grand narratives, and sought a fluid, polyvalent writing style, it is difficult to derive

---

41 Paul Gilroy, 'Diaspora and the Detours of Identity', in Kathryn Woodward (ed.), *Identity and Difference* (London, Thousand Oaks, and New Delhi, Sage Publications, in association with Open University, 1997) pp. 310–41, 329.

42 Edna Longley, 'From Cathleen to Anorexia', in *The Living Stream: Literature and Revisionism in Ireland* (Newcastle-upon-Tyne, Bloodaxe Books, 1994) p. 195.

43 Fritjof Capra, *The Web of Life: A New Scientific Understanding of Living Systems* (New York, Doubleday, 1996) pp. 6–7.

a clear, logical outline of their ideas. However, though their writings are more suggestive than definitive, what is clear from their major work, *A Thousand Plateaus*, is the opposition which they propose between 'rhizomatic' and 'arborescent' culture. The hierarchical system of thought on which Western Enlightenment rationality is founded they term 'arborescent',[44] complete with roots and leaves – like Yeats's 'spreading laurel tree', the symbol of rootedness. Opposed to the organic, totalising implications of 'arborescent thinking' is what they call 'rhizomatic thinking'. The rhizome is a botanical term referring to a horizontal stem, like that of grass. The rhizome root has no apparent source root, it moves outward, not upward, cutting across borders, bridging gaps, making new connections. The principle characteristics of the rhizome include 'connection', 'heterogeneity', 'multiplicity'. The rhizome is mobile, deterritorialised, and undermines the logic of binaries. Associated with the rhizome is another of Deleuze and Guattari's suggestive metaphors – that of the nomad. It is within rhizomatic space that the postmodern nomad operates. The mobile nomad-self traverses and transgresses the familiar binaries of here and there, home and away, self and other. Deleuze and Guattari use the nomad as a metaphor for the unruly forces in society that resist the bounded spatiality of State discipline but, as Steven Best and Douglas Kellner explain, the concept has wide cultural reference:

> Nomads provide new models for existence and struggle. The nomad-self breaks from all molar segments and cautiously disorganises itself. Nomad life is an experiment in creativity and becoming, and is anti-traditional and anti-conformist in character.[45]

Northern Irish poets, especially the younger ones, have, with increasing boldness, ventured beyond the more or less safe ground of inherited territory and 'arborescent thinking' to explore new images of place and identity, new narratives of diversity, inclusiveness, fluidity, migrancy, uncertainty and homelessness. As Tom Paulin puts it in 'And Where Do you Stand on the National Question?': 'I've heard/ Hewitt and Heaney trace us back/ to the Antrim weavers –/ I can't come from *that*'.[46] If Montague and Heaney tend to confirm the binary terms and divisions which have dominated cultural debate, it is possible to see a greater readiness among Protestant-background poets such as Simmons, Mahon, Longley and Paulin, MacNeice before them, and even Hewitt, to undo the usual binary oppositions between home and away, here and there, self and other, and to replace an ideal of continuity with one of productive discontinuity. In their introduction to *Across a Roaring Hill*, a collection of essays on modern Protestant writing, the editors Gerald Dawe and Edna Longley characterise the Protestant imagination in terms of 'a concern with isolation … an imaginative withdrawal from the territory, from the all-Ireland imperative, the unitary state of being', and 'redemptions of isolation in terms of vital individuality, artistic energy, or visions of a basic human community which might transcend and replace trib-

---

44 Gilles Deleuze and Félix Guattari, *A Thousand Plateaus: Capitalism and Schizophrenia*, trans. Brian Massumi (Minneapolis, University of Minnesota Press, 1987) p. 5.
45 Steven Best and Douglas Kellner, *Postmodern Theory: Critical Interrogations* (New York, Guilford Press, 1991) p. 103.
46 Tom Paulin, *The Liberty Tree* (London, Faber) p. 68.

alism and triumphalism'.[47] Some demonstration of these characteristics is to be found among the poets in this study. For example, Hewitt's regionalism attempts to redeem isolation in terms of a vision of 'basic human community' that transcends the usual sectarian dichotomies. Paulin proposes another version of 'basic human community' founded on notions of 'the just state' and 'the vernacular city'. Simmons, dispensing with the usual pious line-up of Irish poetic subjects – place, nation, history, myth, identity – writes about himself, the archetypal Honest Ulsterman, a man at home in his world, spokesman for both 'vital individuality' *and* an implied 'basic human community'. Mahon takes his place in the fiercely individualistic tradition of Protestant writing. With no sacred memory of home to counter the modern sense of fragmentation, and deeply suspicious of any notion of community or belonging, his 'redemptions' are effected in terms of a modernist exile poetics. Michael Longley doesn't fit easily into either the individualist or the communitarian model suggested by the two editors, displaying instead what we might call an ecological imagination that surpasses a merely human frame of reference. His idea of home is certainly 'a matter of choice, of experience, not simply of origins',[48] and in that sense is an individual construct. However, his imagined ground, in keeping with his 'open, non-exclusivist attitudes',[49] continually looks beyond 'human community' to embrace the whole interconnected earthly ecosystem.

Similarly, a generation of younger Catholic-background poets (Muldoon, Carson, McGuckian) has continued the experiment with ambiguous and multiple perspectives on identity, place and belonging, offering powerful critiques from within the discursive realms of postcolonialism, postmodernism and feminism in particular. *Knowing My Place*, the punning title of Muldoon's first collection, an *Honest Ulsterman* pamphlet published when he was still a student at Queen's in 1971, announces the precocious poet's challenge to conventional ideas of place – both his place in the world and in literary tradition. In the writings of this younger generation of poets, traditional, idealised notions of a past when fixed places were (supposedly) inhabited by coherent and homogenous communities give way to alternative place knowledge: Muldoon's vista of mobile meanings and shifting connections, Carson's new urban poetics, McGuckian's provocative reinstatement of 'feminine' places as an alternative to the larger political, cultural and national fields of vision associated with male poets. As against the 'rooted' or 'closed' account of culture and cultural identity, we are made aware of other ways of imagining community belonging which are not centred in the nation-state or the traditional narratives of cultural nationalism but which cut across many of these boundaries, and provide alternative images of identity and culture.

The loosening of the fixed, bounded, rooted conceptions of home and identity has the effect of deterritorialising identity in home, place, region, nation. The traditional bond between Irish poetry and Irish territory is broken, and the poet, no longer able to constitute himself as the subject (or master) of a

---

[47] Gerald Dawe and Edna Longley, *Across A Roaring Hill: The Protestant Imagination in Modern Ireland* (Belfast, Blackstaff Press, 1985) p. iii.

[48] Alan J. Peacock and Kathleen Devine (eds.), 'Introduction', in *The Poetry of Michael Longley* (Gerrards Cross, Colin Smythe, 2000) pp. xiv–xv.

[49] Ibid., p. xv.

space, is unmoored, as are his conceptual co-ordinates. Mobility and displace-
ment produce other, often disruptive or transgressive, poetic personae: hybrids,
resident aliens, exiles, marginals, migrants, urban pedestrians, *flâneurs*, tourists,
travellers, nomads, 'Greens', zappers, surfers and other kinds of cybernaut. We
need to be clear about the differences between some of these categories. The trav-
eller is obviously a privileged figure, while that of migrant or nomad is conven-
tionally less so, and that of the exile – that perennial figure of Irish tradition
– less so again. Unlike the nomad or migrant who is never re-territorialised,
always in transit, exilic experience is inscribed in the dialectic of home and away
and always presupposes the possibility of homecoming. While the word 'exile'
can be applied to either forced or voluntary absence from one's native country,
it generally carries connotations of deprivation, suffering, punishment, solitude,
exclusion and, as Edward Said puts it in his essay 'Reflections on Exile', 'terminal
loss'.[50] In an Irish context, the tropes of exile have traditionally been mobilised to
describe the social, economic and cultural relations of colonial exploitation and
oppression, as well as the experience of physical (diasporic) separation from the
homeland. Exile was traditionally used for political opponents of those in power,
as any number of cases from Ovid to Mandelstam to Hugh O'Neill demon-
strate. A secondary motivation is economic necessity – the theme of section V
of Mahon's 'The Hudson Letter', which pays homage to the ghosts of Irish immi-
grants to New York, such as the young Bridget Moore. The word, however, has
also come to refer to those who for a wide variety of other reasons such as racial
or ethnic conflict, war, famine, drought, career advancement or tax evasion, have
left their homelands to seek survival or a better life elsewhere. The metaphorical
use of the word extends its meaning to any form of displacement, to the point
where the notion of exile is so thoroughly depoliticised that it comes to mean
little more than a subjective feeling, an aspect of the human condition, a designa-
tion of the intellectual, the affluent, the powerful, the 'inner emigré' who chooses
to live in a metaphorical exile from his world.

While the older Catholic generation (Fiacc, Montague, Heaney) write self-
consciously as exiles from within colonialism (*Forms of Exile* was the title of
Montague's first collection of 1958), their successors – Muldoon most explicitly
– have generally resisted the exile label. The note of exile is not confined to
'colonised', Catholic-background poets, but is also discernible as an existential
phenomenon in Protestant-background poets such as Mahon. Yet if alienation
and detachment seem to be the very conditions of Mahon's creativity, the nostalgia
for home which conventionally attends the exilic experience is entirely missing
from his work, and he himself has little time for the stereotypical modes of
colonial victimhood. 'What's the difference between an exile and an expatriate?',
he asks himself, and answers his own question: 'It seems that an Englishman in
France is an expat, but an Irishman is an exile.'[51] Nevertheless, the usual Maho-
nian personae – 'the unreconciled, in their metaphysical pain'[52] – are recognis-

---

50 Edward Said, 'Reflections on Exile', in Russell Ferguson et al. (eds.), *Out There: Marginalization
   and Contemporary Culture* (Cambridge, MA, MIT Press, 1990) pp. 357–66, 357.
51 'A Sense of Place', Nicholas Wroe in interview with Derek Mahon, *Guardian*, 22 July 2006.
52 Derek Mahon, 'Glengormley', *Collected Poems* (Loughcrew, The Gallery Press, 1999) p. 14.

able types of modernist exile, existential figures of banishment and alienation, at home nowhere in the world, yet haunted by the desire for wholeness.

Muldoon shares Mahon's objections to the inflated terminology of 'exile', as in these lines from *The Prince of the Quotidian*:

> In the latest issue
> Of the *TLS* 'the other Seamus', Seamus Deane,
>
> Has me 'in exile' in Princeton:
> This term serves mostly to belittle
> The likes of Brodsky or Padilla
>
> And is not appropriate of me; certainly not
> Of anyone who, with 'Louisa May' Walcott,
> Is free to buy a ticket to his emerald isle
>
> Of choice. To Deane I say, 'I'm not "in exile",
> Though I can't deny
> That I've been twice in Fintona.[53]

Muldoon returns us to political meanings. For Muldoon, exile is a life-or-death condition, as it was for the rebel Russian poet, Joseph Brodsky, whom the Soviet authorities exiled to northern Russia in 1964 and then, in 1972, expelled from Russia altogether; or Heberto Padilla, the Cuban poet who was denounced by Castro's notoriously anti-intellectual regime as 'counter-revolutionary' and subjected to close daily surveillance for a decade, until, in 1980, Edward Kennedy secured his release to the U.S. Muldoon can claim no such involvement with powers that both overwhelm and incite resistance. Nor can he claim to experience the usual feelings of the exile – the sense of loss, the trauma of deracination. His is not the experience of separation as described by Said: 'the unhealable rift forced between a human being and a native place, between the self and its true home: its essential sadness can never be surmounted'.[54] Muldoon does not have this experience because he does not accept the premises on which it rests – the notion of a 'true home'. His displacement to America, he says, is more a matter of choice than coercion: the experience of exile, he also implies, is as likely to be felt in Fintona,[55] Co. Tyrone, as at Princeton, New Jersey. He refuses to be recruited to Deane's postcolonial republican narrative because the traditional tropes of Irish exile are less relevant in an age of global dislocation, when a younger genera-

---

[53] Paul Muldoon, *The Prince of the Quotidian* (Loughcrew, The Gallery Press, 1994).

[54] Said, p. 357.

[55] By playfully suggesting that Fintona, a small place near Omagh, is the back of beyond, Muldoon would seem to be making the Co. Tyrone town into an Ulster mock-heroic version of, as it might be, Ovid's place of exile at Tomis on the Black Sea at the edge of the known world. Or perhaps he is alluding playfully to a passage in one of Benedict Kiely's short stories, 'Bluebell Meadow', where a Protestant woman is telling the story 'about the young fellow who went to the priest to tell him his sins and told him a story that had more women in it than King Solomon had in the Bible and the goings-on were terrible, and the priest says to him, Young man are you married? And the young fellow says back to him, dead serious and all, Naw father but I was twice in Fintona' (*The Collected Stories of Benedict Kiely* (London, Methuen, 2001)) p. 450. Like Kiely's young fellow who knows something about 'wild women', Muldoon knows something about exile, each from his experience of being twice in the semi-mythical Fintona.

tion, beneficiaries of education, new technology and easy travel, now inhabit the global village. The concept of 'exile', Muldoon suggests, harbours an outmoded essentialist myth of homeland. If 'exile' presumes an originary home and the eventual hope of return, Muldoon undoes the stable points of both departure and destination. As Fintan O'Toole puts it: 'The exile's dream of return has no meaning when the homeland is an ex-isle, a place forever gone.'[56] Ireland, says O'Toole 'has been for at least 150 years, scattered, splintered, atomised ... Ireland is a diaspora, and as such is both a real place and a remembered place, both the far west of Europe and the home back east of the Irish-American. Ireland is something that often happens elsewhere ... Emigration makes the borders of the island permeable.'[57] 'Home' is not any one place, language or tradition; it cannot be reduced to unitary notions of Ireland. Rather, 'home' is produced out of the encounter with other places, languages and histories, in the process of which the opposition between home and away, self and other, rootedness and itineracy, is inevitably revised. Ireland is now an 'emerald isle/ Of choice' – a cultural construct with significant American and global dimensions. Hence, Muldoon's interest in cultural and racial hybridity, in boundary-crossing and migrancy. The eliding of Louisa May Alcott, the New England feminist author of *Little Women*, and Derek Walcott, the Caribbean poet who saw himself as a nomad between European and West Indian culture – 'a mulatto of style' – enacts Muldoon's perception of hybrid identity. Walcott's Caribbean heritage is itself notoriously miscegenated as a result of British, French, Spanish, African, East Indian, Dutch – and Irish – influence: Montserrat is known as 'the emerald isle of the Caribbean' not only because of its scenic resemblance to Ireland but also because of the fact that in the seventeenth century Oliver Cromwell began transporting Irish political prisoners there after the defeat of the Irish at the Battle of Drogheda. The Irish interbred with the African slaves, and even today there is the hint of an Irish brogue amongst their descendents on the island, a curiosity to which Muldoon is perhaps alluding in his libretto *Shining Brow*, where Frank Lloyd Wright's black chef from Barbados (called 'Carleton' – perhaps named after the nineteenth-century boundary-crosser, William Carleton, who converted from Catholicism to Protestantism) provokes this question from Mamah: 'Can it be/ that all the natives of Barbados/ speak with an Irish brogue?'[58]

Unhampered by profound nostalgia for roots, and open to the challenges posed by the host culture, Muldoon exhibits more of a migrant or diasporic, as opposed to exilic, subjectivity. Iain Chambers explains:

> 'Migrancy ... involves a movement in which neither the points of departure nor those of arrival are immutable or certain. It calls for a dwelling in language, in histories, in identities that are constantly subject to mutation. Always in transit, the promise of a homecoming – completing the story, domesticating the detour – becomes an impossibility'.[59]

---

56 Fintan O'Toole, 'Setting Foot on Arch Hill', in *The Ex-Isle of Erin* (Dublin, New Island Books, 1996) pp. 157–79, 176.
57 Fintan O'Toole, *The Lie of the Land: Irish Identities* (London, Verso, 1997) pp. 12–13.
58 Paul Muldoon, *Shining Brow* (London, Faber, 1993) p. 62.
59 Iain Chambers, *Migrancy, Culture, Identity* (London, Routledge, 1994) p. 5.

For expatriate postmodern writers such as Muldoon, migration is, in the words of Stuart Hall, 'a one-way trip. There is no "home" to go back to.'[60] Muldoon's journeying never takes him to any definite destination (the Argentina that his father never reached) nor returns him to any definite 'home'. 'Homelessness', says Heidegger, 'is coming to be the destiny of the world.'[61] Migrancy, with its implication of discontinuity, becomes, in Iain Chambers' view, 'a potent theme of modern culture': 'The migrant's sense of being rootless, of living between worlds, between a lost past and a non-integrated present, is perhaps the most fitting metaphor of this (post)modern condition. This underlines the theme of diaspora.'[62] Diasporic writing, which encodes the experience of displacement and dispersal, mediates between the memory of the prior homeland and a sense of attachment to the adopted country. 'Home' is no longer a place, but the poetic space, which is a site of difference. Thus, on the lexical playfields of Muldoon's poetry, history is undone and re-inscribed, identities are broken down and re-combined, traditional forms are re-configured. Endlessly, the poet must map his own place in a world where there is no secure ground of being, no reliable co-ordinates that he can use. The materiality of place is dissolved in textual place, which brings more visibly to the fore the complexity, fluidity and constructed-ness of place, the way place is always a discourse in process.

If the story of contemporary Northern Irish poetry traces a general shift away from Yeatsian notions of rooted identity and the orthodoxy of a closed, unified culture towards a concept of culture as a worldwide web or provisional network of routes, it is worth remembering that the relation between place and culture has never been simple, that there has always been movement, migration and settlement in new places. The origin or 'centre' has always been diasporic, shaped by migration into Ireland, from Tudor Planters to present-day refugees and asylum seekers, and by out-migration, whether to America to escape the Famine or to England in search of work. Places are always linked together by flows of cultural influence that circulate through wider social space, though there is of course unevenness, from place to place, and from time to time, in the scale and intensity of these interconnections. Places are inevitably more or less hybrid, their character always influenced by relations with other places. Bounda-ries are always temporary, always porous, always socially constructed. The idea of a closed national culture has always been challenged and undermined. Not only is the concept of nation and the nation-state a comparatively recent develop-ment in the history of human evolution, but national boundaries are constantly changing to accommodate new political scenarios. The 'narrative of the nation' proclaimed by Irish nationalism calls for a return to a lost Gaelic past, but the ideal of a unified culture is something which never existed, and never will. Yet, illusory or artificial though they may be, these traditional notions of place and identity have proved to be extremely powerful, expressive of the passion for belonging, identity and cultural wholeness. The claims of home and homeland

[60] Stuart Hall, 'Minimal Selves', in L. Appignanesi (ed.), *Identity. The Real Me: Post-Modernism and the Question of Identity*, ICA Documents, 6 (London, ICA, 1987) p. 44.
[61] Martin Heidegger, 'Letter on Humanism', in *Basic Writings* (New York, Harper & Row, 1977) p. 219.
[62] Chambers, p. 27.

have been used to justify violence and atrocity, but they have also provided the ideological impetus for important movements of resistance and liberation. However, moving beyond these territorial concepts of place and belonging, and writing in the midst, or in the aftermath, of the most serious civil disturbance in the history of the state, and in an era of unprecedented migration, globalisation and transculturation, contemporary Northern Irish poets have taken up the challenge of exploring more diverse and open constructions of place, home and identity. If the realities of hybridity, diaspora and nomadism are age-old, it is only recently that a revitalised language of movement and interconnectedness has evolved, including that which informs an exciting new poetics of 'home', to deal with these realities in the contemporary context of radical, rapidly accelerating cultural change.

Chapter 2

PARADIGMS AND PRECURSORS:
ROOTED MEN AND NOMADS

John Hewitt, Patrick Kavanagh, Louis MacNeice

John Hewitt seems a natural starting-point in that nearly all subsequent Ulster poets have looked up to him as a moral exemplar and pioneering figure, the 'daddy of us all',[1] even if they developed a completely different poetics and aesthetic. Hewitt picks up the perennial debate about poetry and place from a distinctively Protestant, Planter point of view:

> In my experience, people of Planter stock often suffer from some crisis of identity, of not knowing where they belong. Among us you will find some who call themselves British, some Irish, some Ulstermen, usually with a degree of hesitation or mental fumbling.[2]

In these, the opening sentences of his essay, 'No Rootless Colonist' (1972), Hewitt speaks for many Ulster Protestants who, aware of Britain's ambivalence towards Northern Ireland, do not feel securely British, and who, perceiving the Gaelic and Catholic emphasis of cultural nationalism in the South, also feel excluded from dominant images of Irishness. In contrast to the glamour of the romantic nationalist narrative espoused by Northern Catholics, the Ulster Protestant, it is often felt, hasn't much of a story to tell, reflective as it is of an historic siege mentality, and structured largely in negative, defensive terms, in contradistinction to the perceived threat of the Catholic, Gaelic Other, North and South. Given Northern nationalists' rejection of Britishness, and Protestant Unionists' lack of an adequate cultural identity, Hewitt turned to the possibilities of territory and landscape viewed as common ground shared by all sections of the community.

Speaking from his 'Planter' position of insecurity and crisis, he declared in his programmatic essay of 1945, 'The Bitter Gourd: Some Problems of the Ulster Writer', that the Ulster writer must be a rooted man:

---

[1] James Simmons, 'Flight of the Earls Now Leaving', in *Judy Garland and the Cold War* (Belfast, Blackstaff Press, 1976) p. 3. The phrase was picked up by Michael Longley, writing in the *Belfast Telegraph* in an obituary tribute, 29 June 1987.

[2] John Hewitt, 'No Rootless Colonist', in Tom Clyde (ed.), *Ancestral Voices: The Selected Prose of John Hewitt* (Belfast, Blackstaff Press, 1987) p. 146. Hereafter abbreviated to *AV* and page references incorporated into the text.

If writers in an isolated group or in individual segregation are for too long disso-
ciated from the social matrix their work will inevitably grow thin and tenuous,
more and more concerned with form rather than content, heading for marvellous
feats of empty virtuosity ... He [the Ulster writer] must be a *rooted* man, must
carry the native tang of his idiom like the native dust on his sleeve; otherwise he
is an airy internationalist, thistledown, a twig on a stream ... An artist, certainly
in literature, must have a native place, pinpointed on a map, even if it is only to
run away from.   (*AV* 114–15)

In a bureaucratic, centralised world, Hewitt looks to the limited region, with its
local geography, history and traditions, as the bedrock of meaning and identity.
As to the question of whether the region is a product of the writers, or the
writers products of the region, it would seem that for Hewitt the individual artist
and the concept of the region are mutually produced. The crucial definition of
regionalism comes in his 1947 essay, 'Regionalism: The Last Chance':

Regionalism is based upon the conviction that, as man is a social being, he must,
now that the nation has become an enormously complicated organisation, find
some smaller unit to which to give his loyalty. This unit, since the day of the clan
is over and that of the large family is passing must be grounded on something
more than kinship. Between these limits lies the region; an area which possesses
geographical and economic coherence, which has had some sort of traditional and
historical identity and which still, in some measure, demonstrates cultural and
linguistic individuality. (*AV* 122)

The problem with Hewitt's 'region' was how to define it. He is deliberately vague.
Is he thinking of the historic province of Ulster, which includes Cavan, Mona-
ghan and Donegal, or is he tacitly endorsing the artificially constructed and
contested six-county statelet of Northern Ireland, which has much less of a claim
to natural, geographical coherence?[3] The essay concludes:

Ulster, considered as a region and not as the symbol of any particular creed, can, I
believe, command the loyalty of every one of its inhabitants. For regional identity
does not preclude, rather it requires, membership of a larger association. And,
whether that association be, as I hope, of a federated British Isles, or a federal
Ireland, out of that loyalty to our own place, rooted in honest history, in familiar
folkways and knowledge, phrased in our own dialect, there should emerge a culture
and an attitude individual and distinctive, a fine contribution to the European
inheritance and no mere echo of the thought and imagination of another people
or another land. (*AV* 125)

In place of an exclusive nationalism, he proposes an inclusive regionalism. The
driving force of Hewitt's thinking was a practical desire to sidestep the age-old
problems of religious and sectarian conflict, and to re-direct the question of
belonging away from the abstract idea of nation and towards a concept of an

---

[3]   In a 1985 interview, Hewitt admitted that his 'Ulster' was really only 'Antrim and Down and a bit
of Armagh, the northeast of Ulster'. In K. Levine, '"A Tree of Identities, a Tradition of Dissent":
John Hewitt at 78', *Fortnight*, 213 (February 1985) pp. 16–17.

inherently pluralist region. As an independently-minded 'dissenter', he was natu-
rally suspicious of the kind of ideological over-determination which nationalism
(Irish or British/Unionist) so often seemed to entail. His regionalist theory was
intended as an alternative to nationalism, whether Yeats's Anglo-Irish cultural
nationalism which excluded Northern Protestants, or Daniel Corkery and D.P.
Moran's philosophy of a Gaelic, Catholic 'Irish-Ireland' which excluded Prot-
estants altogether, or British/Unionist nationalism which excluded Irishness.
Acknowledging the multiplicity of Ulster's culture and history, he attempted to
re-imagine place in a way that would allow both Unionist and Nationalist a sense
of belonging. The region is construed as a paradoxical mesh of overlapping and
divergent belongings that resist unification within either of the existing national
formations.

He uses his own situation to demonstrate this idea of multiple belonging:

> I'm an Ulsterman of planter stock. I was born in the island of Ireland, so second-
> arily I'm an Irishman. I was born in the British archipelago and English is my
> native tongue, so I am British. The British archipelago is offshore to the continent
> of Europe, so I'm European. This is my hierarchy of values and as far as I'm
> concerned, anyone who omits one step in that sequence is falsifying the situa-
> tion.[4]

He emphasises a plural, woven identity, a capacity for holding several alle-
giances simultaneously. His 'both-and' rather than 'either-or' model of social
and political relations chimes with Edna Longley's notion of Northern Ireland
as a cultural corridor, permeated and enriched by both British and Irish cultural
influences. Longley considers that Irish literature reflects such a state of affairs,
even if Northern Irish politics do not, for both Unionism and Nationalism tend
to 'block the corridor at one end ... or the other'.[5] Freed from the essentialist
mystique of the national, the mythic and the tribal, Hewitt's concept of the region
has similarities with Kavanagh's notion of the 'parochial', but where Hewitt's
imagined community is based on a recognition of difference and variety, Kavan-
agh's 'parish' assumes homogeneous community and traditional values. As such,
the concept of the unitary 'parish' cannot readily be applied to Ulster construed
as a frontier-society, a cultural corridor, 'a site riven by the problems, cleavages,
barriers and traffic of history'.[6] Standing on 'riven' Ulster ground, Hewitt doesn't
exclude other – Irish, British or European – contexts, nor does he insist on
any particular political arrangement. Preferring to defer the question of political
structures, he contents himself with cultural retrieval and imaginative explora-
tion of the fractured terrain of his Ulster homeland. From one point of view this
looks like a cop-out, a refusal to face the hard questions, so desperate is the wish
to establish a sense of shared heritage; from another, it can be seen as a strategic
decision to create a breathing space amidst the clamour of sectarian atavisms,

---

4   John Hewitt, *Irish Times*, 4 July 1974.
5   Edna Longley, 'Opening Up: A New Pluralism', in R. Johnstone and R. Wilson (eds.), *Troubled
    Times: Fortnight Magazine and the Troubles in Northern Ireland 1970–1991* (Belfast, Blackstaff
    Press, 1991) pp. 141–4, 144.
6   Edna Longley, *The Living Stream: Literature and Revisionism in Ireland* (Newcastle-upon-Tyne,
    Bloodaxe Books, 1994) p. 60.

a space in which a new language of common ground, rather than division and otherness, might be shaped. Nevertheless, the language in which Hewitt's notion of regional identity is cast reveals the limits of his claim to radicalism. His 'hierarchy of values' suggests a notion of assimilativeness that is more multicultural than *inter*cultural, an acceptance of otherness that does not imply any radical transformation of his 'original' Planter identity. The model of identity which he espoused is based on notions of concentricity, rather than hybridity, as meaning the equal exchange or mutuality of cultures. Throughout his life he adhered to the idea of a 'British solution' to the question of regional identity. Thus, in a 1985 interview given two years before his death, he had this to say:

> I couldn't … happily belong to a Gaelic-speaking Irish republic, because that's not my native tongue, and I don't want to separate it from Britain because the complete body, the corpus of my thought, has come from Britain … The Irish people, before my ancestors came here, were a tribe of cattle-rustlers, fighting each other and burning churches and what not. They wrote very nice songs and some good poetry. I'd like to include them too in the general picture, but they're not the whole of the story.[7]

Hewitt's notions of regionalism are nothing if not contradictory and inconsistent, his variations of emphasis depending on the changing circumstances of his life and the audience he is addressing. His generally Anglocentric views can, on occasion, mutate into more radical-sounding pronouncements, as when, in a letter to John Montague in 1964, he speaks of regionalism as 'a necessary first step to prize Ulster loose from the British anchorage' in preparation for 'unity with the other part of our island' and transformation of Ulster people into 'a special kind of Irish themselves'.[8] Despite his somewhat inflexible terminology of 'hierarchy' and strict 'sequence', at times the self-conscious Planter also wants to be a native Gael. In 'Rite, Lubitavish, Glenaan' (1953), he proclaims himself 'of the Irishry/ by nurture and by birth';[9] in 'May Altar' (1950), he 'hankers for the pagan thorn' (*CP* 115). From early on – in 'Ireland' (1932) – he shows his concern to lay claim to both an Irish and an inclusive European identity. He numbers himself among 'We Irish' who were part of 'the Keltic wave that broke over Europe,/ and ran up this bleak beach among these stones' (*CP* 58). In contrast to the final line of 'Once alien here' ('as native in my thought as any here'), he declares in 'Ireland': 'We are not native here or anywhere' (*CP* 58). Rather than ideas of 'rootedness', he emphasises the importance of movement and migration to the life of a community. Deeply critical of insularity and isolationism, he calls for a continual openness to outside influences in order to avoid fossilisation:

> So we are bitter, and are dying out
> In terrible harshness in this lonely place,

---

7   Levine, pp. 16–17.
8   John Hewitt, letter to John Montague (Spring 1964) John Hewitt Collection, University of Ulster at Coleraine.
9   Frank Ormsby (ed.), *The Collected Poems of John Hewitt* (Belfast, Blackstaff Press, 1991) p. 83. Hereafter abbreviated to *CP* and page references incorporated into the text.

And what we think is love for usual rock,
Or old affection for our customary ledge,
Is but forgotten longing for the sea
That cries far out and calls us to partake
In his great tidal movements round the earth.   (*CP* 58)

Even while seeking to uncover the grounds of a common Ulster identity, Hewitt himself was never quite able to escape the constraints and prejudices of his own Ulster Protestant background. Politically, he situates himself in an English rather than Irish socialist tradition, taking his bearings from the Diggers and Levellers who had sought to bring about a social revolution during the English Civil War, the writings of Thomas Paine and William Cobbett, the English Chartists who had campaigned in the 1840s for workers' votes, and William Morris's utopian socialism. He identifies with the Ulster dissenting tradition, with the 'vertical men who never genuflected,/ the assertors, the protestors', as he put it in 'Rose-blade's visitants and mine' (*CP* 392); with the United Irishmen and northern weaver poets of the late eighteenth- and early nineteenth centuries who exemplified for him an attractive independence of mind. His preferred freedom-fighting narratives are drawn, not from the Irish, but the wider European archive: in 'No Rootless Colonist', he acknowledges only 'a vague sense of romantic Irish nationalism ... our politics looked beyond to the world. Sacco and Vanzetti were, for us, far more significant than any of the celebrated "felons of our land"' (*AV* 150). When he writes about the Glens people, he does so in the manner of English landscape and nature poets, as he himself acknowledges: 'I draw upon an English literary tradition which includes Marvell, Crabbe, Wordsworth, Clare ...' (*AV* 148). Generally, he employs a standard Ulster-English, only cautiously venturing into idiomatic speech or Ulster-Scots dialect usages (as in 'The Bloody Brae'). Rarely does he consider Irish language culture as forming an important part of the Ulster 'weave':

Our speech is a narrow speech, the rags and remnants
Of Tudor rogues and stiff Scots Covenanters,
With a jab or two of glaar from tangled sheugh,
And the cross-roads solo and the penny ballad.
                    ('Overture for Ulster Regionalism', *CP* 512)

'Glaar' (mud) and 'sheugh' (ditch) are Irish words, but a mere 'jab or two' of Irish is sufficient to account for the Irish component of Ulster speech. In a 1981 interview, he spoke with characteristic ambivalence of both willingness and reluctance to broach the Irish element: 'I've wanted somebody to open that door to me because I'm reluctant to open it myself.'[10] He has stood accused not only of concentrating on Planter and Ulster-Scots cultural tradition at the expense of indigenous culture, but of treating the Catholic religion with offensive disdain (though he had little truck with religion of any kind). Rather than dissolving the

---

[10]   John Hewitt, Interview with Daniel J. Casey, *Quarto*, 7 (1980–1) p. 38.

old binaries of Protestant and Catholic, colonist and colonised, his poetry, some readers have concluded, merely reinforces the age-old oppositions.[11]

However, if the question of political correctness can be put aside for long enough, there is much to recommend in Hewitt's poetry – his subtlety, his courage and honesty, his willingness to confront the tensions in Ulster society and in himself, his forthright admission of the difficulty in sustaining the regionalist ideal of a rooted, territorialised identity that was at the same time shared, inclusive and open. The tensions are evident in 'The Colony' (1950), a 140-line poem in decasyllabic blank verse which allegorises regional circumstance as that of a Roman colony at the Empire's waning, and considers how the colonists viewed the situation and the future. The speaker is a Roman colonist, the representative of state power, and it is his version of events which counts. As an expression of the colonist's self-justifying rhetoric, the poem constructs a series of oppositions: civilisation versus barbarism, rationality versus irrationality, cultivation of the land versus neglect, culture versus nature. Civilisation, culture and rationality are the characteristics of the colonist, while the native is projected as barbaric, childlike, superstitious, irresponsible, requiring the assistance, guidance or coercion of the colonial master. Yet, while Hewitt's poem is weighted on the side of Empire and colonialism, it treats colonial stereotypes with considerable subtlety. There is, for example, no attempt to idealise the colonists, who are variously described as 'camp-followers', a 'rabble', and include runaway debtors, tax absconders and opportunistic lawclerks, as well as those seeking freedom 'beyond the ready whim of Caesar's fist', and those fleeing 'for conscience' sake' (*CP* 76). Within the discourse of colonialism, the natives are the savage 'other', the 'wild Irish', a people living outside civilisation. But in the context of the poem's narrative of violent dispossession ('for we began the plunder'; 'We took the kindlier soils' *CP* 77) and enslavement ('Teams of the tamer natives we employed/ to hew and draw, but did not call them slaves' *CP* 78), reference to the native population as 'barbarian tribesmen' (*CP* 77) is not without irony. Throughout, the Roman settler's is an unsettled narrative voice, contradictory and uncertain in its attitudes and pronouncements. Fear of the natives is mingled with guilt for having dispossessed them of their land, which at the same time doesn't prevent the colonist from expressing his deep pride in having developed the land and made it productive. He is touched by the 'old tree magic', but quickly recovers from such 'enchantments', which are branded a sickness: 'but I am not a sick and haunted man' (*CP* 78). Hewitt's satire plays over stereotypical colonial attitudes, such as the idea that the natives can be distinguished 'by pigmentation'

---

[11] The most trenchant attack has come from Sarah Ferris who, in her book, *Poet John Hewitt (1907–1987) and Criticism of Northern Irish Protestant Writing* (New York, The Edwin Mellen Press, 2002), argues that Hewitt's rise to prominence in the early '70s when the Troubles were at their height, was the result of partisan influences, emanating chiefly from the Arts Council and the academy, which sought to create a Protestant alternative to both a compromised ruling class and an ascendant romantic nationalism: 'In a context of rising antipathy towards a "Protestant state", Hewitt's claim to be an atheist, man of the left, cultural visionary and victim of the Ulster "establishment", commended him to northern intellectuals as a uniquely sexy Protestant' (p. 66). The burden of Ferris's argument is to dismantle the myth of Hewitt the 'Perfect Protestant' (p. 4), and to re-present the so-called anti-sectarian, radical socialist evangelist as an essentially conservative crypto-unionist.

(*CP* 78), that 'they breed like flies' (*CP* 78), that their religious practice is mere superstition which 'we snigger at' (*CP* 78). In the last lines of the last section, the speaker sets himself apart from the other colonists by affirming his desire to cohabit peacefully with the natives:

> We would be strangers in the Capitol;
> This is our country also, nowhere else;
> And we shall not be outcast on the world.   (*CP* 79)

But even while wishing to 'make amends' (*CP* 79) for ancient wrongs, the speaker can still sound patronising, as when he refers to the natives' 'swaddled minds' and considers them capable of being 'redeemed/ if they themselves rise up against the spells/ and fears their celebates surround them with' (*CP* 79). The stridency of the poem's final confident assertions suggests an underlying insecurity. Belonging is not something simply to be accepted as natural, a given, as it is for the Catholic poets, but has to be argued for, proved, demonstrated. As John Wilson Foster remarks, the last lines capture 'the planter's brittle certainty with its soft centre of despair'.[12]

Hewitt is as much obsessed by history as Heaney or Montague, but in a different way. Where poets from a Catholic nationalist background are motivated by a revivalist urge to recuperate a lost past and way of life that have become submerged under colonialism, Hewitt is driven to the past by guilt, by the need to provide proofs (of birth, residence, genealogy and personal investment) to justify his claims to nativeness, with regionalism as the mechanism of reconciliation. In 'The Colony', the speaker hopes he can convince the country people that he and his people have changed 'if not to kin, to co-inhabitants' (*CP* 79). The hope is characteristically cautious, and contains a realistic acknowledgement of limits. Similar qualifications and pull-backs appear in other poems. In 'The Watchers' (1950), the speaker closely observes a badger: 'It was as if another nature came/ close to my knowledge, but could not be known' (*CP* 81). 'O Country People' (1950) is a meditation on the gap between the urban speaker and the country people: 'I would be neighbourly, would come to terms/ with your existence, but you are so far'; 'I know the level you accept me on/ .../ But we are no part of your world, your way' (*CP* 73). It is the same sentiment as that expressed by Brian Friel's Hibernophile English colonist, Yolland, in *Translations*: 'I'd always be an outsider here ... I may learn the password but the language of the tribe will always elude me ... The private core will always be ... hermetic, won't it?'[13] But Hewitt is even more emphatic about his alienation:

> I recognise the limits I can stretch;
> even a lifetime among you should leave me strange,
> for I could not change enough, and you will not change;
> there's still be levels neither'd ever reach.   (*CP* 73)

12   John Wilson Foster, '"The Dissidence of Dissent": John Hewitt and W.R. Rodgers', in Gerald Dawe and Edna Longley (eds.), *Across a Roaring Hill: The Protestant Imagination in Modern Ireland* (Belfast, Blackstaff, 1985) p. 141.
13   Brian Friel, *Translations*, in Seamus Deane (ed.), *Selected Plays of Brian Friel* (London, Faber, 1984) p. 416.

Constantly, the polemic of regionalist identity comes under pressure from the poet's awareness of difference and otherness. All the time looking for the grounds of community and commonality, he is forced to acknowledge increasing personal alienation, and political and social division. The signs are there from early on. 'Conacre' (1943), written at the time when he was just beginning to formulate his theory of regionalism from his readings in Le Play, Patrick Geddes and Lewis Mumford (*AV*, 152–3), registers what Foster calls 'reminders of incomplete plantation'.[14] The poem defines 'home' and 'country' in terms of elemental landscape rather than in human terms:

> This is my home and country. Later on
> Perhaps I'll find this nation is my own
> But here and now it is enough to love
> This faulted ledge, this map of cloud above,
> And the great sea that beats against the west
> To swamp the sun.   (*CP* 9–10)

The title, 'Conacre', connotes his uncertainty about 'nation', conacre being land which is leased on a temporary basis (though two later poems, 'Freehold' (1946) and 'Homestead' (1949) suggest a more secure and confident sense of tenure). If 'Conacre' defers the challenge of 'nation', in a later poem, 'The Scar' (1971), he is anxious to claim 'Irish' identity on the dubious grounds that his great-grandmother died from famine fever as a result of responding to a beggarman's cry for help. But, again, otherness is stressed simultaneously with identification:

> Though much I cherish lies outside their vision,
> and much they prize I have no claim to share,
> yet in that woman's death I found my nation.   (*CP* 177)

In one of his best-known poems, 'Once alien here' (1942), difference is reinforced by the Romantic stereotyping of the Catholic peasantry, which leads the poet away from the real lives of these people:

> The sullen Irish limping to the hills
> Bore with them the enchantments and the spells
> That in the clans' free days hung gay and rich
> On every twig of every thorny hedge,
> And gave the rain-pocked stone a meaning past
> The blurred engraving of the fibrous frost.   (*CP* 21)

Contrast this with the description of his own people who, unlike the hill-people, are the entrepreneurs, the shapers, those with tasks to perform, a destiny to fulfil. This race of industrious builders and doers are framed within a strenuous, heavily-accented, consonantal rhetoric: 'Once alien here my fathers built their house,/ claimed, drained, and gave the land the shapes of use ...' (*CP* 20). The final stanza asserts belonging and identity shaped by environment:

---

14   *Across a Roaring Hill*, p. 142.

> So I, because of all the buried men
> in Ulster clay, because of rock and glen
> and mist and cloud and quality of air
> as native in my thought as any here   (*CP* 21)

The poem, having described a divided community and a sectarian landscape, is tensed between asserting belonging and accepting non-belonging. We cannot help feeling that Hewitt's rational, democratic argument is unable to compete with his sense of the existence of authentic (racial and religious) belonging. In the end, an assured image of shared, common ground remains elusive.

'The Glens' (1942) is mostly taken up with expression of the poet's alienation from the country people: 'Not these my people of a vainer faith/ ... / I fear their creed as we have always feared/ The lifted hand against unfettered thought' (*CP* 310). The poem evinces Hewitt's deeply rooted fear of the Catholic Irish – a colonist's fear of those his ancestors had dispossessed, and a dissenter's fear of the power of the Catholic Church. In lines that Heaney was to re-work in 'The Other Side', Hewitt pushes towards a sense of difference that is ultimately unspeakable. In the country he is alone, always on the margins, a spy, a watcher, an outsider:

> I cannot spare more than a common phrase
> of crops and weather when I pace these lanes
> and pause at hedge gap spying on their skill,
> so many fences stretch between our minds.   (*CP 310*)

Only in the last three lines does he change direction, shifting his attention from the people to the landscape as the ground of home, and inspiration of his poetry:

> And yet no other corner in this land
> Offers, in shape and colour all I need
> For sight to touch the mind with living light.   (*CP* 310)

While constantly aware of difference, he evinces a comprehensive understanding of what is needed to bring the two communities in Ulster together. His long dramatic poem, 'The Bloody Brae' (1937), deals with the residual problems of a violent history in a courageous and far-sighted manner. The poem is based on actual events which occurred in 1642 when a Cromwellian force massacred Catholics in Islandmagee. John Hill, an aged soldier troubled by guilt about the murder of a young woman, Bridget Magee, is forgiven by her ghost but charged with having indulged his guilt rather than devoting himself to promoting tolerance in others. Only by such decisive action can the wrongs of the past be expiated and the cycle of violence and distrust broken. Hewitt may well be addressing himself (Frank Ormsby calls attention to the significance of the planter's initials). On this reading, the poem becomes an honest appraisal of the poet's own brand of quiet moderation, a reflection on his own failure to be sufficiently bold and resolute in reaching out to others in the battle against prejudice and injustice.

The failure of his application for Directorship of the Belfast Museum and Art Gallery in 1953 has been the subject of considerable debate. His 'progressive non-sectarianism', Ian Duhig commented, 'cost him a career on his home ground'.[15] However, the view that Hewitt's rejection was an essentially political determination, an expression of repressive Unionist opposition to his radical and socialist ideals, is arguably based on a somewhat mythologised account of what actually may have happened. Sarah Ferris, who has assembled and scrutinised the evidence, is sceptical about such a view,[16] and certainly it is more comfortable to think that one has been ideologically victimised than deemed difficult to work with, which was probably at least a consideration. Between 1957 and 1972 Hewitt lived outside his native Belfast, having accepted the Directorship of the Herbert Gallery and Museum in Coventry. The move to Coventry, he later said, was 'one of the best things that ever happened to me'.[17] In this cosmopolitan city, re-building after the war, he could escape the parochialism of Ulster but not, it would seem, the tensions in his own inheritance and outlook. 'An Irishman in Coventry' (1958) reveals his liberal, socialist approval of the rapidly modernising city and its progressive attitudes:

> A full year since, I took this eager city,
> The tolerance that laced its blatant roar,
> its famous steeples and its web of girders,
> As image of the state hope argued for ...   (*CP* 97)

When his thoughts turn to Ireland and the Irish, familiar feelings of 'rage and pity' re-surface. While he may choose to identify with an 'enclave of my nation' in Coventry, he still remains 'apart'.

> The faces and the voices blurring round me,
> The whiskey-tinctured breath, the pious buttons
> Called up a people endlessly betrayed
> By our own weakness, by the wrongs we suffered
> In that long twilight over bog and glen,
> By force, by famine and by glittering fables
> Which gave us martyrs when we needed men ...   (*CP* 97–8)

His Protestant colonist's need to balance colonial 'wrongs' with the shortcomings of the native is apparent in the ironic enjambment: 'a people endlessly betrayed/ by our own weakness, by the wrongs we suffered'. English Enlightenment tolerance has not modified his contempt for Catholic, nationalist Ireland. Old attitudes remain fixed, inherited certainties prevail over more liberal, non-sectarian instincts.

Placing 'An Irishman in Coventry' alongside John Montague's 'Murphy in Manchester',[18] another poem about the emigrant experience written around the same time, highlights the difference in cultural perspective between the

---

15 Ian Duhig, '"Pictures carried with singing"', *Irish Review*, 12 (Spring–Summer 1992) pp. 165–70, 167.

16 Ferris concludes: '[I]t is possible Hewitt was generally perceived as operating with a professional hubris incompatible with his role as public servant, and that he was considered temperamentally unsuited to manage the diverse priorities of a public resource equitably' (p. 13).

17 John Hewitt, *Quarto*, 7, 1980–1.

18 John Montague, 'Murphy in Manchester', in *Poisoned Lands* (Dublin, Dolmen Press, 1977) p. 18. First published by McGibbon and Kee, 1961.

Planter and the Gael. Hewitt's poem is obviously more directly autobiographical, Montague's more emblematic of a collective mythology. Hewitt's first person narration allows us to see the inner struggle of the speaker, while Montague's third person narration keeps his persona at a distance, views him from the outside, and treats him typologically. In comparison to Montague's poem, Hewitt's contains a more positive view of England and a more critical attitude to Ireland. Hewitt's England inspires hope and confidence. Coventry is a well-ordered place in contrast to Ireland's 'crazily tangled' history, and the poet feels at home there. Murphy, on the other hand, a very different persona from Hewitt's middle-class, cultivated urbanite, is one of Hewitt's country folk, a naïve young man uprooted from his familiar rural surroundings and forced, like so many of his kind, to come to England in search of work. In Manchester he feels confused, lost and alienated. Where Hewitt's persona responds enthusiastically to Coventry's new urban developments, the 'vast glass headlands', 'the comprehensive school', Montague's Murphy experiences English civic pride from the very different standpoint of the colonial subaltern: 'Stares open-mouthed at monuments/ To manufacturers, sabred generals'. For Murphy, the city will mean, not the 'high promise' of Hewitt's urban dream, but continuation of the collective historical experience of loss and exploitation: 'Soon the whistling factory/ Will lock him in:/ Half-stirred memories and regrets/ Drowning in that iron din'. Murphy's (and, by metonymic extension, Ireland's) victimhood is as 'fated' as Ireland's is in Hewitt's poem. 'This is our fate: eight hundred years' disaster', says Hewitt, though his final lines suggest the possibility of a break with determinism. Montague's view of Ireland, as mediated through Murphy, is more idealised, homely and nostalgic than Hewitt's. Montague's tone is softer and gentler. Only in the final lines of Hewitt's poem do the poet's anger and resentment against his 'nation' recede, replaced by resignation and a (forlorn) hope for the future, contained in the romantic, mythological image of Ireland: 'Yet like Lir's children banished on the waters/ our hearts still listen for the landward bells'.

Eventually, Hewitt comes to see the illusoriness of thinking in terms of a bounded region. He was always, as Frank Ormsby remarks, 'an inveterate traveller' (*CP* lxv), and the travelled, cosmopolitan aspect of his life and work should not be underestimated. A sequence of travel poems, first published in the pamphlet *Tesserae* (1967), following a visit with his wife to mainland Greece and the Cyclades the previous year, has the poet uprooted from his native place but finding himself 'at home' amidst the ruins of the classical world. The first poem in *Tesserae*, 'Hand over Hand', introduces a contrasting persona to that of the rooted man: 'Some time now I have felt outside life/ floating like a padded man/ on a slack cable round his capsule/ with neither pull nor drag' (*CP* 51). Notions of attachment and rootedness are replaced by a 'billowing freedom' which 'threatens to/ smother me with euphoria./ Hand over hand eagerly I crawl/ back to uncertainty' (*CP* 51). In 'Mykonos and Epidaurus', the Greek landscape momentarily calls to mind Cuchullain and Ossian,

> But only near the dark green grove
> with the pine-scent and the light airs
> among the fronded fans,

> was I somehow strangely at home,
> receiving, open, myself.   (*CP* 55–6)

In Greece, he is 'strangely at home' (*CP* 56); being 'myself' no longer involves the feeling of being embedded in a region or community.

These poems mark a stage beyond the situation described in the early 'Homestead' (1949), which scathingly dismisses ideas of travel and relocation, emphasising instead the need for stability, rootedness and community. In this poem the poet is preparing to build a house, a 'dwelling, and … an outcrop, part of the place' (*CP* 68). It will, the poet says, be a durable, fixed construction, not mobile like the Ark, which is now a forgotten wreck. The suggestion of a mobile existence with no boundaries or roots is dismissed as living a 'mirage', and prompts a reassertion of the value of local place and tradition, significantly couched in a vigorous Ulster-Scots vernacular: 'No. There is nothing for it but to build right here/ In rough-cut stone and spread a roof of scraws' (*CP* 71). The homestead obviously means more than a natural or physical structure. It is a concept, an ideal, a spiritual and aesthetic space:

> The stonework will be simple, honest and sturdy
> Not showy, not even neat but built to last.
> I go today to the quarry to tryst the stones.   (*CP* 72)

But the attempt to articulate a tolerant, liberal, urbane politics in a time of war is inevitably scored by tension and unease. He is aware of the limits of his own traditional formalist procedures: 'Reality is of a coarser texture;/ the scene collapses absurd,/ lath and canvas' (*CP* 140). In 'The Coasters' (1972), the benign and mannerly address of his earlier regionalist verse gives way to seething anger at those, including himself, who have been chiefly responsible for the disintegration of his ideal – the complacent middle-class of both communities. The title is loaded, suggesting smooth, easy sailing along the shore, keeping to familiar territory, never venturing into deeper water. The rhythm is gentle, light and flowing, the tone contemptuous and bitter. The image is of a progressive, easygoing society, but in reality it is paralysed by self-delusion and hypocrisy, as Hewitt emphasises in repeating the clichéd phrase 'relations were improving' (*CP* 136). Atrophy, not progressiveness, is pervasive. The poem ends with a vision of a diseased, delirious society, complacency obliterated, the slums in turmoil, contagion threatening the 'leafy suburbs':

> Now the fever is high and raging;
> who would have guessed it, coasting along?
> The ignorant sick thresh about in delirium
> and tear at the scabs with dirty fingernails.
> The cloud of infection hangs over the city,
> a quick change of wind and it
> might spill over the leafy suburbs.
> You coasted too long.   (*CP* 137)

While the tone is one of regret for missed opportunities, an air of middle-class liberal angst and helplessness hangs over the whole poem. There is no cure, no hope for the future. Hewitt admits his own shortcomings, his own prejudices and timidity: 'And you who never had an adventurous thought/ were positive enough that the church of the other sort/ vetoes thought' (*CP* 136).

The sense of radical discontinuity inherent in modernity and brought forcefully to the fore by the violence of the Troubles makes him question the relevance of his earlier pastoralism:

> Then I remembered that the nature-poet
> Has no easy prosody for
> Class or property relationships,
> For the social dialectic ...
>
> ('Below the Mournes in May', 1975, *CP* 244)

Likewise, pressure of events forces a revision of the traditional place-name poem. 'Ulster Names' (1950) celebrates the intimate knowledge of particular places in typical regionalist fashion: 'I take my stand by the Ulster names,/ each clean hard name like a weathered stone' (C 386). But 'Postscript, 1984' re-writes the earlier poem in the context of the Troubles:

> Banbridge, Ballykelly, Darkley, Crossmaglen,
> Summoning pity, anger and despair,
> By grief of kin, by hate of murderous men
> Till the whole tarnished map is stained and torn,
> Not to be read as pastoral again. (*CP* 388).

In 'A Local Poet' (1975), he contemplates the undoing of the whole weave of his endeavour – the failure of the vision of community represented by the Rhyming Weavers, the dispelling of the myth of literary Ireland, the inadequacy of his own 'mannerly verses'. Recognition of conflict and disunity makes him self-conscious about his language and procedures. 'Neither an Elegy nor a Manifesto' (1972) presents the struggle to find an 'unrhetorical', 'neutral' and 'unaligned' language that would speak for the whole community, for 'those deliberately gunned down/ and those caught by unaddressed bullets:/ such distinctions are not relevant':

> Bear in mind these dead:
> I can find no plainer words.
> I dare not risk using
> That loaded word, Remember. (*CP* 188)

The poem is a moving, humanist lament in which the rhetoric of 'patriotism, loyalty, martyrdom' is replaced by a tentative exhortation to 'thoughtful response'. But the note of helplessness and hopelessness prevails.

With its strict poetic decorum, its quiet tones and plain style, its distrust of freedom and extravagance, its technique of careful observation and concern for form, Hewitt's is not a poetic equipped to probe the dark recesses of the Ulster conscience or to confront 'the Spirit that plagued us so'.[19] His are the poetics of homestead, disturbed by fears of homelessness, but reluctant to penetrate the dark facts of hatred and division. Heaney has generously acknowledged

---

[19] Seamus Heaney, 'A Northern Hoard', in *Wintering Out* (London, Faber, 1972) p. 39.

Hewitt's exemplary importance to succeeding Northern Irish writers 'as a hinterland of reference, should they require a tradition more intimate than the broad perspectives of the English literary achievement',[20] and Heaney's own poetry has undoubtedly been helped into existence by Hewitt's regionalist experiment. Like Hewitt, he writes poems about landscape and place, about vanishing rural rites and traditional customs, about Ulster's variegated linguistic inheritance. But in his Scandinavian and Viking poems he elaborates a sustained narrative engagement with the powers of the dark, in which he pursues hidden, telluric aspects of language, psyche and race sensibility ('unscarfing/ a zoomorphic wake,/ a worm of thought/ I follow into the mud'[21]), probes his own deepest fears, and the most tabooed knowledges, the unruly, wild energies within the culture. Drawing attention to the unconscious pagan and violent barbarian drives within his Ulster Catholic rural community, he enters the Irish necropolis ('I am Hamlet the Dane,/ skull-handler …'[22]) to investigate the diseased psycopathology of his people. There is a breadth and depth of imaginative vision in Heaney which is lacking in Hewitt. Terence Brown is surely correct in concluding that Hewitt 'remain[s] a minor poet because in the end, despite the integrity of his vision, imaginatively he does not know enough'.[23] Hewitt doesn't know enough about otherness, and isn't sufficiently interested in exploring it. His 'mannerly verses', as he admitted himself, left so much unsaid. 'Simple, honest and sturdy' they may be, but they are locked into stereotypical, essentialist assumptions about Irish culture and identity. Such assumptions would also seem to underlie the conception of Hewitt's and Montague's celebrated 1970 poetry tour around the province, entitled 'The Planter and the Gael'. Although designed to encourage greater cross-community understanding, and hailed by Roy Foster as 'a landmark affirmation of cultural diversity',[24] the tour was very much a project of its time, its very title highlighting fixed and fossilised binary thinking and reflecting pre-given, ethnically defined identities.

*

However, for Ulster Catholic poets like Heaney, it was Catholic Kavanagh rather than 'Planter' Hewitt who was the truly exemplary poet of roots and region. By the time Kavanagh arrived in Dublin in 1939 the Revival was on its last legs though some were still trying to be peasants and ready to hail Kavanagh as the real thing. He, however, was struggling to discard the stereotype of the literary peasant and attempting to give an honest, realistic picture of rural Irish life. Earlier writers such as Yeats or Joyce, writing from a colonial or postcolonial standpoint were, not unnaturally, absorbed by the binary opposition between Ireland and England. Kavanagh's great contribution to Irish poetry was his disregard of the colonial theme, his rejection of the nationalist and Revivalist orthodoxies of rural

---

20 Seamus Heaney, quoted by Michael Longley in 'Poetry', in Michael Longley (ed.), *Causeway: the Arts in Ulster* (Belfast, Arts Council of Northern Ireland, 1971) pp. 106–7.

21 Seamus Heaney, 'Viking Dublin: Trial Pieces', in *North* (London, Faber, 1975) p. 23.

22 Ibid.

23 Terence Brown, 'The Poetry of W.R. Rodgers and John Hewitt', in Douglas Dunn (ed.), *Decades of Irish Writing* (Cheadle, Carcanet, 1975) pp. 81–97, 95.

24 Roy Foster, 'Varieties of Irishness', in M. Crozier (ed.), *Cultural Traditions in Northern Ireland*, March 1989, Belfast, p. 22.

harmony, and his insistence on the artistic validity of the local, the particular and the ordinary. As he famously put it in *Kavanagh's Weekly* in 1952: 'Parochialism and provincialism are direct opposites. A provincial is always trying to live by other people's loves, but a parochial is self-sufficient'.[25] In his essay of 1975, 'From Monaghan to the Grand Canal', Heaney embraces Kavanagh as 'something new, authentic and liberating', a poet who ignored the mythic, historical or literary imperatives that had usually governed Irish writing, and who seemed to have 'wrested his idiom bare-handed out of a literary nowhere'.[26] Heaney identifies in Kavanagh's work a concern with a hidden Ireland, 'a hard buried life that subsisted beyond the feel of middle-class novelists and romantic nationalistic poets, a life denuded of "folk" and picturesque elements', and the word he uses to describe this quality in Kavanagh – 'artesian'[27] – he also applies to his own short-lined verse that drills down into the depths of consciousness and culture. Kavanagh's depiction of Irish rural life, says Heaney, opened new ground, 'raising the inhibited energies of a subculture to the power of a cultural resource'. Again, the tribute to Kavanagh re-cycles self-description, as when Heaney describes his early poetry as 'divination, poetry as revelation of the self to the self, as restoration of the culture to itself'.[28] Clearly, Heaney considered the possibility of being a 'parochial' poet like Kavanagh: 'I have no need to write a poem to Patrick Kavanagh', he is reported to have said, 'I wrote *Death of a Naturalist*'.[29] The echo of Kavanagh's *The Great Hunger* in the opening lines of Heaney's 'At a Potato Digging' has often been noted, but the direction of Heaney's poem suggests the differences between the two poets that would become more evident in Heaney's later work. As Heaney says in his essay, the '"matter of Ireland", mythic, historical or literary, forms no significant part'[30] of Kavanagh's material. Certainly, Kavanagh's title alludes to the Great Famine of the 1840s, and the spiritual hunger of twentieth-century rural Ireland, but *The Great Hunger* remains a poem of its own time and place. Heaney's potato-diggers, however, do lead him towards the 'matter of Ireland', and the poem resolves itself in a mixture of Christian and pagan ritual as the diggers, 'stretched on the faithless ground, spill/ Libations', in propitiation of the 'famine god'.[31]

Another essay of two years later, 'The Sense of Place' (1977), reiterates Heaney's profound sense of gratitude to the older poet:

> Kavanagh's fidelity to the uncompromising, unspectacular countryside of Monaghan and his rendering of the authentic speech of those parts gave the majority of Irish people, for whom the experience of life on the land was perhaps the most formative, an image of themselves that nourished their sense of themselves.[32]

Heaney compares Kavanagh with both Montague and Hewitt. In Kavanagh,

---

25 Patrick Kavanagh, 'Parochialism and Provincialism', in Antoinette Quinn (ed.), *Patrick Kavanagh: A Poet's Country: Selected Prose* (Dublin, Lilliput, 2003) p. 237.
26 Seamus Heaney, *Preoccupations: Selected Prose 1968–1978* (London, Faber, 1980) p. 116.
27 Ibid.
28 Seamus Heaney, 'Feeling into Words', in *Preoccupations*, p. 41.
29 Seamus Heaney, quoted in Dunn (ed.), *Two Decades of Irish Criticism*, p. 35.
30 Seamus Heaney, 'From Monaghan to the Grand Canal', in *Preoccupations*, p. 115.
31 Seamus Heaney, 'At a Potato Digging', *Death of a Naturalist* (London, Faber, 1966) p. 31.
32 Seamus Heaney, *Preoccupations*, p. 137.

Heaney says, 'place names stake out a personal landscape' and are 'denuded of tribal or etymological implications'.[33] In Montague, however, Heaney identifies 'an element of cultural and political resistance and retrieval', and discovers a sacred, tribal, mythologised sense of place that is very similar to his own:

> What is hidden at the bottom of Montague's region is first of all a pagan civilization centred on the dolmen; then a Gaelic civilization centred on the O'Neill inauguration stone at Tullyhogue. The ancient feminine religion of Northern Europe is the lens through which he looks and the landscape becomes a memory, a piety, a loved mother. The present is suffused with the past.[34]

Hewitt, too, Heaney believes, is animated by ancestral memory. Commenting on the way both Montague's and Hewitt's vision founds itself on the archaeological – Knockmany Dolmen in Montague's case, and the similarly megalithic 'broken circle of stones on a rough hillside, somewhere' in Hewitt's – Heaney distinguishes between Montague's 'monocular', 'insular' vision and the 'bifocal' perspective implied by Hewitt's gloss on 'circle of stones': 'for me the archetype of this is the Rolright Stones on the border of Oxfordshire, mingled with the recollection of "Ossian's Grave", Glenaan, Co. Antrim'.[35] In contrast to both Montague and Hewitt, Kavanagh represents a different kind of rootedness, one that does not rely on archaeological symbols or historical myth, but direct, personal engagement with his own time and place. Kavanagh's region, Heaney insists, 'is as deep not as its history but as his own life in it'.[36]

These ideas are somewhat revised in a later essay of 1985, 'The Placeless Heaven: Another Look at Kavanagh', in which Heaney probes the cultural politics of Kavanagh's position. Now Kavanagh is construed as a subversive influence, providing succeeding Irish poets with a sense of identity separate from England, and a poetics that is independent of English models and movements:

> Kavanagh gave you permission to dwell without cultural anxiety among the landmarks of your life ... Without being in the slightest way political in his intentions, Kavanagh's poetry did have political effect. Whether he wanted it or not, his achievement was inevitably co-opted, north and south, into the general current of feeling which flowed from and sustained ideas of national identity, cultural otherness from Britain and the dream of a literature with a manner and a matter resistant to the central Englishness of the dominant tradition.[37]

In the earlier essays, Heaney emphasised Kavanagh's fidelity to the local and the particular, but in the later one he concentrates on how 'all these solidly based phenomena are transformed by a shimmer of inner reality',[38] how the sensuous 'weightiness' of Kavanagh's early poetry is replaced by a visionary 'weightlessness'. In tracing this change of focus in Kavanagh from inner to outer, Heaney could have been sketching the essential pattern of his own career which has simi-

---

33 Ibid., p. 140.
34 Ibid., p. 141.
35 Ibid., p. 147.
36 Ibid., p. 142.
37 Seamus Heaney, *The Government of the Tongue* (London, Faber, 1988) pp. 9–10.
38 Ibid., p. 10.

larly moved from a poetry of earthiness and weightiness to a concern with the marvellous and miraculous, from the 'artesian' to the aerial, from physical place to visionary space, from the home that is given to the home that is found.

*

Where Hewitt is the champion of Ulster rootedness and regionalism, MacNeice is the representative of Anglo-Irish hybridity, exile and migrancy. Commenting on the pattern of MacNeice's career for a review of the *Collected Poems* in the regionalist magazine *Rann*, Roy McFadden echoed Hewitt's strictures on the poet who wasn't a rooted man:

> The only uneasy ghost in Mr. MacNeice's mind is his place of origin. From time to time the poet reverts to Ireland, nostalgically, impatiently, contemptuously – only to set his face firmly again towards the English scene. This retreat from childhood is a pity for, in the absence of any spiritual roots, Mr. MacNeice might well have strengthened his work by allegiance to place ... Allegiance to something beyond one's immediate time is a valuable asset in poetry. Mr. MacNeice is yet to apply for membership for Mr. Hewitt's school of regionalism, and, studying the superstitions and sagas of the forefathers, discover Louis MacNeice.[39]

Recognising, as Hewitt did, the stalemate of Irish politics, MacNeice responded, not by joining the ranks of the regionalists or any other group or movement, but by evolving a migrant poetics of multiple perspectives, ironic distance and verbal ambiguity. Born in 1907 in Belfast, his family moved to Carrickfergus in 1909 where he spent his childhood until he was sent to Sherborne preparatory school in Dorset in 1917. In 1921 he went to Marlborough, and in 1926 to Merton College, Oxford, after which he lectured in classics at Birmingham University, then Bedford College, London, and, from 1941 to 1961, worked as a Features producer in the BBC. His father, a Church of Ireland rector, was a nationalist, and a supporter of Home Rule. This unusual stance, which no doubt alienated his father from his co-religionists, is indicative of the shaping forces of MacNeice's childhood. His identification with any one religious, political or religious sect was further complicated by the fact that both his parents were not originally from Ulster, but the west of Ireland, which in MacNeice's poems figures as an antithesis to Ulster. Living in a limbo between England and Ireland, migrating between the North and the South of Ireland, spending time in various other countries (America, Greece, South Africa, Iceland, India, Pakistan), MacNeice remains always detached, always the sceptical outsider. Not only does he fall short of Hewitt's and McFadden's regionalist requirements, but for some fellow poets and critics he does not qualify as an 'Irish' poet at all. He goes unrepresented in both Montague's and Kinsella's anthologies of Irish poetry and has until recently generally been treated as a minor figure in the Auden-Spender-Day Lewis constellation of English leftist '30s writers. Even granting his Irishness, there remains the question of where in Ireland his home might be. Moving from

---

[39] Roy McFadden, 'Review of *Collected Poems* by Louis MacNeice and *The Edge of Being* by Stephen Spender', *Rann*, 7 (Winter 1949–50) p. 11.

'Carrickfergus' to 'Belfast' to 'Dublin' to 'Western Landscape', we find differing attitudes to very different MacNeice 'homes'.

MacNeice's autobiography, *The Strings are False* (1965), opens on board a transatlantic liner returning from America to war-torn England in 1940, from which point in time and place he proceeds to survey his life in terms of his multiple travels and translocations. He is, he says, 'a mere nomad who has lost his tent'.[40] The advantage of his liminal position as voyager is that it affords him the necessary distance to review his life objectively: 'It was on this same boat I came over in January. Now that there is no hurry I can look back on it as if it were mounted under glass; although at the time I was tense, anxious, muddled, expecting the moon, guilty of the war, so full and so empty of myself' (*SAF* 18). As Tom Paulin notes: 'MacNeice is always crossing the water, and the feeling of unease and displacement, of moving between different cultures and nationalisms, which he paradoxically returns to in his poetry, means that his imagination is essentially fluid, maritime and elusively free'.[41] The sea and the railway, both of which MacNeice remembers vividly from childhood, are symbols of escape, promises of other places and possibilities. Opposed to all fixed positions, he offers a kind of empirical humanism, the actuality of the passing moment: 'And I give you the faces, not the permanent masks,/ But the faces balanced in the toppling wave'.[42] The poem from which these lines are taken – 'Train to Dublin' – consists of a series of sharply observed images, the poet's fleeting perceptions while he is borne swiftly along through the Irish countryside. The sudden vividness and surprise of the various images are more important to him than coherent narratives or *a priori* ideas and concepts. His perspective is that of the tourist in his own land – the persona that he explicitly adopts in another poem, 'Valediction': acknowledging that he 'cannot be/ Anyone else than what this land engendered me', he nevertheless says he will 'acquire an attitude not yours/ And become as one of your holiday visitors' (*CP* 53).

In *The Strings are False*, he expresses a particular affinity with Dublin: 'I am at home in Dublin, more than in any other city' (*SAF* 222). He explores his relation with the city in his poem, 'Dublin', where he casts himself in the role of exile and outsider: 'This was never my town', he says, '[b]ut yet she holds my mind' (*CP* 163) – perhaps because he felt an affinity between Dublin's identity and his own:

> She is not an Irish town,
> And she is not English
> [...]
> Fort of the Dane
> Garrison of the Saxon
> Augustan Capital

---

40 Louis MacNeice, *The Strings are False: An Unfinished Autobiography* (London, Faber, 1965) p. 17. Hereafter abbreviated to *SAF* and page references incorporated into the text.
41 Tom Paulin, 'The Man from No Part: Louis MacNeice', in *Ireland and the English Crisis* (Newcastle-upon-Tyne, Bloodaxe Books, 1984) pp. 75–6.
42 Louis MacNeice, *Collected Poems* (London, Faber, 1987) p. 28. Hereafter abbreviated to *CP* and page references incorporated into the text.

> Of a Gaelic nation,
> Appropriating all.   (*CP* 164)

MacNeice is attracted by the flux and uncertainty of Dublin's history, its protean nature reflecting the fluctuations and indeterminacy of his own identity. Even the language used in the poem reinforces notions of unpredictable variousness, as in MacNeice's characteristic use of paradox: 'Declamatory bronze/ On sombre pedestals', 'seedy elegance', 'glamour of her squalor'.

Any notion of belonging to a bounded place, region or identity is undermined by his sense of uncontrollable flux which disturbs familiar patterns of spatial or historical coherence: 'Even the walls are flowing, even the ceiling,/ Nor only in terms of physics ...', he says in 'Variations on Heraclitus', a poem which ends with:

> I just do not want your advice
> Nor need you be troubled to pin me down in my room
> Since the room and I will escape for I tell you flat:
> One cannot live in the same room twice.   (*CP* 503)

The next poem in the *Collected*, situates him in a 'defamiliarised' world whose solidity dissolves in 'reflections':

> The mirror above my fireplace reflects the reflected
> Room in my window; I look in the mirror at night
> And see two rooms, the first where left is right
> And the second, beyond the reflected window, corrected
> But there I am standing back to my back.   ('Reflections', *CP* 503).

No unambiguous definition, completion or closure is possible in this hall of mirrors. The formal coherence of the poem plays ironically against the incoherence of perceptual experience. As Peter McDonald remarks, 'MacNeice's idea of the "honest" voice was one in which any coherence was consciously provisional.'[43] And there is, of course, MacNeice's own statement in the Introduction to *Autumn Journal*: 'Poetry in my opinion must be honest before anything else and/ I refuse to be "objective" or clear-cut at the cost of honesty' (*CP* 101). Essentialist notions of the single, unified self disintegrate, as in the 'The Taxis' (1979), a dream-poem where the repeated 'tra-la' signals the breaking-up of rational communication, and the self-image reflected back to the speaker is one of a multiple self, unrecognisable and beyond his control:

> As for the fourth taxi, he was alone
> Tra-la when he hailed it but the cabby looked
> Through him and said: 'I can't tra-la well take
> So many people, not to speak of the dog.'   (*CP* 522)

Any possibility of a return to origins, as 'The Truisms' implies, is at best problem-

---

43 Peter McDonald, 'The Falling Castle: MacNeice's Poetry 1936–1939', in Jacqueline Genet and Wynne Hellegouarch (eds.), *Studies on Louis MacNeice* (Centre de Publications de l'Université de Caen, 1988) pp. 27–50, 31.

atic, despite the poem's culminating redemptive image. All that origins have to offer is the box of truisms 'shaped like a coffin', remnants of his father's religion. Returning to his childhood home, 'he arrived at a house/ He could not remember seeing before'. Yet, instinctively, he 'raised his hand and blessed his home', only to find the truisms become suddenly filled with life, and 'a tall tree sprouted from his father's grave' (*CP* 507).

Given this fluid and provisional cast of mind, it is no surprise that MacNeice's attitude to Ireland should be marked by ambivalence, doubt and contradiction. Ireland was the nearest thing to 'home', yet feelings of alienation from his own country left him with a sense of exile as the representative modern condition. The place of childhood, the subject of his poem 'Carrickfergus', is presented in terms of industrial pollution ('stinking of chlorine', 'Smoky Carrick'), cacophonous sound ('hooting', 'clang', 'yelping', 'yapping'), blockage ('bottle-neck'), division and disunity ('Scotch Quarter' and 'Irish Quarter', 'Anglican order' and 'Irish poor'), siege and confinement ('walled', 'banned', 'barred', 'prison ship', 'cage'), oppression and war (the Normans, 'the Chichesters', World War I), defeat and death ('lost sirens', 'funeral cry', 'drowning moon') – all contained within a contradictory regime of orderly quatrains. The opening line establishes the poet's in-between position: 'I was born in Belfast between the mountain and the gantries' (*CP* 69). The fifth stanza elaborates the feeling of the Protestant outsider in Catholic Ireland –

> I was the rector's son, born to the Anglican order,
> Banned for ever from the candles of the Irish poor;
> The Chichesters knelt in marble at the end of a transept
> With ruffs about their necks, their portion sure   (*CP* 69)

– while the last stanza alludes to his feeling of being an Irish outsider in England:

> I went to school in Dorset, the world of parents
> Contracted into a puppet world of sons
> Far from the mill girls, the smell of porter, the salt-mines
> And the soldiers with their guns.   (*CP* 70)

The lines hold in balance notions of escape and confinement, unreality and reality, belonging and not belonging, relief and nostalgia.

'Belfast' offers a picture of an urban wasteland, with its images of monolithic fixity and frozen petrifaction, of life corrupted at its source:

> The cold hard fire of the northerner
> Frozen into his blood from the fire in his basalt
> Glares from behind the mica of his eyes
> And the salt carrion water brings him wealth.
>
> Down there at the end of the melancholy lough
> Against the lurid sky over the stained water
> Where the hammers clang murderously on the girders
> Like crucifixes the gantries stand.   (*CP* 17)

That last image fuses industrialisation and religion in an evocation of noise, violence, cruelty and death. In this nightmarish landscape there is no hope of salvation. MacNeice speaks as an outsider: this is the Belfast which, in the later poem, 'Day of Renewal', he says he 'disowned', to claim for himself 'a different birthplace' (*CP* 309).

'Valediction' contains another picture of oppressive Protestant industrialism, of life hardened into frozen immobility, time and history brought to a deadly standstill:

> See Belfast, devout and profane and hard,
> Built on reclaimed mud, hammers playing in the shipyard,
> Time punched with holes like a steel sheet, time
> Hardening the faces, veneering with a grey and speckled rime
> The faces under the shawls and caps.   (*CP* 52)

The dominant imagery is of changeless, inanimate, unyielding rock, stone, metal: 'Country of callous lava cooled to stone' (*CP* 52). Indignation is not reserved for the North only, for he goes on to denounce the commercial and touristic exploitation of romantic Ireland, with its 'trade-mark of a hound and a round tower' (*CP* 53), its false 'Irish glamour' (*CP* 53) and '[s]ham Celtic crosses' (*CP* 53). Nevertheless, he concedes that Ireland is an intrinsic part of him: 'But I cannot deny my past to which myself is wed,/ The woven figure cannot undo its thread' (*CP* 53). Having made this statement of belonging, he immediately proceeds to undo it: 'I will exorcise my blood/ And not to have my baby-clothes my shroud/ I will acquire an attitude not yours' (*CP* 53). Simultaneously, he accepts Ireland as being what made him what he is, yet wants to 'exorcise' himself of this past. He makes the conscious decision to 'resign' (*CP* 53), yet is powerfully drawn to his homeland, enumerating all the attractions he has resolved to leave. Edna Longley notes that 'Even *in extremis* – "Farewell my country, and in perpetuum" – MacNeice attaches the possessive pronoun to Ireland.'[44]

His irritation with Ireland re-surfaces in Canto XVI of *Autumn Journal*, which sounds like Hewitt's 'An Irishman in Coventry'. Writing during the Munich crisis of 1938, MacNeice was particularly angered by Irish intransigence, North and South, at a time when the whole of Europe was on the brink of cataclysm:

> The land of scholars and saints:
>   Scholars and saints my eye, the land of ambush,
>   The born martyr and the gallant ninny;
> The grocer drunk with the drum,
>   The land-owner shot in his bed, the angry voices
> Piercing the broken fanlight in the slum,
>   The shawled woman weeping at the garish altar.   (*CP* 132

The reference to 'born martyr' mocks the blood-sacrifice tradition of Pearse and the Irish Republican Brotherhood, while 'gallant ninny' recalls the mock-heroics of the likes of Peter Flynn in O'Casey's *The Plough and the Stars* or Christy Mahon in Synge's *Playboy of the Western World*. However, the crescendo of bitterness and aggression quickly modulates into Romantic feelings of attachment and

---

44 Edna Longley, 'Louis MacNeice: The Walls are Flowing', in *Across a Roaring Hill*, p. 105.

nostalgia: 'Such was my country and I thought I was well/ Out of it, educated and domiciled in England,/ Though yet her name keeps ringing like a bell/ In an underwater belfry' (*CP* 132). 'Domiciled in England' is a coldly legalistic designation, deliberately withholding any connotation of homely attachment: Ireland is still '*my* country' (as opposed to the more distanced '*This* England', *CP* 137).

In reaction against all this petrified violence, venality and vulgarity, he chooses the freedoms of exile:

> I come from an island, Ireland, a nation
> Built upon violence and morose vendettas.
> My diehard countrymen, like dray-horses,
> Drag their ruin behind them.
> Shooting straight in the cause of crooked thinking
> Their greed is surfaced with pretence of public spirit.
> From all which I am an exile.   ('Eclogue from Iceland', 1936, *CP* 41)

The dialectic which is at play throughout his work is again evident here: although they are 'diehard' and he is an 'exile', the Irish are still 'my countrymen'. And however angry, appalled or frustrated Irish society makes him feel, Irish landscape is a perennial wonderland. By concentrating on the actual physical world, the miracle of the ordinary, he rises to a pitch of lyrical intensity that carries him beyond the blocked paralysis, stupidity and intransigence of the social world into a visionary realm of lightsomeness, fluidity and freedom:

> But I will not give you any idol or idea, creed or king,
> I give you the incidental things which pass
> Outward through space exactly as each was.
>
> I give you the disproportion between labour spent
> And joy at random; the laughter of the Galway sea
> Juggling with spars and bones irresponsibly,
> I give you the toy Liffey and the vast gulls,
> I give you fucshia hedges and the whitewashed walls.
>
> I give you the smell of Norman stone, the squelch
> Of bog beneath your boots, the red bog-grass,
> The vivid chequer of the Antrim hills, the trough of dark
> Golden water for the cart-horses, the brass
> Belt of serene sun upon the lough.   ('Train to Dublin', *CP* 28)

Here there are unexpected delight ('joy at random'), fun and freedom ('the laughter of the Galway sea/ Juggling … irresponsibly'), children's play ('I give you the toy Liffey'), vivid colours ('fucshia hedges and the whitewashed walls'); hard stone is sensuously evocative; the murder-site of the bog squelches harmlessly under walkers' boots; the 'stained water' of the 'melancholy lough' ('Belfast') is now bathed in 'serene sun'.

As war approaches, Ireland figures as Romantic retreat associated with Lethe, lotus, amnesia:

> Forgetfulness: brass lamps and copper jugs
> And home-made bread and the smell of turf or flax

> And the air a glove and the water lathering easy
>> And the convolvulus in the hedge.
>
> Only in the dark green room beside the fire
> With the curtains drawn against the winds and waves
> There is a little box with a well-bred voice:
>> What a place to talk of War.   ('Cushendun', *CP* 165)

Here Ireland is constructed in terms of pure sensation, in the immediate present tense. A co-ordinate grammatical structure (six 'and's in the space of four lines) enforces a sense of fluid, dynamic perception and complete absorption in the sensual moment without interference from the mediating intellect. In 'Neutrality' (1942), Ireland again figures as an idyllic retreat from the turbulence of the political events unfolding in the outside world. But while acknowledging the magical charms of Irish landscape, MacNeice insists on the moral obligation to confront reality. He takes Ireland to task for her neutrality, her addiction to the Yeatsian 'dream' while the mackerel in her western seas 'Are fat – on the flesh of your kin' (*CP* 203).

MacNeice himself refused to turn his back on history. Despite the attractions of Irish landscape and the essential fluidity of his own imagination, he felt it necessary to engage with the wider problems of urban society and the international situation – the collapse of government in Spain, the rise of fascism in Europe, the spread of Communism, the depredations of capitalism – and committed himself to an idea of community understood as a de-territorialised, egalitarian Utopia:

> Let us dream it now,
> And pray for a possible land
>> Not of sleep-walkers, not of angry puppets,
> But where both heart and brain can understand
>> The movements of our fellows;
> Where life is a choice of instruments and none
>> Is debarred his natural music
> Where the waters of life are free of the ice-blockade of hunger
>> And thought is free as the sun.   (*Autumn Journal* XXIV, *CP* 152)

But Ireland, which demonstrated for him the problems of ideological entrenchment and rigid identity-fixation, exerted an inevitably restraining effect on his own involvements, rendering him rather more circumspect on the issue of political commitment than his colleagues in the 'Macspaunday' quartet of '30s leftist poets in England. At the same time, his social awareness and commitment to communitarian social values prevented him from succumbing to solipsism, nihilism or aestheticism:

> Who am I – or I – to demand oblivion?
> I must go out tomorrow as the others do
>> And build the falling castle;
> Which has never fallen, thanks
>> Not to any formula, red tape or institution,

> Not to any creeds or banks
>> But to the human animal's endless courage.
>>> (*Autumn Journal* II, *CP* 104)

Nevertheless, the idea of 'home' has a steadying influence. In 'Eclogue from Iceland' (1936), the ghost of Grettir, the Icelandic saga hero, counsels the two travellers, Ryan and Craven, versions of MacNeice and Auden, to confront the 'Voice of Europe', the forces of historical flux:

> Minute your gesture but it must be made –
> Your hazard, your act of defiance and hymn of hate
> Hatred of hatred, assertion of human values,
> Which is now your only duty.   (*CP* 47)

For Grettir, this 'assertion of human values' demands a return to 'where you belong'. In urging Ryan to return to his island home as a source of value, Grettir also urges a return to the individual, 'for every country stands/ By the sanctity of the individual will' (*CP* 47). The poem moves toward assertion of a communal vision generated out of the dialectic between roots and mobility. As Edna Longley remarks: 'MacNeice's thirties' utopias had tried, indeed, to conceive the best of British and Irish worlds: to combine the assets of a traditional, rooted, "island" society with a modern fluidity.'[45]

The best of MacNeice's Irish world lay in the West, the supposedly untouched wilderness that Revivalists venerated as the vestigial remains of authentic Ireland, the site of a simple, antique cultural purity free from the pressures of the modern world, a primitive Eden largely unaffected culturally and linguistically by colonialism. MacNeice's sister, Elizabeth Nicholson, has described the importance of the West to both of them:

> … neither our mother nor Louis nor myself felt that we belonged properly to the Ulster community in which we were living. Our parents had both been born and spent their childhoods in Connemara … My father occasionally told us stories of Connemara, but my mother spoke of it so constantly and with such love and such longing that I think it was she who really made it come alive for Louis and myself. It became for us both a 'many-coloured land', a kind of lost Atlantis where we thought we should be living, and it came to be a point of honour that we did not belong to the North of Ireland. We were in our minds a West of Ireland family exiled from our homeland.[46]

If MacNeice's relationship with Ireland acquired the timeless, universal dimensions of myth, it is not the totalising, self-presencing, Yeatsian kind, but a modern myth of loss and exile. Though he may have regarded the West as his ancestral and spiritual home, reality, as Derek Mahon puts it, 'lay elsewhere, in an Ulster childhood and a life's work abroad'.[47] But even the first home in Carrick had

---

45   Edna Longley, *The Living Stream*, p. 146.
46   Elizabeth Nicholson, 'Trees were Green', in Terence Brown and Alec Reid (eds.), *Time Was Away* (Dublin, Dolmen Press, 1974) pp. 13–14.
47   Derek Mahon, 'MacNeice in Ireland and England', in *Journalism* (Loughcrew, Gallery Press, 1996) pp. 21–9, 29.

mythic promise, as the opening of the starkly symbolic 'Autobiography' asserts –

> In my childhood trees were green
> And there was plenty to be seen   (*CP* 183)

– until reality interposes. This bright Edenic world is quickly clouded by maternal loss, psychic disruption, the end of security. The childhood place grows dark and lonely, the poem's pathos heightened by the nursery-rhyme lilt and refrain line '*Come back early or never come*'. In 'Last Before America', personal loss and bereavement (MacNeice's mother died when he was seven) underwrite an alternative cultural myth:

> Both myth and seismic history have been long suppressed
> Which made and unmade Hy Brasil – now an image
> For those who despise charts but find their dream's endorsement
> In certain long low islets snouting towards the west
> Like cubs that have lost their mother.   (*CP* 227)

'Day of Renewal' alludes to the attempted recovery of the Western Eden as a quest for both psychological release and mystical possibility: 'Go west and live. Not to become but be. Still that remains an ideal – or a pretence' (*CP* 309). Desire for the ideal is tempered by a restraining realism. In 'Western Landscape', a poem based on a visit to Achill Island, he identifies with St Brandan the Navigator, 'Brandan, spindrift hermit, who/ Hankering roaming un-homing up-anchoring', sought to 'Distil the distance and undo/ Time in quintessential West' (*CP* 256). Brandan, monk and mystic, is both within and without the world of time: 'One thought of God, one feeling of the ocean,/ Fused in the moving body, the unmoved soul' (*CP* 256). Such wholeness, the poet recognises, is beyond him. 'Western Landscape' is a paean to the erotic, narcotic pull of the West, but ends with reiteration of the exile's awareness of separation and loss: 'Let now the visitor, although disfranchised/ In the constituencies of quartz and bog-oak/ …/ let me, if a bastard/ Out of the West by urban civilization/ …/ let me who am neither Brandan/ Free of all roots nor yet a rooted peasant/ Here add one stone to the indifferent cairn' (*CP* 257).

Whether he is longing for reunion with 'my mother/ Earth' (CP 257) in the West, as in this poem, or, as in 'Valediction', bidding farewell to 'the chequered and the quiet hills' (*CP* 54) around Carrick, there is no escaping the desire for a mythic home grounded in his Irish origins. He can make no final valediction. 'Carrick Revisited' (1945) marks a kind of homecoming and repossession: 'Back to Carrick, the castle as plumb assured/ As thirty years ago …/ But the green banks are as rich and the lough as hazily lazy/ And the child's astonishment not yet cured' (*CP* 224). The poem's geological metaphors ('myself/ In a topographical frame'; 'Like a belated rock in the red Antrim clay') reinforce the notion of embeddedness in the Ulster landscape. However, this acknowledgement is offered in a tone of rueful resignation, in the knowledge of another kind of displacement – his exile from his spiritual home in Clifden, Connemara: 'And the pre-natal mountain is far away' (*CP* 225). Unsurprisingly, the poem does not spell out any final resolution to his crisis of identity. He is still longing for elsewhere. Typical of MacNeice, there is no statement which is not challenged, questioned or undercut. His attitude to Ireland is never uncomplicated, his search for home is never completed. The poetry offers a complex of unresolved attitudes, contradictory and dialectical perspectives. Displacement and dislocation is what drives the poetry, his sense of ambivalent belonging constituting a valuable creative resource. In the late, uncollected 'Prologue', which was to be used in a book of essays entitled *The Character of Ireland*, he speaks of the Irish as the 'inheritors of paradox and prism'.[48] In an earlier prose piece, he explained the peculiar 'prismatic' effect of Irish landscape: 'Owing to the moisture in the air, sunlight in Ireland has the effect of a prism; nowhere in the British Isles can you find this liquid rainbow quality which at once diffuses and clarifies.'[49] The Irish landscape itself supplies him with an image of his sense of the ambiguity and mutability of meaning and identity.

It is MacNeice's cultural complexity, his sceptical intelligence, his insistence on the primacy of the living word over dogma and abstraction that make him a figure of special relevance to recent debates about identity and 'home' in Northern Ireland. Derek Mahon notes how MacNeice's 'example has provided a frame of reference for a number of younger poets'.[50] For these poets, MacNeice represents a refreshing and liberating freedom from regional or national definitions of home, a radical challenge to the conventional modes of Irish poetry. Longley, Mahon and Paulin share, in varying degrees, his Protestant background and English connections, and for all three of these younger poets, as well as for Muldoon, MacNeice exemplifies the poetic potential of what Heaney called 'displacement and unrest'.[51] In his essay on MacNeice, 'The Neolithic Light' (1973), Michael Longley sees MacNeice as 'a touchstone of what an Ulster (that is to say Irish) poet might be'.[52] For Longley, the 'sensuous vividness', 'the riot of imagery' and 'dizzy word-play' are elements of MacNeice's defiant reply to the 'darkness' of his Ulster childhood, an assertion of poetic imagination over determinism. Longley's interest in the idea of constructing a 'home from home' without regard to origins, tribe or roots, puts him in touch with MacNeice's creative, existential sense of the world, as expressed in 'London Rain' (1939):

> Whether the living river
> Began in bog or lake,
> The world is what was given,
> The world is what we make
> And we only can discover
> Life in the life we make.   (*CP* 162)

As Longley remarks in his essay, life for MacNeice 'had to be organic, open to all

48 Louis MacNeice, 'Prologue' (1962), a poem written for a projected study, *The Character of Ireland*, quoted in J. Stallworthy, *Louis MacNeice* (London, Faber, 1996) pp. 488–91.
49 Alan Heuser (ed.), *Selected Prose of Louis MacNeice* (Oxford, Clarendon Press, 1990) p. 151.
50 Derek Mahon (ed.), Introduction, *The Sphere Book of Modern Irish Poetry* (London, Sphere, 1972) p. 12.
51 Seamus Heaney, 'The Pre-Natal Mountain: Vision and Irony in Recent Irish Poetry', in *The Place of Writing* (Atlanta Scholars Press, 1989) pp. 36–53, 47.
52 Michael Longley, 'The Neolithic Light: A Note on the Irishness of Louis MacNeice', in Dunn (ed.), *Two Decades of Irish Writing*, p. 104.

the possibilities. No systems could be imposed'[53] – a statement which summarises Longley's own poetic refusal to align himself with any political, aesthetic or religious creeds, his determination to remain open to the infinite, often surprising, possibilities of life.

Where Longley has never left Northern Ireland, Mahon, like MacNeice, is more of a nomad. As citizen of the world, Mahon's poetic locales include such diverse places as the 'Coleraine triangle', Rathlin Island and the Aran Islands, New York, San Francisco, North Carolina, lower Manhatten, Kyoto and Antarctica. Through his translations and his range of allusion he moves from one time or place or text or art work to another, always conscious of the wider cultural forces circulating through particular manifestations of art, history and literature. Even his constant revising of his poems testifies to a preoccupation with change and process, a resistance, such as we associate with MacNeice, to fixity and completion. As expatriate outsider, Mahon is as much 'a tourist in his own country' as he said MacNeice was: '"A tourist in his own country" it has been said, with the implication that this is somehow discreditable; but of what sensitive person is the same not true? The phrase might stand, indeed, as an epitaph for modern man.'[54] Mahon accepts deracination as the essential condition of modern life and, taking MacNeice as his example, sees it as importantly creative. Mahon's is, as Terence Brown opines, 'a peregrine imagination', an 'emigrant sensibility, perhaps most in exile when actually at home'.[55] Or, as Declan Kiberd has it, Mahon is 'a poet of Belfast, but often by way of disavowal'.[56] MacNeice's *amo atque odi* attitude to Ireland is repeated in Mahon's ambivalent feelings about 'roots' and inheritance. Both poets are inheritors of an environment which is inimical to poetry, yet Ireland haunts their imagination. Mahon's lines in 'Glengormley' – 'By/ Necessity, if not by choice, I live here too'[57] – echo MacNeice's in 'Carrick Revisited': 'what chance misspelt/ May never now be righted by my choice' (*CP* 224). Like MacNeice, Mahon occupies marginal or interstitial positions (strands, sea shores, river banks), and writes about night-crossings, vacations, departures and returns. Reacting against Hewitt's insistence on the need for the Ulster writer to be 'a rooted man' to avoid being merely 'an airy internationalist, thistledown', Mahon comments: 'This is a bit tough on thistledown; and, speaking as a twig in a stream, I feel there's a certain harshness, a dogmatism, at work there. What of the free-floating imagination, Keats's "negative capability", Yeats's "lonely impulse of delight"? Literature is surely more than a branch of ethics. What about humour, mischief, wickedness?'[58] In contrast to Hewitt's (or Heaney's) sense of belonging, Mahon's poems assert a poetic freedom by complicating all stereotypes of identity, projecting them into extreme metaphysical realms beyond human history and the human self, in the end, subverting the very idea of belonging anywhere.

As a *deraciné*, a free-floater, Mahon could see from MacNeice's example that

---

53 Ibid., p. 99.
54 Derek Mahon, 'MacNeice in Ireland and England', in *Journalism*, p. 25.
55 Terence Brown, Introduction to Derek Mahon, *Journalism*, p. 18.
56 Declan Kiberd, *Inventing Irelands: The Literature of the Modern Nation* (London, Vintage, 1996) p. 599.
57 Derek Mahon, 'Glengormley', in *Collected Poems* (Loughcrew, Gallery Books, 1999) p. 14.
58 Derek Mahon, 'An Honest Ulsterman', in *Journalism*, p. 94.

his first duty was to adopt a pose, a style, a way of being in the world. In his essay, 'MacNeice in Ireland and England' (1974), he finds in MacNeice (and that other Anglo-Irish expatriate Samuel Beckett) 'some sort of Irish sensibility' which manifests itself as 'a mordancy ... and a fascination with the fact of language itself'.[59] Mahon quotes Wallace Stevens: '*Natives of poverty, children of malheur,/ The gaiety of language is our seigneur*', and goes on to discuss MacNeice's language in terms of its capacity to render 'the existential tingle of the passing moment',[60] its extraordinary facility for recording surface and sensation, the 'profound super-ficiality'[61] of the poet's vision. For all three poets – Stevens, MacNeice, Mahon – poetry represents the triumph of style over despair. And it is in such terms that Mahon memorialises his Anglo-Irish mentor in 'In Carrowdore Churchyard' (1964), a poem which, coming early on in the *Collected*, has the force of a poetic manifesto. Mahon's elegy is a tender and generous tribute to the older poet. Warmer, more affectionate and reverential than we are used to from Mahon, 'In Carrowdore Churchyard' nevertheless declares, à la MacNeice, that meaning exists ambiguously, riddlingly; that there is no simple correspondence between subject and object, text and world; that indeterminacy pervades our actions, ideas, interpretations, indeed constitutes our world. The poem responds to MacNeice's love of 'things being various', and rehearses the older poet's ironical, sceptical outlook, his pervasive ambiguity, his love of wit and verbal ingenuity, his combination of conversational freedom and intricate formal patterning, his urbane and balanced style:

> This, you implied, is how we ought to live –
>
> The ironical, loving crush of roses against snow,
> Each fragile, solving ambiguity.   (*CP* 17)

Mahon is of course alluding to MacNeice's 'Snow', with its sense of a 'plural' world of constantly shifting possibilities, a world that is incongruous, surprising, 'incorrigible', that refuses to conform to our preordained ideas and theories. While re-registering MacNeice's devotion to immediate, perceptual sensation, his fascination with the surfaces of the phenomenal world, Mahon's poem, as we might expect from an elegy, does in the end assert closure and resolution: 'You lie/ Past tension now, and spring is coming round'. The MacNeicean heritage is guaranteed for posterity, and, unusual for Mahon, the poem looks forward to a hopeful future: 'you bring/ The all-clear to the empty holes of spring,/ Rinsing the choked mud, keeping the colours new' (*CP* 17).

Richard York finds that, in comparison with MacNeice, Mahon's poetry is generally darker, more alienated and solitary, more ambiguous and ironic, bereft of the older poet's political optimism and directly personal touch. In York's view, Mahon's is a bleaker vision of random objects, his sense of apocalypse contrasting with MacNeice's 'there will be sunlight later/ And the equation will come out at last' (*Autumn Journal* XXIV, *CP* 153). York directs us to two MacNeice poems. The first is 'Order to View', a poem which opens with a typical Mahon image

---

59   Derek Mahon, 'MacNeice in Ireland and England', in *Journalism*, p. 21.
60   Ibid., p. 27.
61   Ibid., p. 26.

of a house fallen into dereliction and decay. Suddenly, however, a tree shakes 'like a setter/ Flouncing out of a pond' a horse neighs, the curtains blow out: 'the world was open' (*CP* 170), York comments: 'The opening is unpredictable, miraculous; but MacNeice, unlike Mahon, expects miracles.'[62] In the second, 'The News-Reel', there is a similar 'opening' on the historic level: 'the intrusions/ Of value upon fact, that sudden unconfined/ Wind of understanding that blew out/ From people's hands and faces' (*CP* 204). While agreeing with the general tenor of York's argument, I would simply point to the recent turn in Mahon's poetry, evidenced in his latest volume *Harbour Lights* (the title suggestive of home-coming), in particular the last poem in the collection, a version of Paul Valéry's 'Le Cimitière Marin'. Mahon's 'The Seaside Cemetery' ends with a sudden intuition of value and hope similar to that which York identifies in MacNeice, an affirmation of human will and power which is particularly reminiscent of 'Thalassa', the last poem in MacNeice's *Collected*:

> No, no; get up; go on to the next phase –
> body, shake off this meditative pose
> and, chest, inhale the first flap of the air.
> A palpable new freshness off the sea,
> an ozone rush, restores my soul to me
> and draws me down to the reviving shore ...
>
> The wind rises; it's time to start. A vast breeze
> opens and shuts the notebook on my knees
> and powdery waves explode among the rocks
> flashing; fly off, then, my sun-dazzled pages
> and break, waves, break up with ecstatic surges
> this shifting surface where the spinnaker flocks![63]

MacNeice is undoubtedly the major influence on Muldoon. While embracing Kavanagh's emphasis on the parochial, Muldoon invariably sights the local through global perspectives, and brings to his treatment of traditional Irish material a sceptical, ludic intelligence that is recognisably MacNeicean. In both sentiment and manner, MacNeice's 'Entirely' prefigures Muldoon:

> If we could get the hang of it entirely
> It would be too long;
> All we know is the splash of words in passing
> And falling twigs of song
>   [...]
> ... in brute reality there is no
> Road that is right entirely. (*CP 158–9*)

Even here, in this statement of resistance to fixed ideals, dogmatism and totalism, the typical MacNeicean dialectic is evident. The poem expresses seriously held beliefs but its light tripping rhythm and slangy diction undercut the conven-

---

62 Richard York, 'Louis MacNeice and Derek Mahon', in Kathleen Devine and Alan J. Peacock (eds.), *Louis MacNeice and his Influence* (Gerrards Cross, Colin Smythe, 1998) pp. 85–98, 98.
63 Derek Mahon, *Harbour Lights* (Loughcrew, The Gallery Press, 2006) p. 75.

tional gravity with which such matters are usually expressed. This playful, provisional, serendipitous quality is a staple of the Muldoonian aesthetic. It is hard to read Muldoon's poems supposedly constructed out of marginalia or errata (see 'Errata') without thinking of MacNeice's 'Ode':

> I cannot draw up any code
>   There are too many qualifications
> Too may asterisk asides
>   Too many crosses in the margin
> But as other, forgetting others,
>   Run after nostrums
> Of science art and religion ...   (*CP* 58)

Neither poet can subscribe to any fixed ideological code because any absolute narrative 'forget[s] the others'. Fixities cannot accommodate a fluid conception of life; they ignore the 'qualifications' and 'asides' which are all too likely to constitute the substance of a MacNeice or Muldoon poem. Though addressing his newborn son, MacNeice could also be speaking to his literary son: 'Must become the migrating bird following felt routes/ ... / And so come to one's peace while the yellow waves are roaring' (*CP* 58).

MacNeice figures as one of the transients in Muldoon's poem '7, Middagh Street', and features in Muldoon's introduction to the *Faber Book of Contemporary Irish Poetry* as spokesman for a detached, cosmopolitan perspective against F.R. Higgins' nationalistic, atavistic, 'blood and soil' conception of poetry. Muldoon's affinity with MacNeice is reflected in the generous representation which he proceeds to give MacNeice's work in the anthology. MacNeice was the kind of poet who, instead of serving an ideal of tribal or national purity, responded to the world perceived as 'flux', as 'incorrigibly plural', thus providing a model for succeeding poets such as Muldoon who was similarly opposed to ideas of a monolithic, homogeneous, unified culture, and insisted instead on the interstitial, hybrid nature of place, and the dispersed, displaced nature of the subject. This refusal of centre and closure is signalled formally in '7, Middagh Street', a poem taking its title from the address of Auden's brownstone Brooklyn house which, during the 1940s, was temporary home to Auden and his lover Chester Kallman, the striptease artist Gypsy Rose Lee, Carson McCullers, Benjamin Britten, Salvador Dali and MacNeice – all deracinated, drifting émigrés: 'The roots by which we were once bound/ are severed here, in any case,/ and we are all now dispossessed'.[64] Fluidity, indeterminacy and metamorphosis are the controlling compositional principles. Salvador Dali becomes 'O'Daly'; Wystan declares: 'I will not go back as *Auden*', having just considered that his patriotic parents might now be 'tempted to rechristen/ their youngest son/ who turned his back on Albion/ a Quisling',[65] though, as Ben recalls, he has already been renamed as 'Parsnip' (in Evelyn Waugh's *Put Out More Flags*), 'H. W. Austin' the tennis-player by a government Minister, and confused with Winston (Churchill) by Carson McCullers. Notions of perpetual cultural exchange are suggested in

---

the way phrases from Masefield, Yeats, Lorca, Beckett, Crane, Herrick and others are imported, re-configured and re-contextualised. Against this background, Muldoon plots the course of his poem which, like the quinquereme of Nineveh, circulates freely through a series of mobile figures and tropes that constitute an intricate pattern of internal echoes and repetitions, steering a passage through a sea of other texts, recuperating and ingeniously transforming them. The words which end one monologue are picked up and developed in a new context in the first lines of the next one. None of the seven voices is allowed to dominate, the poem, like MacNeice's *Autumn Journal*, refusing completion and definitive meaning – not even in the debate between Wystan and Louis about Yeats, which has attracted considerable critical speculation. Wystan's forceful

> As for his crass, rhetorical
>
> posturing, 'Did that play of mine
> send out certain men (*certain* men?)
>
> the English shot … ?
> the answer is 'Certainly not'.

– is answered by Louis' measured

> … poetry *can* make things happen –
> not only can, but *must* – [66]

The opposing views are held in suspension, without clear resolution. The very notion of sure and certain knowledge is, right to the end, a joke. When Louis, having 'left by the back door of Muldoon's'[67] (echoing Dali's earlier statement: 'In October 1934/ I left Barcelona by the back door'[68]), finds himself and the quinquereme-poem in Harland and Wolff's shipyard in Belfast, Muldoon the poet comically undermines the Cyclopian foreman's dogmatic certainty:

> 'MacNeice? That's a Fenian name.'
> As if to say, 'None of your sort, none of you
>
> Will as much as go for a rubber hammer
> Never mind chalk a rivet, never mind caulk a seam
> On the quinquereme of Nineveh.[69]

Written against such fixity and intransigence, Muldoon's poem opens up a utopian space in which, as Corcoran puts it, 'sexual, social and political categories circulate and slide'.[70]

*

The spirits of Hewitt, Kavanagh and MacNeice hover over succeeding Northern poets in their negotiations between the local, the regional, the national and the

---

[66] Ibid., p. 192.
[67] Ibid., p. 193.
[68] Ibid., p. 185.
[69] Ibid., p. 193.
[70] Neil Corcoran, in *Louis MacNeice and his Influence*, p. 131.

global. Each of these older poets represents a different form of resistance to the metanarratives of nationalism, Irish or Unionist/British. In the unresolved dialectic between the sense of displacement and the longing for home, there are at one end of the spectrum Hewitt's regionalism and Kavanagh's parochialism as versions of the territorial option which construes place as the unifying ground of identity; at the other, is the example of MacNeice's de-territorialised dwelling in in-between worlds, a position which, rejecting both Kavanagh's monocular vision of place and Hewitt's demand for rootedness, embraces otherness, migrancy and plurality in the struggle for identity and meaning.

Chapter 3

JOHN MONTAGUE: GLOBAL REGIONALIST?

Born in Brooklyn in 1929, shipped back at the age of four to Co. Tyrone where he was raised by his paternal aunts while his elder brothers stayed with their natural mother seven miles away, John Montague from an early age knew all about feelings of dispossession and exile. From his childhood Garvaghey home to boarding-school in Armagh, then to University College Dublin, then Yale, then to various American universities as poet and teacher, then three years in Paris as correspondent for the *Irish Times*, then back to Dublin in 1967, then sixteen years teaching in University College Cork interspersed with frequent visits to America and France, he continues to lead a mobile life, with bases in France, Cork and New York. Experience and outlook have combined, Montague claims, to make him the quintessentially modern Irish poet:

> My amphibian position between North and South, my natural complicity in three cultures, American, Irish and French, with darts aside to Mexico, India, Italy or Canada, should seem natural enough in the later-twentieth century as man strives to reconcile local allegiances with the absolute necessity of developing a world consciousness to save us from the abyss. Earthed in Ireland, at ease in the world, weave the strands you're given.[1]

Reacting against both extremes of a closed regionalism (which he simplistically associates with Frost and Heaney) and a boundless globalism (as exemplified by Pound), Montague insists:

> the real position for a poet is to be global-regionalist. He is born into allegiances to particular areas or places and people, which he loves, sometimes against his will. But then he also happens to belong to an increasingly accessible world ... So the position is actually local *and* international.[2]

Such a self-description opens up an expectation of a progressive concept of identity, one which is not static but dynamic process, a construct, a 'weave' made up of diverse strands. He hints at a dissolving of old (D.P. Moran or Daniel Corkery 'Irish-Ireland'-style) borders or divisions that create an 'us' and 'them' opposi-

---

[1] John Montague, 'The Figure in the Cave', in *The Figure in the Cave* (Dublin, Lilliput Press, 1989) pp. 18–19. Hereafter abbreviated to *FC* and page references incorporated into the text.

[2] Adrian Frazier, 'Global Regionalism: Interview with John Montague', *The Literary Review*, 22, 2 (Winter 1972) pp. 153–74, 17.

tion. Identity, he would seem to say, does not have to be single or unique, but can be a site of diversity and internal conflict, its distinct mixture of wider and more local relations ensuring against homogeneity and producing a global sense of local. 'Global regionalism' is brought forward as the mechanism for making Irish poetry responsive to changing social conditions.

Poetically, Montague's rootedness is evident in both his Yeatsian concern with the cultural past and his loving, Kavanaghesque attention to the local and particular. Yet he has little interest in exploring the concept of regionalism, and alludes disdainfully to what he sees as the folksiness of Hewitt's project: '[T]he Ulster regionalist bit got my goat because it usually meant writing about your cottage in the country or, indeed, only people east of the Bann. So the whole doctrine seemed to me spurious, F.R. Higginsy.'[3] His internationalism, spurred on by a desire to free Irish poetry from both Yeatsian orthodoxies and colonial English influence, links him with world poetry:

> … an Irish poet should be familiar with the finest work of his contemporaries, not just the increasingly narrow English version of modern poetry, or the more exten- sive American one … I would say that my contemporaries are not just the Irish poets I admire, but those with whom I feel an affinity elsewhere, Ponge in France, Octavio Paz in Mexico, Gary Snyder and Robert Duncan in San Francisco.
>
> (*FC* 219)

Though he has lived for twelve years in France and translated the work of French writers such as Jouve, Char, Ponge, Guillevic and others, his chief influences are indubitably the great American modernists – Pound, Williams, Olson, Duncan, Snyder, Bly, Berryman, Roethke – whom he has claimed as kindred spirits:

> I have always read people like Whitman and Crane with grateful recognition. And with American poets, like those whom I met in Iowa in the halcyon days of the Workshop, from Berryman to Dickey and Snodgrass, or much later in the releasing freedom of San Francisco in the sixties, with Snyder and Duncan and McClure, I have always felt a strong sense of kinship. (*FC* 17)

Unlike Muldoon, whose America is very much an historical and social entity as well as a literary inheritance, Montague's America is primarily a literary phenom- enon. Montague's imagination is never absorbed by American place and land- scape as it is by the Irish scene, and it is not so much his everyday experiences of American life that provide the grist to his poetic mill as his readings of, and personal association with, contemporary American poets. What Montague shared with these poets was the sense of a cultural crisis, an awareness that poetry needed once again to become disruptive, critical of its culture, of its past, and of itself. The poetic conservatism of his Irish contemporaries is a theme to which he returns in his essay, 'In the Irish Grain' (1974), the title deliberately echoing Williams' *In the American Grain*. In the essay, Montague praises the new poets of the fifties (Kavanagh, Clarke, Kinsella) who 'began to write without

---

3   Dennis O'Driscoll, 'An Interview with John Montague, 1988, originally printed in the *Irish University review*, 19, 1 (1989); repr. *Agenda*, Irish Issue, John Montague Supplement, 40, 1–3, pp. 52–74, 54.

strain, a poetry that was indisputably Irish (in the sense that it was influenced by the country they came from, its climate, history, and linguistic peculiarities) but also modern', while identifying in the next generation of poets, who came from the North (Longley, Mahon, Heaney, Simmons), a tendency towards 'an epigrammatic neatness which shows the influence of the limiting British mode' (*FC* 125). Montague's call for an alternative to British formalism, like Williams' affirmation of an 'American idiom', may thus be seen, in the words of Paul Bowers, as 'a declaration of poetic and national independence'[4] from traditional English models. The American influence on Montague is not just a matter of technique, but of creative attitude. The American preoccupation with such questions as 'What is an American?' and 'What is an American poet?', which arise as part of the process of decolonisation, is replicated in Montague's similar exploration of what it means to be Irish, and to be an Irish poet.

In Montague's poem, 'William Carlos Williams, 1955', Williams is hailed as a kind of poetic mentor summoning the young Montague to his vocation. It is Williams who 'made the gesture/ (of manumission, almost)/ seem so instinct-/ ively natural'[5] – an allusion to the American poet's decisive role in liberating poetry from traditional, predetermined English poetic modes. In 'A Note on Rhythm' (1972–3), Montague expresses his dissatisfaction with the confinement of the traditional English iambic line:

> I am sure that there was a specific relationship between Elizabethan language and the iambic line which no longer holds true as an example of how to harness an energy ... There is an inhibiting traditionalism in contemporary poetry this side of the Atlantic which saps inventiveness. It is only a habit of mind which makes us expect a poem to march docile as a herd of sheep between the fence of white margins ... (*FC* 48)

Against this portrait of the artist as a model farmer, Montague declares his affinity with the looser American poetic in which content dictates its own shape and rhythm rather than being forced into a preconceived form.

> I believe very strongly that a poem appears with its own rhythm ... I think of a poem as a living thing, which one must aid, not forceps-haul into birth. This sense of the organic nature of a poem goes with the conviction that rhythm and line length should be based on living speech. (*FC* 48)

Montague's pronouncement echoes Charles Olson's 1959 declaration that 'FORM IS NEVER MORE THAN AN EXTENSION OF CONTENT'[6] which echoes Robert Creeley but also Waldo Emerson's elegant aphorism over a hundred years before: 'For it is not metres, but a metre-making argument that makes a poem'[7] – a staple of Romantic theory generally. In his Preface to *The Rough*

4 Paul Bowers, 'John Montague and William Carlos Williams: Nationalism and Poetic Construction', *The Canadian Journal of Irish Studies*, 20, 2 (December 1994) pp. 29–44, 33.
5 John Montague, *Born in Brooklyn* (Fredonia, NY, White Pine Press, 1991) p. 76.
6 Charles Olson, 'Statements on Poetics', in Donald Allen (ed.), *The New American Poetry 1945–1960* (University of California Press, 1999), pp. 386–97, 387.
7 Ralph Waldo Emerson, 'The Poet', in *Selected Essays*, edited by Larzer Ziff (London, Penguin Classics, 1982) pp. 259–84, 263–4.

Field, Montague declares that 'living in Berkeley introduced me to the debate on open-form from *Paterson*, through Olson, to Duncan',[8] and in his loose, dynamic, short line poems, he proceeds to Hibernicise Olson's theory of 'Projective' or 'open' verse in which syntax is shaped by sound, rhythm is dictated by natural breathing and thinking, sense relies on direct movement from one perception to another, not rational argument or rhetoric, and the reader's consumption is guided by the poem's typography. Pound, Williams and Olson specialised in the vivid recreation of the world around them in a condensed imagistic form of communication. Montague's own techniques of concrete, imagistic precision take from both the American aesthetic and, much closer to home, the example of Patrick Kavanagh's close-up attention to the miracle of the commonplace. Indeed, Williams echoes Kavanagh in describing poetry as a matter of 'lifting to the imagination those things which lie under the direct scrutiny of the sense, close to the nose'.[9]

The danger in the localist or particularist focus is that poems might become a series of isolated fragments unable to speak beyond their own moment. One way in which Montague, again following the American poets, sought to develop an encompassing poetry was through his experiment with the poetic sequence which, according to M.L. Rosenthal, is 'the decisive form'[10] toward which all the developments of modern poetry have tended. From Crane (*The Bridge*), Eliot (*The Waste Land*), Pound (*The Cantos*), Williams (*Paterson*), Olson (*The Maximus Poems*), Lowell (*Notebook 1967–1968*) and Berryman (*77 Dream Songs*), Montague discovered the long poem sequence that was made up of a loosely coordinated arrangement of lyrics and prose pieces which tend to interact as an organic whole. The American poetic sequence is obviously very varied, but what all these writers have in common is a desire to find ways to hold some sort of balance against an acute awareness of decline, disintegration and anomie. The sequence allows for the expression of a fragmented modern sensibility, but also the desire for tragic or epic scope. Liberated from a narrative framework, the modern sequence provides a sense of inclusiveness or transcendence by orchestrating conflicting energies and holding them in resonating equilibrium.

Following Williams and Olson, Montague combines Whitmanian epic with the techniques of Imagism and collage. *Paterson* includes verse, prose, drama, excerpts from books and newspapers, letters, interviews and local history. *The Maximus Poems* are even more deregulated, various and slackly discursive than *Paterson*, even more strongly representative of 'open form'. Olson arranges his words, lines, phrases and stanzas freely over the page, in a method which he described as 'composition by field' – a method to which Montague perhaps alludes in his title *The Rough Field*. Both Williams' and Olson's long poems have been criticised for their looseness of organisation, their lack of coherent structure and unifying voice: similar charges have been levelled, with some justification,

---

8   John Montague, *Collected Poems* (Loughcrew, The Gallery Press, 2003) p. 5. Hereafter abbreviated to *CP* and page references incorporated into the text.
9   William Carlos Williams, 'Kora in Hell', in Webster Schott (ed.), *Imaginations* (New York, New Directions, 1970) p. 14.
10 M.M. Rosenthal and Sally M. Gall, *The Modern Poetic Sequence: The Genius of Modern Poetry* (New York, Oxford University Press, 1983) p. 3.

against *The Rough Field*. Montague's long poem, far from being the kind that marches docile as a herd of sheep between the fences of white margins, replicates the collage-like text of the Americans, interspersing prose throughout the poetry, and using the page as a space for visual and typographical experimentation. Nevertheless, he is never as promiscuously experimental as either Olson in *The Maximus Poems*, or even Williams in *Paterson*, and is, in fact, closer to Crane's more traditional lyric form in *The Bridge*, though here too he would have found, in Crane's marginalia – some in prose, some poetry – a model for his own collage-like techniques. Crane's long poem showed Montague the value of a central poetic symbol to focus an historical, socio-political meditation, and the American's typographical eccentricities, such as his repeated use of the stepped short line and capitalised words, proved attractive to Montague in giving prosody a visual dimension. Section VI of *The Bridge*, for example, ends:

> Leaf after autumnal leaf
> > break off,
> > > descend –
> > > > descend – [11]

Crane's spatial sense of words on the page (including the withholding of a final full-stop) is reproduced in Montague's climactic statement of irrecoverable loss in *The Rough Field*:

> with all my circling a failure to return
> to what is already going,
> > going
> > > GONE   (*CP* 81)

One of the most important lessons to be learned from the Americans, as far as Montague was concerned, was the way rootedness could be combined with openness. Williams always insisted on the inextricable connection between man and place: 'a man in himself is a city', Williams says in the 'Author's Note' which prefaces *Paterson*, 'beginning, seeking, achieving and concluding his life in ways which the various aspects of a city may embody'.[12]

The man is indeed the city, Parterson referring both to the city (which is not unlike Williams' home town of Rutherford, New Jersey) and the protagonist (who is not unlike the poet himself). Rooted in a concept of democratic individualism coming down from Whitman, American epic demonstrated how the poet-protagonist could be a representative figure – representative of both his people and his place. Olson's more than 300 poems of varying length written over a twenty-year period also demonstrated for Montague a poetry that was a kind of autobiographical and historical geography based on the local – on the detailed, immediate and particular life of a community (the sea-faring community of Olson's home-town of Gloucester, Massachusetts); a poetry rooted in a vibrant all-encompassing sense of place, devoted to the uncovering of the

---

[11] *The Complete Poems of Hart Crane*, ed. Waldo Frank (New York, Doubleday Anchor Books, 1958) p. 52
[12] William Carlos Williams, *Paterson* (New York, New Directions Books, 1963) npn.

mythical *genius loci* – 'the primal features of those founders who lie buried in us',[13] to use Olson's words. Here was a poetry that viewed the present through ancient cultural paradigms, and was driven by a broadly nationalistic motive, though the single location was intended to serve as microcosm of the whole human condition. Echoes of all this, including Olson's tendency to didacticism, are readily apparent in Montague's epic verse. Like the Americans before him, Montague in *The Rough Field* and *The Dead Kingdom* uses the materials of his personal life and a deeply ingrained sense of place to construct a cultural myth. The hero is the poet himself, the details of the poet's life expressive of the larger crisis of culture. Montague isn't given to the kind of dramatic ventriloquism and adoption of personae that we associate with Berryman in the *Dream Songs* or Olson in *The Maximus Poems*; he is more obviously political than Williams, and in this regard more like Crane and Olson; he displays affinities with Crane's visionary quality, Williams's democratic impulse and Olson's sweeping sense of history. But where the Whitmanian American epic is prompted by a desire to reaffirm the promise of the New World (Olson, for instance, describes himself as 'an archaeologist of morning'[14]), Montague's is expressive of the 'backward look', and is embedded in Old World postures of suffering, loss and defeat. Though he follows the example of the American epic in placing the poet-historian himself at the centre, there is, in Montague's case, less a sense of a poet writing himself into an identity, than of a poet writing out of a pre-conceived one. The American poets are engaged in a dynamic process of self-discovery through a poetry that re-discovers 'America': Montague, less genuinely 'open' than the Americans, is committed to tropes of endless 'circling' and 'return'.

This concern to see himself as representative of his culture, to turn auto-biography into the spiritual biography of his times, also links Montague with the American confessionals, especially Robert Lowell, whom he met while a student at Yale in 1953–4. In Lowell's ground-breaking *Life Studies*, Montague saw how a poet could revolutionise his own poetic. In Lowell's case this involved a turn away from a compressed, ironic formalism towards a freer, more self-revealing, colloquially direct expression, while still managing to retain the ambitious histor-ical sweep that he had cultivated in earlier books. Lowell's influence was three-fold: his extraordinary candour (in dealing with family and personal details), his technical experiments (in devising a controlled and supple free verse), and his political conscience (Lowell was the epitome of American rebelliousness, whether against his family's Protestant New England heritage that he saw as oppressive and irrelevant, or against what he considered to be the immorality of the Vietnam War). He, like Ginsberg, Duncan and many others who voiced their disaffection with America during the Vietnam War years and the period of civil and racial disturbance in the late 1960s, opened up a faultline that ran all the way to Garvaghey:

> Lines of protest
> lines of change

---

[13] Charles Olson, quoted in Donald McQuade et al. (eds.) *The Harper American Literature*, vol. 2 (New York, HarperCollins, 1993) p. 1906.

[14] Charles Olson, *Additional Prose* (Bolinas, 1974) p. 40.

a drum of beating
   across Berkeley
all that Spring
   invoking the new
Christ avatar
   Of the Americas
Running voices
   Streets of Berlin
Paris, Chicago
   Seismic waves
Zigzagging through
   A faulty world   (*CP* 72)

The spirit of resistance, protest and consciousness-raising was concentrated particularly in the mythological West Coast poets, many of whom Montague had met at Berkeley in the '50s and '60s: Alan Ginsberg, Robert Bly, Gary Snyder, Robert Duncan. Montague was present at Ginsberg's first reading of *Howl*: 'I came back into the Ireland of the later 1950s which was not very liberated, and there was no point trying to deploy a "Howl" technique yet.'[15] Ginsberg and the Beats were important to Montague for the example they set in fighting against both private inhibitions and public censorship. In poems such as 'The Cage', 'A Muddy Cup', 'A Flowering Absence' and 'The Locket', Montague indulged the impulse towards the personal, sometimes to the point of the confessional, in dealing with his own childhood and family background, and his own ambivalent feelings towards his parents. Poems such as 'The Current' lifted the veil on adolescent male sexuality in rural Ireland. 'The Siege of Mullingar' declared that '*Puritan Ireland's dead and gone,/ A myth of O'Connor and O'Faolain*' (*CP* 67). The poems in *Tides* explored marital tension with a candour unusual in Irish poetry. Receptive to the renewed spirit of post-war American rebelliousness, the modernist cult of the personal, the confessional impulse, Montague's poetry registered something of the new transatlantic feelings of freedom, individualism and resistance to traditional values, though he was never as radically personal as the Ginsberg and Duncan who wrote shockingly about their homosexuality, or the Lowell who wrote about illness and madness, or the Sylvia Plath whose poetry was a form of controlled hysteria.

Montague is at his most intimately confessional in *The Dead Kingdom* where he journeys back to the primal source of his sense of displacement and exile, his mother's rejection of him. Contradictory feelings of anger, guilt, fear and incestuous desire surround his representation of the maternal body:

Mother, my birth was the death
Of your love life, the last man
To flutter near your tender womb;
A neonlit barsign winks off & on
Motherfucka, thass your name. (*CP* 181)

---

[15] Frazier, p. 157.

This fierce rhetoric of loss and despair, and its framing within a specific historical and cultural tradition, recall Ginsberg's elegy for his immigrant Jewish mother, though, as Elizabeth Grubgeld discerns, 'in their rendering of parental betrayal, Montague's elegies are more akin to those of Lowell and Berryman than to the transfiguring grace of Ginsberg's "Kaddish"'.[16] *The Dead Kingdom*, a long poem which is both 'on the road' in typically American fashion, and 'strikes inwards and downwards' like the 'pioneers' in Heaney's 'Bogland',[17] amalgamates the expansive American journey or quest poem, and the concentrated and contracted archaeological and artesian modes of Irish poetry. As the poet drives from his home in Co. Cork, through the midlands to the North of Ireland to attend his mother's funeral, the mythic landscapes of childhood, of ancient slaughter and primal evil function as 'deep images' through which he explores intimate psychic pain. 'All poems are journeys', says the American confessional poet and proponent of the 'deep image' theory, Robert Bly (whom Montague met at the Iowa Writers Workshop in 1954). Bly's first collection, *Silence in the Snowy Fields* (1962), opens with a car journey through the American Midwest, the trip across the prairie landscape becoming an exploration of dark zones of consciousness, solitude and silence. What Montague learned from the Americans was how the *dinnseanchas* tradition, which gives *The Dead Kingdom* its basic structure, could be modernised by incorporating within this ancient form an intense subjectivity that penetrates beneath and beyond the personal, the local and the temporal, to reveal the elemental forces which rule all our lives.

Commenting on Robert Duncan's trilogy, *The Opening of the Field* (1960), *Roots and Branches* (1964) and *The Bending of the Bow* (1968), Montague remarks: 'How curious it was to have gone as far as San Francisco to find someone who believed in magic like Yeats, and who persisted in the great romantic vision of Blake and Shelley!' (*FC* 16). Duncan's interest in a poetry of dreams, myths, visions and magic derives from his Theosophist upbringing, and it is this Yeatsian Duncan whom Montague remembers in 'Beyond the Liss' (*A Chosen Light*, 1967), a dream-narrative of fairy enchantment and Ovidian metamorphosis dedicated to Duncan. Nevertheless, one wonders if what Montague is responding to is anything more especially American than a shared indebtedness to Blake, Shelley and Yeats. Montague rarely mentions influential *texts*, referring rather to influential *poets*, the American influence on his work tending to manifest itself in general, pervasive ways, in terms of poetic style and attitude, rather than in terms of intertextual specifics, notwithstanding a few poems which do depend on direct allusion to prior American texts ('Division: *I.M. Theodore Roethke*', which refers to Roethke's 'The Meadow Mouse', and 'A Ballad for John Berryman', which features Berryman's alter ego, Henry, in the *Dream Songs*), and still others where it is impossible to know whether the intertextual relation was in Montague's mind at the time of writing his poem (i.e. implied intertextuality) or

---

16 Elizabeth Grubgeld, 'John Montague's *The Dead Kingdom*', in Thomas Dillon Redshaw (ed.), *Well Dreams: Essays on John Montague* (Omaha, Creighton University Press, 2004) pp. 276–88, 286.

17 Seamus Heaney, 'Bogland', in *Opened Ground: Poems 1966–1996* (London, Faber, 1998) p. 41. Heaney tells of writing 'Bogland' to propose the bog as 'an answering Irish myth' to the American myth of the frontier and the West. See Heaney, *Preoccupations: Selected Prose 1968–1978* (London, Faber, 1980) p. 55.

is something which occurs to the reader (i.e. inferred intertextuality). Obviously, a text can be illuminated by comparing and contrasting it with just about any other, this inferred kind of intertextuality being more a critical technique than a textual object, legitimised in the end by the significance of the comparisons or contrasts that are drawn.

On this logic, we might (tentatively) place Montague's 'For the Hillmother' beside one of Duncan's best-known poems 'Often I am Permitted to Return to a Meadow', the first poem Montague would have come across in *The Opening of the Field*. Montague first:

> Hinge of silence
>   creak for us
> Rose of darkness
>   unfold for us
> Wood anemone
>   sway for us
> Blue harebell
>   bend for us
> Moist fern
>   unfurl for us
>   ...   (*CP* 261)

Now Duncan:

> Often I Am Permitted to Return to a Meadow
>
> as if it were a scene made-up by the mind,
> that is not mine, but is a made place,
>
> that is mine, it is so near to the heart,
> an eternal pasture folded in all thought
> so that there is a hall therein
>
> that is a made place, created by light
> wherefrom the shadows that are forms fall.
>
> Wherefrom fall all architectures I am
> I say are likenesses of the First Beloved
> whose flowers are flames lit to the lady.[18]

Duncan demonstrates for Montague how a visionary poetry can also be modern; how poetry, as Duncan put it, could be 'a ritual referring to divine orders'[19] and yet speak to a secular age. Montague's poem is resoundingly Irish, strongly echoing both the Marian litany and ancient Irish nature poetry, but it is also indebted, literally as well as metaphorically, to American 'field composition': literally, in the way nature is presented as the agent of vision, the means of 'return' to the source, the gateway to the sacred mysteries; metaphorically, in the use of free verse to convey the inflections of individual speech. Like Duncan's,

---

[18] Robert Duncan, *The Opening of the Field* (New York, New Directions, 1973), p. 1.

[19] David Allen (ed.), *The New American Poetry 1945–1960* (University of California Press, 1999) p. 433.

Montague's verse has a dynamic, provisional quality that turns the poem into an open field, a site of vital possibility, in which the poet re-writes the world in his own terms. Both poems rely on a loose, open syntactical structure, eschewing compound sentences and favouring simple, repetitive structures in which each object is valued in and for itself. Traditional metres are stretched, made more open. Duncan manages an inner coherence through the repetition of motifs, sounds, images and phrases. Montague deploys an active, present-tense grammar with no punctuation, and elaborates a subtle echolalia of antiphonal phrase-pulsations to fulfil the role of more traditional methods of providing unity and coherence. Both poets work, not with argument or narrative, but a series of sharply visualised dream-images, and an incantatory language and idiom. The intention is the same as that which lies behind that prototypical piece of 'field composition', Whitman's *Leaves of Grass*: to express the longing for – better still, to conjure into existence – the much-desired union between self and world. The sacred merges with the sensual and the sexual, the Christian with the pagan and the Platonic. Both Duncan and Montague are in thrall to a mythical female principle, the lover and mother, the female Muse – 'the Lady', 'the First Beloved', the 'Queen Under the Hill' in Duncan's poem, and, in Montague's, the primeval Earth Mother, who is also linked with Mother Ireland and the Virgin Mother. But Duncan's poem is more thoroughly modernist, for he displays a self-consciousness about his own poetic procedures that is absent in Montague. Ultimately, 'Often I am Permitted' is a poem about poetry, Duncan's deliberately Stevensian phrasing used to emphasise the idea of the fictive, the 'as if' virtual reality of 'a scene made-up by the mind'. By contrast, Montague's is a more grounded poem, his voice more consistently that of the suppliant, the Yeatsian or Blakean *vates* rather than the Duncanian *makar*.

Montague's sacramental vision of nature, which is recognisably part of Irish tradition, was confirmed and updated for him by those American poets whose revitalisation of the Romantic view of nature and celebration of wilderness formed the basis of the ideology of American literary nationalism. One of the chief exponents of the contemporary American back-to-nature movement is the logger, forester and farmer, Gary Snyder, with whose Buddhist and native Indian-oriented eco-philosophy Montague has professed a special affinity: 'I accept the Celtic/Hindu idea of natural rhythms. I accept the North American Indian notion that God speaks through nature, the oldest values in the world as Snyder says in *Earth Household*; which we violate wholesale' (*FC* 13). The Montague who complained about the depredations visited upon the Irish landscape by an advanced capitalism that was eating up the small farms and driving motorways through the rural areas understood Snyder's eco-warrior's outrage against the abuse and exploitation of nature as well as people. But, again, the strongest influence may originate much nearer to home, as Montague himself concedes in this reference to Snyder: 'I heard what I had not yet heard in America – a young man reading poems about physical work. That seemed to link up with where I'd come from, with Patrick Kavanagh. He was reading poems about logging, about working in the fields.'[20] In a revealing comment, Montague indicates the limits

---

[20] Frazier, p. 157.

of his American influences: explaining that while he was at first impressed by Snyder's 'visionary mysticism', he says he found that the American's aesthetic 'was not quite right' for him because 'he (Snyder) would have resisted the very idea of a completed poem ... whereas, like Yeats, I felt that a good lyric should be clicked shut like a box'.[21]

A pervasive American presence in Montague's poetry is that of the confessional and visionary Theodore Roethke. Roethke's connection with Heaney has often been noted, as when John Haffenden suggested to the author of 'Digging' and 'Bogland': 'Much of your poetry speaks of atavism, genetic memories, about digging back into roots ... I've always felt this is very close to Ted Roethke.'[22] Montague is very close to Roethke too, and for the same reasons: Roethke's sensuous evocation of nature, his concern to penetrate to the preliterate roots of being, his sense of unity with cosmic forces. A series of so-called 'greenhouse poems' in his second collection, *The Lost Son and Other Poems* (1948), presents the young Roethke, lost among the plants and flowers, roots and stems of his father's 'greenhouse' world (Otto Roethke ran the family horticultural business and owned extensive greenhouses in Saginaw, Michigan). In a free verse format of variable line lengths and strongly alliterated speech, Roethke mimics natural processes, and asserts the correspondence between human and vegetable:

> I can hear, underground, that sucking and sobbing,
> In my veins, in my bones I feel it –
> The small waters seeping upward,
> The tight grains parting at last.
> When sprouts break out,
> Slippery as fish,
> I quail, lean to beginnings, sheath-wet.[23]

Heaney's and Montague's identification with the natural world is presented in a similarly intense and dramatic manner. There is, for example, Heaney's memory of being lost in the pea-drills, 'a green web, a caul of veined light, a tangle of rods and pods, stalks and tendrils, full of assuaging earth and leaf smell, a sunlit lair'.[24] His close, sensuous relation with the landscape is described in terms of 'betrothal', 'initiation' and re-birth, just as Roethke, leaning towards his beginnings, still 'wet' from the slime of the womb, chrysalis, or sheath, finds renewal in the feeling of being part of a vast natural process of becoming. Absorbing both Roethke and Heaney, Montague celebrates a wet, green, silent world too, using a similarly mystical language to describe Sweeney's 'slow dance': 'Then the dance begins, cleansing, healing ... the earth begins to speak ... the branch of the penis lifting, the cage of the ribs whistling ... In wet and darkness you are reborn ... your breath mingling with the exhalations of the earth, that eternal smell of

---

21 John Brown, *In the Chair: Interviews with Poets from the North of Ireland* (Cliffs of Moher, Salmon Publishing, 2002) p. 51.

22 John Haffenden, *Viewpoints: Poets in Conversation* (London, Faber, 1981) p. 62.

23 Theodore Roethke, 'Cuttings (later)', *Theodore Roethke: Collected Poems* (New York, Anchor Books, 1975) p. 35.

24 Seamus Heaney, 'The Sense of Place', in *Preoccupations: Selected Prose 1968–1978* (London, Faber, 1980) p. 133.

humus and mould' (*CP* 258). Further clarification of the meaning of Sweeney's 'slow dance' is provided by an essay on Roethke which Montague included in his memoir *Company: A Chosen Life*. The essay, entitled 'Dance On, Dance On', alludes both to the Yeatsian dream of unity in the dance, and to a line from Roethke: 'everything comes to One/ As we dance on, dance on, dance on'.[25]

In the essay, Montague comments on the fact that Roethke does not simply celebrate childhood pantheistic intimacy with his 'greenhouse' world, but also registers the latent threat in nature. This terrible knowledge is equally part of Heaney's vision (see 'Death of a Naturalist') and Montague's sense of the fault-lines that disrupt the green Eden of his childhood. As Montague puts it in his essay: 'But it was not all simple child's-eye memories of growth in a green place, Saganaw, Michigan, or Garvaghey, County Tyrone … Here was a poet who was determined to go the whole hog, dense with physical memories of the soiling of childhood, full of little comforting cries and invocations against the dark powers.'[26] The last of the series of so-called 'greenhouse poems' in *The Lost Son*, 'Frau Bauman, Frau Schmidt, and Frau Schwartz', is an affectionate recollection of an important source of comfort for the young Roethke. Daniel McAllister shows the way the 'floristic alchemy'[27] of these gardeners is mirrored in Heaney's descriptions of the women making butter in 'Churning Day' and the activity of the eponymous thatcher with his 'Midas touch'. Montague points to his own more personal connection with Roethke's poem '… like myself Ted had known the spell of childless old women, "These nurses of nobody else … (who) plotted for more than themselves." I could be back in my restoring Garvaghey home with my aunts …' (*C* 155). 'Frau Bauman, Frau Schmidt, and Frau Schwartz' not only recalls Montague's poems about his aunts, such as 'The Little Flower's Disciple' or 'Still Life, with Aunt Brigid', but also bears comparison in both attitude and style to other poems such as 'Like Dolmens Round My Childhood' or 'The Wild Dog Rose'. The three greenhouse workers are life-givers, carers, nurses, muses, the memory of them representing a powerful extension of the past into the ever-changing present. 'Frau Bauman, Frau Schmidt, and Frau Schwartz' begins with the word that closes Montague's *The Rough Field* – 'Gone'. The three women, though 'Gone', 'still hover' over the present. Taking on the fecund powers of earth mothers, they become mysteriously transubstantiated mythic figures, like the old people whom Montague remembers. Roethke's poem showed Montague and Heaney how the small and intimate details of the personal life could be transformed into a resonant, vital mythology, how the actual could be recreated without destroying it.

In the second half of 'Dance On, Dance On', Montague recalls Roethke visiting him in Herbert Street, Dublin, in the summer of 1960, and the two of them exchanging drafts of work in progress. At the time, the 29-year-old Montague was working on his second book *Poisoned Lands*, the American on his 'North American Sequence' (eventually published posthumously in 1964). From the

---

25 Theodore Roethke, 'Once More, the Round', in *Collected Poems*.

26 John Montague, *Company: A Chosen Life* (London, Duckworth, 2001) p. 155. Hereafter abbreviated to *C* and page references incorporated into the text.

27 Daniel McAllister, 'The Influence of American Poets on John Montague, Seamus Heaney, Derek Mahon and Paul Muldoon' (unpublished PhD thesis, University of Ulster, 2007) p. 96.

drafts of 'North American Sequence', Montague would have seen how Roethke, in returning for the last time to the greenhouse world of childhood, did so within the larger context of the entire North American continent, just as the young Irish poet in his long sequences, *The Rough Field* and *The Dead Kingdom*, was to set personal memory within the larger context of public history. Both Roethke's and Montague's exploration of roots involve dreamlike journeys to the interior regions of the self. 'North American Sequence' charts a journey of healing of the self in which the speaker, ravaged and vulnerable, attempts a characteristically American transcendental reintegration of self and nature. In the poem's loose progression, its tentative, unfixed form at once cohering and dispersing, Roethke dramatises a constant process of dissolution and renewal: 'I am renewed by death, thought of my death',[28] he says. A similar idea is elaborated by Montague in, for instance, one of the poems in *Tides* – 'But/ Everything dies into birth' ('Undertow', *CP* 254) – and in a later sea poem, 'The Hag's Cove': 'that hectic glitter of decay,/ that gluttonous moil of creation,/ to be smashed on the rocks,/ broken down and built again'.[29] Roethke's poem pursues a transcendent vision of wholeness that remains perpetually elusive, and the poet learns to accept the provisional and artificial nature of his repeated visionary syntheses. He closes his sequence with the symbol of a single wild rose struggling out of a thorny tangle of undergrowth, growing toward clarity out of confusion: 'A single wild rose, struggling out of the white embrace of the morning-glory'.[30] It is an objective and emotionally satisfying expression of an inner synthesis, evocative of the greenhouse roses of the poet's childhood. Montague's 'The Wild Dog Rose' moves toward a similarly compressed and visionary conclusion, its culminating symbol available only to the poet who writes from deep down in his environment. Transplanted from Eliot's English country garden, and Roethke's cliff edge, and supported by the rich liturgy of Catholicism, Montague's rose symbolises an ideal beauty of a distinctively Irish kind. Montague, like Roethke, is drawn to the big themes and the big poem but, like Roethke, his gift was really for small-scale lyricism, vivacity of observation, convincing and exact description, intense scrutiny of nature and people, sensitivity to the 'minimals' (Roethke's 'The Meadow-Mouse') and 'small secrets' (title of a Montague poem). And indeed it was these aspects of Roethke's poetry which Montague especially praised in his essay.

Roethke's long poem offers a way of reading one of Montague's short poems, 'Roethke's Ghost at Roche's Point' (*Drunken Sailor*), which evokes a typically Roethkean correspondence between self and seascape, the natural world of wind, fish and birds becoming a symbolic psychic landscape. Montague, too, contemplates the elemental waters, as he has done over many years, registering his fear of the dark organic processes and of death. The movement in 'Roethke's Ghost at Roche's Point' from stilled expectancy, through intimations of death and disorder, to the apocalyptic lunacy of 'that flaring cry – / as the night finds tongue// under the driving moon' (*DS* 17), to the final ordering image of the lighthouse, parallels the drive towards integration and harmony in Roethke's poetry. Roethke's 'figure

---

28 Theodore Roethke, 'North American Sequence', in *Collected Poems*.
29 John Montague, *Drunken Sailor* (Loughcrew, The Gallery Press, 2004) p. 14. Hereafter abbreviated to *DS* and page references incorporated into the text.
30 'North American Sequence', in *The Collected Poems*.

glowing on its own' at the beginning of the poem prefigures the final image of the lighthouse – Roethke viewed as both haunting presence and guiding beacon in the Irish poetic landscape.

It is now the accepted critical wisdom that Montague is one of the most important modernisers and internationalisers of the Irish poetic tradition. In the opinion of Edna Longley: 'More than any poet of his generation he opened up channels between the Irish and English tradition, between regional and cosmo-politan allegiances, between Ulster and Irish perspectives.'[31] And similar large claims are made by Gregory Schrimer: 'It is only a slight exaggeration to say that the poems that Montague published in the 1950s and 1960s almost single-handedly led Irish poetry out of the Sargasso Sea of provincialism in which Montague found it and into the increasingly cosmopolitan world of post-war poetry beyond the shores of Ireland ... The extraordinary flowering of Irish poetry during the last three decades, built in part on the foundation laid by Montague, has produced a literary environment in which worldliness, sophis-tication, and a generally pluralistic view of Irish culture are more or less taken for granted, part of the cultural air that the contemporary Irish poet, Montague included, breathes almost unconsciously.'[32] These critics take their cue from Montague's own polemic, but in assessing the extent of his internationalism, it is well to recall D.H. Lawrence's advice: Never trust the teller, trust the tale. Just how much of a challenge to narrow definitions of Irish poetry does Montague's own work really represent? And just how inclusive is his localism, especially when it aspires to public poetry?

*

Like Heaney, Montague continually looks back to childhood and the idea of a sacral world which, as Heaney put it, still retained 'some vestigial sense of place as it was experienced in the older dispensation'.[33] Both poets present a totemistic, hieratic, legendary landscape 'instinct with signs' of folkloric belief. This sense of place, Heaney has suggested, is 'the foundation for a marvellous or a magical view of the world, a foundation that sustained a diminished structure of lore and superstition and half-pagan, half-Christian thought and practice'.[34] In Montague's poem 'The Northern Gate' (*Tides*, 1971), the speaker 'tried to follow' (*CP* 250) the owl into the rural night, into the pagan, folkloric Gaelic past, into a mental landscape beyond the gate which separates town and country, the *pagus* from the civilised world. The gate gives access to the 'North', the dark and troubled home ground of the poet's childhood, the atavistic depths of his own being. Out of his fleeting perceptions of the owl, the speaker imagines a 'feathered ghost', a spirit of place who occupies the space between dream and reality. Heaney, too, in 'The King of the Ditchbacks' follows the 'trespasser'[35] Sweeney, taking a path

---

[31] Edna Longley, blurb of *Selected Poems* (London, Penguin, 2001).

[32] Gregory A. Schrimer, '"A Richly Ambiguous Position": Re-viewing *Poisoned Lands, A Chosen Light*, and *Tides*', in Thomas Dillon Redshaw (ed.), *Well Dreams: Essays on John Montague* (Omaha, Creighton University Press, 2004), pp. 81–94, 82.

[33] Seamus Heaney, 'The Sense of Place', in *Preoccupations: Selected Prose 1968–1978* (London, Faber, 1980), p. 133.

[34] Ibid.

[35] Seamus Heaney, *Opened Ground*, p. 238.

through a barred gate into the marginal pagan and cultural Gaelic ground, just as in earlier poems he had been drawn into the trail of the servant boy ('Servant Boy') or the 'geniuses who creep out of every/corner of the woodes and glennes'[36] ('Bog Oak'). In 'The King of the Ditchbacks' the speaker is 'translator' as well as 'trespasser', reading in the signs of the rural landscape an ancient Gaelic text, a dark, othered sensibility: 'just beyond the hedge/ he has opened a dark morse/ along the bank'. If, as Montague says, 'the whole landscape [is] a manuscript/ We had lost the skill to read' (*CP* 33), poems such as 'The Northern Gate' and 'The King of the Ditchbacks' are doors into the dark, into the cave of night, the dark kingdom, the green world of the mythic past.

In dedicating 'The King of the Ditchbacks' to Montague, Heaney associates the older poet with the spirit of Sweeney, the pioneer who sought to move beyond the accepted limits. Both poets have identified with the mythic hag-ridden wild-man who was in conflict with the Church and in touch with the earthy forces, but Montague is anxious to out-Sweeney Heaney. In his review of Heaney's *Sweeney Astray*, 'Tarzan Among the Nightingales', he criticises Heaney for being too 'literary' and not 'lunatic' or 'wild' or 'Irish' enough: 'he (Heaney) does not, it seems to me, possess the crucial gift or wound of a grafted tongue; part of his mind does not think naturally in Irish … his concern is more with the effect in English than the force of the Irish … Although he may live in a lunatic land, Seamus Heaney seems to me eminently sane, both as man and poet.'[37] For Montague, Mad Sweeney is 'the secret genius behind not only Irish but modern literature in English, a lunatic note undermining our sense of reality'.[38]

Inscribed in a traditional rural culture and a pagan, Catholic metaphysics, the imagination of both Heaney and Montague is deeply scored by awareness of loss and change. Their poetry stems from a nostalgic, elegiac 'backward look'. Both write poems about traditional rural folkways, about mummers, water-carriers, forges, about places and placenames as the bearers of history and ancestry, about the 'heart land' (the title of a recent Montague poem), about neighbours, local people and family members. Like Heaney, Montague continually returns to his personal past, *à la recherche du temps perdu*. Just as Heaney found in the felled chestnut tree a memory 'ramifying forever' ('Clearances' viii), so for Montague the loss of his mother is 'a flowering absence' ('A Flowering Absence'): memory and imagination are magical faculties through which absence is converted into presence, loss and emptiness into plenitude. In 'A Graveyard in Queens', Montague keeps faith with family despite dispersal and death. 'First Landscape, First Death', from his most recent collection, *Drunken Sailor* (2004), evokes memories of a dead father, a dead aunt, a dead neighbour. But this landscape also affords 'gentle nourishment' and 'still gives solace'. Though the poet moves 'light-footed between/ cities', he is 'stopped suddenly by/ the sight of some distant hill/ or curving twilight river, to see/ on a ghostly mound, my abiding/ symbol, a weathered standing stone'. The significance of place to identity is for Montague symbolised by the dolmen – 'the weathered standing stone' – as it is

---

36 Ibid., p. 44.
37 John Montague, 'Tarzan Among the Nightingales', review of Heaney's *Sweeney Astray*, *Fortnight*, 200 (December 1983) p. 27.
38 Ibid.

for Heaney by the omphalos, 'the stone that marked the centre of the world'.[39] In Montague's poetry, as in Heaney's (but not in Kavanagh's), landscape has a cultural and political meaning. Both Montague and Heaney see themselves as the custodians and celebrants of a lost culture, a lost history and heritage; for both, identity is profoundly embedded in ancestral terrain and native culture. In times of doubt, Montague takes it upon himself to reaffirm the lost centre, as he does in dedicating his finely worked poem 'Hearth Song' to Heaney who, in *The Place of Writing*, had lamented the loss of the hearth in Irish homes: 'the transition from a condition where your space, the space of the world had a determined meaning and a sacred position, to a condition where space was a neuter geometrical disposition without any emotional or inherited meaning. I watched it happen in Irish homes when we first saw a house built where there was no chimney, and then you'd go into rooms without a grate – so no hearth, which in Latin means focus.'[40] Montague's answering poem affirms continuity with the past, and does so in the same way as Heaney does, through a redemptive, healing aesthetic, symbolised by the cricket 'throbbing and trembling in darkness/ a hearth song of happiness'.

> Rising from beneath our feet,
> Welling up out of the earth,
> A solitary, compulsive song
>
> Composed for no one, a tune
> Dreamt up under a flat stone,
> Earth's fragile, atonal rhythm.   (*CP* 298)

Compare Heaney's attentiveness to his whispering landscapes, or his intuition of the 'undersong' in the 'Lightenings' section of *Seeing Things*:

> Beneath the ocean of itself, the crowd
> In Roman theatres could hear another
> Stronger groundswell coming through ...   ('Lightenings', iv)[41]

In both Heaney and Montague there is the consolation of a deeper, truer life going on beneath the public world of history and politics. Rather than presenting history in linear, teleological terms as something developing towards a predetermined goal, both poets concentrate on a present moment still in touch with its depth.

But Montague is aware of the dangers of sentimentality in the 'backward look'. He refuses to acquiesce unquestioningly in the received myth. 'The Source' (*The Rough Field*, 1972), dramatises the attempt to return to 'the central heart' of the landscape, provocative of childhood memories and ancient myth ('ancient trout of wisdom', 'bird of all knowledge'). But Montague unceremoniously dispels the atmosphere of hushed awe and reverence in which Heaney communes with mystery. In 'Kinship' (*North*, 1975), Heaney's quasi-sexual intrusion of the spade into the bog – 'As I raised it/ the soft lips of the growth/ muttered and split,/ a tawny rut/ opening at my feet/ like a shed skin,/ the shaft wettish/ as I sank

---

39   Seamus Heaney, 'Mossbawn', in *Preoccupations*, p. 17.
40   Seamus Heaney, *The Place of Writing* (Atlanta, GA, Scholars Press, 1989) p. 71.
41   Seamus Heaney, *Seeing Things* (London, Faber, 1991) p. 58.

it upright' – brings him to 'the edge of centuries', where he stands 'facing a goddess'.[42] Contrastingly, Montague's journey to 'the source' takes place in a debased context of drunken debauchery, in which we find the poet 'plung[ing]' and '[crash[ing]' boisterously through the darkness, 'singing/ In a mood of fierce elation'. His probing of the dark depths of 'a pool of ebony water' is described with the same kind of erotic intensity that we find in Heaney ('Legend/ Declared a monster trout/ Lived there, so I slipped/ A hand under the fringe of/ Each slick rock, splitting/ The skin of turning froth'), but Montague finds 'nothing' in his search for the mythical heart of his place – 'nothing but that/ Wavering pulse leading to/ The central heart where/ The spring beat, so icy-cold' (*CP* 51). He rejects the temptations of 'legend', suggesting that meaning depends not on the traditional lore of the collective myth-kitty but on the individual's direct imaginative engagement with the world. Penetration to 'the source' involves making oneself susceptible to nature's magic, a prerequisite for which is the suspension of rational mind – 'The seventh sense of drunkenness' (*CP* 52), a heightened or defamiliarised state of awareness which the poet celebrates elsewhere in poems such as 'The Hag's Cove' (*Drunken Sailor*). The resources of personal memory and imagination succeed where collective mythology fails: 'As I plod/ Through the paling darkness/ Details emerge, and memory/ Warms'.

Much of the interest of Montague's poetry lies precisely in his ambivalent attitude to both tradition and modernity. The poet is both absorbed in and distanced from his home place. Poetry can, as Heaney put it, 'continue, hold, dispel, appease';[43] but the imagination is wayward, it is a potentially destabilising force, as likely to undermine as to confirm cherished ideas, images and myths. Like Heaney in 'Terminus' ('Two buckets were easier carried than one/ I grew up in between'[44]), Montague is caught between two worlds, life and art. In 'The Water-Carrier' Montague's speaker is 'balanced as a fulcrum between two buckets', drawing water from the spring, a symbol of poetic inspiration rooted in his childhood memories of rural Ulster: 'Recovering the scene, I had hoped to stylise it,/ Like the portrait of an Egyptian water-carrier'. But he recognises that mere recollection and reflection is not enough. Experience only achieves its full meaning when reality is impregnated by imagination:

> I sometimes came to take the water there,
> Not as return or refuge, but some pure thing,
> Some living source, half imagined and half real
>
> Pulses in the fictive water that I feel. (*CP* 189)

The Stevensian 'fictive water' is a 'living source' because it springs from actual experience. Memory is inevitably a creative, fictionalising, mythologising (and potentially falsifying) faculty. The great challenge is not to let rhetoric displace reality. In 'Tim' Montague praises the old horse for 'denying rhetoric with your patience,/ forcing me to drink/ from the trough of reality' (*CP* 208). But while committing himself to 'reality' – 'the struggle with casual/ Graceless unheroic

---

[42] Seamus Heaney, *North* (London, Faber, 1975) p. 42.
[43] Seamus Heaney, 'Glanmore Sonnets' II, *Opened Ground*, p. 164.
[44] Seamus Heaney, 'Terminus', *Opened Ground*, p. 295.

things' – the poet recognises art's ritualising function. In 'A Bright Day', 'the only way of saying something/ Luminously as possible' is not through 'the accumulated richness/ Of an old historical language', but 'a slow exactness/ Which recreates experience/ By ritualising its details' (*CP* 225). Thus, if poems such as 'The Shan Bhean Bhoct' and 'The Wild Dog Rose' move towards emblem and ritual, the mythicising impulse is rooted in carefully observed realistic portraiture which produces something rather different from traditional nationalist iconography. Memory supplies, not romantic female images of traditional Ireland, but pictures of crazed and lonely old people whom the poet has known – Maggie Owens, Mary Moore, Mary Mulvey. 'Like Dolmens Round My Childhood', with its echo of Yeats's line in 'Under Ben Bulben' – 'Ancient Ireland knew it all'[45] – rejects the older poet's idolisation of the past. Montague's picture of the past is a combination of affectionate and uncompromisingly honest recollection. Beginning with detailed close-ups, he then pulls back to re-configure the fragmentary images into ritual and symbol, thereby achieving some measure of control over the raw and often difficult facts of experience.

> Ancient Ireland indeed! I was reared by her bedside.
> The rune and the chant, evil eye and averted head,
> Fomorian fierceness of family and local feud.
> Gaunt figures of fear and friendliness,
> For years they trespassed on my dreams,
> Until once, in a standing circle of stones,
> I felt their shadows pass
> Into the dark permanence of ancient forms.   (*CP* 13)

'Old Mythologies' (the title taken from Yeats's 'The Coat' – 'I made my song a coat/ Covered with embroideries/ Out of old mythologies'[46]) debunks the heroic imagery of nationalist myth, re-imagining the ancient Gaelic warriors 'To bagpiped battle marching,/ Wolfhounds, lean as models,/ At their urgent heels'. As Seamus Deane remarks: 'Montague claimed that Kavanagh "liberates us into ignorance", by which he meant, among other things, that he liberated a whole generation of Irish writers from the erudite, the esoteric and the sometimes overpowering mythological systems of the writers of the revival.'[47] Montague seeks in his own poetry to continue this work of liberating the imagination from the Yeatsian grand narratives of Irish nationalism. In 'Patriotic Suite 10' the sound of O'Riada's traditional Irish music evokes, not a sense of cultural wholeness or rejuvenation, but a demeaning sentimentalism: 'The gloomy images of a provincial catholicism …/ wound in a native music/ curlew echoing tin whistle/ to eye-swimming melancholy/ is that our offering?' The music conjures up images of the mythic west, but the very last line of the poem suddenly makes us aware that the speaker is listening to the music on the radio of 'a self-drive car'. The imagery of car and radio signals the modern journey of the exile uprooted from his home place, but still hankering after stable ground, the resonances of a mythic

---

45 W.B. Yeats, *Selected Poems* (London, Macmillan, 1975) p. 206.
46 Ibid., p. 63.
47 Seamus Deane, 'John Montague: The Kingdom of the Dead', in *Celtic Revivals* (London, Faber, 1985) p. 147.

past, in a disintegrated modern world. Access to the primal Irish psyche now ironically depends on the technology of a modern commodity culture, in which traditional values have to fight for public attention against the rival attractions of a growing 'Gross National Product' and a general modernising tendency in the sphere of artistic culture: 'is that our offering?' the poet asks in reference to O'Riada's music, 'While all Europe seeks/ new versions of old ways,/ the hammer of Boulez swing-/ ing to Eastern harmonies./ From 1960 the Gross National Product ...' (*CP* 68). Montague registers his scepticism about the possibility of ever being able to repossess the past, and a doubt about the wisdom of even trying, given the dangers of nostalgia and regression. The poem balances longing for an original wholeness with awareness of the need to adapt to new conditions. Recalling the harsh conditions of rural life in 'Epilogue', he explicitly rejects the bogus pastoral of the Irish past (though this is not his last word on the matter): 'Only a sentimentalist would wish/ to see such degradation again:/ heavy tasks from spring to harvest; the sack-cloth pilgrimages under rain/ to repair the slob-bery gaps of winter/ with the labourer hibernating/ in his cottage for half the year/ to greet the indignity of the Hiring Fair' (*CP* 80). In a review of Heaney's *Selected Poems*, Montague criticises the younger poet for trying to escape from a rapidly changing modern world into a sentimental pastoralism, 'as if Gold-smith had celebrated the ideal Auburn only, and not its desolation'.[48] For all his careful evocation of tradition, rural landscape, folk custom, Montague's quest for 'the source' is conducted in full awareness that the idea of a centre is fictive. While this knowledge may at times frustrate, it is also creatively enabling. In 'The Plain of Blood' (*Drunken Sailor*), the speaker sets off in quest of what Foucault calls an 'archaeology of knowledge': '... our most fearsome legend./ We went in search of him/ .../ halting to follow the lost/ stone alignments of Moytura/ .../ This mythic battleground' (*DS* 69). The archaeological image implies a vein of 'truth' lying waiting to be disinterred as opposed to the Foucauldian recognition that history is a dynamic construct of discourses designed to produce specific knowledges of the past. Montague's poem acknowledges that the past can never be available in pure form, only in the form of narratives and representations. The idea of a single, authoritative version of the past is displaced by an awareness of the constructedness of myth, and the need to revise the images of the past in the light of new historical circumstances. Aloft on 'the wings of the imagination' the speaker journeys into the Irish heart of darkness, determined to discover 'beauty' as well as 'terror', sunlight as well as darkness. The object of his search is Crom Cruach (which means bloody crescent or bloody bent one and is mentioned in the sixth-century *Dinnseanchas* in the *Book of Leinster*), the most ancient and venerated god of all the various tribes of Ireland. The god was worshipped in idol form on Moyslacht (the plain of adoration or destruction) in Co. Cavan. Situated around him were twelve smaller idols made of stone while he was gold. To him the early Irish are supposed to have sacrificed one third of their children on Samhain (1 November) to ensure the fertility of their land, though there is no evidence to prove or disprove this theory. The idols were extremely ancient even in Patrick's time around AD 500, and, according to tradition, it was he who

---

48 John Montague, 'The Poet's Workshop', *The Guardian*, 27 November 1980, p. 11.

destroyed them and worship of them. Crom Cruach was believed to be a sun god, and it is the life-giving rather than the destructive forces associated with the god that Montague chooses to emphasise: 'here was no sullen dark god/ but a shining central stone/ .../ the Sun God and His seasons,/ an Irish Apollo pouring/ down His daily benison' (*DS* 74–5). With a nod to the problematical nature of historical knowledge ('"There's them", he says, "that believe/ there was no human sacrifice, there was/ no Plain of Slaughter or Blood./ 'Twas all invented by the Christians/ to change old gods into new demons"' *DS* 73), Montague's intervention aims to re-write tradition for his contemporary world. He does so by transforming a god of horror into a foundational symbol of life, hope and unity: 'Sure it's only one step to the border./ They were all one people living here/ .../ They hoisted this stone upright there/ long before the Christians came' (*DS* 73–4). The poem, with its alternative interpretation of the presiding Irish deity, is a radiant, affirmative response to the earlier poem, also entitled 'The Plain of Blood', in *The Dead Kingdom* (1984). The earlier 'The Plain of Blood' invokes 'malignant Cromm' as the source of Ireland's present Troubles, but then proceeds to dismiss myth invoking instead a reinterpretation of the present situation in terms of a colonial and sectarian politics: 'wise imperial policy/ Hurling the small people s/ against each other, Orange/ Order against Defender,/ neighbour against neighbour,/ blind rituals of violence,/ our homely Ulster swollen/ to a Plain of Blood' (*CP* 155). Returning to myth in the later poem, Montague exploits the doubts and uncertainties in the historical record to re-write the earlier 'mournful auld poem, *The Dead Kingdom*' ('Last Court'). The re-constructed narrative of the Plain of Blood – the last poem in his last collection – clears away outmoded or unhelpful myths and stereotypes and, starting with the poet's own personal experience of the 'plain of blood' in the actual present, attempts a revisioning of Irish tradition that could contribute to a more optimistic future. Montague, it would seem, is no more willing to accept a fatalistic view of Irish historical myth than he is to accept a sentimentalised one.

Yet while interrogating old mythologies, he never entirely puts them to route for he cannot ever completely accept the rapidly changing, disorienting and deeply uncongenial world of colonial modernity. He sees a deserted countryside and laments the way the land has been bought up for new road construction. While acknowledging that the hardship of farming life has been eased by the introduction of new technology such as tractors, milking machines and grain silos, he decries the break-up of traditional rural values. He welcomes the liberated atmosphere of the Mullingar fleadh ('The Siege of Mullingar') yet opposes the artificiality of the Garvaghey dance hall ('The Dancehall'). His detachment from the past never completely cancels out the plangent note of elegy: 'Yet something mourns', he says, as he contemplates 'a world where action had been wrung/ through painstaking years to ritual' (*CP* 80). The fate of his ancestral rough field is linked to that of Goldsmith's deserted village. 'In all my wanderings round this world of care', Goldsmith's narrator intones, 'I still had hopes, my long vexations past,/ Here to return – and die at home at last.'[49] But the ending of

---

[49] Oliver Goldsmith, 'The Deserted Village', in *Poems and Essays* (London, Groombridge and Sons, 1858) p. 25.

'The Deserted Village' emphasises the erosion of traditional values and natural rhythms, the destruction of a traditional rustic idyll by the forces of modernisation : 'E'en now the devastation is begun,/ And half the business of destruction done;/ E'en now, methinks, as pond'ring here I stand,/ I see the rural virtues leave the land'.[50] In a 1962 essay, 'Oliver Goldsmith: The Sentimental Prophecy', Montague describes 'The Deserted Village' as a 'lament of the returned exile' (*FC* 67), a vision of destruction and waste which sees the end of the narrator's childhood and his dreams of escape and peaceful retirement. The fall of Auburn implies the disruption of 'a divine order' (*FC* 66), the loss of 'a pastoral Eden' (*FC* 66). Goldsmith's theme is the destruction of 'rural virtues', 'spontaneous joys', 'piety' – even poetry itself: 'And thou, sweet poetry, thou loveliest maid,/ Still first to fly where sensual joys invade!/ Unfit, in these degenerate times of shame,/ To catch the heart or strike for honest fame'.[51] The closing lines of *The Rough Field* express a similar sense of failure: 'Our finally lost dream of man at home/ in a rural setting! ... with all my circling a failure to return/ to what is already going/ going/ GONE' (*CP* 81). The rural past, and the poetry in which it has been reconstructed, fall under the hammer of commercial modernity. An historic process of colonial dispossession, combined with the renewed outbreak of violence in the North and the encroachment of advanced capitalism, it would seem, have silenced the poetic spirit. *The Rough Field* ends by arresting process, freezing it into an emblematic moment of eternal circling, expressive of the traditional nationalist nostalgia for a home transcending the torn ground of historical and political strife.

Coming to prominence in an age of electronic mass media and transnational capitalism, Montague's totalising tribal and nationalistic approaches, his mythopoeic and antiquarian concerns, his constant circling of grounded, rural communal origins, place him in outright or ironic opposition to the forces of modernisation. Even while various international influences were drawing him beyond Kavanagh's parish, he was at the same time engaged in the recuperation of revivalist narratives of Irishness based on notions of the continuity of tradition, a concept of the poet as tribal bard, and an old-fashioned sectarian politics. The epigraph to his essay, 'The Figure in the Cave', comes from a poem, 'Roots', by John Berryman:

> Young men (young women) ask about my 'roots'
> As if I were a *plant* ...
>
> I can't see it. Many are wanderers,
> Both Lawrences, Byron, & the better for it.
> Many stay home forever: Hardy: fine.
> Bother these bastards with their preconceptions ...
>
> I'd rather live in Venice or Kyoto,
> Except for the languages ...   (*FC* 1)

While implicitly aligning himself with Berryman's mobile poetics and dismissal

---

[50]   Ibid., p. 34.
[51]   Ibid.

of regionalism, Montague's own poetry can at times suggest undue attachment to roots and traditional community, which he is still looking for even in Cork, however much he may try to convince us that his parish can be anywhere. We need to be alert to the difference between Montague's polemic of modernisation and Americanisation, which is the aspect of his poetics that he emphasises in his prose writings, and his actual poetic practice. In the context of the Berryman poem, the opening line of Montague's essay – '*With all my circling a failure to return*': but to where?' (*FC* 1) – is nothing if not disingenuous. Is there ever really any doubt that what Montague is circling is always the ancestral home, even if it exists now only in imagination, and even if his peregrinations take in other places and other potentially destabilising perspectives and procedures?

In poems such as the early 'Portrait of the Artist as a Model Farmer' (*Poisoned Lands*) he mocks the kind of enervating provincialism that seemed to him to characterise Irish poetry in the 1950s, yet Montague's own poetry remains rooted in inherited tradition and 'sense of place'. Like many poems in his most recent volume, 'Slievemore' returns to the poet's native region. Section 3 of the poem first appeared in *Tides*, under the title 'King & Queen':

> Jagged head
> Of warrior, bird
> Of prey, surveying space
>
> Side by side
> They squat, the stern
> Deities of this place ...   (*DS* 64)

Montague's description of the landscape of southeast Tyrone is conveyed in the loose triadic stanza associated with William Carlos Williams. But where Williams emphasises endless, de-centred process, Montague's Slievemore figures an aboriginal, sacred centre presided over by 'guardian forms', 'stern deities':

> Blunt fingers
> Splay to caress
> A rain-hallowed stone
>
> Towards which
> The landscape of five parishes
> Tends, band after band
>
> Of final
> Peewit haunted,
> Cropless bogland.   (*DS* 65)

The central organising symbol of the 'rain-hollowed stone' orders the surrounding landscape in a much more fundamental way than Wallace Stevens' jar in Tennessee. More like Heaney's 'untoppled omphalos',[52] Montague's ancient, pagan dolmen image, associated in his mind with the nearby O'Neill inauguration stone at Tullyhogue Fort, stakes and centres the imagination, identity, culture and poetry. The vocabulary of 'warrior', 'guardian forms', 'deities of place',

---

52 Seamus Heaney, 'The Toome Road', *Opened Ground*, p. 150.

'rain-hallowed stone', 'parishes' and 'haunted bogland' springs from the kind of atavistic feeling that the revivalist F.R. Higgins believed poetry should be all about – poetry as 'blood-music that brings the racial character to mind'.[53] It is not the language that one would normally associate with a self-avowed moderniser. Montague may express his admiration of 'the diversity of American poetry, its daring directness in pursuit of a language to accommodate modern experience' (*FC* 189), but his own formal hieratic style and patrician attitude is a far cry from the variety and flexibility of poetic speech that we find in modern American poetry.

'The Road's End', the first poem in the 'A Severed Head' section of *The Rough Field*, displays an imagistic concentration and exactitude that is reminiscent of Williams' 'The Red Wheelbarrow':

> Only the shed remains
> In use for calves, although fuschia
> Bleeds by the wall, and someone has
> Propped a yellow cartwheel
> Against the door.   (*CP* 32)

Michael O'Neill sees the 'yellow cartwheel' reference as 'a moment of puckish homage to Williams' red wheelbarrow', which, O'Neill argues, saves Montague's poem from 'over-solemnity'.[54] For Williams, 'so much depends/ upon' not some great abstract idea, but the humble details of the life before his eyes. There are 'no ideas but in things', and attention is concentrated on the individual object or event, caught at a particular point in time and space. Williams's poem has a painterly quality suggestive of a leisurely, professional detachment which is quite different from Montague's more aggravated engagement with the scene before him. The red wheelbarrow does not stand for something else, it is uniquely itself. But Montague wants us to see his yellow cartwheel and other evocative images – deserted cabins, dilapidated shed, slumped thatch, dusty flags – as symbolic of the past, 'shards/ Of a lost culture' (*CP* 32). In Montague, however, 'small secrets' (the title of one of his poems) bespeak larger secrets, poems reconstruct the platonic manuscript of place we've lost the skill to read. For Williams, all there is are the patterns that may be discovered in a world of discrete particulars; but Montague's melancholy description (which the allusion to Williams does little to alleviate) is both generated out of, and made to serve, the grand narrative of Irish nationalism, with its mythology of the defeat of the Irish folk-spirit and of Irish sovereignty, symbolised by the severed head – the lost leadership of the O'Neills. The fragmentary forms of the modernist aesthetic are put to use to enunciate the familiar themes of Irish colonial loss – the lost past, a lost culture, a lost population. And a lost language, as in these lines from 'A Grafted Tongue':

> (Dumb,
> bloodied, the severed

---

[53] F.R. Higgins quoted by Paul Muldoon in his Introduction to *The Faber Book of Contemporary Irish Verse* (London, Faber, 1986) p. 18.

[54] Michael O'Neill, 'John Montague and Derek Mahon: The American Dimension', *Symbiosis: A Journal of Anglo-American Relations*, 3, 1 (1973) pp. 54–61, 56.

head now chokes to
speak another tongue –

   As in
a long suppressed dream,
some stuttering garb-
led ordeal of my own)

   An Irish
child weeps at school
repeating its English. (*CP* 37)

Montague's poem is an example of Olsonian 'Projective' verse, based on the prin-
ciples of particularity and immediacy, and the idea of a poem as a continuous,
performative process. Montague's short, irregular, free-verse lines and compact
stanzas disrupt normal flow of meaning by breaking word units across line
breaks and stanza breaks and even breaking words in the middle, in a manner
reminiscent of Olson or e.e. cummings. The disruption also takes place on the
level of punctuation and syntax. The poem develops stumblingly; it drifts and
stutters; crowding stresses and pauses convey the speaker's struggle for articula-
tion. Ironically, the liberated forms of modern American poetry, re-deployed
in an Irish context, express the constrained utterance of the colonially grafted
tongue. Despite Montague's combination of American and Anglo-Irish poetics,
the poem sees hybridity, not as potentially fruitful intermarriage, not as healthy,
liberating and creative crossing of languages and perspectives, but as the painful
excoriation of an authentic Irishness.

In *Drunken Sailor*, something continues to mourn. 'Last of the House' is a
haunting, sentimental lament for a lost Gaelic past, a lost tribe, the title based
on the Irish phrase *An Fear Deireanach den tSloinneadh* ('The Last of that Family
Name'). The landscape is 'numinous', the ground of a shared but diminished
culture, redolent of the life of the poet's people, disinherited and dispossessed.
The poem itself is an affirmation of 'stubborn continuity' in the face of the 'fierce
calamity' (*DS* 47) of an encroaching colonial modernity. From the beginning,
Montague has seen the poet as having a special relationship with his people. He
is the representative writer of the nation, insisting, as Corkery had done before
him, that there is a continuity between individual and national identity: 'Is the
writer the people's voice?' Corkery asked, 'has there ever been, can there be, a
distinctive literature that is not a national literature?'[55] Thus, in his Introduction
to the 1979 edition of *The Rough Field*, he grandly calls himself 'the last bard
of the O'Neills', the exemplary spokesman, or dramatic conduit, for his nation,
dedicated to the task of revealing the community to itself.

Another elegy from the same collection, 'Demolition Ireland', continues a
perennial theme in Montague's work. As a lament for the demolition of 'Ireland',
both physical and mythical, the poem goes back to the ironic 'Hymn for the New
Omagh Road' (*The Rough Field*). The hidden Ireland, originary ground, the 'dear
perpetual place', is falling to the modernisers and developers who are respon-
sible for the de-magicking of an ancient, sacral landscape. The poem, written in

---

[55] Daniel Corkery, *Synge and Anglo-Irish Literature* (Cork, 1931) p. 2.

the most traditional of poetic forms – the sonnet – registers the poet's fear of newness and otherness, his desire to hold on to the 'primaeval dream' (*DS* 45). This poem, too, concludes with an assertion of romantic faith in the 'stubborn continuity' of the life-force: 'But see, the rushes rise again, by stealth,/ tireless warriors, on the earth's behalf'. In 'Hermit', 'stubborn continuity' manifests itself in nature's processes of 'endless death, ceaseless birth' (*DS* 18). Montague posits a principle of identity of mind and nature in his suggestion of a correlation between the gradual emergence of a poem and the slow processes of nature in the surrounding world: 'Intellect and universe/ held briefly in tune' (*DS* 18). The apotheosis of the self is realised to the extent that the poet recognises his identity with nature, his implication in 'the pull and swirl of the current' ('The Current'[56]) – a typically Wordsworthian or Emersonian notion of the 'life-force', the 'Universal Being spread o'er all'. Out of the poem's tranced stillness and mood of susceptibility arises the image of another kind of standing stone – the lighthouse, 'upright and defiant/against the night' (*DS* 18), imperious phallic symbol of the 'well-made poem' itself, one of the 'night structures' which bring life and light to old chaos.

The poem immediately preceding, 'Roethke's Ghost at Roche's Point', ends with a similar climactic reference to a lighthouse: 'as the night finds tongue/ ... / under the driving moon/ by the lighthouse dome' (*DS* 17). These repeated references to the lighthouse appear strangely ironical beside another poem, 'The Hag's Cove', in which the poet identifies with the drunken sailor who despises lighthouses. The drunken sailor is a Sweeneyesque figure who flouts authority and convention, who wants to go his own way, heedless of all expectation and good reason. The Captain is so drunk that he is unable to control his vessel and it founders on the rocks. The incident is now a 'hushed pub legend' (*DS* 15), testimony to the power of language to recreate actual events and give them a new kind of life. However, the drunken sailor is a confused figure in unintended ways. Far from representing some kind of poetic ideal of freedom from rational control and social responsibility, the Captain is prosaically 'drunk in his bunk', simply unconscious of what is going on around him. Yet, as the closing lines make explicit, the drunken sailor is a figure of the poet: 'what shall we do with *this drunken sailor/ early in the morning?*' As an experimental poet who has sought to modernise and internationalise Irish poetry, Montague might well see himself as something of a drunken sailor who tacks and veers from straight lines. But for all his questioning of the traditional rules of Irish poetry, he remains perceptibly attached to an essentialist vision of place as the stable ground of identity. Where MacNeice revels in 'the drunkenness of things being various', Montague's renegade imagination is held in check by his bardic ambitions. For all his claims to 'drunken' freedom, the poet operates within a continuous ideological framework. In the last two lines the poet coyly entertains the image of himself as a hopelessly wayward and irresponsible case, but the poem, despite its fragmented, polyvocal form, is not at all 'drunken' or out of control. As the title emphasises, the poet situates himself within the 'old mythologies' of Irish

---

[56] John Montague, *Smashing the Piano* (Loughcrew, The Gallery Press, 1999) p. 30. Hereafter abbreviated to *SP* and page references incorporated into the text.

tradition, subject to the whims of the ravening sea-hag of Irish legend who is particularly associated with the Beare Peninsula in Co. Cork. She is the *cailleach bhéarra*, the goddess of sovereignty and fertility, the pagan mother of the physical landscape. For Montague, it would seem, the drunken Captain is exemplary because he has 'allow[ed]' himself 'to be swallowed again,/ repossessed by nature's thick sweetness' (*DS* 15). The hapless sailor is at one with the great processes of nature in which death and life, decomposition and re-composition are inextricably connected: '*(Over the steeped, heaped seaweed/ the flies sing their song of harvesting)*' (*DS* 15). But it is James Simmons, with his version of the same legend in 'The Old Woman of Portrush', who is more of a drunken sailor than Montague.

Montague is too rooted a poet to be a convincing drunken sailor or lunatic Sweeney. Or magic carpet rider. *Smashing the Piano* (1999) has a number of poems – 'Araby, 1984', 'The Straying Blackthorn', 'Magic Carpet', 'Landing' – about travelling, specifically flying, as a metaphor for the imagination in flight. The panoptic bird's-eye or godlike perspective gives rise to feelings of lightness, exhilaration and visionary freedom, reminiscent of those found in Heaney's flying poems, beginning with 'Honeymoon Flight' and including 'A Kite for Michael and Christopher', the Sweeney poems, and *Seeing Things*. Flying is expressive of the desire for escape from social responsibility, from history and politics. It is an image of transcendence made possible through the magical force of imagination, the etymological connection between magic and imagination reinforced by Montague's fondness for seeing the aeroplane as 'our flying carpet' (*SP* 52), a 'magic carpet' (*SP* 79). These poems, in which modern air travel is magicked and mythologised, alternate with others about Margaret Thatcher, Bobby Sands and the Omagh bomb which are rooted in the very different idiom of contemporary history and politics, the contrast designed to keep alive the central dialectic of this collection – the tension between the sense of social obligation and the impulse to creative freedom.

'Araby, 1984' testifies to the international scope of the poet's experience and poetic reference, but the 'other' in the poem – 'the hot colours and confusions of Bombay', 'emigrant workers queuing for Dubai' (*SP* 52) – is always held at a safe distance, the object of a tourist's (or Joycean outsider's) curiosity rather than the source of a potential metamorphosis of the self. The cultural 'other' is figured only in emblematic, almost epigrammatic, terms ('lone wolf Kurdistan', 'disputed glitter of Sophia's dome', 'saffron robes of holy men'), in a poem of typological evocations. Even the poet's partner is denied real life: 'Our ship glides above all as in a dream,/ a mayfly light on the Heraclitean stream,/ as you rest your head's gilt casket on my arm'. She is a precious ornament, symbolically linked with the aeroplane itself (*'Morning Jewel'*), rather than a human being.

In 'Magic Carpet', detachment from the known world once again leads not to a complexification of the self through engagement with the 'other', but escape into a transcendent dream-time: 'dreaming time/ had finally stopped, meanness/ been put to rout, the world/ become safe for lovers' (*SP* 79). A Heaneyesque note of caution is sounded, as the speaker asks 'is this paradisal gleam, this Dantean/ spaceship, yet another form of deception?' But doubt is outweighed by the sense of buoyancy and exhilaration. Despite disappointment and failure, the speaker, Gatsby-like, holds to the dream 'as my little personal plane beats on' (*SP* 80).

The poem, concerned with 'dream-/ ing a haven that is suddenly real', expresses a longing that runs through the whole volume, the exhausted desire for the end of history.

In 'Magic Carpet' the speaker is 'in no hurry/ to come hurtling, or sailing down', but in 'Landing', the last poem in the collection, he looks forward to a return to earth which is now viewed in terms of precious gems – 'jewel caskets' and 'lampstrings of pearls': '*how the floor of* earth *is thick inlaid!*' (*SP* 82). The language of Shakespearian romance displaces the overt nationalist idiom that more usually characterises Montague's sense of place. 'I race homewards/ towards you, beside whom I now belong,/ ... / my late, but final anchoring', the speaker says, no longer 'circling to return' but assured of anchorage in his loved one. For Montague, as for Robert Frost, 'earth's the right place for love'. Love is what gives meaning to 'home' and 'belonging'.

Difference and otherness are suppressed in the urge towards transcendence. The poet's engagement with feminine otherness in his love poems is no more convincing than his negotiation with the tribal other in his public poems. For Heaney, otherness lies inside as well as outside the tribe, and he draws attention to the unconscious pagan and violent barbarian drives within his Ulster Catholic rural community, pursuing the most tabooed knowledges within the culture, probing the diseased psychopathology of his people ('the Spirit that plagued us so'[57]) in a series of dark and powerful poems, including 'Funeral Rites', 'North' and 'Viking Dublin: Trial Pieces'. Montague develops no such sustained and radically troubling critique of his own tribe, nor does he display any such tortured ambivalence in referencing his own tribal affiliation. But what he does share with Heaney, along with such other Ulster writers with a strong regionalist base as Brian Friel and Michael McLaverty, is a tendency to ignore the presence of the Protestant 'other' in the North, a constituency for or about which neither poet has little interest in speaking. Montague's poetic terrain, like Heaney's, is remarkably sparsely populated by the so-called majority community, and, when the two poets *have* turned to Catholic-Protestant relations, they have done so in remarkably similar ways. In Heaney's 'The Other Side', the Protestant neighbour, a somewhat unsubtle personification of the Planter, unwittingly asserts his sense of superiority to his Catholic neighbour in terms of farmland, language and religion, referring to his Catholic neighbour's 'scraggy acres', speaking with a 'fabulous, biblical dismissal/ that tongue of chosen people',[58] and making the observation that Catholics are not guided by the Bible. However, Heaney's picture affirms neighbourliness and community. He portrays with sympathy the Protestant farmer's feeling of uneasiness as he waits in his Catholic neighbour's yard until the prayers are over and he can pay his social call. In Montague's 'The Errigal Road', 'old Eagleson', a Protestant farmer, and his Catholic neighbour are walking through their 'shared landscape', and lament the violence of the Troubles. The Protestant tells his Catholic neighbour that when he returns to the Republic he should tell the people there that Protestants and Catholics can still be friends: '"Tell them down South that old neighbours/ can still speak

---

[57] Seamus Heaney, epigraph to 'A Northern Hoard', in *Wintering Out* (London, Faber, 1972) p. 39.
[58] Ibid., p. 34.

to each other around here"/ & gives me his hand, but does not ask me in' (*CP* 271). The gesture of friendship is again compromised by a sense of distance and unease. Ultimately, both poems seem to valorise difference rather than challenge the immutability of sectarian division. For both, identity is given, stable and ethnically defined. As John Goodby puts it: 'In the work of Montague and Heaney … insistence on an identity confronting difference confirms the binary terms or "timeless" divisions, which have dominated cultural debate, rather than undoing them'.[59] Goodby concludes that 'fossil rhetorics contradict a thematics of change, fluidity and openness', with the result that '*The Rough Field*, for all its major achievement, fails in its epic attempt at representative inclusivity.'[60] Patrtick Crotty, in reference to Montague's treatment of amorous and historical themes, voices a similar opinion: 'Though his (Montague's) handling of those themes is strongly modernist in terms of style, it is rather traditionalist in ideation, leaving his work open to the charge that it reproduces stock nationalist and masculinist tropes without subjecting them to any particularly energetic species of interrogation.'[61] The strongest criticism comes from Peter McDonald, who accuses Montague of resorting to the usual media stereotypes. In 'A New Siege', McDonald says, 'second-hand images stand in for straightforward contempt', and 'bull-voiced bigotry' is taken to represent 'the essential nature of Ulster Protestantism': 'The loudest, and least acceptable, manifestation of the tradition is insisted upon as its most essential expression. Yet there is something itself "bull-voiced" about such depictions, as can be seen when Montague's poem, written throughout on the auto-pilot of prejudice and "history", is compared with Derek Mahon's "Ecclesiastes".'[62]

McDonald overlooks those poems in which Montague distances himself from the collective historical consciousness, but he has a point that the rigorous self-interrogation that forms the substance of much of Mahon's poetry is not the characteristic Montague mode. Comparing the two poets, Mahon, we might say, is less inclined to 'trade self-knowledge for/ a prelapsarian metaphor,/ love-play of the ironic conscience/ for a prescriptive innocence'.[63] For while admitting the impossibility of ever repossessing the past, even conceding that the idea of a source or centre is fictive, Montague nevertheless keeps returning to prelapsarian metaphors and invocations of a prescriptive innocence. If he has learned from Joyce the potential of a cosmopolitan realism and detachment, the prospect of renewal is always contained within traditional ideological structures of thinking and feeling. In 'A Response to Omagh', one of the 'Civil Wars' sequence in *Smashing the Piano*, the poet asks, 'Who can endorse such violent men?' (*SP* 77): on the opposite page another poem pays tribute to Bobby Sands. In the final poem of the sequence, entitled 'Sunny Jim', the poet's pronounce-

59 John Goodby, *Irish Poetry since 1950: From Stillness into History* (Manchester University Press, 2000) pp. 145–6.
60 Ibid., p. 148.
61 Patrick Crotty, 'Montague Bound: A Note on *Collected Poems*', in Redshaw (ed.), *Well Dreams*, pp. 376–92, 381.
62 Peter McDonald, *Mistaken Identities: Poetry and Northern Ireland* (Oxford University Press, 1996), pp. 84–5.
63 Derek Mahon, 'Beyond Howth Head', in *Collected Poems* (Loughcrew, The Gallery Press, 1999) p. 53.

ment on his father's politics – 'Your fierce politics I decry' (*SP 77*) – has to be placed alongside earlier poems of explicit race hatred such as 'The Sound of a Wound' (*The Rough Field*): 'This bitterness/ I inherit from my father, the/ swarm of blood/ to the brain, the vomit surge/ of race hatred' (*CP 42*). If there is a less angry note sounded in his more recent work, that is perhaps because, 'weary/ of discords, heart-sick for harmony', exhaustions have nominated peace. 'Last Court' (*Drunken Sailor*) is an affectionate tribute to his dead brother in which the poet is nevertheless at pains to distance himself from the traditional 'narrow' family attitudes epitomised by his brother: 'against your patriarchal views,/ I assert the right of love to choose,/ from whatever race, or place. And of verse/ to allay, to heal, our tribal curse, that narrowness' (*DS 60*). But the poetry seems reluctant to accept 'the reality of the North as a frontier-region, a cultural corridor, a zone where Ireland and Britain permeate one another'.[64] 'Border Sick Call' crosses state borders, but not the more fundamental religious or tribal ones. Montague's is a poetry which seems either to reinforce old divisions, or to smooth over conflict and difference in pursuit of a transcendent master narrative. In an essay of 1985 he speaks of 'the unpartitioned intellect', an idea of Irish unity based on tolerance and acceptance of diversity highly reminiscent of Friel and Field Day's concept of the 'Fifth Province' or Homi Bhabha's 'Third Space':

> So I would like to introduce a new element into the discussion of Anglo-Irish litera-
> ture, an inclusiveness towards which we might all aspire, a passionate welcoming,
> a fertile balance. The unpartitioned intellect is a sensibility which is prepared to
> entertain, to be sympathetic to, all the traditions of which our country can be said
> to be composed ... Let us declare an end to all narrowness, in our thoughts at
> least. The unpartitioned sensibility would be able to accept, or listen to, the many
> voices, agreeable and disturbing, which haunt our land. 'The isle is full of noises',
> but they should be made to blend, as a symphony contains its dissonances, struc-
> tures of healing. (*FC 40*)

Even granting the sincerity of Montague's expressed intentions, his terminology, with its complicating postcolonial or pre-colonial connotations, is unfortunate, for it is trapped within the old discursive fields of (Northern) Irish colonial politics. His prelapsarian metaphor of the 'unpartitioned intellect' implies a rolling back or suppression of history and politics, and embracement of what J.W. Foster calls 'a politico-spiritual impossibility – a mythic landscape of beauty and plenitude that is pre-Partition, pre-Civil War, pre-famine, pre-Plantation and pre-Tudor'.[65] Montague may from time to time interrogate received narra-tives of Irishness, nation, home, belonging, exile, sexuality, religion, but invari-ably he takes refuge in old mythologies and traditional discursive systems. While demonstrating an openness to cosmopolitan influences, what he sought was not a continual process of 'making it new' but a modernisation of Irish tradition within a nationalist framework. In his extra-poetical pronouncements, he is one moment emphasising fealty to his traditional community, the next downplaying

---

64 Edna Longley, 'From Cathleen to Anorexia', in *The Living Stream* (Newcastle-upon-Tyne: Bloodaxe Books, 1994) p. 195.
65 J.W. Foster, 'The Landscape of Three Irelands: Hewitt, Murphy and Montague', in Elmer Andrews (ed.), *Contemporary Irish Poetry* (Houndmills, Macmillan, 1992) pp. 145–67, 150.

the importance of his native place, insisting that 'home' can be anywhere: 'any place you have lived, loved and suffered is your parish' (*FC* 9–10). It is precisely this tension between the local and the global, earthy nativism and airy internationalism that gives his work its distinctive quality and special interest.

Chapter 4

SEAMUS HEANEY AND PAUL MULDOON:
OMPHALOS AND DIASPORA

For a number of younger Irish poets, notably Paul Muldoon, Heaney has been the 'strong precursor' in whose shadow they have visibly struggled to clear their own poetic space and assert their own sense of autonomy and priority. The 'belated' poets' anxiety of influence and determination to define themselves against the example of the father-poet have undeniably led to the opening up of exciting new directions in Irish poetry. For Heaney, embedded in a traditional rural culture and a Catholic nationalist metaphysics, and influenced by the example of fellow Ulster poets, Kavanagh and Hewitt, culture and identity are immanent in place, and dislocation is the source of a profound anxiety. Heaney's poetry is driven by the Romantic search for a culture organically rooted in an authentic landscape. Having learnt from Kavanagh the social and artistic validity of the parochial and the peripheral, Heaney restores to the poetry of place the sense of myth and history, the element of cultural and political celebration and critique that are absent from Kavanagh's work. Stimulated by Hewitt's Protestant Planter version of Ulster rootedness, Heaney develops his own answering Catholic Gaelic myth of continuity grounded in the transcendental reality of place. Recuperating the impulses of the revival, which presupposed some intact inheritance from the past, he strives to affirm continuity and stability against the dominant perceptions of a sceptical, secular modernity. Muldoon, while sharing Heaney's Catholic, nationalist, rural background and Queen's University education, belongs to a younger generation which, having grown up in a period marked by an accelerated and unprecedented transnational movement of people, information, cultures, commodities and capital, is suspicious of essentialist notions of place, and more susceptible to postmodernist modes of construing culture and identity.

The Omphalos

For Heaney, place is the primal and primary determinant – the ground – of identity for both self and community, especially in times of disturbance, and in a context of historical colonialism and encroaching modernity: 'We have in Ireland an element of stability – the land, an element of instability – the people.

It is to the stable element that we must look for continuity.'[1] Disavowing the discontinuous cultures of the modern city, commerce and modernity, Heaney seeks an alternative in the assumed continuity of place, 'authentic' community and submerged Gaelic/pagan folk culture of his rural 'first world'. In his early autobiographical essay, 'Mossbawn', he lays claim to 'natural' or 'original' or autochthonous identity with the land:

> I would begin with the Greek word, *omphalos*, meaning the centre of the world, and repeat it, *omphalos, omphalos, omphalos*, until its blunt and falling music becomes the music of somebody pumping water at the pump outside our back door.
>
> (*P* 17)

The essay emphasises rootedness in place and community, in a sacred, feminine landscape:

> I remember, too, men coming to sink the shaft of the pump and digging through the seam of sand down into the bronze riches of the gravel, that soon began to puddle with the spring water. The pump marked an original descent into the earth, sand, gravel, water. It centred and staked the imagination, made its foundation the foundation of the *omphalos* itself ... ratifies this hankering for the underground side of things. (*P* 20)

In his now famous 'Open Letter' (1983), Heaney makes explicit his poetic intentions:

> My *patria*, my deep design
> To be at home
> In my own place and dwell within
> The proper name.[2]

Assuming the persona of the colonial subject, Heaney, unlike Joyce who wished to fly the nets of home, declares for a poetry of reclamation and return.

The early *Death of a Naturalist* is a *recherche du temps perdu*, Heaney's title indicating the preoccupation with loss – a lost time, a lost childhood, a lost intimacy with the natural world, a lost language and culture. The poetry, rooted in a Heideggerean sense of homelessness, is a mourning for the passing of the grand narratives of the past, but also contains the promise of loss redeemed. Heaney's excavatory, recuperative aesthetic reflects the conventional nationalist view that the dislocation of the present is a colonial consequence of the loss of a pristine Gaelic past. Displaced from origins, from family and community, from a traditional folkloric ethos and magical world-view, he reconstitutes himself in a literary culture through which he seeks to recuperate and re-enter the 'first place'. Haunted by loss and absence, yet longing for an originary firm ground, he attempts to use the evocative power of language to conjure into existence the lost world of the past. Though renowned for his powerful realism, Heaney is funda-

---

[1] Seamus Heaney, 'The Sense of Place', in *Preoccupations: Selected Prose 1968–1978* (London, Faber, 1980) pp. 131–49, 149. Hereafter abbreviated to *P* and page references incorporated into the text.
[2] Seamus Heaney, *An Open Letter* (Field Day Theatre Pamphlets, 1983).

mentally a poet of dream. From out of the mists of time he summons the ghostly presences of the forgotten 'mound-dwellers',[3] the 'moustached dead' (*OG* 44), the 'servant boy' (*OG* 47). The more intense the feeling of displacement, the more urgent the effort to re-establish connections with the ancestral past. In 'Bogland' 'the wet centre is bottomless' (*OG* 42), but in 'Gifts of Rain', searching for the 'lost fields' (*OG* 50) of Gaelic culture, he finds that the ancient alluvium, submerged beneath the colonial flood, 'blooms up to his reflection'. Language, place and identity are intimately connected, and in a series of place-name poems he seeks to recover the lost past. These place-name poems invoke the local narratives of the dinnsheanchas which can 'possess the land emotionally and imaginatively without any sense of ... titular ownership'.[4] 'Anahorish' is, significantly, '*My* place of clear water' (*OG* 46). 'Broagh' acknowledges a plural history, the language of the poem embodying the successive invasions which have shaped land, language and identity, but the 'O' at the centre of both placename and poem inscribes a kind of original possession, a feminine presence, the indestructible *omphalos*. The poem ends with the reference to 'that last/ *gh* the strangers found/ difficult to manage' (*OG* 54), emphasising, not interaction, but difference and self-enclosure, the sense of exclusion that the Englishman Yolland felt in Friel's *Translations*: 'I may learn the password but the language of the tribe will always elude me ... The private core will always be ... hermetic, won't it?'[5] Like Friel, Heaney suggests that Gaelic place-names contain some degree of essentialism, some kernel of truth that belongs to a Golden Age that was lost at the time of colonisation.

Travel

The car, which appears early on in Heaney's work, might be thought to signal the journey of the migrant poet away from the farm, tribe, community, into the modern world. Instead, however, the poet, 'inclined to the appetites of gravity',[6] remains remarkably resistant to the adulterating influence of 'the other', remarkably faithful to his home ground. In 'The Peninsula' the car drive provides the metaphorical space in which the exhausted landscape of the poet's familiar world is revivified in memory and in writing. In 'Tollund Man', travel leads not to fresh new seeing, as in 'The Peninsula', but merely confirms a radical dislocation: nationalist nostalgia for a Gaelic Eden is overwritten by the disturbing, timeless narrative of tribal violence. In 'Westering', a poem written during his year spent at Berkeley in 1971, his California dreaming under 'Rand McNally's "Official Map of the Moon"' (*OG* 80) quickly lands him back in Ireland, as he recalls a Good Friday car journey through Co. Donegal. The poet's physical distancing of himself from 'home' produces 'a loosening gravity'. In California,

3   Seamus Heaney, 'Anahorish', in *Opened Ground: Poems 1966–1996* (London, Faber, 1998) p. 46. Hereafter abbreviated to *OG* and page references incorporated into the text.
4   Nuala Ni Dhomhnaill, 'Dinnsheanchas: The Naming of High or Holy Places', in Patricia Yaeger, *The Geography of Identity* (Ann Arbor, University of Michigan Press, 1996) pp. 408–432, 431.
5   Brian Friel, *Translations*, in Seamus Deane (ed.), *Selected Plays of Brian Friel* (London, Faber, 1984) pp. 377–451, 416.
6   Seamus Heaney, 'Kinship', in *North* (London, Faber, 1975) p. 43. Hereafter abbreviated to *N* and page references incorporated into the text.

he can imagine 'untroubled dust', an ambiguous phrase which may refer to a vision of a peaceful homeland free of the Troubles, or of a people whose religious piety reduces them to a state of immobility, a living death. 'What nails dropped out that hour?' the poet asks, reflecting on both orthodox penitence and his own new-found freedom from the bonds of orthodoxy, imaged in the roads which 'unreeled, unreeled' (*OG* 81). If the poem recalls Donne's 'Good Friday, 1613. Riding Westward', in which the poet prays for forgiveness for his neglect of God, symbolised by his journey westward away from the rising 'Sun', that is, the Risen Son/Christ, 'Westering' ends, not with spiritual renewal and reconsecration, but with the querulous poet's sense of an unsettling and ambiguous freedom. Muldoon's 'Good Friday, 1971. Driving Westward' rewrites both Donne and Heaney. Replacing Heaney's earnest soul-searching with metaphysical wit and idiomatic playfulness, Muldoon projects the tension between freedom and responsibility into the opposition between the male speaker/driver and the girl he picks up on a Good Friday journey westward across the border into Co. Donegal. If Donne's salvation lies in the East, Muldoon's unregenerate speaker believes 'It was good going along with the sun',[7] that is, following the natural cycle; he is 'happy' in the West, in Gaoth Dobhair, in the pagan, animistic, pre-Christian world evoked by the Donegal Gaeltacht. The girl's confession of guilt, which is clumsily endowed with Christian significance through the references to 'the death of more than lamb or herring' (*P* 20), disrupts and undermines monologic male authority, yet is made to appear embarrassing and foolish: 'She stood up there and then, face full of drink,/ And announced that she and I were to blame/ For something killed along the way we came./ Children were warned that it was rude to stare,/ Left with their parents for a breath of air' (*P* 20). At the same time, the male speaker's confident, 'happy' agnosticism is also undercut by the insistence on his failure to see: 'But I had seen nothing, perhaps a stick/ Lying across the road. I glanced back once/ And there was nothing but a heap of stones' (*P* 19–20). The question of what actually happened on the road (symbolic crucifixion? political atrocity?) is left unresolved in the manner of such Frostian mysterious narrative poems as 'The Fear'. The single, authoritative centre and voice in both Donne and Heaney is rejected in favour of complexly ironic kinds of fragmentation. Muldoon's poem, predicated on a kind of metaphysical uncertainty, is an early example of his resistance to the fixed position, his 'distrust of the definitive', his embracement of the ambiguous thrill of travel and border-crossing. Where Heaney's journey westwards loops swiftly back, via the moon and memory, to home, Muldoon's westering involves an intense and potentially self-de(con)structive engagement with otherness.

The suggestion of betrayal and guilt in 'Westering' becomes acutely explicit in 'Exposure', a meditation on Heaney's move across the border from Belfast to Glanmore, Co. Wicklow, in 1971. He calls himself an 'inner emigré' (*OG* 144), constituting his identity in traditional political and colonial terms: 'I am neither internee nor informer/ .../ a wood-kerne escaped from the massacre'. He is not a republican activist nor a traitor to the republican cause; he is like one of

---

7   Paul Muldoon, *Poems 1968–1998* (London, Faber, 2001) p. 19. Hereafter abbreviated to *P* and page references incorporated into the text.

the Gaelic outlaws of Elizabethan times with whom he sought kinship in the earlier poem 'Bog Oak'. 'Alphabets' charts the process whereby the poet learns how he and his world are all socially and historically constructed by cultural and linguistic sign systems. The poem ends with the poet as astronaut viewing the world from his space capsule, seeing 'all he has sprung from,/ The risen, aqueous, singular, lucent O/ Like a magnified and buoyant ovum' (*OG* 294). The poem itself is a circle, finally returning the mature poet's grand meta-perspective to the child's formative experiences of place, family, community and language on the Mossbawn farm: 'like my own wide pre-reflective stare/ All agog at the plasterer on his ladder/ Skimming our gable and writing our name there/ With his trowel point, letter by strange letter' (*OG* 294). No matter how far he may travel, or how estranged or unhappy he may feel at home, Heaney never gives up on the dream of roots and origins. The bid for freedom is always attended by guilt and doubt. Something of this tension between displacement and groundedness is projected into his account of the adventures of Sweeney Astray, Heaney's figure of 'the artist, displaced, guilty, assuaging himself by his utterance … an aspect of the quarrel between free creative imagination and the constraints of religious, political, and domestic obligation'.[8]

In his latest volume, *District and Circle* (2006), he submits to the 'appetites of gravity', many of the poems in the collection returning to the home ground of childhood and the tropes of roots and origins: 'Plant it, plant it,/ Streel-head in the rain'.[9] However, the title poem, set in the London Underground, elaborates an image which is the antithesis of rooted existence and stable identity. The poet, situated in the flashing, noisy, unreal world of the Underground, which is the symbol of both the subterranean passage of colonial history and a rapidly accelerating (post)modernity, struggles for space and balance. His only point of personal contact or mutual recognition is the busker playing the tin whistle – a figure of subaltern marginalisation within the modern metropolis, Murphy in London.[10] The complex pattern of rhyme and half-rhyme such as we find in the last section of the poem – the echo of 'circle' in 'growl', 'treble', 'centrifugal', and of 'district' in 'socket', 'relict' and 'flicker-lit' (*DC* 17–19) – reinforces the sense of an all-encompassing (cultural, historical, linguistic) network, symbolised by the labyrinthine Underground, within which the poet is inscribed. 'District', a word which he more commonly uses to refer to the home parish (as in 'making/ the rounds of the district' in 'To Pablo Neruda in Tamlaghtduff', *DC* 64) and 'circle', which before was associated with the omphalos, the natal origin ('the black O/ in *Broagh*') are reconstructed through the recodifying of traditionalist discourse in the semiotic system of (post)modern capitalist consumerism. But the poet's urban experience remains deeply scored by his rural Irish origins, as his language suggests: a train strap is 'a stubby black roof-wort' (*DC* 18), his arm swinging on the strap is 'like a flail' (*DC* 19), shutting doors 'growl' (*DC* 19), he regards himself as a 'relict' (19); his father still keeps stumbling behind him and will

---

8   Seamus Heaney, 'Introduction', in *Sweeney Astray* (Derry, Field Day Publications, 1983) p. viii.
9   Seamus Heaney, 'Planting the Alder', in *District and Circle* (London, Faber, 2006) p. 60. Hereafter abbreviated to *DC* and page references incorporated into the text.
10 'Murphy in Manchester' was the title of a poem by John Montague, in *Collected Poems* (Loughcrew, The Gallery Press, 2003) p. 193.

not go away: 'My father's glazed face in my own waning/ And craning' (*DC* 19). Modernity is intimidating, hostile, de-personalising and characterised by loss: authenticity lies in the sacred past, in the pastoral Irish Eden from which he has been expelled:

> And so by night and day to be transported
> Through galleried earth with them, the only relict
> Of all that I belonged to, hurtled forward,
> Reflecting in a window mirror-backed
> By blasted weeping rock-walls.
> Flicker-lit.   (*DC* 19)

The Colonial Other

Heaney loves the English language and has generously acknowledged his debt to the English literary canon, yet there is no mistaking the deep sense of trauma resulting from a history of territorial, linguistic and cultural colonialism which is registered in his work. In 'The Toome Road' he speaks in the voice of the resentful native claiming his originary ground against the colonial invader: 'O charioteers, above your dormant guns,/ It stands here still, stands vibrant as you pass,/ The invisible, untoppled omphalos' (*OG* 150). In 'Traditions', English colonial influence is figured as rape and despoliation. The stereotypical nationalist treatment of Protestant/Catholic encounter in poems such as 'The Other Side' and 'A Constable Calls' emphasises difference and irredeemable otherness. In 'The Other Side', the description of the Protestant neighbour, constituted within a puritan, settler, text-based culture, is almost satirically reductive: 'His brain was a whitewashed kitchen/ hung with texts, swept tidy/ as the body o' the kirk' (*OG* 60). The man's only direct speech, referring to his Catholic neighbour's land – 'It's poor as Lazarus, that ground' – is glossed as a 'fabulous, biblical dismissal/ that tongue of chosen people' (*OG* 59). So completely fashioned is the Protestant farmer in terms of his religious heritage that he has little independent existence, unable, it would seem, to think or speak for himself. There is rather less condescension shown in Heaney's characterisation of his own side and its feminised, ritualised Catholicism. At the end, the gesture of friendship towards the historic enemy, though delicately and poignantly handled, is trapped within traditional attitudes: the speaker thinks of asking his neighbour about 'the price of grass-seed' (*OG* 61), instinctively relegating the Protestant farmer to the role of mercantile colonist whose interest in the land is presumed to be merely economic, as opposed to that of the native who is bound to the land in a sacramental relationship that is 'lived, illiterate and unconscious' ('The Sense of Place', *P* 131).

In 'A Constable Calls', the policeman is the official representative of 'the ministry of fear' (*OG* 134). Everything about the policeman – the 'fat black handlegrips' of his bicycle, his 'heavy ledger', 'the polished holster/ With its buttoned flap, the braid cord/ Looped into the revolver butt' (*OG* 137), his 'baton-case', his 'snapping the carrier spring/Over the ledger' (*OG* 138) – perceived through the eyes of the child, betokens the power of the Protestant, unionist statelet within which the Catholic community feels trapped and vulnerable. The constable has called to register the 'tillage returns/ In acres, roods and perches' (137): that is, to record Irish resources within an empirical, British system of measurement and control. Heaney's poem is reminiscent of Friel's *Translations*, where the visiting English survey team is engaged in measuring and mapping the Irish terrain so that it can be brought within the administrative and political control of colonial England. Corresponding to the map and the name-book in Friel's play is the constable's 'domesday book' (*OG* 138), an apocalyptic image of colonial English power. The poem ends ambiguously – 'His boot pushed off/ And the bicycle ticked, ticked, ticked' – an image suggestive of the inexorable process of the law, but also intimating incipient violence. The poetry, conditioned by colonial fear and resentment, is resistant to contamination and hybridity in the circulation of cultures ('a wake of pollen/ drifting to our bank, next season's tares' *OG* 137). It is to Muldoon that we must look for an alternative aesthetic designed to explore the mutations that lead to unexpected extensions and configurations of both personal and collective identity.

Myth and Vision

The essentialist, totalising tendencies in Heaney find expression in his preoccupation with myth. With the aid of such ahistorical, mystical concepts as 'spirit of place', 'territorial numen' and 'archetypal pattern' he attempts to evolve an ordering narrative in which to place the contemporary violence in Ulster. Yet, though Heaney saw himself as engaged in a project of 'politicising the terrain' and advocated a view of poetry as 'revelation of the self to the self, as restoration of the culture to itself', he was never entirely comfortable as a spokesman for his people. Critics such as David Lloyd[11] and Ciaran Carson[12] who accuse him of suppressing differences and discontinuities in the effort to construct a fixed and unified identity ignore the way the poetry embodies tension – the tension between the claims of 'the collective historical experience' and those of 'the emergent self'. Increasingly, Heaney finds it difficult to sustain his vision of a nurturing primal place and original autochthonous tradition. 'Parable Island' records the difficulty of ever knowing the 'truth' of place, history and identity. 'Truth' is simply power masking itself: 'the subversives and collaborators/ always vying with a fierce possessiveness/ for the right to set the "island story" straight'.[13] However, this postmodern turn is accompanied by a renewed emphasis on the creative possibilities opened by the awareness of loss: 'The island sustaining us seemed to hold firm/ Only when we embraced it *in extremis.*/ All I believed that happened there was vision' ('The Disappearing Island', *OG* 324). The poet's sense of displacement from origins into the linguistic, discursive and ideological

---

11 See David Lloyd, '"Pap for the dispossessed": Seamus Heaney and the Poetics of Identity', in Elmer Andrews (ed.), *Contemporary Irish Poetry: A Collection of Critical Essays* (London, Macmillan, 1992) pp. 87–116.

12 See Ciaran Carson, 'Escaped from the Massacre?', *The Honest Ulsterman*, 50 (Winter 1975) pp. 183–6.

13 Seamus Heaney, 'Parable Island', in *The Haw Lantern* (London, Faber, 1987) p. 10. Hereafter abbreviated to *HL* and page references incorporated into the text.

systems of the modern world co-exists with a continued longing for transcend-
ence, a persistent faith in poetry's redemptive capability. While acknowledging
that 'vision' may simply be illusion – 'seeing things' in the colloquial sense – he
doesn't completely surrender the possibility of transcendence offered by place
and poetry. The earthly home, however desecrated or disfigured, is transformed
into a placeless heaven. Writing about Kavanagh's later poetry, Heaney recalls a
place where a much-loved chestnut tree was cut down:

> ... [I]t was not so much a matter of attaching oneself to a living symbol of being
> rooted in the native ground; it was more a matter of preparing to be unrooted, to
> be spirited away into some transparent, yet indigenous afterlife. The new place was
> all idea, if you like; it was generated out of my experience of the old place but it was
> not a topographical location. It was and remains an imagined realm, even if it can
> be located at an earthly spot, a placeless heaven rather than a heavenly place.[14]

This is not an image of being uprooted, atomised and dispersed as flotsam and
fragments on the troubled currents of modernity. Rather, it is an image of the
transformation of emptiness into plenitude, time into timelessness, absence into
presence. The mythical centre, the *omphalos*, is re-discovered in the super reality
of the text. Heaney reaffirms his faith in the redemptive power of poetry under-
written by the memory of the lost home.

The Critique of Nativism

By setting up a presumed 'authenticity', symbolised by the *omphalos*, to be held
against the corruption of colonial modernity, Heaney, as we have seen, risks
merely reproducing the existing power relations in reverse, constructing another
monologue, another mode of ethnocentricity, enforcing difference in terms of a
re-nominated 'other'. As Edward Said remarks:

> Nativism, alas, reinforces the distinction by revaluating the weaker or subservient
> partner. And it has often led to compelling but often demagogic assertions about
> a native past, history or actuality that seems to stand free not only of the colonizer
> but of worldly time itself ... to accept nativism is to accept the very radical, reli-
> gious and political divisions imposed on places like Ireland, India, Lebanon, and
> Palestine by imperialism itself.[15]

Muldoon's poetry represents an alter/native text that is prepared to undertake
the endless journey between different cultures and languages, thereby creating
a world of process in which language, identity, tradition, nation, and politics
are scattered, and we are inducted into a hybrid state and composite culture.
For Heaney and Muldoon, the de-colonisation of culture means two different
things. Heaney, mourning the passing of an archaic Gaeldom from within the

---

[14] Seamus Heaney, 'The Placeless Heaven: Another Look at Kavanagh', in *The Government of the Tongue* (London, Faber, 1988) pp. 3–14, 4. Hereafter abbreviated to *GT* and page references incorporated into the text.

[15] Edward Said, 'Yeats and Decolonization', in D. Walder (ed.), *Literature in the Modern World* (Oxford University Press, 1990) p. 38.

perceived decay of the colonial present, sees poetry as a means of recuperating an essential culture that existed before the historical moment of colonisation. By contrast, Muldoon entertains the idea of absorbing different, far-flung histories into a complex and syncretic present composed of cross-cultural transfigurations. Heaney emphasises the value of a sense of historical continuity in dealing with the contemporary world, while for the younger generation of poets like Muldoon the challenge of postmodernity is precisely how to live with an irredeemable discontinuity. Forced to recognise that there is no uninterrupted inheritance, Heaney still views the remnants of the Gaelic past as the source of a unique tradition rather than elements in a range of diverse histories that have to be continually recomposed. In Muldoon's very different understanding of tradition, Heaney's identification with a unitary sense of belonging is a nostalgic illusion. Muldoon chooses uncertainty over the desire for certainty, a poetics that is always destined to be incomplete, exposed, but not immobile. In doing so, he dispels the sacramental sense of place, essentialist notions of identity, and nostalgic visions of lost plenitude.

American Connections

Both Heaney's and Muldoon's writing home has been conducted from geographical and cultural perspectives outside Ireland, mostly from America, where both have lived for extended periods, and where Muldoon continues to live as a naturalised American citizen. Both poets' writing home has been profoundly shaped by American influences, influences which, let it be said, were already being absorbed long before either Heaney or Muldoon had any direct, first-hand experience of the country. While international influences on both poets have been manifold and are in the end incalculable, the first and formative one, and the profoundest and most pervasive one, is indubitably American, and it is the influence of one American in particular – Robert Frost. Frost's role in Heaney's and Muldoon's constructions of place is especially interesting because the American's influence operates in almost diametrically opposed ways on the two Irish poets.[16] As a New England farmer poet speaking in his own regional voice about country lore and the practicalities of rural labour, Frost (along with Kavanagh) proved for Heaney the possibilities of regional Irish pastoral autobiography. But more than that, Frost played an important role in the shaping of Heaney's mature ideas about the nature and function of poetry. To bolster

---

[16] Rachel Buxton, in *Robert Frost and Northern Irish Poetry* (Oxford and New York, Clarendon Press, 2004), organises her excellent study to highlight Heaney's and Muldoon's contrasting appropriations of Frost in terms of 'acoustic' and 'design': 'where Heaney is affected principally by Frost's "acoustic", Muldoon has taken inspiration from Frost's approach to "design"' (p. 6). While it is undoubtedly true that Frost's 'acoustic' – his theory of 'the sound of sense' – and his poetic experiment with vernacular speech rhythms had an important liberating influence, both politically and psychologically, on a young Irish poet looking for non-English models, it is also true that Heaney, caught in the upheaval of the Troubles, found a congenial rationale in Frost's idea of poetry as a 'momentary stay against confusion': 'design' as well as 'acoustic'. Equally, while an increasingly elaborate and playful patterning is a central feature of Muldoon's aesthetic, his poetry is influenced by Frost's stress on the importance of living speech, and the example of his dramatic voicing or ventriloquism: 'acoustic' as well as 'design'.

his concept of the 'redress of poetry', Heaney turns to a Frost poem, 'Directive', in which, says Heaney, Frost offers a view of poetry as 'a clarification, a fleeting glimpse of a potential order of things "beyond confusion" … The poem provides a draught of the clear water of transformed understanding and fills the reader with a momentary sense of freedom and wholeness'.[17] In 'Directive', the journey takes the narrator to a deserted farmstead on a mountainside. Here are to be found the remains of a house and a playhouse where the children played their games of make-believe. For Heaney, 'Directive' is a poem about the relationship between art and life:

> He [Frost] convinces us that the playhouse has the measure of the other house, that the entranced focus of the activity that took place as make-believe on one side of the yard was fit to match the meaning of what happened in earnest on the other side, and in doing so Frost further suggests that the imaginative transformation of human life is the means by which we can most truly grasp and comprehend it.
>
> (*RP* xv)

The space between farmhouse and playhouse is, in Heaney's terms, 'the frontier of writing' – 'the line that divides the actual conditions of our daily lives from the imaginative representation of those conditions in literature, and divides also the world of social speech from the world of poetic language' (*RP* xvi). Heaney's poem, 'From the Frontier of Writing', records, in the transit across the border, a rites of passage into a realm of freed speech. Through art, Heaney is telling us, we can be taken out of ourselves, beyond everything familiar. Such transcendence has to be earned through the poet first submitting himself to the challenge of the actual. As Frost put it in another poem, 'Servant to Servants', 'the best way out is always through'.[18] 'Through' is the key word. At the border check-point the narrator feels 'subjugated, yes, and obedient'. But experience happens twice. On crossing the frontier of writing, 'Suddenly you're through, arraigned yet freed', moving beyond common understanding, the guarded limits, 'past armour-plated vehicles, out between/ the posted soldiers flowing and receding/ like tree shadows into the polished windscreen' (*OG* 297).

These ideas of 'transformed understanding', transcendence, 'redress' or 'momentary stay against confusion', however much he may desire or be tempted by them, mean little to Muldoon: 'I've never understood some of these notions about art – "the end of art is peace" – … none of these ideas mean anything to me'.[19] Such ideas, Muldoon believes, are more appropriate to religious than to

17 Seamus Heaney, *The Redress of Poetry: Oxford Lectures* (London, Faber, 1995), p. xv. Hereafter abbreviated to *RP* and page references incorporated into the text. For further Heaney references to Frost's notion of poetry as 'a momentary stay against confusion', see also: *RP* 198; *Preoccupations*, p. 193; and 'Above the Brim', in Joseph Brodsky, Seamus Heaney and Derek Walcott, *Homage to Robert Frost* (London, Faber, 1997) p. 66. Hereafter abbreviated to *HRF* and page references incorporated into the text.

18 Robert Frost, 'A Servant to Servants', in *Selected Poems*, ed. Ian Hamilton (London, Penguin, 1973) p. 65.

19 'Lunch with Paul Muldoon', interview with Kevin Smith, *Rhinoceros*, 4 (1991) pp. 75–94, 90. Muldoon was no doubt aware of the genealogy of the phrase, 'The end of art is peace', which is cited by Heaney in 'The Harvest Bow' (*OG* 184) and in the epigraph to *Preoccupations*, which is

literary discourse: 'This may be largely an emotional response to the baggage of my religious upbringing – all these ideas of "solace" and "succour", never mind "restitution" and "redemption", which are perfectly appropriate to religious, but not, I think, literary discussion.'[20] No, what Muldoon is attracted to is something else in Frost. In his well-known essay, 'The Figure a Poem Makes', Frost describes a concept of poetry that seeks to accommodate the 'unforeseen' within the 'predestined':

> The figure a poem makes. It begins in delight and ends in wisdom. The figure is the same as for love. No one can really hold that the ecstasy should be static and stand still in one place. It begins in delight, it inclines to impulse, it assumes direction with the first line laid down, it runs a course of lucky events, and ends in a clarification of life – not necessarily a great clarification, such as sects and cults are founded on, but in a momentary stay against confusion. It has an outcome that though unforeseen was predestined from the first image of the original mood – and indeed from the very mood. It is but a trick poem and no poem at all if the best of it was thought first and saved for the last. It finds its own name as it goes and discovers the best waiting for it in some final phrase.[21]

Heaney and Muldoon take different things from Frost's statement. Heaney emphasises Frost's notion of achieved equilibrium, imaginative resolution, organic wholeness, homecoming. Even in Part II of *Seeing Things* ('Squarings'), where the Transatlantic influence is most strongly apparent in Heaney's poetry, the overriding aim is still to raise a voice 'That might continue, hold, dispel, appease' ('Glanmore Sonnets' II, *OG* 164). 'Squarings' demonstrates a more relaxed and looser style than is common in Heaney, a suppressed lyricism that is close in tone to the irregular, speech-like style of William Carlos Williams. In his handling of the long, constellatory form, Heaney has no doubt learnt from the modern American masters of epic comedy, from Lowell's *Notebook*, composed of unrhymed loose blank verse sonnets, a form which Lowell said allowed him 'rhetoric, formal construction and quick breaks'; or John Berryman's sonnet or 'dream song' sequences, in which we are aware simultaneously of the intensity of effort to deal honestly with the chaos and urgency of private feelings, and of the obsession with form. 'Everything flows', Heaney says in one of the poems ('Squarings' xxvii, *OG* 374); 'Improvise. Make free', he commands himself in another ('Squarings' v, *OG* 361). He celebrates the serendipitous and the random, what he calls 'the music of the arbitrary' ('Squarings' v, *OG* 361). Yet, while evincing a characteristically American concern with freedom, lightness and spaciousness, he emphasises the need for order and 'vision', or transcendence. The poems are what Heaney calls 'Squarings', a term he remembers from playing marbles as a child: 'anglings, aimings, feints and squints/ ... / Test-outs and pull-backs, re-envisagings' ('Squarings' iii, *OG* 360); but 'Squarings' also

---

a quotation from Yeats's essay, 'Samhain, 1915' (in *Explorations*), Yeats having taken the phrase from the pious Coventry Patmore.

[20] Paul Muldoon, 'Getting Round: Notes towards an *Ars Poetica*', *Essays in Criticism*, 48, 2 (April 1998), pp. 107–28, 126.

[21] Robert Frost, 'The Figure a Poem Makes', *Robert Frost: Poetry and Prose*, ed. Edward Connery Lathem and Lawrance Thompson (New York, 1973) pp. 393–6.

connotes rectilinear structure, such as that of the house his father had planned in 'Squarings' xxxiii: '"Plain, big, straight, ordinary, you know"/ A paradigm of rigour and correction,/ .../ Rebuke to fancifulness and shrine to limit ...' (*OG* 378). The architecture of the sequence, which is made up of 48 poems organised in four sections of twelve poems, each poem consisting of four three-lined stanzas, is itself an embodiment of the Frostian 'stay against confusion', an image of the 'bastion' which Heaney attempts to secure against the flux of life: 'Sink every impulse like a bolt. Secure/ The bastion of sensation. Do not waver/ Into language. Do not waver, in it' ('Squarings' ii, *OG* 359). 'Squarings' i, opens the sequence with an image of a lost home – the 'tumbled wallstead' from Wordsworth's 'The Ruined Cottage' – and bathes it in rain and a dazzling, estranging light: 'Shifting brilliancies ... // Bare wallstead and a cold hearth rained into –/ Bright puddle where the soul-free cloud-life roams' (*OG* 358). All that remains is 'Unroofed scope. Knowledge-freshening wind' – an absence that is yet invigorating when viewed in the light of Wordsworthian imagination. The images of deliquescence and freedom are held within the secure structure of the 12-line form. The next poem, 'Squarings' ii, which is also focused on the broken-down house, urges, at an explicit level, the need for structure and renovation, while conveying these ideas within a fairly free, unrhymed verse form, and in a broken, disjointed speech. Taken together, the two poems comment on each other in a way that is typical of the dialogic structure of the entire sequence. 'Squarings' thus becomes a complex, multifaceted image of the tension between fluidity and architecture that informs all of Heaney's poetry. His explanation of what he intended in the sequence replays Frost's notion of the 'predestined' and the 'unforeseen':

> The 12-line form felt arbitrary but it seemed to get me places swiftly. So I went with it, a sort of music of the arbitrary that's unpredictable, and can still up and catch a glimpse of a subject out of the blue. There's a phrase I use, 'make impulse one with wilfulness': the wilfulness is in the 12 lines, the impulse in the freedom and shimmer and on-the-wingness.[22]

'Squarings' xxiv, a powerful evocation of the haunting stillness of a deserted harbour, images Heaney's poetic ideal which lies in a silent, tremulous, state of 'equilibrium, brim'. The poem presents a scene of 'perfected vision' in which the irreconcilables are finally reconciled:

> Air and ocean known as antecedents
> Of each other. In apposition with
> Omnipresence, equilibrium, brim.   (*OG* 373)

The image is taken from Frost's 'Birches'

> He learned all there was
> To learn about not launching out too soon
> And so not carrying the tree away

---

[22] Seamus Heaney, interview with Blake Morrison, 'Seamus Famous: Time to be Dazzled', *Independent on Sunday*, 19 May 1991.

Clear to the ground. He always kept his poise
To the top branches, climbing carefully
With the same pains you use to fill a cup
Up to the brim, and even above the brim.
Then he flung outward, feet first, with a swish,
Kicking his way down through the air to the ground.[23]

Here we have an image of Heaney's desired condition of defying 'the appetites of gravity' and, Sweeney-like, 'walking on air'. It is an image of linguistic and imaginative surplus or free 'supply'. The exhilaration of operating 'above the brim', of moving beyond the normal rational controls and entering upon new-found freedoms is the subject of many Heaney poems, which at times recall the language of 'Birches'. 'A Basket of Chestnuts', for example, recreates in the movement of its verse the 'shadow-boost', the 'giddy strange assistance' that happens when you swing a loaded basket. There is a rhythm that lightens the burden of reality: 'The lightness of the thing seems to diminish/ The actual weight of what's being hoisted in it'.[24] Or there's the poem 'Wheels within Wheels', where he remembers how he used to set his bicycle upside down and turn the pedal until it 'began to sweep your hand ahead/ Into a new momentum', the action granting 'an access of free power' (*OG* 355). Or, perhaps closest of all to 'Birches' in its recreation of child's play, there's Heaney's 'The Swing', 'A lure let down to tempt the soul to rise'.[25] Though 'we favoured the earthbound', the swing exerted a powerful attraction, and, by virtue of technique and determination that are described with Frostian precision, 'In spite of all, we sailed/ beyond ourselves':

To start up by yourself, you hitched the rope
Against your backside and backed on into it
Until it tautened, then tiptoed and drove off
As hard as possible. You hurled a gathered thing
From the small of your own back into the air.
Your head swept low, you heard the whole shed creak.   (*SL* 49)

Where Heaney finds in Frost support for his concept of poetry as 'redress', 'equilibrium, brim', 'perfected vision', 'reconciliation', Muldoon responds to the impulsive, serendipitous, improvisatory dynamic of Frost's poetry, the American's refusal of fixed attitudes and forms, his recognition of the importance of chance in creativity, the need to let a poem find its own shape and meaning. In both poets' work, the speaking voice with its chatty familiarity and natural rhythms departs from, but always ultimately returns within, a strict formal patterning, thus enacting the tension between 'accident' and 'design', the 'unforeseen' and the 'predestined'. Both poets trust wildness, indirection and circumnavigation to bring them home to form. As Frost said of the poetic life: 'The way will be zigzag, but it will be a straight crookedness … He will be judged as he does or doesn't

---

23 Robert Frost, 'Birches', *Selected Poems*, pp. 81–2.
24 Seamus Heaney, 'A Basket of Chestnuts', in *Seeing Things* (London, Faber, 1991) p. 24. Hereafter abbreviated to *ST* and page references incorporated into the text.
25 Seamus Heaney, 'The Swing', in *The Spirit Level* (London, Faber, 1996) p. 48. Hereafter abbreviated to *SL* and page references incorporated into the text.

let this zig or that zag project him off out of his general direction'.[26] In his poem, 'I Remember Sir Alfred', Muldoon also rejects the undeviating simplicity of the straight line prized by politicians, revolutionaries and construction workers, and images his own poetic method as one of 'singleminded swervings' (*P* 82). For Muldoon, 'slips' (a central metaphor in 'Yarrow'), 'errors' (the theme of 'Errata' in *Hay*),[27] 'veerings from, over, and back along a line, the notions of di-, trans-, and re-gression'[28] can be importantly creative and productive of new meaning.

In his interview with John Haffenden, Muldoon makes explicit his sense of affinity with Frost, referring particularly to Frost's hidden complexity, the deceptive simplicity of his language, and his love of mischief-making: 'But the most important thing for me in Frost was his mischievous, sly, multi-layered quality under the surface.'[29] Interestingly, in the very same interview, 'mischief-making' is the term Muldoon uses to describe his own poetry:

> I've become very interested in structures that can be fixed like mirrors at angles to each other – it relates to narrative form – so that new images can emerge from the setting up of the poems in relation to each other: further ironies are possible. I hope the mischief I make is of a rewarding kind, not that of a practical joker, and will outline the complexities of being here.[30]

This concept of poetry as a hall of mirrors in which the source-image is always indeterminable accounts for Muldoon's elusiveness and avoidance of any kind of dogmatic assertiveness. Yet, not wishing to be thought of as a poet lost in the postmodern funhouse, he hopes his mischief will be of the 'rewarding kind'.

Frost's 'multi-layered quality' relates to his idea of poetry as metaphor – the 'saying one thing and meaning another, saying one thing in terms of another, the pleasure of ulteriority'.[31] Muldoon evinces a similar interest in discovering relationships between apparently unrelated things, whether in terms of the Frostian parable poem or far-fetched conceit, or the use of rhyme and intertextual allusion. Encryptment is, according to Muldoon, a characteristic feature of the Irish literary tradition, from as far back as Amergin, the 'first poet of Ireland', who demonstrates 'the urge towards the cryptic, the encoded, the runic, the virtually unintelligible' (*TII* 5). Behind this urge we may discern the poet's wish to hold the world at arm's length, to keep the secret core of self safe from prying eyes, to avoid an over-earnestness that allows him the right to play. Experience is given objective shape either by dramatic, narrative or other figurative means. The poetry remains 'classical' in its detached control of tone and emotion. Both Frost and Muldoon specialise in a poetry that is neither personal confession nor personal expression but an ingenious, brave attempt to formulate what seems incoherent

---

26 Robert Frost, 'The Constant Symbol', in Lathem and Thompson, p. 405.

27 For discussion of Muldoon's 'implication of poetry in error', his constant recognition of 'the imminence of imperfection', see John Kerrigan, 'Paul Muldoon's Transits: Muddling through after *Madoc*', in Tim Kendall and Peter McDonald (eds.), *Paul Muldoon: Critical Essays* (Liverpool University Press, 2004) pp. 125–49.

28 Paul Muldoon, *To Ireland, I* (Oxford, Oxford University Press, 2000) p. 5. Hereafter abbreviated to *TII* and page references incorporated into the text.

29 John Haffenden, *Viewpoints: Poets in Conversation* (London, Faber, 1981) p. 134.

30 Ibid., p. 136.

31 Robert Frost, 'The Constant Symbol', Lathem and Thompson, pp. 400–401.

and formless. 'Every poem', Frost said, 'is an epitome of the great predicament: a figure of the will braving alien entanglements.'[32] By loading himself with ever more severe constraints of rhyme and verse pattern, Muldoon becomes a figure of the Frostian poet as performer, testing himself and his resources, engaging in an act of daring, risking everything to show his poise. The greatest freedom is to be found within the maximum of constraint.

The 'mischievous, sly, multi-layered quality under the surface' that Muldoon admired in Frost is precisely the quality in Muldoon to which Heaney draws attention. Heaney refers to the younger poet's 'delight in the trickery and lechery that words are capable of', adding that 'What he [Muldoon] has to say is constantly in disguise, and what is disguised is some conviction like this: the imagination is arbitrary and contrary, it delights in its own fictions and has a right to them' (*P* 213). 'All the fun's in how you say a thing',[33] says the local farmer to his townee visitor in Frost's 'The Mountain'. This and other lines from Frost's poem are quoted verbatim by Muldoon in 'The Country Club', as part of a conversation between the narrator and a local doctor, whose name, Lee Pinkerton, is an amalgam, according to Edna Longley, of Robert Lee Frost and the famous detective agency.[34] The speakers in Frost's and Muldoon's poems refer to a mountain stream which is 'cold in summer, warm in winter', and explain the phenomenon as follows:

> I don't suppose the water's changed at all.
> You and I know enough to know it's warm
> Compared with cold, and cold compared with warm,
> But all the fun's in how you say a thing.[35]

Both speakers make the point that the saying itself bears little resemblance to the reality of the situation, and can in fact falsify the reality. What is important is the individual's frame of reference at any given point in time (Muldoon's intertextual allusiveness itself representing a playful manipulation of different frames of reference). The object is never completely independent of the subject. Words have this pernicious effect on our perception that they tend to fix definition when in fact the object or event that is being observed and defined exists in time, and as such is always subject to change and alteration. Frost's/Muldoon's lines emphasise the reductiveness of language which forces us to see the world as one thing only, not as multitudinous and contradictory. Our understanding and explanation of experience can only be provisional and unreliable, for reality always overflows any particular narrative formulation of it. Muldoon's poem is itself an illustration of the impossibility of holding any firm convictions, or asserting any kind of definitive 'truth'. It is premised on a view of the inherently paradoxical nature of all beliefs and their susceptibility to change in a different frame of reference. 'The Country Club' secretes, we are led to believe, a hidden narrative, but unlike Heaney, who asserts (at the end of 'The Peninsula') his

---

[32] Ibid., p. 405.
[33] Robert Frost, 'The Mountain', in *Selected Poems*, p. 53.
[34] Edna Longley, '"Varieties of Parable": Louis MacNeice and Paul Muldoon', in *Poetry in the Wars* (Newcastle-upon-Tyne, Bloodaxe, 1986) p. 225.
[35] Robert Frost, *Selected Poems*, p. 53.

faith in being able to 'uncode' experience through the transformative power of the imagination, Muldoon resolutely refuses to provide the key to revelation, or even resolution. The reader's efforts to uncover hidden meanings, track down references and expose submerged connections between images are undoubtedly valuable, but, as Clair Wills says, 'the danger here lies in the assumption that the poems wrap everything up, or create a balanced whole, which may be coded but can be unravelled with enough time and ingenuity. What this approach misses is the poetry's concern with the failure to articulate, with something fallen away, with things that don't add up.'[36]

Favouring the longish poem in the form of the pastoral eclogue or dramatic dialogue allowed Frost to embrace the ambivalences, oppositions and contradictions of everyday life, and to demonstrate the mischievous, sly, multi-layered quality which attracted Muldoon. Frost's vernacular voice finds its natural expression in the dramatic narrative poem which is not usually Heaney's preferred mode, but one which Muldoon has readily adopted:

> I'm very interested in the narrative, the story, and in wanting almost to write novels in the poem. I like to think that a whole society is informing the lines of a poem, that every detail is accurate. And I'm interested in the dramatic persona. I like using different characters to present different views of the world.[37]

Muldoon's 'The Merman', a poem of Frostian simplicity and allegorical resonance, also explores the subject of boundaries, frontiers and limits, and does so in a typically Frostian manner. Muldoon counterposes the viewpoints of the farmer/narrator and merman, as Frost balances the two viewpoints of his farmer/narrator and neighbour in 'Mending Wall'. In both poems, opposites are held in ironic tension; in neither poem is the narrator's viewpoint clearly superior to that of the 'other'; in neither is there resolution or closure. Typically, the Muldoon poem, like the Frost poem, emerges out of the interplay of its parts, which are held in the figure the poem makes. On one level, 'The Merman' is a parable of sectarian incomprehension and mistrust, like Heaney's 'The Other Side', but Muldoon dissolves time and place into symbolic fantasy and linguistic play, eschewing any of the obvious kinds of treatment of the Northern situation. Referring to Muldoon's playfully and cryptically oblique approach which saves him from partisanship, Heaney comments: '[Muldoon's] swerves away from any form of poker-faced solidarity with the political programmes of the Northern Catholic minority (from which he hails) have kept him so much on his poetic toes that he has practically achieved the poetic equivalent of walking on air.'[38] Heaney sounds almost envious, as if Muldoon was able to write out of the free, creative imagination that the older poet longed to be able to indulge, but always felt guilty about when he did.

If Muldoon is drawn to narrative, his narratives are fragmented, elliptical and skewed in much more radical ways than anything found in Frost. Long poems

---

[36] Clair Wills, *Reading Paul Muldoon* (Newcastle-upon-Tyne, Bloodaxe, 1998) p. 23.
[37] Haffenden, p. 133.
[38] Seamus Heaney, 'The Pre-Natal Mountain: Vision and Irony in Recent Irish Poetry', in *The Place of Writing*, Emory Studies in the Humanities (Atlanta, GA, Atlanta Scholars Press, 1989) pp. 36–53, 47.

such as 'Immram', 'The More a Man Has', 'Madoc' and 'Yarrow' dispense with linearity, cause and effect, progress, teleology, resolution and reason; instead, Muldoon experiments with a heteroglossic, circular, dialogised, intertextualised narrative held together by an evermore complex architectural structure of rhyme and repetition. Wound into the elaborate circular and repetitive structures of 'Yarrow' is a reference to Frost's 'The Most of It':

> in Frost's great poem, 'The Most of It', the 'talus'
> refers not to a heel,
>
> of course, but the cliff-face or scarp
> up which his moose or eland
> will so memorably rear – 'rare',
>
> my da would have said – while the Cathedral of Ero-
> tic Misery, like that of Rheims,
> will soon be awash in blood, in blood and sacred oil.   (*P* 385–6)

Richard Poirier describes 'The Most of It' as a poem 'in which a wandering figure tries to locate a "home"', and fails because '"life" is being asked to do some or all of a "poet's" work'.[39] The speaker, or would-be poet, calls to the universe and waits for an original voice, but hears only the 'copy speech' of his own voice:

> And nothing ever came of what he cried
> Unless it was the embodiment that crashed
> In the cliff's talus on the other side ...[40]

The 'embodiment' is an immensely forceful, animal, mythical presence, but the poem ends hovering between the dismissive and affirmative meanings of '– and that was all'. The poem was originally entitled 'Making the Most of It', yet Frost's speaker is an indifferent 'maker', whether because of lack of imaginative responsiveness or incapacity in the face of the unknown and unnameable. Muldoon, however, is the kind of poet who is committed to an ideal of poetry and 'truth' as 'made' things. He makes the most of what chance brings, of what lurks in the verbal underbrush. He searches for the 'truth' that may be located in the slide between 'talus' as heel and 'talus' as spur of land, between the different meanings of 'cliff' and 'scarp', 'moose' and 'eland', 'rear' and 'rare', Frost's version of events and his own. For this is all there is to set against a universal destruction intimated in the references to the Cathedral of Erotic Misery in Hanover that was firebombed during World War II, and the Cathedral of Rheims that was devastated during World War I. Muldoon attempts to 'make' a home, but not by demanding a 'return', 'counter-love, original response'. That would be asking too much. That, in fact, would be closer to the kind of aspiration that we find in Heaney. In 'On the Road', for example, Heaney is engaged in a Sweeney-like journey through geology and history in search of origins, and imagines a 'book of changes' in which a lost archaic spirit, symbolised by the picture of a drinking

---

[39]   Richard Poirier, *Robert Frost: The Work of Knowing* (New York, Oxford University Press, 1977) p. 159.
[40]   Robert Frost, *Selected Poems*, p. 198.

deer incised in rock in 'the deepest chamber', is brought noisily back to life: 'I would meditate/ that stone-faced vigil/ until the long dumbfounded/ spirit broke cover/ to raise a dust/ in the font of exhaustion' (*OG* 288).

Crossings

In an environment of certainties, defined identities and allegiances, Muldoon takes delight in exploring uncertainty, ultimately crossing boundaries and blurring identities. In 'The Boundary Commission' he uses the image of the village where the border runs down the middle of the street to question Heaney's essentialist sense of place. 'The Boundary Commission', says Edna Longley, 'challenges the binary terms of Heaney's "Other Side" by reducing territorial maps to absurdity'.[41] While Longley obviously has Catholic, nationalist place-making in mind, Muldoon's title refers to the Boundary Commission established by the Anglo-Irish Treaty at the end of the Anglo-Irish War in 1921, the purpose of which was to draw the border between the Irish Free State and Northern Ireland. From the beginning, the commission was a controversial body, and in the end had little more than a virtual reality. Nationalists hoped it would secure substantial transfer of border land from Northern Ireland to the Free State, while Unionists opposed its establishment altogether. Fearing further civil unrest, the British, Irish and Northern Irish governments agreed to suppress the commission's report, and the existing border that had been drafted earlier in the Government of Ireland Act (1920) was ratified in 1925. The village of Pettigo on the Fermanagh/Donegal border, to which Muldoon refers in his poem, is an example of the kind of anomaly thrown up by Partition. 'The Boundary Commission' reflects on the fact that boundaries do not represent any eternal or essential truth about places, but are socially and politically constructed and serve particular purposes. The image of the shower of rain stopping cleanly across the lane like a wall of glass that had toppled over jokily suggests that natural features or forces do not naturally constitute boundaries either. In describing this boundary as running down the middle of the street with the proverbial butcher and baker in different states, Muldoon points to the way boundaries absurdly (but inevitably) cut across other flows and relationships which construct a particular place. The places that boundaries define are not discrete but depend on their relationship with other places. In the context of the village community, the idea of exclusion, difference and 'otherness' imposed by a remote external authority is made to appear not just ridiculous but surreal. In reality, there are no closed places. Boundaries are always artificial. The poem mirrors the Muldoonian aesthetic which is founded, not on the principles of 'othering' or exclusionism, but of productive interrelationship and openness. His representations emphasise movement and mixing, permeability of boundaries, the intersection of diverse cultural resources and influences, complex patterns of interconnection. For Muldoon, no place, no culture, no identity is 'pure'. The figure in the poem, confronted by the arbitrary construction of place, is wondering 'which side, if any, he should

---

[41] Edna Longley, *The Living Stream* (Newcastle-upon-Tyne, Bloodaxe, 1994) p. 211.

be on' (*P* 80). Detachment, non-alignment, neutrality would seem to be reasonable options in a situation where the centre no longer holds, where there is no undissipated, monological ground of being. Identity is not to be found in artificially bounded spaces, whether geographical, national, personal or aesthetic. Home is not the place of cultural wholeness as claimed by nationalist ideology, whether Irish or British. Muldoon's poetry defies the search for originary absolutes, for authentic manifestations of a stable, unchanging, given identity; for pristine, pure customs and traditions. In Heaney's poem, 'The Given Note', the music, redolent of place and the Gaelic past, is a gift from the other world. The music comes off the bow 'gravely' (*OG* 36) – seriously, but from the graves too, confirming ancestry and continuity. In 'The Lass of Aughrim', Muldoon, exemplifying the dynamics of a transnational modernity, transposes the traditional Irish air (closely associated with Joyce's story 'The Dead') to the Amazonian forests where, reinterpreted by the natives, it is played 'to charm/fish from the water'. The reassuring signs of home appear radically defamiliarised and re-formed. The Irish traveller's initial 'delight' at hearing the sound of home in alien surroundings is further ironised by the discomfiting information, vouchsafed by 'Jesus', that the flute on which the melody is played 'was the tibia/of a priest/ from a long-abandoned Mission' (*P* 160). By deconstructing the naive speaker's position in the poem, and re-inscribing traditional culture within an economy of endless transcultural exchange, Muldoon historicises our understanding of the idea of the 'given note'.

When Heaney writes about border-crossing (as in 'From the Frontier of Writing'), he thinks in terms of an opposition between fixed entities – here and there, self and other – and explores the possibility of achieving that momentary peace in which the difficult conflicts of everyday life may be magically resolved in the self-contained, transcendent poetic symbol. He takes Frost's image of the birch-swinger seesawing between heaven and earth, the Herculean and Antaean sides of personality, to illustrate his concept of 'redress' – 'that general inclination to begin a countermove once things go too far in any given direction' (*HRF* 74). Where Heaney, following Frost, swings between heaven and earth, Muldoon shows how the one inheres pluralistically in the other. In Muldoon's poem 'Mules', for example, the mare has 'feet of clay' yet a 'star' burned on her forehead. The donkey is associated with Christianity, though it takes Christ to his death. The afterbirth – 'like some fine, silk parachute' – contradicts the idea that the mule 'sprang from earth', suggesting instead that it fell from the sky. The union between mare and donkey suggests a union of pagan and Christian, but also between Catholic and Protestant (the donkey belonging to the neighbour called 'Parson'), and between the two men who become themselves hybrids of animal and human: 'It was as though they had shuddered/ To think, of their gaunt sexless foal/ Dropped tonight in the cowshed' (*P* 67). Muldoon dissolves conventional binary oppositions, collapsing clear-cut distinctions between different orders of being, and accepts their intermingling as a fact of life and a condition of writing. Heaney, on the other hand, holds them apart, anguishing over their proper relation in a socially responsible poetry. As Muldoon makes clear, hybridity is both a potential ('Should they not have the best of both worlds?') and a 'fall', a degeneracy producing a 'sexless' foal, an hermaphrodite offspring unable to reproduce, predestined to be 'neither one thing or the other'. In contrast to Muldoon's 'both/and' hybrid constructions, Frost retains an 'either/or' logic, thus keeping alive the idea of choice between worlds, between one thing and another. In the canonical 'The Road Not Taken' the speaker has a choice between two roads, chooses one road and eliminates the other ('sorry I could not travel both/ And be one traveller'[42]), aware that a direction and destiny are assumed with the first choice laid down ('knowing how way leads on to way'), yet preoccupied with the road not taken rather than the one that is taken. Muldoon's speaker usually has no choice, his course is predestined, as the central trope of 'rowing around', circular voyaging, would suggest; yet as poet, Muldoon entertains more possibilities than Frost. Most noticeably in his long quest poems, Muldoon chooses – simultaneously – many roads, thus creating diverse futures, diverse times which also fork and prolif-erate. In doing so, he stakes an even more insistent, or perhaps more desperate, claim to imaginative freedom within a governing destiny, which is itself, as 'October 1950' suggests, formed out of chance and contingency. Reflecting on the randomness of the moment of his conception, Muldoon, while acknowl-edging that the past determines the future, emphasises the unknowability of origins, with the inevitable result that he is 'left in the dark':

> Whatever it is, it all comes down to this;
> My father's cock
> Between my mother's thighs.
> Might he have forgotten to wind the clock?
>
> Whatever it is, it goes back to this night,
> To a chance remark
> In a room at the top of the stairs;
> To an open field, as like as not,
> Under the little stars.
> Whatever it is, it leaves me in the dark.   (*P* 76)

Though 'left in the dark', Muldoon is nevertheless free to imagine 'anything wild or wonderful', to explore a whole network of roads leading to and around the putatively originary home.

A Hermeneutics of Suspicion

Against Heaney's faith in the magical, healing power of poetry, Muldoon, even while he is drawn to such claims, is deeply suspicious of myths and visions. In 'Kinship', Heaney, in a spirit of ceremonial reverence, stands 'at the edge of centu-ries/ facing a goddess' (*N* 42): Muldoon, in 'Aisling', rewrites the Gaelic vision poem, transforming the traditionally venerated figure of Cathleen Ni Houlihan into an unidentifiable female who infects her lovers with disease or, as in the case of 'the latest hunger-striker' (*P* 126), lures them to self-destruction. Heaney's visionary reclamation of his rural childhood is mocked by Muldoon in poems like 'Trance' (the title ironically deflating the very notion of vision), where Muldoon's

---

[42]   Robert Frost, 'The Road Not Taken', *Selected Poems*, p. 77.

childhood memory of Christmas Eve, 1954 is linked to hallucinogenic experience and Siberian shamanic mushroom ritual. In 'Belderg' Heaney indulges his excavatory, archaeological impulse to uncover the hidden ground of contemporary Ulster, and ends with the image of Ygdrassil of Norse mythology, 'a world-tree of balanced stones,/ Querns piled like vertebrae./ The marrow crushed to grounds' (*N* 14) – the quernstones, like the 'untoppled' *omphalos*, affirming a surviving originary being, even though its vital core has been fragmented into 'grounds'. Muldoon replies with a poem called 'Ygdrassil', mocking Heaney's longing for vision and myth. In 'Ygdrassil', the grand public project of the poet's ascent of Ygdrassil is interrupted and displaced by a series of micro-narratives expressive of unruly subjective and libidinal energies. Vision is reduced to drug-induced hallucination, the fanciful prophecy of a Russian invasion of Ulster:

> Yet the lichened
> tree trunk will taper
> to a point where one scrap of paper
> is spiked, and my people yearn
> for a legend:
>
> *It may not be today*
> *or tomorrow, but sooner or later*
> *the Russians will water*
> *their horses on the shores of Lough Erne*
> *and Lough Neagh.* (*P* 119)

Instead of offering the people a consolatory nationalist myth of home, Muldoon introduces fantastical notions of invasion, contamination and hybridity. Muldoon's fables and parables enunciate, not explanatory myths, but a hermeneutics of suspicion in which the metanarratives of history, identity and place all come under deconstructive scrutiny. Unlike Heaney's home, or even the home of Frost's 'Directive', Muldoon's home, as Clair Wills says, is 'not a place of security and groundedness, but a shifting and unstable terrain'.[43]

Movement and Migrancy

In Muldoon's poetry, the Heaneyesque vision of return to an original place, articulated in terms of nature, divinity, mother earth, the ancestors, is supplanted by themes of movement and migrancy. Where Heaney subscribes to the identity of place and evinces a longing for coherence, origin and closure, Muldoon relishes the dialogue of difference, enthusiastically mobilising such potent tropes of modernity as those of displacement, dislocation, and composite, cosmopolitan identities. In his interview with John Haffenden, Muldoon (in an echo of Larkin's poem 'The Importance of Elsewhere'), emphasised the importance of always 'going somewhere else':

---

[43] Wills, p. 23.

One of the ways in which we are most ourselves is that we imagine ourselves to be going somewhere else. It's important to most societies to have the notion of something out there to which we belong, that our home is somewhere else … there's another dimension, something around us and beyond us, which is our inheritance.[44]

James Clifford elaborates on the significance of this redefinition of home in terms of itineracy and otherness:

If we rethink culture … in terms of travel, then the organic, naturalizing bias of the term culture – seen as a rooted body that grows, lives, dies, etc. – is questioned. Constructed and disputed *historicities*, sites of displacement, interference, and interaction, come more sharply into view.[45]

'Why Brownlee Left' is an image of precisely this transition – traditional rural culture with its 'organic, naturalizing bias' left stunned and silent by the impact of the new emergent culture of 'travel', 'disputed historicities' and 'displacement'. The poem opens up a silence, a space, an interrogation, the Heaneyesque grand narrative of rural coherence transformed, transposed and translated into a collection of mysterious traces. Muldoon plays a joke on his readers, promising explanation in his title but using the poem to generate ambiguity and mystification in what is a species of anti-narrative, a poetic 'immram' or 'rowing around' that leads nowhere. Muldoon turns the moment of departure into perpetual departure, transporting us beyond a comforting rationality and morality that might have provided an explanation or ending.

In an age of unprecedented geographic mobility and technological advance, the individual's relationships with place have become multiple, tenuous and provisional. Even more decisive than origins in the determination of our identity is the potentially far-flung network of relationships in which we have been, and are presently, inscribed. Muldoon's 'Quoof' measures identity in spatial as well as temporal terms. Diasporic identity, we see, is at once both local and global. By placing the discourses of 'home' and 'dispersion' in creative tension, the poem inscribes a homing nostalgia while simultaneously critiquing Heaneyesque discourses of fixed origins. The poem explores the shifting and overlapping boundaries of the migrant subject and the challenge of evolving new languages to mediate between different worlds. It opens with an act of translation (*transfero* – I carry across) that has occurred countless times in the past – 'How often have I carried our family word/ for the hot water bottle/ to a strange bed' (*P* 112) – the carrying across of a private childhood language into the world of the contemporary metropolis, which ironically is itself a postcolonial site – 'New York City'. Also drawn from the margins into the 'melting pot' of New York is the 'girl who spoke hardly any English', and who therefore exceeds the limits of the speaker's world altogether. To name is to possess, to domesticate: the girl remains irredeemably other – 'unspeakable', as elusive as 'the yeti' – because she escapes the control of the speaker's language, as the syntactical slippage in

44   Haffenden, p. 141.
45   James Clifford, *Routes: Travel and Translation in the Late Twentieth Century* (Cambridge, Mass., Harvard University Press, 1997) p. 25.

the sestet would suggest. It is the speaker's fear of difference – whether sexual, racial or cultural – which prevents communication and produces the other as monstrous. Nevertheless, the echo of 'yeti' in 'yet to' in the last line of the poem contains a recognition (and enactment) of the evolutionary nature of language and a prospect of future assimilation: 'My hand on her breast/ like the smouldering one-off spoor of the yeti/ or some other shy beast/ that has yet to enter the language' (*P* 112). The sestet, not having a main verb, is left suspended in time, between memory and fantasy, its 'action' reverberating in an 'eternal interim' ('Lull', *P* 81).

Heaney's move from Belfast to Co. Wicklow was what prompted his adoption of the persona of the birdman Sweeney. Muldoon answers by rhyming Muldoon with Mael Duin, the hero of the eighth-century voyage poem *Immram Mael Duin*. Where Heaney invokes the Heaney/Sweeney identification to explore his own migrant solitude, his own love of place, his melancholy sense of loss and uprootedness, Muldoon uses the Old Irish mythological hero parodically to present his postmodernist peregrinations around contemporary America. Where Heaney uses ancient myth to express continuity, Muldoon uses it to emphasise discontinuity and uncertainty. Muldoon's journeys are erratic, unpredictable and circling. Situated in the gap between the real and the imaginary, his itinerary criss-crosses both temporal and spatial boundaries, exploring roads not taken as well as those that are taken. Following the outline of *Immram Mael Duin*, 'Immrama' and 'Immram' are journey poems in quest of a lost father, prompted, Muldoon tells us, by a dubious story of his father's aborted decision to emigrate to Australia in the 1930s:

> It's an image that's troubled me for ages, since it underlines the arbitrary nature of so many decisions we take, the disturbingly random quality of so many of our actions. I would speculate on my father's having led an entirely different life, in which, clearly, I would have played no part. And suddenly my poems were peopled by renegades, some of them bent on their idea of the future, some on their idea of the past. All bent, though. All errantly going about their errands.
>
> I seem to remember my father telling me that he determined once to emigrate to Australia. Now he tells me it was a hen's yarn. Either he, or I, must have made it up.[46]

Where in Heaney's poetry the father is an idealised, exemplary figure of root-edness in the land, in tradition and the past, Muldoon releases his father from the limitations of the actual, imagining alternative life histories for him, thereby turning him into a metamorphic mystery-man, associated with emigration and exile. Like Brownlee, the father in 'Immrama' has suddenly and unexpectedly 'disappeared', leaving an absence which the poem proceeds to fill. The factual record of the father's life with which the sonnet begins is displaced in the sestet by an exoticised re-imagining of the father's other 'renegade' life in the Nazi underworld of Brazil.

In 'Immram' (*P* 94–102), his father, the 'mulish' farm labourer, is trans-

---

46 Paul Muldoon, 'Paul Muldoon writes ...', *The Poetry Book Society Bulletin*, 106 (Autumn 1980) p. 1.

formed into an equally exotic character – a dangerous international drug smuggler. 'Immram' is another poem which is ostensibly about the quest for origins, the search for the father, but is in fact a travesty of any metaphysics of origins or authenticity. The poem, set in the famously decentred city of Los Angeles, inscribes a circular movement, ending as it began in Foster's pool-room. In the original legend, the voyager sailed in search of enlightenment, eventually meeting an old hermit who urges him to give up his desire for vengeance on his father's murderers. Muldoon satirises the quest for enlightenment through his description of the search for heaven using 'angel dust', and the new religion of 'The Way of the One Wave'. The eventual source of enlightenment is a decrepit Howard Hughes father-figure, ensconced in the penthouse of the Park Hotel, who declares 'I forgive you', and then abruptly calls for a dish of Baskin-Robbins ice cream. In Muldoon's poem, a perpetual movement of transmutation and transformation disperses the transparency of truth and the poetry of origins. Inheritance isn't simply destroyed or erased but rewritten and re-routed. The poetry is a re-citing and re-siting of tradition, a witty and ingenious re-membering of fragments and traces of historical and cultural knowledge. Traditional lyric and narrative forms, including the sonnet and sonnet sequence, are radically re-worked. While the quest theme and circular, episodic structure are based on *Immram Mael Duin*, the setting and narrative voice are modelled on Raymond Chandler and the conventions of *film noir*. There are parodic references to Byron, Tennyson's 'The Voyage of Maeldune', MacNeice's radio play *The Mad Islands*, *The Odyssey*, *The Tempest*, the biblical story of Susanna and the elders, Wallace Stevens' version of the same story in 'Peter Quince on the Claviar', Howard Hughes's *The Hidden Years*. Out of these diverse sources, Muldoon constructs a hybridised, carnivalesque, multi-voiced language, which powerfully conveys an attitude of irony and cynicism characteristic of a non-rational, disjunctive, postmodern world. The poem demonstrates the way Muldoon uses the past: while acknowledging traditional resources (including aspects of poetic form), he is aware of the dangers of entrapment, and claims his own artistic freedom through an iconoclastic reworking of the formal and narrative structures of his sources, incorporating parody and surrealism, elaborate digressions, hallucinogenic experience, ironic vision, ambivalence and equivocation, alternative histories, pyrotechnic linguistic displays, international analogies and historical parallels, which unsettle given meanings and open up the potential of a liberated future. Through this process of 'rowing around' Muldoon explores the tensions between freedom and subjection, authority and dispersal, power and powerlessness.

'The More a Man Has' (*P* 127–47) likewise eschews any stable epistemological point of view or coherent truth. Just as Brownlee left without explanation, so characters appear in 'The More a Man Has' without explanation or context. Identities merge or remain indeterminate until we are forced to conclude that Muldoon is 'throwing the very concept of "identity" into question'.[47] Formally and linguistically, the poem enacts 'seemingly endless possibilities of change and transformation'.[48] In the contingent world of the poem, identity is multiple,

---

[47] Tim Hancock, 'Identity Problems in Paul Muldoon's "The More a Man has the More a Man Wants"', *Honest Ulsterman*, 97 (Spring 1994) pp. 57–64, 57.
[48] Wills, p. 108.

forged in discontinuous, heterogeneous histories. Caught up in a *bricolage* of seemingly incompatible discourses, we must fill in the gaps, try to make sense of the poem's disjunctive narrative and ever-shifting constellations of meaning. Traditions and roots are important, not for themselves, but as part of a complex, scattered inheritance that may be re-worked and played with. The picaresque protagonist is the metamorphic Gallogly, a Sweeneyesque outsider who breaks all the rules, a fugitive in a 'thorn-proof jacket' who is 'drawn out of the woods/ by an apple pie/ left to cool on a window sill' – like Sweeney, perched on a sill, gazing longingly upon the comforts of home that are denied him. Sweeney's highly lyrical and romantic eulogy to Glen Bolcain is re-written as comic anti-pastoral:

> He will answer the hedge-sparrow's
> *Littlebitofbreadannocheese*
> With a whole bunch
> Of freshly picked watercress,
> A bulb of garlic,
> Sorrel,
> With many-faceted blackberries,
> Gallogly is out to lunch.   (*P* 134)

The protean Gallogly is referred to as a 'gallowglass', the name given to the mercenary soldiers of Viking origin who, between the thirteenth and seventeenth centuries, hired themselves out to Irish and Scottish Highland chieftains, and who distinguished themselves during the sixteenth century in the Irish wars against the English. But Gallogly goes under different names, even that of the colonial 'English'. 'Gallogly' may also be a version of 'Oglala', the Indian tribe to which, perhaps, Mangas Jones belongs, though there are alternative suggestions that the avenging Indian may be a Mescalero Apache or a Winnebago 'Trickster'. Perhaps Mangas Jones is Gallogly's romanticised alter ego. Like the Trickster, Gallogly is the source of a disruptive sexuality which subverts monolithic discourse, whether that of tradition, politics or history. Also like the Trickster, he sometimes appears in animal rather than human form. Identity, we may conclude, is something which is constantly formed and re-formed, on the move, in transit, unable to be confined within any single definition or traced to any originary source.

Alluding to Heaney's 'Broagh', Muldoon mocks the notion of the possibility of a return to some kind of 'authentic', originary state complete with its own racial/tribal RSP:

> Gallogly lies down in the sheugh
> to munch
> through a Beauty of
> Bath. He repeats himself, *Bath,*
> Under his garlic-breath.
> *Sheugh,* he says, *Sheugh.*
> He is finding that first 'sh'
> Increasingly difficult to manage.
> *Sh*-leeps. A milkmaid sinks
> Her bare foot

> To the ankle
> In a simmering dung hill
> And fills the slot
> With beastlings for him to drink.   (*P* 135)

In Muldoon's poem, Heaney's 'O' – the 'pure' source – becomes a 'slot' in a dung hill filled with 'beastlings' – the word a shifting signifier of Old English derivation, a variant of 'beestings' which, according to the *Oxford English Dictionary*, can mean either 'the first milk drawn from a cow after parturition' or 'a disease caused by imbibing beastlings'. Where Heaney is haunted by the ghosts of an authentic nationalism, Muldoon rejects the idea of an 'original', grounding presence and thinks in terms of extensive, multiple histories and 'adulterated' cultures, languages and identities.

The question of his own allegiance, especially when it involves acquiescence in communal atrocity, troubles Heaney. He anguishes over the question in 'Punishment', where he probes his divided feelings about communal violence against those who transgress the tribal dictate, whether Iron Age adulteress or the young girls of the present-day who are tarred and feathered for going out with British soldiers. In 'The More a Man Has', Muldoon re-writes 'Punishment', comically muddling our understanding of the situation, refusing to construe it in the straightforward tribal and political terms which exercise Heaney:

> Someone on their way to early Mass
> Will find her hog-tied
> To the chapel gates –
> O Child of Prague –
> Big-eyed, anorexic.
> The lesson for today
> Is pinned to her bomber jacket.
> It seems to read *Keep off the Grass*.
> Her lovely head has been chopped
> And changed.
> For Beatrice, whose fathers
> Knew Louis Quinze,
> To have come to this, her perruque
> Of tar and feathers.   (*P* 130)

Muldoon keeps out of his poem and concentrates on the victim herself. His tone is witty, ironic and playful. 'Anorexic' links the girl with both the republican hunger striker and the debased goddess of Ireland in 'Aisling'. 'Bomber jacket' relates to drugs as well as bombs. The comic punning continues with the warning '*Keep off the Grass*', which, though it might apply to police-informing, is more likely in the context of the poem to refer to drug-taking, since Beatrice is a devotee of 'a psilocybin god'. As well as devotee, the girl is herself an ironic figure of the divine, addressed as 'Child of Prague', the distinctive feature of this miraculous statue being the tiara on the Holy Infant's head. The reverential tone of Heaney's approach to the ancient bog victim is replaced by Muldoon's mockery of Church authority ('The lesson for today'). Using the general form of the sonnet which, like the girl in the poem, is shockingly 'chopped/and changed',

Muldoon experiments with a scandalous hybridisation of heterogeneous languages and discourses, transgressing moral as well as aesthetic and political boundaries. Heaney's poem weighs liberal humanist outrage against instinctual understanding of atrocity: Muldoon makes us aware of the ethical relationship between the subject and the (tricky, lecherous) language which subjects.

With Muldoon we may speak not only about the writing of travel ('Immrama', 'Immram', 'The More a Man Has') but also about the travel of writing. Poetry, language, identity derive from movement. In poems such as 'Immram' and 'The More a Man Has' the poet sets forth into the unknown in the hope that, from the experience of transit, some surplus or excess may be discovered which opens up unforeseen horizons of possibility. Poetry is a journeying, a constant meta-morphosis as language requires, in which empirical reality is invested by doubt and dislocation, and the usual narrative modalities are playfully reworked. There is no single frame or map, no single language or authority, no straight course to be followed. Movement and multiplicity unsettle any tendency towards 'truth' or 'knowledge'. For what, above all, Muldoon shares with Frost, is a suspicion of dogmatic or monologic truth, of systems and system-building, of all grand narra-tives which impose a totalising (and therefore falsifying) myth on the world. 'The More a Man Has' ends with reference to Frost's 'For Once, Then, Something':

> 'They foun' this hairy
> han' wi' a drownded man's grip
> on a lunimous stone no bigger than a ...'
>
> 'Huh'. (*P* 147)

Frost doesn't know whether he saw a transcendent truth at the bottom of the well, or a mere pebble of quartz. 'For Once Then Something' ends with a series of questions, not confident assertions, bespeaking the speaker's uncertainty: 'What was that whiteness?/ Truth? A pebble of quartz? For once, then, some-thing'[49]) Muldoon's final 'Huh' is an even stronger rejection of absolute 'truth', a contemptuous dismissal of all that the characters in the poem have died for. Compare these endings with that of Heaney's 'Personal Helicon', the title itself foregrounding the traditional romantic notion of the poet as divinely inspired. Looking into the dark depths of the well, Heaney discovers the source of his poetic power and ends with a ringing affirmation of faith in the self-presencing power of 'rhyme'. Referring specifically to the closing lines of 'Directive' – 'Here are your waters and your watering place./ Drink and be whole again beyond confusion' – Heaney describes Frost's poetry as 'a poetry which gives access to origin' (*HRF* 72). Heaney could as well have been describing his own poetry. In the later poem 'A Drink of Water', he rededicates himself to the originary, feminine creative and life-giving force, symbolised by the water from the Moss-bawn pump, Heaney's Irish omphalos: 'Where I have dipped to drink again, to be/ Faithful to the admonishment on her cup,/ *Remember the Giver*, fading off the lip' (*OG* 151). Muldoon's poem, 'Tea', written on the poet's re-location to America, also echoes Frost's 'Directive': 'All I have in the house is some left-over/

---

[49] Robert Frost, *Selected Poems*, p. 131.

squid cooked in its own ink/ and this unfortunate cup of tea. Take it. Drink' (*P* 198) – but the sacramental force of the gesture in Muldoon's last line is undercut by the sense of depleted resources and colonial anxiety (in the echoes of the Boston Tea Party).

Diasporic Identity

There is arguably much more of America in Muldoon than in Heaney. Heaney, though he has lived for extended periods in the States, has tended to absorb America second-hand, through the influence of its poets – chiefly Frost and Lowell – rather than directly in terms of life style, landscape, history and language. Unlike Heaney, Muldoon grew up on American culture, and his poetry from the beginning evinces his transatlantic interest. What is especially notable are those aspects of America to which he is drawn – the frontier, Native America, multicultural America, being on the road ('Immram', 'The More a Man Has'), American popular culture (see *General Admission*,[50] a collection of song lyrics, including 'My Ride's Here', co-written with Warren Zevon and recorded by Bruce Springsteen). Muldoon's America is the polyvocal, heteroglossic 'melting pot' that he celebrates in 'Yarrow':

> To the time I hunkered with Wyatt Earp and Wild Bill Hickok
> on the ramparts of Troy
> as Wild Bill tried to explain to Priam
>
> how 'saboteur' derives from *sabot*, a clog;
> to the time we drove ten thousand head from U-Cross
> to Laramie with Jimi and Eric riding point.   (*P* 356)

Such poetry declares a contemporary Irish culture that knows no borders, that is porous and diffuse.

In 'Madoc', the biographical context of which is Muldoon's migration from Ireland to begin a new life with his Jewish wife in America, he explores all kinds of hybridity, interconnection and 'mixed marriage' – between old and new worlds, fact and fiction, nationalism and imperialism, poetry and politics, poetry and philosophy, lyric fragment and epic narrative. Fusing different kinds of discourse – published memoir, poetic fantasies, detective story, western, historically recorded events, historical fictions – he explores stories of interracial sex, the politics of intercultural encounters, the possibilities of cultural analogy and historical parallel. At the same time he resists any totalising ambition. The parenthetical titles of the individual poems, some of them no more than fragments, are the names of philosophers, but 'Madoc – a Mystery', doesn't add up to a coherent philosophy: it is, rather, as Muldoon has said, a 'madcap history of Western thought', filtered through the perceptions of 'some kind of

---

[50] Paul Muldoon, *General Admission* (Loughcrew, The Gallery Press, 2006).

Sunday philosophy buff'.[51] His two central characters represent the extremes of assimilation and separatism: Coleridge mixes with the Indians and 'goes native'; Southey adopts a strict, authoritarian attitude and becomes increasingly resistant to native American influences. Edna Longley and Neil Corcoran have suggested that in the contrast between Coleridge and Southey, Muldoon is allegorising the difference between his and Heaney's relationship with America. More certifiable are the reverberations created between the colonisation of America and that of Ireland, though as the inclusion of the Scots-Irish scout Alexander Cinnamond in the pantisocratic experiment implies, Irish emigrants were themselves at the heart of the colonialist enterprise. Referring to the historic position of the Irish in New York, Ronald Bayer and Timothy Meagher have this to say:

> Throughout their history in New York, the Irish have been at the border of the ins and outs, interpreting one to the other, mediating, sometimes including, sometimes excluding. They have been both victim and victimiser, 'other' and definer of the 'other', and, paradoxically, sometimes played both roles simultaneously.[52]

British colonial language in the nineteenth century, as Fintan O'Toole has shown, frequently conflated the savagery of the native Irish and that of the native American. At the same time, the Irish were at the forefront of the white myth of the American West, distinguishing themselves as clearers of wilderness and killers of Indians. Exemplifying a characteristic both/and hybrid identity, Irish-Americans are 'natives and conquerors, aboriginals and civilisers, a savage tribe in one context, a superior race in another'.[53]

Muldoon's pantisocratic settlement is called 'Ulster' and it collapses in a miasma of betrayal and violence. The poem acknowledges colonial depradation, but, as in 'Immram' or 'The More a Man Has', the writing defies both linear progressivism and any simple doom-laden notions of timeless circularity. The oppressive weight of historical continuity, and its metaphysics of tradition and truth, are broken up by tropes of historical discontinuity and transcultural counterhistory, by fantasy and linguistic playfulness. Exploring ideas of linear progressivism and historical continuity, Paul Gilroy, in his book, *The Black Atlantic: Double Consciousness and Modernity*, uncovers 'a syncopated temporality – a different rhythm of living and being' in the black Atlantic diaspora. Gilroy cites Ralph Ellison, author of *Invisible Man*:

> Invisibility, let me explain, gives one a slightly different sense of time, you're never quite on the beat. Sometimes you're ahead and sometimes behind. Instead of the swift and imperceptible flowing of time, you are aware of its nodes, those points where time stands still or from which it leaps ahead. And you slip into the breaks and look around'.[54]

---

[51] Lynn Keller, 'An Interview with Paul Muldoon', *Contemporary Literature*, 35, 1 (Spring 1994) pp. 11–12.

[52] Ronald Bayer and Timothy Meagher, *The New York Irish*, 1966; quoted in Fintan O'Toole, *The Ex-Isle of Erin* (Dublin, New Island Books, 1996) p. 134.

[53] Fintan O'Toole, *The Lie of the Land: Irish Identities* (London, Verso, 1997) p. 33.

[54] Paul Gilroy, *The Black Atlantic: Double Consciousness and Modernity*, p. 281.

In 'The Key', a prose-poem which programmatically precedes 'Madoc', Muldoon. explores a similar colonial experience of temporal and perceptual difference or 'defamiliarisation' from the point of view of the Irish emigrant experience in America. An Irishman, Foley, is at work in Los Angeles on a 'remake' of the film *The Hoodlum Priest*:

> Foley was working on a sequence involving a police line-up, in which the victim shuffled along, stopped with each suspect in turn, then shuffled on. At a critical moment, she dropped a key on the floor. Foley was having trouble matching sound to picture. (*P* 197)

'The Key', which opens into the postmodern culture of the simulacrum, is, as Clair Wills says, about the difficulties in making connections – between sound and picture, occurrence and its representation, the subject and his world. Just as Foley is having problems in matching sound to picture, the prose-poem itself is a detailed narration of events that never happened. The poet imagines himself recalling Foley to his roots (in words which are a parodic 're-make' of an earlier Muldoon poem, 'Brock'), and Foley rounding on him, urging him to stop 'defending that same old patch of turf' (a 'post-production' of James Joyce's words to Heaney in the last section of 'Station Island') and embrace the new American reality. Foley, the poet is forced to admit, 'has had some strange effect on me. These past six months I've sometimes run a little ahead of myself, but mostly I lag behind, my footfalls already pre-empted by their echoes' (*P* 198). 'The Key' opens up breaches in the 'imperceptible flowing' of hegemonic discourse, and marks those moments in which diasporic subversions, counter-histories and off-beat cultural and poetic critiques originate. What 'The Key' suggests and 'Madoc' illustrates is that in syncopated time, new stories can be told, alternative identities can be forged, different futures can begin to be imagined, in an interminable process of 're-making' and 'post-production'.

'The Briefcase', one of the poems following 'The Key' in *Madoc*, contains both the possibility of creative freedom and a suggestion of the postmodern construction of poetry as an endless intertextual recycling of culture. The briefcase appears in 'Madoc' as the 'valise' (*P* 203) which belongs to Southey, is passed from one person to another, eventually ending up back with Southey, and replicates itself and its contents ('All except for a dog-eared letter in cuttle-/ ink' *P* 288). South, a character linked up to a retinograph and through whose 'eye'/'I' the fragmentary narrative is relayed, also has a valise containing a mysterious 'scrap of paper' (*P* 321) – 'the first/ inkling of this poem' (*P* 202) – which is 'repossessed' by the Unitel thought police back in Ireland. We may also recall that it was in a 'powder-blue attaché-/case' (*P* 128) that the American Indian, Mangas Jones, attempted to smuggle the Frostian 'pebble of quartz' – 'the truth?' – into 'The More a Man Has'. However, the primary intertextual connections are with Heaney. 'The Briefcase' is dedicated to Heaney, and may be read as a 're-make' of those Heaney poems such as 'Sandstone Keepsake', 'Granite Chip' and 'Stone from Delphi'[55] about objects construed as almost magical repositories of the past.

---

55 The most obvious link is with Heaney's 'The Schoolbag', in *Seeing Things*, which, since it was published in 1991, a year after *Madoc*, may be seen as a Heaney 're-make' of 'The Briefcase'.

Significantly, the briefcase, evocative of the older poet, is held 'at arm's length' (*P* 202). Heaney's portentous lines on Michael McLaverty – 'fostered me and sent me out, with words/ Imposing on my tongue like obols' ('Fosterage', *OG* 142)) – which emphasise a sense of words as having a sacramental weight and power – are mocked by Muldoon, who says he doesn't want to set his briefcase down 'to slap my pockets for an obol' for 'the cross-town/bus'. 'The Briefcase' also recalls Heaney's 'Lough Neagh Sequence', about the transatlantic migrations of eels from the Sargasso Sea to Lough Neagh. The eelskin briefcase, quickened into life after a rainstorm, threatens to 'strike out along the East River/ for the sea. By which I mean the "open" sea' (*P* 202) – lines which recall the advice Joyce gives the poet at the end of Heaney's 'Station Island': 'When they make the circle wide, it's time to swim/ out on your own and fill the element/ with signatures on your own frequency,/ echo soundings, searches, probes, allurements,/ elver-gleams in the dark of the whole sea' (*OG* 268). By letting go of his briefcase/poem, the speaker fears it may attempt a Heaneyesque return to origins; or, contrarily, that it may swim out into the 'open' spaces of American life and poetry, and lose touch altogether with origins, inheritance and traditional form (which is the direction Muldoon's poetry takes in 'Madoc').

The eelskin briefcase coming back to life like the panther in another Muldoon poem ('The Panther') suggests a wild, primitive energy that cannot entirely be extinguished or transformed by the civilising forms, whether of colonisation, domesticity or poetry. Muldoon pictures 'the last panther in Massachusetts' (*P* 200) hanging in the kitchen of his house as a trophy-symbol of the triumph of colonisation and civilisation. But the wild spirit of the panther is still alive despite the speaker's confidence that 'it was brought to justice' and his attempts to treat it as an unthreatening plaything ('the tippy-tip of its nose'). This image of an elemental, native force refusing to die – 'The air under the meat-hook –/ it quakes, it quickens' (*P* 200) – replays a familiar Heaney trope found, for instance, in 'Badgers', where the poet hears 'duntings under the laurels' (*OG* 158) and acknowledges the 'other' in himself, the stirrings of the dark forces of violence and barbarism that lie beyond the pale of enlightened society: 'the bogey of fern country/ broke cover in me' (*OG* 158). Heaney identifies with the atavistic forces, but Muldoon refuses the gesture of solidarity: situated in his kitchen in a house built by an early Scots-Irish settler, 'Ephraim Cowan from Antrim', Muldoon's speaker occupies the place of the colonist and feels complicit in the history of Irish-American colonialism.

Probing the uncanny displacements of diaspora historicity, memory, narrativity and poetics, Muldoon reveals homecoming, not as return to or recovery of a source or centre, but as a combination of here and there, self and other. Home becomes a matter of fluid improvisation. 'The Mudroom' extends 'Quoof''s quasi-autobiographical investigation into the experience of displacement, dispersion and transculturalism. The mud room in American homes is a kind of cloakroom where muddy boots are left, a *zona media* 'at the border of the ins and outs'. Muldoon's title is provocative of 'muddle', 'mid', 'Muldoon' – perhaps even 'The Mud Vision', a poem in which Heaney laments the contemporary neurosis of a people displaced from a traditional, rural cultural inheritance and a pagan, magical sense of the world into a technological, secular modernity: 'What might have been origin/ We dissipated in news' (*OG* 322). At the centre of Muldoon's poem is the self-questioning, disrupted and decentred subject, cut off from the homelands of tradition, living between worlds, caught on a border that runs through every aspect of his life, the image of which is the 'wheel of Morbier' (*P* 395), a round of cheese crossed by a blue-green seam of pine-ash. Focusing on the intersections of histories and memories, Muldoon suggests the dispersal of origins and their translation into new, more extensive configurations. The cluttered, shifting, haunted 'mudroom' of the poet's life and art is a site of inter-minable exchange between a scattered historical inheritance and a heterogeneous present. The diverse contents of this home away from home (portable skating-rink, Bogota blanket, wheel-felloe, gefilte fish, boxes of seventies albums, six-packs of beer, Abraham's altar and seven-branched candlestick, Virgil's *Georgics*, his father's boots), and the linguistic variety of the writing used to describe it ('haggaday', 'afikomen', 'quadriga', 'mishegaas', 'scammony') express the complex transnational networks built from multiple attachments. Ireland is not simply left behind but enters into relationship with a contrapuntal modernity and a heterotopic future.

'At the Sign of the Black Horse, September 1999', the last poem in *Moy Sand and Gravel*, is written in Yeatsian eight-line stanzas, a 're-make' of Yeats's 'Prayer for My Daughter'. Just as Yeats, from the safety of his tower, prays for his daughter in the midst of the howling storm, symbolic of the turmoil of the time, so Muldoon tenderly pictures his children in the aftermath of Hurricane Floyd, even echoing and re-working some of Yeats's phrasing – 'the haystack-/ and roof-leveling wind, bred/ on the Atlantic',[56] 'Asher sleeps on', 'Asher slept on, half hid/ under the cradle hood', 'his soul less likely than ever to recover radical innocence and learn at last/ that it is self-delighting', 'No obstacle but Gregory's wood/ and one bare hill', 'If there's no hatred in a mind ...', 'Once more the storm is howling'. But where Yeats prays that his daughter may remain 'Rooted in one dear perpetual place',[57] Muldoon's poem celebrates a durability and resilience that thrive on migrancy and deracination. Yeats's ideal is 'a house/Where all's accus-tomed, ceremonious':[58] Muldoon is 'happy that the house I may yet bring myself to call mine/ is set on a two-hundred-and-fifty-year-old slab', but also 'happy that, if need be, we might bundle a few belongings into a pillow slip/ and climb the hill and escape'. Yeats's concentration on an exclusively Anglo-Irish style of ceremony and custom, symbolised by the 'rich horn' and 'spreading laurel tree', has to make room for Muldoon's more diverse heritage that includes the Jewish 'bris' (ritual circumcision), kosher cooking, 'Midrash' (rabbinical commen-tary on the Torah), and 'menorah' (the branched candelabrum used in Jewish worship). These references, however, do not imply orthodoxy, but the opposite – the speaker's transgression and dissent from orthodoxy: 'By which authority did we deny Asher a mohel?'; 'a peaked cap enquiries about the orthodox/ posi-tion on the eating of white-lipped peccary'; 'You ignore the Midrash/ by which

---

56 Paul Muldoon, 'At the Sign of the Black Horse, September 1999', in *Moy Sand and Gravel* (London, Faber, 2002), 73–90. Hereafter abbreviated to *MSG* and page references incorporated into the text.

57 W.B. Yeats, *Selected Poetry*, edited by A. Norman Jeffares (London, Macmillan, 1974) p. 102.

58 Ibid., p. 103.

authority?' The Jewish references emphasise Muldoon's embrace of pluralism and difference, the assumption that the self has meaning only in interrelation with otherness. A self-conscious, hybridised poetic language cross-fertilises the diverse languages of which it is composed.

Punctuating Muldoon's poem are the constant intrusions of the busy public world – 'No Way Out', 'No Children Beyond This Point', 'Please Secure Your Own Oxygen Mask/ Before Attending To Children', 'Do Not Fill/ Above This Line', 'Don't Walk', 'Keep Out', 'Keep Clear', 'All Directions'. These signs of a fixed and regimenting social order keep breaking in on the poet's thoughts, which, in contrast, flow and swirl like the millrace produced by the canal in flood. The flooded canal brings to mind the Irish navvies who died building it, Irish famine victims, the sufferings of the Jews in Auschwitz, the memory of a stillborn son. In the face of his living son, Asher, the poet sees the confluence of tribal histories, Irish and Jewish, enacted in the rhyming of 'Magherafelt' (site of a long history of civil violence, from the Rebellion in 1641 to the detonation of an IRA van bomb in 1993) and 'yellow felt' (the star worn by pogrom Jews):

> When we wheeled the old Biltrite baby carriage
> to the brink this morning, I was awestruck to see in Asher's glabrous
> face a slew of interlopers
> not from Maghery, as I might have expected, or Maghera, or Magherafelt
> (though my connections there are now few and far between),
> but the likes of that kale-eating child on whom the peaked cap, *Verboten*,
> would shortly pin a star of yellow felt … (*MSG* 74–5)

Throughout the poem, key words, phrases, images and motifs are repeated and recombined in a fugue-like or kaleidoscopic pattern. Temporal, spatial and cultural gaps are abolished. A highly flexible metrical line registers the inflections of the speaking voice and turns the poem into an open field of possibility. The loose syntax tends towards long, trailing sentences, which are arranged in repetitive, co-ordinate structures or in disjointed, appositional forms, without the kind of complex subordination that is used to organise perceptions and events in a hierarchical order, or to imply rational, intellectual control of the material. Ideas of mixed marriage, hybridity and migrancy are embodied in a richly heteroglossic language, reflective of the American melting-pot, as these, the closing lines of the poem, illustrate:

> when the cry went up from a starving Irish schlemiel who washed an
>   endosperm
> of wheat, deh-dah, from a pile of horse-keek
> held to the rain, one of those thousands of Irish schmucks who still loll,
>   still loll and lollygag,
> between the preposterous tow-path and the preposterous berm. (*MSG* 90)

The lines incorporate Yiddish-American slang ('schlemiel' – a born loser; 'schmuck' – a fool, from the Yiddish word for a penis, which associates with 'endosperm'), scientific or technical terminology ('endosperm' – the albumen of a seed; 'berm', from French and German – the bank of a canal opposite the tow-path), nonsense words ('deh-dah'), Ulster-Scots ('keek' – dung); Americanisms ('lollygag', a word of unknown etymology, meaning to loiter, or to kiss and cuddle [*OED*]); formal Latinate vocabulary ('preposterous', from Latin *prae* (before), and *posterus* (coming after), meaning 'contrary to nature, reason or common sense; obviously wrong, foolish, absurd' [*OED*]). These words, as Muldoon uses them, 'want to find chimes with each other, things want to connect', and so we have 'cry' echoing in the first syllable of 'Irish' and in 'pile'; 'endosperm' finding a rhyme in 'preposterous berm', 'wheat' in 'keek', 'loll' in 'lolly-'; the 'l's in 'schlemiel' recurring in 'pile', 'held', 'loll', 'still' and 'lollygag', the k-sound in 'cry' reappearing in 'keek', 'schmucks' and almost in the last syllable of 'lollygag'. The effort is to bring diversity into a harmonising net of sound, to discover in language its 'inherent' rhymes, repetitions and patterns. The almost frantic polyglottism, with the poetry sounding more and more like a cross between Joyce's *Finnegan's Wake* and Lewis Carroll's 'Jabberwocky', reflects the struggle for comprehensiveness and crystallisation, which always remain elusive. Muldoon's phrasing – 'still loll,/ still loll and lollygag'- might put one in mind of Whitman ('I loafe and invite my soul,/ I lean and loafe at my ease'[59]). There is, in fact much about Muldoon's poem that recalls Whitman: not just the long, free verse lines, flexible enough to register the inflections of individual speech; the loose syntactical structures and listings; the cumulative series of references and vivid snapshot images which call attention to the minute particulars of experience; the active grammar that favours the present participle in order to emphasise continuing process; the refusal of literary and cultural boundaries, the openness to what is other, summed up in Whitman's assertion 'I am large, I contain multitudes', and in Muldoon's humorous description of himself as 'the goy from the Moy'. The whole open-ended, provisional nature of 'At the Sign of the Black Horse' grows out of a Whitmanian conception of the poem – and of life – which is a distinctively American conception of the need to 'make it new', to restore and renew perception. Muldoon's poem, hovering between Whitman's free verse and a highly disruptive use of a traditional Yeatsian stanza and metrical pattern, produces feelings of surprise, of stimulating discord. The Yeatsian form is rendered more open and malleable, in response to a highly personal, idiosyncratic and anarchic notion of the poem's purpose.

Muldoon de-commissions boundaries and rejoices in heterogeneity and difference. Ideas of ethnic, racial or cultural 'purity', normalised by boundary fetishism, are replaced with the discourse of 'hybridity', which has biological and racial connotations, but only in terms of diversity, mixing and dispersion. A diasporic poetics acknowledges entanglement and replaces the hierarchical language of majority and minority, master and subaltern, coloniser and colonised with concepts of equal, indissoluble and often hidden relationship. Behind Muldoon's constantly mobile, migrant perspective, his refusal to think of 'here' and 'there' as fixed and opposite terms, is a view of movement and process as a primary mode of being in the world. His poetry models flexible ways of belonging, and a concept of community as a balancing act on the border between

---

[59] Walt Whitman, 'Song of Myself', in Donald Hall (ed.), *A Choice of Whitman's Verse* (London, Faber, 1989) pp. 23–83, 23.

rootedness and disintegration. Poetry thus becomes an active strategy to circumvent the false choices – between exile and engagement, free imagination and social conscience – that nationalism has traditionally imposed upon the Irish poetic.

Chapter 5

PADRAIC FIACC AND JAMES SIMMONS

Padraic Fiacc (real name Patrick Joseph O'Connor) was born in 1924 on the Lower Falls in Belfast. The family moved to East Street in Belfast's Markets area, where he spent his first five years. He grew up in two cities, Belfast and New York. His father was involved in the IRA during the sectarian violence of the late 1920s and had to flee to New York. Reluctantly, his wife, accompanied by her two young sons, joined him a few years later in 1929, at the onset of the Depression. When the father's grocery business went bankrupt, the family had to move to the Hell's Kitchen ghetto, a veritable melting pot of nationalities – Irish, Italians, Latin Americans, Jews, Russians and Germans. Here the sensitive young poet was early introduced to the brutalising urban realities of crime, violence, drug abuse and other social problems. 'Standing Water (A Rag)' describes the transatlantic journey:

> Punting into Nova Scotia
> Nineteen and Twenty Nine, girl
> Mother's delph face *creaks*, cracks ...
> (I'm breaking in two myself at five!)[1]

America stirs none of the usual immigrant feelings of excitement about fresh new starts and hopeful futures, only a deadly sense of oppression ('A yellow wolf cold/ Sits on the leaden Atlantic' *RP* 89), and apprehension ('The Russian Orthodox priest who/ Has a beard, is the Bogey Man/ Will put me in his bag/ Is "America" the Bury Hole he'll/ Put me in if I cry?' *RP* 89). Written in the present tense, and trailing off inconclusively in ellipses, the poem constructs a timeless emblem of entrapment and entombment, on whichever side of the Atlantic ('A back street womb wall won't/ Let me climb over it./ We stare at the brick Hali-/ fax sky'). The fragmentation of normal syntax and poetic form indicates a profound psychic tension, which is further reflected in the pervasive imagery of creaking, cracking and breaking. From the beginning, the poet establishes a characteristic persona, that of the terrorised victim, the vulnerable child seeking shelter in the maternal presence: 'I cling hard tight onto/ A Belfast flapper's strong/ Wrist bone' (*RP* 90).

---

[1]   Padraic Fiacc, *Ruined Pages: Selected Poems*, ed. Gerald Dawe and Aodán MacPóilin (Belfast, Blackstaff, 1994) p. 89. Hereafter abbreviated to *RP* and page references incorporated into the text.

Disillusionment with New York and the American Dream meant that the young Fiacc looked for another version of home, and his gaze returned to Ireland, not the Ireland of his own actual early experience – Belfast's Catholic slums and sectarian violence – but Romantic Ireland, the image of which had been kept vividly alive in his imagination by his mother, who read Yeats's poems and sang Irish songs to him. Padraic Colum, who was at the time living and working in New York, took an interest in the fledgling poet's work, and encouraged Fiacc to 'write of your own people – dig in the garden of Ireland'.[2] In 1946 Fiacc abandoned his studies for the priesthood at St Joseph's Seraphic Seminary, Calicoon, in New York state, and returned to Belfast, where he has spent most of the rest of his life.

His early poetry recreates an idealised, timeless Gaelic past, pre-invasion, pre-colonial, which takes its inspiration from Yeatsian Celticism and the Irish monastic tradition, with its love of nature and interest in mythological themes. In poems such as 'Storm Bird', 'Trying to Study Philosophy', 'A Wonder', 'Luck', 'The Boy and the Geese', 'Patrick Turns the Sod', 'At Autumn Birds of Passage', 'Jackdaw', 'Fionn's Spring', 'North Man' and 'At Night the Snow', the elemental world is viewed with preternatural clarity, with a painter's attentiveness to patterns of light and colour and movement. These poems show not only the influence of Gaelic models, but also the influence of American poets such as William Carlos Williams, yet manage to convey Fiacc's own genuinely personal appreciation of nature in a style that is notable for its simplicity and economy of means, its clean, sharp images, closely observed and freshly rendered. 'Tenth-Century Invasion' pictures the scene after raiding Norsemen have vandalised an Irish monastery, killing the monks and stealing their sacred manuscripts. To the poet, the most grievous loss of all is a monk's song inscribed in a drowned Bible's margin:

> Bells ring throughout the book
> At the bottom of the lough
>
> Gold running over the
> Ruined page
>
> Drowned
> Emerald and lilac ink
>
> From the song written in
> The shaft of the sun
>
> In the moment on the
> Margin
> Never to be sung.   (*RP* 57)

Inevitably, Fiacc's is a poetry of loss. Intruding upon the romantic pastoral myth are the nightmare realities of urban squalor, psychic disturbance and sectarian violence:

---

[2]   Quoted in Michael McKernon. (ed.), *Padraic Fiacc, Sea: Sixty Years of Poetry* (Belfast, Multimedia Heritage Press, 2006) p. 12.

> I rise and stalk across the scarred with storm
> -erected daisies, night in the north, grass.
>
> My water-coloured twilit-childhood island
> -scape barricaded with circles of rain-rusted
> Orange, coiled to kill, barbed wire.   ('The Wrong Ones', *RP* 137)

The European post-war urban wasteland is given a specifically Irish inflection, the blasted Belfast cityscape mythologised into a symbol of a lost Gaelic civilisation, scene of a fall from an archaic purity and innocence into the horror of the modern world: 'In all the land the lack/ Of what was whole' ('The Ghost', *RP* 61). 'Haemorrhage' takes as its epigraph lines from Joyce's poem 'Tilly': 'I bleed by the black stream/ For my torn bough' (*RP* 81), suggesting the poet's sense of a lost culture haemorrhaging into the black stream of modernity, leaving only ghost-like figures such as himself to haunt the contemporary landscape: 'The moonlight gets an un/ -earthly white Belfast man' (*RP* 81).

Gerald Dawe nominates 'First Movement' as a pivotal poem, marking, in its description of the sea, which symbolises some vast, environing threat, Fiacc's 'disintegrating relationship with the world around him' ('Introduction', *RP* 6):

> And to the east where morning is, the sea
> And to the west where evening is, the sea
>
> Threatening with danger
>
> And it would always darken suddenly.   (*RP* 75)

In seeking to transcribe as directly and exactly as possible this sense of danger and sudden darkening, Fiacc evolves a poetic shaped by the modernist experiment of contemporary American and European poets. His condensed, intuitive form of communication shakes off the constraints of predetermined verse and the tyranny of conventional notions of representational art. Working intently upon the data of his own sense experience, he attempts a cubist-like re-structuring of perception, a dissociation and rearrangement of the elements of concrete reality. Dispensing with normal narrative connections, he relies on rapid, compacted associations of sharply etched images, a sinuous, elliptical syntax, and rhythms and cadences directly expressive of a particular moment and voice. In 'Glass Grass' he speaks of how his fellow poets find his poems 'cryptic, crude, dis/ - tasteful, brutal, savage, bitter' (*RP* 131). 'The Ditch of Dawn' records the anguish he felt at the sectarian murder of a young twenty-year-old poet friend, Gerry McLaughlin, who lived about a mile away from Fiacc's home in Glengormley, and who was shot dead on his way to work in April 1975:

> How I admired your bravado
> Dandering down the road alone
> In the dark yelling, 'I'll see
> You again, tomorrow', but
>
> They pump six bullets into you.
>
> Now you are lying in a mud
> Puddle of blood, yelling.

'There is no "Goodbye",
No "Safe Home"
In this coffin country where
Your hands are clawed ...'   (*RP* 143)

The colloquial idiom, direct address and direct speech, along with the use of the present tense, recreate the remembered scene in all its painful vividness and immediacy. The open, relaxed movement of the first few lines is quickly arrested with the heavily stressed line that imitates, in its brutal simplicity, the pump-action gunfire that killed the young victim. The metre is slowed and broken with repeated, heavy stresses, and becomes more congested with the rhyming that begins with 'but', continues through 'pump' and 'bullets', and thickens in the closely-occurring 'mud', 'puddle' and 'blood'. With dream-like clarity, the event of the past is held in what appears to be an inescapable, timeless present:

How can I tell anyone
I'm born, born lying in
This ditch of a cold Belfast dawn
With the bullet-mangled body of
A dead boy
         And can't
Can't get away?

The ironic objectivity of the first part of the poem gives way to direct expression of personal pain, which is reminiscent of Beckett's bleak vision of birth astride of a grave. The poet, transfixed by grief, is unable to provide a resolution or move towards any kind of transcendent understanding of what has happened. Rather, the poem is aware of its own inadequacy, and the inadequacy of words generally ('There is no "Goodbye",/ No "Safe Home" ...). There is no emotion, no formal or aesthetic ritual, no language which can deal with the terrible event:

         A young
Brit soldier wanders
Over to my old
         Donkey honk
Of bitter *Miserere* of
Dereliction on the street:

'What is it mate, what is it?

WHAT'S WRONG?'   (*RP* 143–4)

The poet bitterly mocks his own lament ('my old/ Donkey honk') which is incapable of providing relief or solace, or conferring understanding or dignity on the senseless death. He is unable to lift his grief out of abjection. The religious connotations of '*Miserere*' mean nothing. The poem's modernist typographical self-consciousness, its broken lines, ellipses and use of capitalisation reflect both the crisis of modern society and the psychological disintegration of the speaker devastated by grief. The poet, far from attempting to distance himself from the event in order to achieve some control over his feelings and attain a new level of consciousness, wants instead to render the dramatic reality of suffering and loss, unmitigated, unmediated and unredeemed. Significantly, at the end of the poem, it is the British soldier who speaks and the poet who is silent, unable to answer the moment or rise above an intolerable situation. Powerless to resolve his acute personal predicament, the poet condemns himself to isolation and silence. In this respect, Fiacc specialises in a kind of poetry that is quite unlike the usual form of the elegy, which we expect to transcend death and loss, to restore equanimity by purging the emotions and rediscovering life's basic goodness: grief transformed into resignation and renewal.

Heaney, himself a master-elegist of the Troubles and a poet who throughout his career has been much concerned with the proper role of the poet in time of war, provides a useful point of comparison. Confronted with 'insoluble conflict', Heaney sees poetry as a way of achieving 'symbolic resolution', and prefaces his essay, 'Place and Displacement: Reflections on Some Recent Poetry from Northern Ireland' (1984), with a quotation from Anthony Storr's introduction to Jung's psychology:

> Jung describes how some of his patients, faced with what appeared to be an insoluble conflict, solved it by 'outgrowing' it, by developing a 'new level of consciousness'. He writes: 'Some higher or wider interest appeared on the patient's horizon, and through this broadening of his outlook the insoluble problem lost its urgency. It was not solved logically on its own terms, but faded out when faced with a new and stronger life urge.'
>
> The attainment of this new level of psychological development includes a certain degree of ... detachment from one's emotions. 'One certainly does feel the affect and is shaken and tormented by it, yet at the same time one is aware of a higher consciousness looking on which prevents one from becoming identical with the effect, a consciousness which regards the affect as an object, and can say "I *know* that I suffer."'[3]

Northern Irish poets, in Heaney's view, demonstrate this 'higher consciousness':

> The only reliable release for the poet was the appeasement of the achieved poem. In that liberated moment, when the lyric discovers its buoyant completion, when the timeless formal pleasure comes to its fullness and exhaustion, in that moment of self-justification and self-obliteration the poet makes contact with the plane of detached consciousness where he is at once intensified in his being and detached from his predicaments. It is this deeper psychological compulsion which lies behind the typical concern of Northern Irish poets with style, with formal finish, with linguistic relish and play.[4]

Rather than seeking to outgrow pain and conflict, Fiacc seems to want to 'identify himself with the effect', to immerse himself in suffering, in the urgencies of the present – which is also the eternal – moment. Historical process is brought to the standstill of the timeless present. The poem, incapable of development,

3   Seamus Heaney, 'Place and Displacement: Reflections on Some Recent Poetry from Northern Ireland', in Elmer Andrews (ed.), *Contemporary Irish Poetry: A Collection of Critical Essays* (Houndmills, Macmillan, 1992) pp. 124–44, 124.
4   Ibid., p. 129.

becomes the elaboration of a static image. Even Fiacc's entire oeuvre shows little development, each new volume re-cycling old poems that first made their appearance up to half a century or more earlier. No 'higher or wider interest' – history, heritage, cultural identity, tradition – is capable of providing a context, or broadening the poet's outlook so that his raw emotion might be absorbed and transformed. Since he is concerned with a static, unchanging human condition, causes and contexts are of secondary importance. Violence is diagnosed as a symptom of absolute evil lurking in the hearts of us all: 'I'm polluted/ With the poison of violence, born and bred into it/ ... / The Black is in my lungs now, and in my poems' ('Glass Grass', *RP* 130–1). He sees himself caught in a permanent condition from which there is no escape: 'I go on nightmaring/ Dead father running. There is a bull/ In the field' ('Son of a Gun', *RP* 87).

The experience of a Fiacc poem is pitiful and sentimental: it is not tragic. The ideal tragic vision can never be pessimistic, for pessimism negates life. The emotion aroused by a tragic poem is productive and insightful. But Fiacc's view of life appears unrelievedly pessimistic. His suffering is simply meaningless suffering. He arouses a useless pity that consumes itself in simply being felt. He is overpowered by circumstance, his fate is inevitable. Invariably, therefore, he adopts the persona of victim, often with a considerable degree of self-loathing and self-pity. The tellingly named 'Night of the Morning' ends with this Yeatsian self-presentation:

> Like a child outside of our
> Little town in time, crying
> 'Yes/No, this is my tribe,
> This is my clan. By these pre
> - arranged bones, I live and think,
> By this skull on a stick, I am
>
> 'Womb-wall-barricaded
> Bulldozed-down man.' (*RP* 134–5)

In 'Son of a Gun' he identifies with the suffering Christ, the poem's epigraph taken from François Mauriac: '*Woe to the boy for whom the nails, the crown of thorns, the sponge of gall were the first toy*' (*RP* 87). 'The Wrong Ones' adumbrates a similarly fixed, unchanging identity, and a universal image of a battle-scarred urban wasteland, divided and dangerous, where no help or home is available:

> I'll be a 'son of a gun' for ever now.
> For ever now I'll never be right. I'm one
> Of the Wrong Ones.
>   No one will help
> The rubber-bullet-collecting kids.
> No one will help the grim
> - faced teenaged British soldiers or young
> Cops, hating the being hated.
>   We all
> Go down the road now sharp and small
> As razor blades ...
>   I pick my steps across

> My backstreet childhood as a soldier would pick
> His steps across a little mine-filled field. (*RP* 137)

Unable to move beyond the surge of disruptive feeling, he condemns himself forever to the role of 'Son of a Gun', 'Wrong One', Christ-like martyr, 'Internee' (the title of another poem). The only available posture is that of abjection, as spelt out in 'Dirty Protest'. Dismissing genteel bourgeois sociology, the Fiacc persona looks for a more visceral grammar of hurt, a primitive language of the body:

> The social worker, the part-time
> Student teacher and/or
> University lecturer
> Volunteer to help –
> Fob me off with words
> As the prison GP with Aspro –
> But how can *they* tell where it hurts?
>
> My left ball, my right ball,
> My bellyhole, my arsehole?
>
> Fixed like the crucified: writhing;
> Not able to rest; immobile, yet
> Sucked down; yet yanked back up
> To wherever you are
>
> Blown up, thrown down born alive. (*RP* 146–7)

His most recent collection, *Semper Vacare* (1999), would seem to promise a more spacious vision, if the book's marketing blurb is anything to go by: 'Yet, taking its title from the dictum of Saint Benedict, *Semper Vacare* (translated as "always make space"), sees Fiacc deepening his vision with an emphasis on personal, human and natural renewal, of a world where life goes on even in the midst of despair and death.'[5] Jung's ideas about our need to distance ourselves from our emotions so that we can achieve 'higher consciousness' re-phrases in psychological language a similar process to that which Benedict formulated in spiritual and theological terms in his 'Rules' for monastic life in the sixth century – the need to separate ourselves from everyday human cares and contacts in order to make room for the essential, which is God. The Latin word 'vacare' has connotations of being vacant or empty, being at rest, being free and unoccupied, being in a state of contemplative openness to ultimate reality. It suggests withdrawal from outward temporal, functional preoccupations, placing ourselves at a distance from things so that we can survey them from a point of vantage without being swamped by partisan interests or personal feelings. However, this suggestion of wider perspectives is undercut by Fiacc's second epigraph. It is taken from a 1974 TV play by Alun Owen in which a detective apprehending a young English black stowaway tells him: '*There's no such place as Africa! That*

---

5   Padraic Fiacc, *Semper Vacare* (Belfast, Lagan Press, 1999). Hereafter abbreviated to *SV* and page references incorporated into the text.

boat's going to Belfast!' (*SV* 57) – lines which would seem to tell us that there's no such place as home, no possibility of escape or rest or renewal. The poem ends, not with the attainment of a broader, more serene, more purely contemplative attitude to life, but with re-assertion of humanity's inescapably determined, victim state, which renders all endeavour futile:

> You go, I go. Goodbye,
> Our fate never belongs to us alone,
>
> Always to others. (*SV* 58)

*

One of Fiacc's severest critics has been fellow poet and editor James Simmons, who took particular exception to Fiacc's *The Wearing of the Black: An Anthology of Contemporary Ulster Poetry*,[6] and the accompanying essay, 'Violence and the Ulster Poet'.[7] Simmons objected to what he perceived to be Fiacc's opportunistic and parasitic obsession with the violence of the Troubles, and to the apparent assumption that Ulster's history has left the Ulster poet with nothing else to write about but terror, panic, bullets and murder. In his review of *The Wearing of the Black*, Simmons alludes to the reasons Fiacc offers in his introduction for compiling the anthology: 'Mr Fiacc is "posing the question ... how deeply can contemporary violence enter a poet's inner being?" by presenting poets "touched by violence"'.[8] Having noted that Fiacc includes a far larger number of poems by himself than any other poet, Simmons caustically entitles his review 'The Man Most Touched', and proceeds to lambast the editor, not only for blatant self-aggrandisement and journalistic portentousness, but 'pretentiousness, bad taste and confusion'.[9] 'Most literary people I know', says Simmons, 'have little time for him; but he seems to be on good terms with a younger generation of Belfast poets. I respond to his intensity and sharp insight, although many poems tail off into hysteria, are not properly worked on.'[10] These strictures need not be altogether surprising coming from a fellow poet of such different background and outlook. Indeed, it would be hard to imagine two artistic temperaments more different than those of Fiacc and Simmons: Simmons, with his libertine philosophy, his concern to entertain and to be accessible, his articulate fluency and epigrammatic wit, his reliance on conventional poetic means; Fiacc, the exponent of a neurotic demotic of fragmented, elliptical intensities created in direct response to the chaos of immediate history, both personal and communal. The simplicity and naturalness of Simmons's own best verse, 'tough reasonableness and lyric grace/ together',[11] contrasts starkly with the bitter, raw emotion

---

6 Padraic Fiacc, *The Wearing of the Black: An Anthology of Contemporary Ulster Poetry* (Belfast, Blackstaff Press, 1974).

7 Padraic Fiacc, 'Violence and the Ulster Poet', *Hibernia* (6 Dec. 1974) p. 19.

8 James Simmons, 'The Man Most Touched', in *The Honest Ulsterman*, 46–47 (Nov. 1974 – Feb. 1975) pp. 66–71, 67.

9 Ibid., p. 68.

10 Ibid., p. 70.

11 James Simmons, 'Didn't He Ramble', in *Poems 1965–1986* (Loughcrew, The Gallery Press, 1986) p. 95. Hereafter abbreviated to *P* and page references incorporated into the text.

of Fiacc's. If Simmons's poetry is 'Constantly Singing',[12] Fiacc's is a 'Missa Terribilis'.[13]

Yet, Simmons, though in a different way, is as shocking as Fiacc, as bent on scandalising conventional morality as Fiacc is on disturbing bourgeois complacency about the nature of violence. For all their differences, each poet has staked his reputation on being the quintessential 'Honest Ulsterman': Fiacc, in his resolve to confront the horror of the Troubles head on, and to bear testimony to the evil of violence and the grim conditions of poverty and sectarian hatred in which it is spawned; Simmons, in the 'atrocious honesty' (blurb on back of *Constantly Singing*, 1980) of his confessional reflections on the pleasures and pains of love.

For Simmons, a bad odour surrounds the pessimistic modernist vision which has infected Fiacc and derives from T.S. Eliot. Simmons's long poem sequence, 'No Land is Waste', is a direct reply to Eliot's pessimism in 'The Waste Land'.

> I've knocked round London, and it puzzles me:
> Where does his lurid vision touch reality?
> 'What are the roots that clutch, what branches grow
> out of this stony rubbish? I don't know.
> What roots? What stony rubbish? What rats? Where?
> Visions of horror conjured out of air.[14]

Like Eliot's poem, Simmons's is also something of a symphonic composition, a montage of images, memories, portraits, dramatic scenes and musings. But where Eliot wanders across the barren landscape of a secularised existence seeking renewal, or where Fiacc conveys a static, nightmarish vision of Belfast, Simmons records, not the horror of life, but its essential goodness, its infinite variety and endless fascination: 'I felt, and still feel, life was good to me' (*JG* 41). The large cast of characters in 'The Waste Land' becomes absorbed into the poem's general symbolic pattern, but Simmons is chiefly interested in his characters as real live human beings. Contemptuously dismissive of Eliot's cerebral aloofness, Simmons finds no want of energy or zest for life in the hollow men of the contemporary world: '*Oh, Stearns, come round to meet the boys tonight,/ to see the hollow men get full and fight*' (*JG* 51). Like Eliot, Simmons re-works his sources. Section 10 of 'No Land is Waste' follows Part II, 'A Game of Chess', in

---

[12] James Simmons, *Constantly Singing* (Belfast, Blackstaff Press, 1980).

[13] Padraic Fiacc, *Missa Terribilis* (Belfast, Blackstaff Press, 1986). I am indebted to Norman Vance for pointing out that 'Missa Terribilis' (the '"Terrible" Mass') alludes to the Catholic Mass used for the Feast of the Dedication of the Basilicas of St Peter and St Paul on 18 November which takes its title from the first word of the Introit (Genesis 28. 17) where Jacob says 'Terribilis est locus iste: hic domi est, et porta coeli; et vocabitur aula Dei' (Terrible is this place: it is the house of God, and the gate of heaven; and it shall be called the court of God). Fiacc thus sets up the possibility that Belfast could be terrible in the religious sense of producing awe, and that it could therefore be considered as a gate of Heaven, capable of being celebrated as such in the ritual of verse. Alternatively, the religious connotations of the title may be taken ironically rather than piously: Belfast could be terrible because it is a hell-on-earth, its poetry a diabolic black mass of despair and death. Either way, Fiacc's title typifies a portentous, hieratic idiom which contrasts sharply with Simmons's light and unpretentious folksiness.

[14] James Simmons, *Judy Garland and the Cold War* (Belfast, Blackstaff, 1975) p. 41. Hereafter abbreviated to *JG* and page references incorporated into the text.

Eliot's poem, which follows Shakespeare's famous lines describing Cleopatra on her barge in Act 2 Scene ii of *Antony and Cleopatra*. Eliot wants to draw a contrast between the passionate and tragic Cleopatra whom Shakespeare describes in expansive, sunlit, natural surroundings ('The barge she sat in, like a burnished Throne,/ Burnt on the water …') and the hysterical, neurotic modern woman pictured in a dim interior setting, amid mirrored reflections and surrounded by art-works, more mock-heroic Belinda than heroic Cleopatra. Simmons turns her into a sexy young customer in a beauty parlour:

> The chair in which the lady now reclines
> is polished leather bound in clamps of chrome. (*JG* 51)

In Shakespeare: 'A strange invisible perfume hits the sense'; in Eliot: 'In vials of ivory and coloured glass/ Unstoppered, lurked her strange synthetic perfumes,/ Unguent, powdered, or liquid – troubled, confused/ And drowned the sense in odours …';[15] in Simmons:

> Not all the smells are beautiful, a faint
> witness of something scorching taints the air.
> But, oh, the fun of it. The comfort of being cared for
> without responsibility.
>   Infinite pleasure,
> guaranteed results, a price she can
> foresee and well afford. She will, she will
> be wonderful: a grateful customer. (*JG* 52)

Eliot's 'synthetic perfumes' loses the romantic connotations of Shakespeare's 'strange, invisible perfume', and the sudden, sensuous potency of Cleopatra's perfume is reduced to a 'confusion' and 'drowning' of the senses. Thus, Eliot emphasises the degeneration of an original energy. Simmons restores the sensual vitality of the Renaissance, freed of puritan guilt. Where Eliot is intent on diagnosing what is pitiful, vicious or pathological in modern civilisation, and is engaged in a process of agonised moral questioning, Simmons is content to register sheer delight in the life of the senses and the magic of the commonplace. In the final section of 'No Land is Waste', he declares his determination to trust to his own talent and not be swayed by outside influences, to dedicate himself to the hard discipline of creativity: 'Work is what matters, and knowing how to endure' (*JG* 58).

One of the most powerful and pervasive influences for any Northern Irish poet of modern times is Seamus Heaney, and it is against Heaney's pre-eminent presence that Simmons has felt compelled to define himself. Where Heaney's poetry is shaped by the traditional concerns of the Irish poet – history, myth, nation, identity, place – Simmons is absorbed by the here and now, by everyday middle-class life, by personal relations and the particular quality of individual experience. No fierce loyalties – whether to nation, church, family, history or place – inform Simmons' work. He has none of Heaney's (or Montague's, or

---

15 T.S. Eliot, 'The Waste Land', *The Complete Poems and Plays of TS Eliot* (London, Faber, 1981) p. 64.

even Hewitt's) pious regard for familial, tribal or communal inheritance, but sees himself as a rootless, sceptical, commonsensical individual, the archetypal 'Honest Ulsterman', unburdened by tradition or conventional morality. With its concentration on the personal and the domestic, the poetry is narrow in its range, and, even taking into consideration his two latest collections, *Mainstream* (1995) and *The Company of Children* (1999), there's not much development in tone, attitude or theme. His subjects are marriage, seduction, adultery, jealousy, lust, erotic daydream, divorce, renewal, memory, children, friends, poetry. These matters he approaches with a refreshing candour, resisting any temptation to strike romantic or heroic poses, other than ironically. In 'Written, Directed by and Starring …', he confesses:

> My break will come; but now the star's mature
> His parts need character and 'love' is out.
> He learns to smile on birth and death, to endure:
> It's strange I keep the old scripts lying about.
> …
> It's hard to start upon this middle phase
> when my first period never reached the screen,
> and there's no end now to my new screen-plays,
> they just go on from scene to scene to scene. (*P* 42)

Even in this relatively early poem from his second collection, *Late But in Earnest* (1967), the persona is middle-aged, retrospective as well as looking forward, openly accepting of his own mediocrity and failure. The poet stakes his appeal on being able to present sufficiently engaging 'character'. To this end, he adopts a variety of tones and attitudes – irony, self-mockery, bitter self-justification, wit and humour, rueful realism, didactic moralising, anger, tenderness – but the voice is consistently without cynicism or guile, expressing itself in an unpretentious, colloquially prosaic language that is technically competent but imaginatively low-key:

> I'm tempted into a Byronic fluency
> That might be fun, but seems a truancy
> From the true subject …
>   Clarity
> Is what I hunger for, along with truth
> And homeliness …[16]

This hunger for no-nonsense rational clarity is what links Simmons with the English Movement poets. As *New Lines* editor, Robert Conquest, opined in relation to post-war English poetry before the Movement, 'the most glaring fault awaiting correction' was 'the omission of the necessary intellectual component from poetry'[17] (Dylan Thomas being the obvious example of the unintellectual or irrational). In concert with the Movement, Simmons's poetry is aligned to

---

16 James Simmons, 'Living in Portrush', in *The Company of Children* (Cliffs of Moher, Salmon Publishing, 1999) p. 31. Hereafter abbreviated to *CC* and page references incorporated into the text.

17 Robert Conquest, 'Introduction', in *New Lines* (London, Macmillan, 1957).

everyday speech and experience, exhibits a similar suspicion of theory, abstraction, pretension and imprecise suggestiveness, a similar resistance to religious or metaphysical belief, a characteristically cautious, restrained, sometimes self-mocking tone, a facility for witty debunkery. But in 'For Philip Larkin', he ponders on the essential difference between himself and the chief of the Movementeers, accusing Larkin of merely playing at nihilism and despair: 'you relished what you hated':[18]

> You made a pact to tell no lies,
> Faustus of that bleak generation,
> and played at being terrified
> of life, and died before you died,
> a poet without inspiration,
> the object of the exercise.   (*M* 71)

Simmons echoes Saul Bellow's denunciation of modern pessimism in *Herzog*:

> Let us set aside the fact that such convictions in the mouths of safe, comfortable people playing at crisis, alienation, apocalypse and desperation, make me sick … We love apocalypses too much, and crisis ethics and florid extremism with its thrilling language.[19]

And, like Bellow, seeks redress in a reconstituted humanism, the liberal heresy of belief in man.

Like Hewitt, whom he admired, Simmons adopted a stance of prosaic ordinariness that risked producing a poetry of prosaic statement. Nevertheless, his best work is invigorated by an idiomatic and dramatic energy, and by keen observation and precise detailing. His reliance on conventional forms closes him off from more exciting and unpredictable poetic possibilities, but he repeatedly demonstrates an ability to handle the traditional resources of quatrain, sonnet, couplet, epigram and parable with economic wit and irony. Blurring the boundaries between poetry and popular song and balladry, he revamps our conception of public poetry. His commitment is to 'the word of life', the quintessential expression of which he hears in the music of the jazz and bluesmen whom he celebrates in 'Didn't He Ramble':

> But the word of life, if such a thing existed,
> Was there on record among the rubbish listed
> In the catalogues of Brunswick and H.M.V.,
> Healing the split in sensibility.
> Tough reasonableness and lyric grace
> Together, in poor man's dialect.
> Something that no one taught us to expect.
> Profundity without the po-face
> Of court and bourgeois modes. This I could use
> to live and die with. Jazz. Blues.   (*P* 95)

---

[18]   James Simmons, *Mainstream* (Upper Fairhill, Galway, Salmon Publishing, 1995) p. 70. Hereafter abbreviated to *M* and page references incorporated into the text.
[19]   Saul Bellow, *Herzog* (Harmondsworth, Penguin, 1985) pp. 316–17.

By embracing the blues aesthetic, which derives from slavery, Simmons identifies with a music that, whatever the quantum of racial agony, represents a glorious affirmation of unquenchable human spirit in the face of injustice and adversity. His readiness to include references to popular culture as well as to high cultural luminaries, along with his use of vernacular speech and tones, and the highly personal, confessional nature of his subject matter, bespeak an essentially democratic imagination keen to make its intellectual and emotional mark directly and immediately.

Though there are a number of fine Troubles poems ('Claudy', 'The Ballad of Ranger Best', 'The Ballad of Gerry Kelly: Newsagent'), 'Ulster Today', from his most political collection, *The Long Summer Still to Come* (1973), declares a fundamental political disinterest:

> Sitting at my desk among papers
> I wonder nothing that troubles the TV news
> moves me to write ...
> I have nothing to add:
> The stones hurt, the smiling boys are boys,
> The farcical and painful history of Ireland
> Is with us, unchanged. If the next bomb
> Kills *me* it will still be irrelevant.[20]

The confessional mode can at times seem wilfully – even chillingly – indifferent to the larger world beyond the self, as in 'Bloody Sunday':

> When speakers dissipate their breath
> demanding basic inalienable rights
> I know we are in for a boring night
> And morning paper headlines of death.   (*LSSTC* 20)

For Simmons, political ideology is merely the new Puritanism, inherently authoritarian and life-denying:

> Social reform by revolution
> Is the morning's great pollution.
> In new disguise, trying to infect
> My infant liberty, I see a sect
> Of hateful puritans. Hate! Hate!
> Is the only hope they contemplate.
>   ('To Certain Communist Friends', *LSSTC* 18)

Intransigent or blinkered alignment with sectional interests can produce no true freedom. The only real 'revolution' lies, not in politics, but in culture. The Belfast-based arts magazine that he inaugurated in October 1969, *The Honest Ulsterman*, originally had as its subtitle (until withdrawn on police advice) 'a handbook for a revolution'. For Simmons, meaningful social change could only

---

[20]   James Simmons, *The Long Summer Still to Come* (Belfast, Blackstaff Press, 1973) p. 22. Hereafter abbreviated to *LSSTC* and page references incorporated into the text.

be brought about by fundamental change in individual hearts and minds, by commitment to life rather than death, creativity rather than hate:

> Bill Broonzy, Armstrong, Basie, Hodges, Chet
> Baker, Garner, Tommy Ladnier,
> Jelly Roll Morton, Bessie Smith, Bechet,
> And Fats Waller, the scholar-clown of song
> Who sang *Until the real Thing Comes Along.*
> Here was the risen people, their feet
> Dancing, not out to murder the elite.   ('Didn't He Ramble', *P* 96)

Simmons's confidence in the resources of the personal life, his self-conscious individualism, is inevitably accompanied by impatience with the usual Irish piety surrounding issues of religion, history, nation. In 'Cloncha', a visit to the ancient monastic site near Culdaff in Co. Donegal is remembered, not for its archaeo-logical or historical interest, but for the erotic dalliance between the two visitors, the poet and his girlfriend, as they search for the ruins. Section 3 of the poem consists of a litany of place-names in the Inishowen peninsula which, again, are recalled, not for their cultural or historical significance, but as representing the co-ordinates of the speaker's youthful adventuring:

> Our hero's Arcady was here
> with the bleak moors and strands,
> for forty years near enough,
> the Derry hinterland
> between Foyle and Swilly,
> from Malin to Buncrana
> to Greencastle to Shrove,
> Moville and Carndonagh.   (*P* 157–8)

Commenting on the importance of place to Protestant poets (Yeats's Co Sligo, Hewitt's Glens of Antrim, Richard Murphy's Connemara and High Island) Terence Brown suggests that all such expressions of the Protestant 'topological imperative' can be read 'as insecure assertions of an Irish identity established through association with place that a man or woman of Catholic nationalist stock feels no need to make'.[21] However, when Simmons 'searched for anecdotes/ to establish his rights there' (*P* 158), and recites his family connections in the area, his conclusion is that 'Nothing of this was his or him' (*P* 159). Such ironic distancing of himself from the usual topographical and genealogical claims in Anglo-Irish poetry leads to this forthright re-figuring of Irish landscape, not in terms of mythology, ancestry or community, but the individual's private life, the sensuous excitements of 'the present moment':

> All he could offer honestly
> was a private childhood, secrecy,
> a boy drifting alone through fern
> forests and alder groves, smoking

---

21 Terence Brown, 'Poets and Patrimony: Richard Murphy and James Simmons', in Gerald Dawe and Edna Longley (eds.), *Across a Roaring Hill* (Belfast, Blacklstaff, 1985) pp. 182–95, 182.

> his first woodbine above Carrig Cnoc,
> a consciousness apart from ancestors
> and local inhabitants, a stranger
> at home in the present moment
> happily, then as now. He was luring
> a girl near his heart in this
> occupied country of his. (*P* 159)

His 'occupied country' is his heart, not Ireland: not politics, but the personal life, is the truly important subject of poetry: 'I sing of natural forces,/ marriages, divorces' (*P* 161). He can write with great feeling and sensitivity about the various places where he has lived and worked and visited throughout his life, but there's no 'great good place' that grounds his whole being in the way the mythologised landscapes of Heaney and Montague do.

Heaney represents the kind of tribal piety that Simmons detested, as his controversial essay, 'The Trouble with Seamus', makes clear. In the essay, Simmons sets out to explain why he doesn't 'get much pleasure'[22] from Heaney, accusing him of either endorsing a tribal position or making vague gestures towards the inevitability of carnage. Sympathy with the tribe, Simmons argues, has been allowed to blunt the moral sense and corrupt humane judgement, resulting in a culpable ambiguity in Heaney's response to atrocity. Heaney, according to Simmons, is an old stick-in-the-mud whose muddled political thinking has disqualified him as 'an ally in the general struggle to liberalise and reform Ulster'.[23] Resorting to verse parody in 'Intruder on Station Island', Simmons shows himself no more predisposed to take account of the tensions in Heaney than he was in the essay. In the poem, Simmons unceremoniously intrudes upon Heaney's sincere self-questioning about being a poet in 'Station Island'. Heaney's poem consists of a series of dream encounters between the pilgrim poet and a number of familiar ghosts. In Simmons's version, supposedly spoken by Heaney, another ghost makes an appearance:

> I expected the next ghost to shake hands
> Would equal in fame my previous advisers.
> Yeats? Swift? No, they were Protestants.
>
> Imagine my chagrin to feel leather, on bone,
> A boot up my arse from a former rugby player,
> Shade of a Catholic policeman I had known. (*M* 82)

Using this unlikely and unwelcome poetic commentator, Simmons proceeds to puncture the restrained Dantean tones of Heaney's original. Adopting the *terza rima* format that Heaney took from Dante, Simmons mocks Heaney's grand cultural mission and, with Kavanaghesque irreverence, wonders at the absences in Heaney's work: where are the Protestants? Where are the ordinary human impulses?

---

22 James Simmons, 'The Trouble with Seamus', in Elmer Andrews (ed.), *Seamus Heaney: A Collection of Critical Essays* (Houndmills, Macmillan, 1992) pp. 39–66, 39.
23 Ibid., p. 50.

And weemin? Ye must have had many a wee frolic
With hot things in Harvard and the West Coast,
But never a mention, or if there is it's symbolic! (*M* 82)

Heaney stands accused of exploiting the exotic appeal of rural activities and
artefacts, of history and etymology, in order to make a name for himself and
secure an international market. Alluding to 'An Open Letter' in which Heaney
objected to being labelled a 'British' poet, Simmons ridicules Heaney's uncharac-
teristic outburst of patriotic feeling with reminders that Heaney uses an English
publishing house, and that for all his protesting that his 'passport's green',[24] he
didn't refuse permission to have his poems included in *The Penguin Book of
Contemporary British Poetry* (1982). It is Craig Raine, editor of the aforesaid
anthology, who helps Heaney escape, Sweeney-like, from the intruder's uncom-
fortable questions:

How to escape without giving offence was my pain!
To aid me the air stirred my blow-dried hair
As a helicopter whose pilot was Craig Raine

Descended. The nonentity melted in whipped air. (*M* 83)

Simmons's deflationary parody is clever and funny, but it is unfairly reductive.
Heaney's attitude to the conventional pieties of his Catholic upbringing isn't one
of simple unquestioning reverence as Simmons implies. Simmons concentrates
only on Heaney's persistent nostalgia for a primordial home and takes no account
of how that longing is crossed with a contrary, very modern Heideggerean feeling
of 'not-being-at-home'.

To Heaney, Montague and other poets from a Catholic nationalist background,
the value of roots is that they can provide anchorage and stability, a link with 'a
shared and diminished culture'.[25] For Simmons, however, roots merely threaten
to strangle the free spirit and crush natural human feeling. The first stanza of
'A Risen Poet: A Review' summarises the poet's attitude: 'About filthy roots he
never/ has much to say –/ the charcoal burner's hut's/ light years away' (*JG* 6).
Another poem, 'Roots', is an emblematic and cautionary, if somewhat fanciful,
tale about a young Presbyterian girl who became pregnant by a circus performer
in Coleraine and as a consequence had to endure the usual opprobrium of her
family and community. Simmons's libertarian outlook sets him at odds with the
narrowness and intolerance of puritan Ulster. Only by severing the bonds with
such a debilitating inheritance can love and humanity flourish: 'We married,
though, and live in Queensland now,/ as free as if we'd dropped out of the sky'
(*P* 33).

A number of poems turn on the apocalyptic idiom of his own tribe's evan-
gelical wing. In 'The Farther Shore' an old woman contemplates the 'old phrase
from the hymnal', but rejects its otherworldly emphasis, insisting instead on the

[24] Seamus Heaney, 'An Open Letter', in Field Day Theatre Company, *Ireland's Field Day* (London, Hutchinson, 1985) pp. 23–9.
[25] Seamus Heaney, 'The Sense of Place', *Preoccupations: Selected Prose 1968–1978* (London, Faber, 1980) p. 141.

value of this actual human world, even though it exists for her now mainly as memories:

> My mind is brimming always
> With childhood, children, grandchildren; but I want no more
> Of the good life God gave me. The farther shore
> Is a real place where we spent our holidays.   (*P* 188)

'The Harvest is Past' also takes its title from an evangelical text. Here, the message of the prophets of doom is challenged by the poet's direct counter-assertion of the value of the present moment, his re-affirmation of the basic goodness of life, and grateful celebration, at this middle stage of his life, of his wife's pregnancy. 'Eden' re-writes the biblical story of paradise lost, casting a joyless and judgmental God in the role of the outcast, the denier of life and humanity:

> The unprejudiced world was what those two lacked,
> And of course they avoided the huge pathetic back
> Of God. To this day He is standing there,
> Banished. There *was* a world elsewhere.   (*P* 152)

The poem which immediately follows, 'After Eden', re-constructs the Fall in the highly personal terms of the poet's expulsion from the family home after an affair, and tells the story of the blame-game between man and woman that began with Adam and Eve.

As well as Protestant religious texts, Simmons re-figures Protestant political texts. His poem 'Ulster Says Yes' plays on Paisley's famously rejectionist mantra of 'Ulster Says No'. Simmons acknowledges Protestant guilt and injustice, and goes some way towards recognising the justification of direct action, but calls for a sense of proportion:

> One Protestant Ulsterman
> Wants to confess this:
> We frightened you Catholics, we gerrymandered,
> We applied injustice.
>
> However, we weren't Nazis or Yanks,
> So measure your fuss
> Who never suffered like Jews or Blacks,
> Not here, not with us ...   (*P* 197)

From Simmons's low-key common sense perspective, the claims of poets such as Heaney and Paulin, who have suggested a connection between the repression suffered by artists in Russia and Eastern Europe under Communism and the situation of poets in Unionist Northern Ireland seem exorbitant. As Simmons comments in his essay on Heaney: 'When Heaney compares himself to Owen and Mandelstam ... he is surely on a wrong tack. Mandelstam would not have suffered in Ulster and Owen would have been with the Peace People.'[26] If, in 'Ulster Says Yes', he questions the popular rhetoric of civil rights, he does so,

---

[26] 'The Trouble with Seamus', p. 64.

not from a sectarian, tribal standpoint, but to preserve the rational spirit of Enlightenment secularism.

Simmons' practice of refurbishing and reinvigorating prior texts is undertaken not only in relation to those of his own tribe, but the master texts of Gaelic tradition as well. 'The Old Woman of Portrush' is a re-writing of the ninth-century poem 'Lament of the Old Woman of Beare'. In the ancient poem, the old woman is represented as a nun bemoaning her past youth, and associated with the goddess of sovereignty, with Irish topography and landscape, especially the Beare peninsula in Co. Cork, and with harsh weather, winter winds, mountains and wilderness. In Simmons's poem, despite the passing reference to his old woman as 'Kathleen ni Houlihan' (*P* 170), she is less a sovereignty figure, more a pagan fertility goddess, or goddess of place, but primarily a real old local woman whose intense sensuality is implicitly contrasted with the puritanical Protestant environment in which she is located, much as Austin Clarke, in his version of the legend in 'The Young Woman of Beare', contrasts his transgressive female figure with the puritanical Catholicism of his time. Simmons's poem is an effective piece of ventriloquism. His old woman of Portrush is a highly attractive figure, spirited, sharp-sighted and unsentimental, her picturesque demotic veering at times into comically scandalous self-denigration:

> I drank champagne with toreadors
> who fucked me stupid through the night.
> Now with retired dames I doze
> in the TV lounge's frigid light.   (*P* 172)

Another example of Simmons's interest in re-appropriating Gaelic tradition for his own contemporary purposes is his poem 'Lament for a Dead Policeman', a re-working of Eibhlín Dubh's famous eighteenth-century *Caoineadh Airt Uí Laoghaire*. In his version, Simmons sets out to include a murdered RUC man in the tradition of Irish keening, lament and martyrology. Art O'Leary was a Kerryman who fell foul of the Penal Laws, was hunted down by the Sheriff of Cork and shot by Crown forces. Simmons' dead Catholic RUC man, shot by the IRA, is lamented by both his devoted Protestant wife and his Catholic sister. Again, the emphasis falls, not on politics, but on the personal, human story of loss and grief, which Simmons distributes even-handedly on either side of the sectarian divide.

The tradition of Irish balladry is invoked in another poem, 'Claudy', which deals directly with the violence of the Troubles, describing the effects of three IRA car-bombs which exploded in the small Co. Derry town of Claudy in 1972, killing nine people, including three children. The poem was written to be sung and, in its vernacular simplicity, its chilling understatement, its controlled anger and deeply felt compassion, it has become one of the most widely known of Troubles poems. The poem opens on a peaceful rural scene. Then the explosions. Then the laconic descriptions of individual men, women and children suddenly destroyed or terribly injured as they go about their daily business. The reserved style heightens the horror. With bitter irony, Simmons drives home his sense of the absurd and grotesque waste of human life.

Fiacc and Simmons are contrasting types of the 'Honest Ulsterman'. Where

Fiacc's honesty lies in the dark, neurotic intensities of his apprehension of unchanging evil and violence, the power of Simmons's poetry consists in a buoyant and virile optimism, a deeply rooted confidence in humanity, that carry him from poignant elegy, through moods of anguish at marriage gone sour, to joyous celebration of new love. Fiacc is a product of the modern poetic revolution in Europe and America, his poetry expressive of an essential homelessness. Simmons is accessible, shrewd and funny, the laureate of a fundamental at-homeness in the world – even the troubled world of Ulster. Where Fiacc's poetry, in its discontinuity, fragmentation and conflict, contains the tragic recognition that 'home' has disappeared and that he is condemned to a perpetual state of Heideggerean estrangement, anxiety and 'uncanniness', Simmons, without recourse to the Heideggerean doctrine of 'blood and soil', affirms the possibility of an authentic Being-at-home, a contented dwelling without roots.

Chapter 6

MICHAEL LONGLEY'S ECOPOETICS

Heaney and Longley: Nativism and Naturalism

In Heaney's poetry, nature, childhood and the collective past are powerfully fused. His 'sense of place' stems from ideas of belonging to and dwelling in 'one dear perpetual place'. The landscape inspires Heaney, not just because it is natural (in the ecological or universalist sense), but also because it is native. His early readings – and creative misreadings – of Wordsworth serve to clarify his own relationship with place and allow him to claim the English poet as a poetic fosterer. Commenting on Wordsworth's famous passage in *The Prelude* –

> The hiding places of my power
> Seem open; I approach, and then they close,
> I see by glimpses now; when age comes on,
> May scarcely see at all; and I would give,
> While yet we may, as far as words can give,
> A substance and a life to what I feel:
> And I would enshrine the spirit of the past
> For future restoration.[1]

– Heaney elaborates an idea of poetry as archaeology, an exhumation not only of personal but collective memory:

> Implicit in these few lines of poetry is a view of poetry which I think is implicit in the few poems I have written that give me any right to speak: poetry as divination, poetry as revelation of the self to the self, as restoration of the culture to itself; poems as elements of continuity, with the aura and authenticity of archaeological finds, where the buried shard has an importance that is not diminished by the importance of the buried city; poetry as a dig, a dig that ends up bearing plants.[2]

In attempting to identify the 'hiding places of his power', Heaney extends Wordsworth's personal focus to more social concerns, revealing his own essentially psychological and cultural sense of place. What is lost is a specifically human and historical landscape. Innocence, security, peace, happiness, plenitude are

---

[1]   William Wordsworth, *The Prelude*, Book XI, lines 336–43 (Oxford, Oxford University Press, 1970) p. 215.
[2]   Seamus Heaney, 'Feeling into Words', in *Preoccupations: Selected Prose 1968–1978* (Faber, London, 1980) p. 41.

imprinted, first on a particular landscape, and then, in a powerful extension, on a particular (Gaelic) era of the rural past, which is now associated with a lost identity, lost relations and lost certainties. The emphasis falls on the social and linguistic constructedness of nature, to which the poet turns in a time of dispossession and social division. His description of fellow Irish poet, John Montague, as clearly applies to himself: Montague's place names, says Heaney,

> are rather sounding lines, rods to plumb the depths of a shared and diminished culture. They are redolent not just of his personal life but of the history of his people, disinherited and dispossessed. What are most resonant and most cherished in the names of Montague's places are their tribal etymological implications.[3]

Like Montague's, Heaney's experience of landscape is erotic, chthonic, pagan: 'among the stones,/ under a bearded cairn/ a love-nest is disturbed,/ catkin and bog-cotton tremble// as they raise up/ the cloven oak-limb,/ I stand at the edge of the centuries/ facing a goddess'.[4] The present is impregnated by the past. The poems about bog bodies and fertility rites testify to Heaney's fascination with the ancient feminine religion of Northern Europe in which the landscape becomes 'a memory, a piety, a loved mother'.[5] His are haunted, whispering landscapes filled with the crepitating murmur of 'soft voices of the dead',[6] traversed by the ghostly figures of servant boy, the 'moustached dead'[7] and the old mound-dwellers. Nature is part of an archaic, unchanging world of immanence. Heaney may start off with careful, empirical description, but the thrust of his work is towards the mythic and transcendent. Nature is equated with the goddess; it is bride to the human bridegroom; it is Nerthus, Earth Mother, Mother Ireland.

Longley's imagination serves no such pagan queen, no mystique of the national, no mythic or tribal imperatives. Where Heaney speaks out of a shared historical experience, with a religious – recognisably Catholic – sense of his vocation, Longley aspires to a different kind of authority based on individual perception, and the tact and fidelity of his devotion to the details of the world around him. Where Heaney's Co. Derry is conceived in essentially communal terms, as the ground of meaning and identity, Longley's West is a wonderland that is inexhaustibly rich and strange, a constant challenge to the poet's powers of imaginative understanding and formal inventiveness. Longley's approach can thus never be anything other than open and improvisatory, its authority guaranteed by the elegance and precision of his expression. Where Heaney is always conscious of the 'public' role of the poet, and has probed and debated that role in his poems and essays over the years, Longley is not exercised in the same way by questions about the poet's responsibilities to society. He has no interest in either politicising the terrain or in reading it politically or historically. His poems are sprinkled with place-names, but Longley's place-names do not come freighted with political significance. 'On Slieve Gullion' rehearses the ancient lore

---

3   Seamus Heaney, 'The Sense of Place', *Preoccupations*, p. 141.
4   Seamus Heaney, 'Kinship', *North* (London, Faber, 1975) p. 42.
5   Heaney, 'The Sense of Place', p. 141.
6   Seamus Heaney, 'Gifts of Rain', *Opened Ground: Poems 1966–1996* (Faber, London, 1998) p. 52.
7   Seamus Heaney, 'Bog Oak', *Opened Ground*, p. 44.

of place, but where for Heaney, 'hoarder of common ground',[8] these stories have a part to play in the creation of an Irish cultural identity, Longley feels removed from the old heroic legends, as much of a stranger as the British soldier who 'sweats up Slieve Gullion'.[9] 'Because of my English connection' (his parents were Londoners who moved to Belfast in 1927), Longley explained in a 1996 interview, 'I am slightly ill at ease in Ireland, and the same applies in England because I am from Ireland. In this community which I am still exploring and trying to understand I still feel a bit of an outsider'.[10] This simultaneous understanding of native tradition and distance from it allows for a kind of complex seeing that Longley valued in the poetry of Louis MacNeice:

> Because of his Irish and English viewpoints MacNeice was able to respond with flexibility and objectivity to the complexities of Ireland, her 'jumble of opposites', her 'intricacies of gloom and glint'.[11]

Belfast is where Longley was brought up and where he worked (as Arts Council official, 1970–91), but the holiday cottage that he has rented for many years in Carrigskeewaun, Co. Mayo is his 'home from home'. In a 1995 interview, he observed: 'Home is Belfast. Belfast is home. I love the place. The city, the hills around it, County Down, County Antrim. My home from home is in Mayo. But home is Belfast ... My sense of Ireland continues to develop as I discover more of it. It's as simple as that ... I hate the notion that there are degrees of Irishness'.[12] As Alan Peacock remarks: 'His two homes (and in this open, non-exclusivist attitude there could logically be more) are not therefore alternatives, but foci within a network of experiences, judgements, choices and relations'.[13]

In Irish literary history 'the West' is an idealised locale, the place of authentic, primordial 'Irishness'. The rural cottage in the West signified historic continuity, roots in the soil, the ancestral home. It formed the iconic basis of the idealisation of rural family life, which was regarded as the cornerstone of the nation. Artists such as Paul Henry, ideologues such as De Valera, and commercial interests such as the Irish Tourist Board have all contributed to the popularisation of the imagery of the West, and the transmutation of the Irish cottage into a romanticised and clichéd symbol of Irish nationalism. Longley's West, however, is a personally imagined world, freed of territorial significance and national meaning. Testimony to the provisional nature of his dwelling in the West is the fact that his Mayo 'home from home' has been for many years a cottage that he has rented rather than owned. No abstract iconographic place, no idealised pastoral idyll, the West in Longley's poems is visualised in terms of specific, carefully observed details:

8   Seamus Heaney, 'Gifts of Rain', p. 52
9   Michael Longley, 'On Slieve Gullion', *Collected Poems* (London, Jonathan Cape, 2006) p. 158. Hereafter abbreviated to *CP* and page references incorporated into the text.
10 'Interview with Michael Longley' (Neil Johnston), *Belfast Telegraph*, 30 Jan. 1996.
11 Michael Longley, 'The Neolithic Light: A Note on the Irishness of Louis MacNeice', in Douglas Dunn (ed.), *Two Decades of Irish Writing* (Cheadle Hulme, Carcanet Press, 1975) pp. 101–2.
12 'An Interview with Michael Longley', by Dermot Healy, *The Southern Review*, 31 (July 1995) 558–9.
13 Alan Peacock, 'Introduction', in Alan J. Peacock and Kathleen Devine (eds.), *The Poetry of Michael Longley* (Gerrards Cross, Colin Smythe, 2000) p. xv.

> Beneath a gas-mantle that the moths bombard,
> Light that powders at a touch, dusty wings,
> I listen for news through the atmospherics,
> A crackle of sea-wrack, spinning driftwood,
> Waves like distant traffic, news from home ...   ('The West', *CP* 69)

The balancing phrases that end each stanza – 'News from home' and 'home from home' – challenge and complicate any simple understanding of the meaning of 'home': the speaker, self-consciously listening and observing, attempts to locate himself in relation to two homes. Sitting in his cottage, he is haunted by intimations of death and violence, the fragility of life: moths 'bombard' the gas-mantle; light 'powders, at a touch, dusty wings'; the internal rhymes in 'atmospherics', 'crackle' and 'sea-wrack' contain the echo of gunshots; driftwood is 'spinning' like a gunshot victim; 'waves like distant traffic' suggests the way the poet can be in two places at the same time. Longley's situation in the West is not an absconding from, or betrayal of, his Belfast home. Rather, 'home' and 'home from home', Belfast and the West, must be read together simultaneously because these categories are mutually constitutive and contingent. Traditionally, the private and interior space of the home has been imagined as a safe place removed from the political tensions of the public world. But Longley complicates such simple binary thinking. His 'homes' have porous walls. He blurs the boundaries between private and public space as he does between 'home' and 'home from home'. Thus, in 'Wounds', a 'shivering boy ... wandered in' (*CP* 62) from the violent streets to desecrate the domestic order of the home; while in 'Wreaths', a civil servant 'was preparing an Ulster fry for breakfast/ When someone walked into the kitchen and shot him' (*CP* 118). Similarly, in 'The West', the public news from 'home' infiltrates the private space of the 'home from home'. The cottage in the West is a place of both rest and disturbance. A sense of global interconnectedness undoes the usual binaries of inner and outer, urban and rural, East and West, North and South. The second stanza moves from the poet listening for news from home to watching himself through a 'sandy lens'. By distancing himself from 'home' he creates a space for new possibilities of self to emerge. In probing an alternative 'home', he also probes an alternative self. The watched self, which is absorbed by, and emerges from, the landscape, is described as 'Materialising out of the heat-shimmers'. Longley's West unsettles and expands identity, which forever eludes full definition: he finds his way 'for ever along/ The path to this cottage'. This emergent sense of self owes nothing to cultural myth and everything to the concrete particulars of the place he loves: 'its windows,/ Walls, sun and moon dials'. The reference to 'sun and moon dials', while existing credibly as naturalistic description, ultimately places the cottage in a vast cosmological context far beyond the frames of any particular cultural myth or political ideology.

Another poem, 'Remembering Carrigskeewaun', reverses the perspective of 'The West', and emphasises the elsewhereness and precariousness of the Mayo 'home from home':

> Home is a hollow between the waves,
> A clump of nettles, feathery winds,
> And memory no longer than a day

When the animals came back to me
From the townland of Carrigskeewaun,
From a page lit by the Milky Way. (*CP* 170)

In finding 'home' in the diverse particulars of locale, in epiphanic 'spots of time', the poet deconstructs totalising, centralising concepts of home. 'Home' has no more certainty than 'a hollow between the waves'; it is understood in terms of process rather than as a fixed and given reality. It comes off the 'page', an inevitably linguistic construct, but it is not merely a matter of language: it is closely associated with the waves, the plants, the animals, the winds and stars. The allusion to the 'Milky Way', like the reference to 'sun and moon dials' in 'The West', situates home in the context of the whole created universe. The poetry, we might say, negotiates with natural reality what 'home' might be, and, in doing so, constructs a perspective whereby human life is viewed in wide ecological contexts. This perspective defines Longley's ecocentric sense of home and history, which, as I shall argue, is expressed not only conceptually but also in terms of poetic method, and carries with it its own kind of political comment.

Dwelling Poetically

Eco-poetics asks in what respects a poem may be a making (Greek *poiesis*) of the dwelling-place – the pre-fix eco- is derived from Greek *oikos*, "the home or place of dwelling"[14]   (Jonathan Bate, 2000)

For Longley, the notion of home is not based on birthright or divine sanction; it isn't a given: home always has to be constructed, built up through a process of personal, emotional and imaginative attachment. In this respect, Heidegger, often hailed as a precursor of contemporary ecocriticism, is relevant. The later Heidegger returned obsessively to a phrase used by the German Romantic poet Friedrich Hölderlin: 'poetically man dwells on this earth'. 'Poetry', Heidegger asserts, 'as the authentic gauging of the dimension of dwelling, is the primal form of building. Poetry first of all admits man's dwelling into its very nature, its presencing being. Poetry is the original admission of dwelling.'[15] Authentic human existence depends on 'dwelling', a term which he invokes against both subjective idealism ('poetic dwelling is a dwelling "on this earth"'[16]) and Cartesian dualism, which had effectively dismantled the organic universe, driving a wedge between subject and object, and establishing the rationale for a view of the earth as valuable only insofar as it could be mastered and exploited. Poetry builds up the very nature of dwelling because it works through 'presencing' not representation: it is a form of being. Longley exemplifies the Heideggerean idea of language as a revealing or unconcealing of the essence of nature, a conjuring up of the condition of dwelling. The *Dasein* of the flora and fauna about which

---

[14] Jonathan Bate, *The Song of the Earth* (London, Picador, 2000) p. 75.
[15] '… Poetically Man Dwells …', in Martin Heidegger, *Poetry, Language, Thought*, trans. Albert Hofstadter (New York, Harper Colophon, 1971) pp. 211–29, 227.
[16] Ibid., p. 218.

Longley writes so sensitively and precisely is unconcealed in the *Dasein* of his poems, in the directness with which they speak the language of the earth. He becomes a dweller by seeking to know and celebrate an immediate, specific place in Co. Mayo, his 'home from home', as fully and honestly as possible, to bring to it the patient, respectful observation and inquiry of the natural historian, the undeviating attentiveness and delight of the lover contemplating his loved one. Through poetry he wants to live as close to the land as possible, to be in touch with its earth, its waters, its winds, its plants and animals, to learn its ways, to be guided by its laws, to make its rhythms his own. Nature is not simply made the vehicle for feelings originating in himself. He adjusts himself to things, not things to himself. His relationship is not one of possession, imposition, domination or superiority. Rather, he grants land and plants and animals their separateness, independence and autonomy, their 'otherness', acknowledging their resistance to anthropomorphic control. That is why his poetry is sometimes obscure, its connections too fractionally achieved for easy readerly consumption.

'Galapagos' is a strange sort of love-poem which uses the metaphysical conceit of treating the loved one as newly discovered land.

> Now you have scattered into islands –
> Breasts, belly, knees, the mount of Venus,
> Each a Galapagos of the mind
> Where you, the perfect stranger, prompter
> Of throw-backs, of hold-ups in time,
>
> Embody peculiar animals –
> The giant tortoise hesitating,
> The shy lemur, the iguana's
>
> Slow gaze ...   (*CP* 49)

Where John Donne's lady in 'To His Mistress Going to Bed' is held in the confident gaze of the male speaker, in 'Galapagos' it is the 'homesick scientist' on board the *Beagle* who is the object of 'the iguana's/ Slow gaze'. Everything in this transitional location is undermined, dislocated and provisional. Neither the loved one, 'scattered into islands' as strange and remote as the Galapagos, nor the landscape is amenable to moralised description or coherent narrative. The structure of a Longley poem is rarely classically sequential but more characteristically a matter of 'throw-backs, of hold-ups in time'. Instead of narrative we have lists, taxonomies, patterns, patchworks and networks. Instead of identity we have 'scattering', 'unravelling', evanescence and vanishing. Landscape, as the poem of that title asserts, is 'A place of dispersals':

> Here my imagination
> Tangles through a turfstack
> Like skeins of sheep's wool:
> Is a bull's horn silting
> With powdery shells.
>
> I am clothed, unclothed
> By racing cloud shadows,
> Or else disintegrate

> Like a hillside neighbour
> Erased by sea mist. (*CP* 91)

Here, Longley speaks not for settled and rooted identity, but for a self in process, of being absorbed by its surroundings. Contrary to Heaney's faith in the grounding force of place, Longley's landscape undoes the settled nature of an identity rooted in its own place of origin. Neither the self nor the environment in which it is situated is stable, but contradictory subjects that shift and change within different frames of interpretation or areas of experience. The fluid, associative structures, the deliquescence of language, the changes of angle of vision, the subtle syntactical manoeuvres suggestive of the movement of the poet's thoughts deconstruct any formulation which would imply the mind's control of a shifting, independent world. In a world of flux and mingling, the landscape can only be read momentarily, in glimpses or snatches:

> For seconds, dawn or dusk,
> The sun's at an angle
> To read inscriptions by:
> The splay of the badger
> And the otter's skidmarks
>
> Melting into water
> Where a minnow flashes:
> A mouth drawn to a mouth
> Digests the glass between
> Me and my reflection.

The 'readings' can never be gathered into 'grand narratives' of place, history or culture. Marks melt into water; the light is only right 'for seconds'; subject and object converge and coalesce, dissolve in water, itself fluid and transparent.

In 'Metamorphoses' ecological time and process challenge human epistemological concepts:

> A boulder locked in a cranny,
> A head without a face, she waits
> For rain to hollow out a font
> And fill her eye in, blink by blink. (*CP* 140)

Longley's ecohistory confounds the relative boundedness and narrowness of the usual human, andropocentric perspectives, confirming Andrew Dobson's introductory remarks in *The Green Reader*: 'The science of ecology teaches us that we are part of a system that stretches back into an unfathomable past and reaches forward into an incalculable future.'[17]

---

[17] Andrew Dobson (ed.), *The Green Reader* (London, 1991) p. 8.

The Naïve and the Sentimental

'Poets will either *be* nature, or they will *seek* lost nature.'[18]
(Freidrich Schiller, 1795)

In his essay, 'On Naïve and Sentimental Poetry', which has become something of a foundational text of 'Green Studies', Schiller distinguishes between two kinds of poetry, the 'naïve' and the 'sentimental': the 'naïve' reflecting an originary, childlike sense of oneness with nature, the 'sentimental' referring to a more self-conscious, self-reflective (rather than excessively emotional) relationship in which one's feelings *about* nature – the yearning for oneness – signifies alienation from nature. 'Naïve' poets (Homer, Goethe) were realistic, affirmative; 'sentimental' poets were elegists for whom poetry was always a metaphysics of loss, rupture, distance. For Schiller, 'culture should lead us back to nature',[19] the exemplary poetic form being the pastoral idyll.

Carrigskeewaun is Longley's Arcadia, a kind of modern pastoral, an alternative to the tensions of urban life in Belfast. 'Carrigskeewaun', Longley says, 'is unbelievably beautiful, it's the most magical place in the world for me. It's the Garden of Eden and I often think about it.'[20] Poems such as 'Metamorphoses', 'Mountain Swim', 'Meniscus' and 'On Mweelrea' illustrate Longley's quality as a 'naïve' poet, whose oneness with the natural environment is confirmed by the power of love. Landscape is the place where subject and object dissolve into each other, where we renew our bonds with each other and the earth. In this eroticised ecopoetry, the pervasive imagery is of fusion, fluidity, coalescence, communion, marriage. 'On Mweelrea' begins: 'I was lowering my body on to yours/ When I put my ear to the mountain's side'; and ends:

> Behind my eyelids I could just make out
> In a wash of blood and light and water
> Your body colouring the mountainside
> Like uncut poppies in the stubbly fields.   (*CP* 142)

Mesmerically, Longley plays with ideas of the interdependency of the natural and the human, mind and body, life and death. The lovers find themselves absorbed in the landscape, finally becoming that landscape. Poems such as 'On Mweelrea' are of course at several removes from the ecology of Mayo: they belong to the *logos* and not the *oikos*, and in that sense they are 'sentimental'. Nevertheless, the sense of oneness with the world is presented as direct experience rather than belonging to a lost time or imagined idyll for which the poet elegiacally yearns. The consciousness which experiences the poetic image becomes 'naïve' in Schiller's sense of merging with, rather than feeling self-consciously apart from, nature.

Yet, Longley's pastoral does not consistently signify harmony and innocence. Landscape, as the poem of that name insists, may disperse identity in unsettling

---

[18] Friedrich Schiller, 'On Naïve and Sentimental Poetry', trans. Julius A. Elias, in H.B. Nisbet (ed.), *German Aesthetic and Literary Criticism* (Cambridge, Cambridge University Press, 1985) p. 191
[19] Ibid., p. 184.
[20] www.teachnet.ie/ckelly/poetspeaks.htm

ways and 'rip thought to tatters' (*CP* 91). Pastoral, as Peter McDonald reminds us, 'is a sophisticated, and not a naïve, genre of poetry'[21] because it readily lends itself to becoming a point of vantage from which to survey the urban world. And, as we have seen, Longley in his cottage in Carrigskeewaun is not deaf to the 'political' resonances which reach him from the front line in Belfast. Characteristically, however, his relation to his earthly home is not one of nostalgic or elegiac yearning (as in Heaney), but intimate connection, on all levels of his being, with the ways of nature. Where Irish nature poetry has traditionally been a poetry of rural community, Longley's concern is not with society, rural or otherwise, but with the natural world, which provides him with an endless supply of images for human relations. When Jonathan Bate, paraphrasing Schiller, says that 'Art is the place of exile where we grieve for our lost home upon the earth',[22] it is necessary to point out that for Longley the home on earth is only lost post-mortem – and perhaps not even then, for in his recent verse, where the theme of mortality weighs more heavily than before, he wants to extend the earthly home 'for ever'.

A favourite trope of Longley's elegies is the return to nature after death. In poems such as 'Marsh Marigolds *in memory of Penny Cabot*', 'Petalwort *for Michael Vinney*', 'An October Sun *in memory of Michael Hartnett*', 'Woodsmoke *for Helen Denerley*', 'White Water *in memory of James Simmons*', 'Heron *in memory of Kenneth Koch*', the human figure is de-centred, and subsumed into the natural scene. The poem becomes a kind of imaginary ecosystem, the point about ecosystems being that they do not have a centre, they are networks of relations. Thus, 'Petalwort *for Michael Vinney*' follows the dead man's ashes 'swirl[ing] along the strand/ .../ Around the burial mound .../ ... through dowel-holes in the wreck –/ Into bottles but without a message, only/ Self-effacement in sand, additional eddies' (*CP* 290). The only heaven there is exists in this world: 'There's no such place as heaven, so let it be/ The Carrickshinnagh shoal or Caher/ Island' (*CP* 290). 'Above Dooaghtry' is a kind of self-elegy, in which the poet envisions the burial of his own ashes as a return to nature, a merging into the timeless landscape. The poet longs to *be* nature, to dissolve the Cartesian split between subject and object, to be dissolved into the ecosystem, assimilated into the environment.

> Let boulders at the top encircle me,
> Neither a drystone wall nor a cairn, space
> For the otter to die and the mountain hare
> To lick snow stains from her underside,
> A table for the peregrine and ravens,
>
> A prickly double-bed as well, nettles
> And carline-thistles, a sheeps' wool pillow,
> So that, should she decide to join me there,

---

[21] Peter McDonald, 'Faiths and Fidelities: Heaney and Longley in Mid-Career', in Fran Brearton and Eamonn Hughes (eds.), *Last Before America: Irish and American Writing* (Belfast, Blackstaff Press, 2001) p. 8.

[22] Bate, p. 73.

Our sandy dander to Allaran Point
Or Tonkeera will take for ever. (*CP* 289)

A love poem as well as an elegy, 'Above Dooaghtry' views love and death, like life
and death, not as antitheses, but as continuing process. Situated within a network
of biological, ecological and social interrelations, the poet resists the Wordswor-
thian attempt to go beyond things themselves towards a transcendental signified,
whether that signified be the great spirit of the universe that 'rolls through all
things' or the poet's own unifying imagination. The poet asks for no more than
the ordinary and everyday – 'for ever'. Heaney dislocates nature to a transcen-
dental, ahistorical domain, separated from the real world: the felled chestnut tree
becomes 'a bright nowhere',[23] the natural world 'a placeless heaven'.[24] But Longley,
adopting the view of ecocriticism, challenges the self-serving idea that nature
is, first and last, an imaginative or textual construct, to be etherealised out of
existence completely. His elegies remain rooted in the earth. There is a sense of
arbitrariness about the selection of elements that constitute these poems. Rather
than attempting some kind of picturesque mastery over the landscape, he follows
an inner vision, pursuing what the ecologist James Lovelock has called 'the Gaia
hypothesis', the idea that the whole earth is a single, vast, interconnected, living
ecosystem.

Self-regulating balance and wholeness are the ecopoetical way, as is evident
from his earliest poems: 'I fight all the way for balance –/ In the mountains'
shadow/ Losing foothold, covet the privilege/ Of vertigo' (*CP* 22), he writes in
'The Hebrides', a poem which takes its bearings from Lowell's 'The Quaker Grave-
yard in Nantucket', Hart Crane and George Herbert. 'Persephone' presents nature
in its forbidding, winter aspect. Landscape is a picture of chaos and destruction
('strew', 'broken home', 'delirium', 'numskulled' *CP* 21). It is crossed by the
sinister, predatory figures of 'weasel and ferret, the stoat and fox'. But the poem
implies a persistent order amidst the chaos and cold, with its references to the
mole's 'buildings' and the swallows' 'home'. The bat and squirrel know how to
adapt to difficult conditions – they are 'the welladjusted and skilled'. The silent
predators are graceful, beautiful creatures. The poem suggests a balanced natural
world: order and destruction, threat and beauty. Persephone, the corn-goddess,
dies each year but returns from the underworld to restore the fertility of the
land. There is, the poem suggests, a basic duality in nature, which is enacted in
the carefully disordered iambic pentameter, the tendency of the tightly enclosed
couplets towards the looseness of half-rhyme. Contemplating the adaptations to
their environment of the leopard and giraffe in 'Camouflage', the poet concludes:
'Such attributes a balanced world conceives,/ Itself reflected, its streams reflecting
these' (*CP* 10). The animals seem to be perfectly at home in their world, and
this harmonious relationship is reflected in the regularity of the stanza form,
iambic measure and rhyme scheme. But it is not a fixed world. The animals
live amid 'change' and 'risk'. Balance and wholeness require constant adjustment
and readjustment – a willingness to be mobile, adaptable, improvisatory. Out of

---

[23] Seamus Heaney, 'Clearances' VIII, *Opened Ground*, 314.
[24] See Seamus Heaney, 'The Placeless Heaven: Another Look at Kavanagh', in *The Government of
the Tongue* (London, Faber, 1988), pp. 3–14.

these intuitions of the flowing, continuous unity of all creation, Longley builds his poetic which, especially from *Gorse Fires* (1991) onwards, displays a more easy-going confidence than is usually to be found in the earlier work, a lighter touch in handling the longer line of hexameters and alexandrines, and sinuous modulations of syntax.

Organic Form

Its title and positioning as the opening poem in *The Ghost Orchid* gives the short four-lined 'Form' something of the force of a poetic manifesto:

> Trying to tell it all to you and cover everything
> Is like awakening from its grassy form the hare:
> In that make-shift shelter your hand, then my hand
> Mislays the hare and the warmth it leaves behind.   (*CP* 197)

'Form' refers to both the home of the hare and the form of the poem. The attempt to 'tell it all' is always paradoxically a concealing, as the ambiguous 'cover' in the first line intimates. 'Awakening' is also ambiguous, suggesting both calling forth and scaring away. Frustration and failure are the key notes of a poem which registers a Heideggerean sense of linguistic crisis: 'Language and linguistics', Heidegger wrote, 'have been caught fast in these rigid forms, as in a net of steel'.[25] 'Form' speaks of the need to free language from rigid forms. Longley is concerned that language can trap us into adopting pre-conceived forms of thought when it should be flexible and responsive to the fugitive, breathing reality of the natural world. The danger lies in thinking of the world as a static, given, fixed object rather than as having active agency. The elusive hare escapes 'form', the human attempt to 'shelter' it and enjoy its 'warmth'. However provisional, improvisatory or open the form constructed by human hands may be, the human 'shelter' can never be adequate simply because it is human. The challenge is to devise a language that is as sensitive and flexible as possible to respond to a shifting, unpredictable world of infinite variety and fragile beauty. The 'form' knows no national or cultural boundaries; it exists in fact somewhere between reality and dream, as the later 'Irish Hare' suggests:

> Amid São Paulo's endless higgledy concrete
> I found in a dream your form again, but woven
> Out of banana leaf and Brazilian silence
> By the Wayana Indians, as though to last.   (*CP* 315)

The eponymous 'The Ghost Orchid', which Neil Corcoran has described as 'one of Longley's most delicate lyrical figurings', demonstrates the poet's sensitivity to nature's exquisite vulnerability:

---

[25] Martin Heidegger, *An Introduction to Metaphysics*, trans. Ralph Manheim (Yale University Press, 1959), p. 53.

Added to its few remaining sites will be the stanza
I compose about leaves like flakes of skin, a colour
Dithering between pink and yellow, and then the root
That grows like coral among shadows and leaf-litter.
Just touching the petals bruises them into darkness.   (*CP* 234)

This 'little hymn to fragility, ephemerality and evanescence', says Corcoran, 'reminds us of the ecology implicit in Longley's whole output and endeavour'.[26] The poem, as Corcoran observes, 'brings nature and poem self-consciously together', to the point of virtual identification. The poem declares the poet's determination to make room ('stanza' means room or home) in his poetry for the natural world, and, like 'Form', it raises the question of how the organic (orchid) can be accommodated within man-made structures (stanza). Typical of Longley's poetry, nature in 'The Ghost Orchid' is a place of literal reference or an object of retrieval or contemplation for its own sake before it partici-pates in any formal or symbolic or ideological discourse. As a lyric meditation on the luminous natural image, the poem is devoted to realising, attentively and tentatively, the materiality of the natural world – though 'materiality' seems almost too substantial a term for such a fragile thing as the ghostly orchid – in language which assumes a pre-eminently mimetic or reflective function. Yet while remaining ecocentrically in touch with its environmental origins, Longley's earth-language acknowledges unavoidable distance, difference, absence and loss. The poet knows that the stanza he composes stands in for the actual thing, that his poem is a displacement of the orchid into the ghostly domain – the virtual reality – of language.

This concern to hold the human and non-human in close creative rapport informs one of Longley's best-known poems, 'The Ice-Cream Man'. The poem, which consists largely of an extended list of Burren wild flowers, constitutes another of Longley's 'wreaths' for the dead, in this case an ice-cream man shot dead by the IRA on Belfast's Lisburn Road:

I named for you all the wild flowers of the Burren
I had seen in one day: thyme, valerian, loosestrife,
Meadowsweet, tway blade, crowfoot, ling, angelica,
Herb Robert, marjoram, cow parsley, sundew, vetch,
Mountain avens, wood sage, ragged robin, stitchwort,
Yarrow, lady's bedstraw, bindweed, bog pimpernel.   (*CP* 192)

The style is quiet and serene. There is no metaphorical virtuosity, no syntac-tical complexity, only a naïve wonder conveyed through the list of wild flowers presented as they occur in memory, without subordination, categorisation or comment, in one long sentence. A more complex subordinating structure would have suggested a more ambitious, active play of mind, a desire to order and control experience: here, the movement is leisurely, receptive, open. With this apparent withdrawal of the mediating consciousness, poetry becomes a direct function of local and earthly, bodily and material existence. By limiting textual

---

26 Neil Corcoran, 'My Botanical Studies: The Poetry of Natural History in the Poetry of Michael Longley', in Peacock and Devine (eds.), p. 119.

activity to childlike naming of wild flowers, Longley challenges the complacent culturalism which renders flora and fauna subordinate to the human capacity for signification. Nature is not merely something produced by language but is granted its independent existence. Flower and word, nature and text, are one. The poem 'naturalises' culture, insisting on a necessary reciprocity between poetry and earth, whereby the two combine to offer their salvific balm to humankind. The earth needs the poets, as Rilke stresses in the ninth Duino elegy, to name its parts, reveal its being:

> For when the traveller returns from the mountain-slopes into the valley,
> he brings, not a handful of earth, unsayable to others, but instead
> some word he has gained, some pure word, the yellow and blue
> gentian. Perhaps we are *here* in order to say: house,
> bridge, fountain, gate, pitcher, fruit-tree, window,
> at most: column, tower? ... but to *say* them, you must understand,
> oh to say them *more* intensely than the Things themselves
> ever dreamed of existing.[27]

To say the earth is to save (not manipulate and master) the earth is to save ourselves from destruction.

The organicist equation of nature and poetry is the explicit theme of poems such as 'Sycamore' in which Longley, like those earlier 'momentary botanists of the battlefield',[28] Keith Douglas and Isaac Rosenberg, sings the song of the earth in celebratory defiance of the atrocity on the battlefields of the Somme.

> The sycamore stumps survived the deadliest gales
> To put out new growth, leaves sticky with honeydew
> And just enough white wood to make a violin.
>
> This was a way of mending the phonograph record
> Broken by the unknown soldier before the Somme
> (Fritz Kreisler playing Dvorak's 'Humoresque').
>
> The notes of music twirled like sycamore wings
> From farmhouse-sheltering-and-dairy-cooling branches
> And carried to all corners of the battlefield.   (*CP* 307)

The music of the violin, which is metonymic of the poem itself, offers the ideal or intellectual form of nature. To make the violin, it is necessary to use the 'white wood' of the sycamore. In its violin-form the tree transcends its broken condition and original particular location and makes music which is 'carried to all corners of the battlefield'. Music/poetry crosses boundaries, no-man's land, nations: the 'unknown soldier' (British? German?) plays a German playing Czech music. The notes of music are 'like sycamore wings': art is an attempt to recover the very thing which has been destroyed so that it can be 'mended'; the music tells of 'farmhouse' and 'dairy' – the *oikos*, the place of dwelling that is being

---

[27] 9th Duino Elegy, in *Selected Poetry of Rainer Maria Rilke*, trans. Stephen Mitchell (London, Picador, 1987) p. 201.

[28] Corcoran, p. 104.

laid waste by war. Nature and poetry combine to propose a necessary dream. Longley's ecopoetics asks us to imagine an alternative to the darkness of death and destruction.

Longley explicitly thinks of his poems in terms of an organicist or ecological epistemology: 'I'm interested in forms that are, if you like, more organic. I wouldn't want to think that the forms in my earlier books are inorganic but I have now to let the poems happen. There's very little deliberation in what I do. It's the difference between trimming a hedge and building a wall.'[29] In the animal and vegetative world of Longley's poetry, the poem is viewed as process, its rhetorical patterns arising organically, as do the patterns in nature, both the poem and the nature it reflects being living systems. In this view, poetry by its very nature is a biological medium, a rhythmic pattern in which past and present are in constant interaction, a realm of imagination outside the physical framework of space-time, a world reflecting the rhythms of the mind and of life itself. There is no element that is not connected to the overall effect of the whole: the poem itself is like the network concept of ecology. Network thinking is distinctly a-causal and non-linear. It is based on the principle of mutual interdependence and non-separability, which Longley acts out in terms of his use of metaphor, his techniques of fusion, juxtaposition and parallelism, his fluid handling of time, place and identity, his subtle syntactical manoeuvres, his self-conscious intertextuality, his panoptic historical, cultural and geographical perspectives. The usual binary oppositions – joy and loss, life and death, evanescence and continuity – are held within a synoptic view whereby the poet contemplates existence as a network of necessarily interdependent parts, or as a living organism in which each part operates in the context of the whole.

Interdependency and interconnectedness characterise not only the structure of individual poems but whole collections. In a 1998 interview, he explained the non-linear 'patchwork' principle of organisation which has been a feature of his collections since then:

> In my first four books I had indulged a tendency to write short intense lyrics and then arrange them in sequences. Something different began to happen in *Gorse Fires* – some kind of involuntary denial of that urge to string poems together in rosaries. The book emerged like a big patchwork. I wanted any given poem to draw resonances from other poems ten or twenty pages in front or behind. I was aiming for a deeper cohesiveness. In more confident moments the books looks to me like one big poem, although each piece has its own title and independence.[30]

The idea of the 'one big poem' suggests a poet who has learnt to dwell more securely with himself, his home(s) and his environment. The structure, which Longley refers to as a 'patchwork', might also be described as that of a 'topological network', which makes manifest connections that would be suppressed within a classically sequential temporal structure, and which, according to Michel Serres, is the kind of ecological topology which structures time and the weather.[31]

---

[29] 'An Interview with Michael Longley: "Au Revoir, Oeuvre"' (Peter McDonald), *Thumbscrew*, 12 (Winter 1998/9) p. 2.

[30] Ibid.

[31] See Bate, pp. 110–11.

Nevertheless, we have to be careful with applying environmentalist termi-
nology to Longley's poems: notions such as 'organic', 'ecological balance',
'ecosystem', should not be allowed to reintroduce, by way of non-literary termi-
nology, idealised literary assumptions of nature as inherently creative, harmo-
nious and peaceful. Longley's poetry grows out of close, intense interaction with
nature. He refers to a natural reality, not the idylls of the pastoral or sublime,
and uses his poetry to remind us of non-human perspectives of birds, animals,
trees, flowers, mountains. His wilderness, while reflecting longing and desire, is
no pristine romanticised enclave, even though at times he has to remind himself
of this:

> I forgot the pale butterwort there on the ground
> Spreading its leaves like a starfish and digesting
> Insects that squirm on each adhesive tongue and
> Feed the terror in your eyes, your smoky blue eyes.
>
> ('Pale Butterwort', *CP* 244)

Nature is savage and disturbing, as well as erotically beautiful. 'The Lapwing'
bases its aesthetics in a concept of pollution and ecological threat:

> Carrickskeewaun in May light has unsettled me.
> Each butterwort flourishes an undertaker's lamp
> For the poisoned swan unfolding on David's pond ...   (*CP 243*)

And the poem after that, 'The Comber', emphasises, not easy continuity and
interconnection between human and natural worlds, but difference and other-
ness. The poem begins by recognising nature's ever-changing, deliquescent,
unpredictable movement – 'A moment before the comber turns into/ A breaker
– sea-spray, raggedy rainbows ...' (*CP* 243) – yet manages to freeze-frame a
sudden image of unusual closeness between human and natural before the
transcendental moment of oneness crashes back into the flux of time. In this
magical, 'suspended' moment of 'water and sunlight', speaker and otter meet,
'without my scent/ In her nostrils, the uproar of my presence,/ My unforgivable
shadow on the sand' (*CP* 243), the language poised between the exhilaration of
epiphany and the sad recognition that he can never feel completely at home in
the world.

Green Ireland

Clearly, Longley's ecopoetics do not conform to any preconceived system, political
or otherwise. Where Heidegger's later career is marked by a controversial politi-
cisation of his ecopoetics and development of a nationalistic theory of dwelling,
Longley remains true to the Heideggerean concept of *poiesis* as a disclosing or
unconcealing of dwelling, free from any 'enframing' history, theory or political
system. Longley sets out not with a set of assumptions or proposals about the
world, but a concern to reflect upon what it might mean to dwell on this earth.
In this sense he exemplifies Jonathan Bate's concept of the ecopoet:

> The poet's way of articulating the relationship between human-kind and envi-
> ronment, person and place, is peculiar because it is experiential, not descriptive.

Whereas the biologist, the geographer and the Green activist have *narratives* of dwelling, a poem may be a *revelation* of dwelling. Such a claim is phenomenological before it is political, and for this reason ecopoetics may properly be regarded as pre-political. Politics, let us remember, means 'of the *polis*', of the city. For this reason, the controlling myth of ecopoetics is a myth of the pre-political, the prehistoric: it is a Rousseauesque story about imagining a state of nature prior to the fall into property, into equality and into the city.[32]

But Longley knows that we live after the fall, and that nowhere, not even Carrigskeewaun, is an ideologically-free zone. Unlike the Marxist or feminist poet, he has no explicit political message, but he is still concerned with effecting an (ecological) revolution of consciousness, as he made clear in a comment in a 2004 issue of *Resurgence,* a journal which advertises itself as 'the leading international forum for ecological and spiritual thinking', and to which Longley is a regular contributor:

> The most urgent political problems are ecological: how we share the planet with the plants and the other animals. My nature writing is my most political. In my Mayo poems I am not trying to escape from political violence. I want the light from Carrigskeewaun to irradiate the northern darkness. Describing the world in a meticulous way is a consecration and a stay against damaging dogmatism.[33]

In the Northern Irish context, ecopoetics propose an alternative socio-political model to the traditional dogmatics of Protestant v Catholic, Unionist v Nationalist. A sense of global and ecological interconnectedness replaces the old sectarian allegiances. Bate illustrates the force of ecological politics in the context of the 1989 'Velvet Revolution' in Czechoslovakia which, he argues, owed more to air pollution in Prague than the existence of the Iron Curtain: 'the political significance of air pollution demands a rethinking of the categories. The political map has been redrawn and it is time for literary criticism to politicize itself in a new way'.[34] In proposing an 'ideology' based on an imaginative reunification of mind and nature, Longley goes beyond, in many ways goes deeper than, the political model that is normally used in thinking about 'the northern darkness'. By dissolving the traditional link between nature and nation, and awakening his reader to cooperative participation within the entire community of human and non-human planetary life, he gives the concept of 'Green' Ireland a new meaning.

The 'light from Carrigskeewaun' illumines a new way of comprehending the world. Carrigskeewaun offers the poet images of resilient nature which can provide consolation in the midst of death and darkness, but his focus on nature and the pastoral is more than an escape from violence and politics: the Carrigskeewaun poems refract his concern for what's happening on the other side of his island. Carrigskeewaun opens up new perspectives on reality, especially on man as an ecological being. His poems express a kind of semi-religious awe in

---

[32] Bate, p. 266.

[33] http://www.resurgence.org/resurgence/issues/longley225.htm

[34] Jonathan Bate, 'From "Red" to "Green"', in Laurence Coupe (ed.), *The Green Studies Reader* (London, Routledge, 2000), pp. 167–72, 169.

respect of the natural world, and implicitly counter hierarchical power structures and social schemes of dominance. Instead of seeking to control the world, ecocriticism suggests the value of co-existing with it and insists on our complete biological and spiritual dependence on it. In those Carrigskeewaun poems which refer to the community, or to representative individuals, we find a remnant of the organic society such as Wordsworth described in his *Guide to the Lakes*: a 'pure Commonwealth; the members of which existed in the midst of a powerful empire like an ideal society or an organized community, whose constitution had been imposed and regulated by the mountains which protected it'.[35] The Carrigskeewaun poems contain no pictures of brutal hardship, ferocious loneliness or hideous violence such as we find in Montague or Kavanagh: the main focus of Longley's attention is the natural rather than the social order. In Carrigskeewaun he situates himself as a citizen of the whole world, not just a citizen within society, and thinks in terms of centuries, or millennia, under the gaze of eternity, in an attitude of humble openness to nature's revelation and autonomy:

> The other thing I think we have to do is to avoid being parochial in a human way, thinking only in terms of ourselves. The huge issue facing us as a species is how we get on with the other animals. I write about them, I hope, with reverence and wonder as a way of giving them space in my poems. I'm saying we have to give them space in our lives and share our space on the globe with them. We're not civilized unless we look after them, the animals, which is why I like to write about them, and celebrate them.[36]

Longley's poetry is a language about our earthly dwelling place, a place from which we have been divorced, and to which poetry can return us. The Longley poem respects traditions, draws on a sense of continuity and organicism that has been subverted by much contemporary poetry with its postmodern suspicion of grand narratives and celebrations of beauty. He argues for a more direct and visceral response to what poetry can do than is usually advocated in the academy:

> I wrote an elegy for an ice-cream man on the Lisburn Road who was murdered by the IRA; I read it on the radio, and I got a letter some time later from the murdered man's mother, a very beautiful letter. My poem ends with a list of twenty-one flowers – I'd never counted them – and it begins with a shorter list of ice-cream flavours. She said, I wouldn't have noticed, but there were twenty-one flower names in my poem and there were twenty-one ice-cream flavours in her son's shop. She signed herself The Ice-Cream Man's Mother. When I published my poem 'Ceasefire' in the *Irish Times*, I got a letter from the father of Paul Maxwell, the sixteen-year-old boy who had been blown up with Lord Mountbatten. Those letters matter more to me than any amount of criticism I might receive in literary journals or attention in the public world.[37]

---

35 *Wordsworth's Guide to the Lakes: The Fifth Edition (1835)*, ed. Ernest de Selincourt (Oxford, 1906, repr. 1977), p. 68.
36 'Michael Longley: An Interview with Margaret Mills Harper', *Five Points: A Journal of Literature and Art* http://www.wbdelsol.com/Five_Points/issues/v8n3/ml.htm
37 McDonald, p. 6.

Longley's sense of public accountability is rooted in a commitment to poetry's referential function which contemporary literary theory has tended to marginalise. At a time when the academy is dominated by cultural studies, with its insistent and self-conscious intellectualising, its demotion of nature to a linguistic construct, merely another text to be read and dismissed, severed from the natural reality to which it refers, Longley offers something different from postmodern scepticism. It is, however, something which, in refusing to conform to the standard critical and cultural paradigms which govern contemporary literary production, has rarely received its due attention or proper evaluation.

Chapter 7

DEREK MAHON: 'AN EXILE AND A STRANGER'

Mahon's relationship with his home place is profoundly troubled and ambiguous. Uneasy with the Protestant culture from which he sprang, and without access to the racial landscape in which his fellow Northern Catholic poets could situate themselves, he epitomises the displaced Northern Protestant for whom ideas of community are highly problematic. Like MacNeice, he is the existential outsider, more familiar with feelings of alienation than those of belonging. Without a community to which he can feel he belongs, he is drawn to romantic outsiders, bohemians, the forgotten and neglected. Thus, he celebrates De Quincey, Edward Dowson, Marilyn Monroe, the forger, the frightened birds in 'Four Walks', the gypsies who are indifferent to national boundaries and the conventional social code. And there are in his own family individuals such as 'Grandfather' and 'My Wicked Uncle' who represent a kind of outlawry with which he identifies. Rather than taking his bearings from a specifically Irish poetic tradition, he draws from a diffuse array of Irish, British, American and European models. His migrant cosmopolitanism is the antithesis of Heaney's rootedness. Where Heaney's landscapes are lushly rural, Mahon's are bleak, post-apocalyptic wildernesses or frozen Antarctic wastes offering little imaginative nourishment or spiritual solace. The mythic West is unable to provide the spiritual home it does for MacNeice or Longley; the natural world is as likely to confirm his aliena- tion as enchant him with its beauty. In 'Day Trip to Donegal', the speaker feels no sense of romantic attunement to nature: instead, the elemental experience of sea, wind, waves and storm makes him think of 'agony and heartbreak', the exis- tential void, and merely serves to highlight his alienation and disorientation: 'At dawn I was alone far out at sea/ Without skill or reassurance'.[1] 'Brighton Beach' recalls a similar trip to Donegal, when the speaker is again the outsider, displaced and unconnected: 'you talked/ For hours to fishermen/ You had worked with while I,/ Out of my depths in those/ Waters, loafed on the quays' (*CP* 154). In 'Aran'/'In the Aran Islands', a contrast is drawn between the traditional singer who is 'earthed to his girl', to the land, his music and tradition, and the alien- ated poet who identifies with the lone 'crack-voiced rock-marauder' (*CP* 37), the bird in flight, belonging nowhere. The speaker, while he may appreciate the West, resists the temptation to immerse himself in it. 'Achill' is another poem

---

[1]   Derek Mahon, *Collected Poems* (Loughcrew, The Gallery Press, 1999) p. 25. Hereafter abbreviated to *CP* and page references incorporated into the text.

which takes its title from a place, but which pictures the 'disconsolate' (*CP* 156) poet, solitary and agitated on Achill, thinking of his children on other islands, holidaying in the Aegean. 'Thinking of Inis Oírr in Cambridge, Mass.'/'Recalling Aran' articulates a recognisably modernist exile poetics in which displacement becomes the prerequisite of creativity:

> A dream of limestone in sea-light
> Where gulls have placed their perfect prints.
> Reflection in that final sky
> Shames vision into simple sight;
> Into pure sense, experience.
> Atlantic leagues away tonight,
> Conceived beyond such innocence,
> I clutch the memory still, and I
> Have measured everything with it since.   (*CP* 29)

Memory heightened by distance produces a luminous, idealised image (significantly devoid of human presence) which is valuable not only as a snapshot of home, but, like the aesthete's 'cold dream/ Of a place out of time' in 'The Last of the Fire Kings' (*CP* 65), as an exemplary dream-distillation of experience into an artistic perfection, finality and purity. Mahon's poem recalls lines from Heaney's 'The Peninsula':

> ... Now recall

> The glazed foreshore and silhouetted log,
> That rock where breakers shredded into rags,
> The leggy birds stilted on their own legs,
> Islands riding themselves out into the fog

> And drive back home, still with nothing to say
> Except that now you will uncode all landscapes
> By this: things founded clean on their own shapes,
> Water and ground in their extremity.[2]

Both poets elaborate a similar displacement aesthetic strategy involving the creation of a pure space which exists outside history where experience can be given significant form.

Yet, the trope of insularity is ambiguous, signifying not only separation from family, country, tradition and history, but the impossibility of separation: no man is ever really an island. 'Rathlin' tells of another day trip, this time to the island off the North Antrim coast. The poem opens dramatically: 'A long time since the last scream was cut short –' (*CP* 107). The intimation of a violent past, abruptly silenced at the end of the first line, nevertheless resonates in the air, while the poet proceeds to describe the island as now representing a peaceful alternative to the troubled present: 'Bombs doze in the housing estates/ But here they are through with history'. The poet thinks of himself as a visitor in his own

---

[2] Seamus Heaney, 'The Peninsula', in *Opened Ground: Poems 1966–1996* (London, Faber, 1998) p. 21.

land, his description of his arrival on the island carrying with it hints of threat, disturbance and invasion: 'the report/ Of an outboard motor at the pier/ Shatters the dream-time and we land/ As if we were the first visitors here'. If the poet's journey to the island signals his desire to escape from history, the last stanza returns to 'the last scream', suggesting the impossibility of such escape. The reference is to the infamous massacre in July 1575 of 600 women and children of the Scottish MacDonnell clan who had taken refuge on Rathlin after the Earl of Essex ordered a force under the command of Sir Francis Drake to attack Sorley Boy MacDonnell, then a growing political threat to Elizabeth I. In the end, the poet departs in confusion: 'We leave here the infancy of the race,/ Unsure among the pitching surfaces/ Whether the future lies before us or behind'. Where Heaney finds solace in an historical and communal identity, Mahon remains a figure of alienation and profound uncertainty.

Heaney believes he can re-enter the past and re-establish communal identity: Mahon, by contrast, questions the idea of a reassuring continuity with the past and the idea of a cultural identity rooted in tradition. 'Lives' is dedicated to Heaney, but mocks the archaeological aesthetic that supports Heaney's quest for genealogy and origins. 'Lives' is a playful fantasia of metamorphosis and migrancy in which the speaker rehearses the story of his multiple incarnations, first as a prehistoric torc of gold, then as a bump of clay on a Navaho rug, then a stone in Tibet, then a tongue of bark in darkest Africa. 'So many lives' (*CP* 45), the speaker self-importantly declares, but these previous lives amount to nothing more than the detritus of history. The poem ends with a satirical portrait of the poet as anthropologist who thinks he can plumb the genealogical mysteries. Weighed down by the trappings of his historical research, he is forced to conclude: 'I know too much/ To be anything any more' (*CP* 45). Where Heaney identifies reverentially with the Iron Age bog victims, Mahon debunks the 'insolent ontology' (*CP* 46) that presumes to be able to understand the way the past informs the present. Identity is multiple, shifting, and no-one should presume to know how it may be encoded. For Heaney (like Yeats) the past offers the promise of cultural identity based on the retrieval of tradition; for Mahon (like Joyce) it opens the possibility of cultural difference, of being always otherwise.

Mahon's poetry travels widely, moving between Belfast, Dublin, London, Japan, Delft, Treblinka, Tomis, North Carolina, Manhattan, Rome, Kinsale – yet it partakes in what he called the 'homeward gravitation in Ulster poetry'.[3] The early work, though set mostly in Belfast and the seaside places of counties Antrim and Down, is written from perspectives in London or the United States. While situated elsewhere, he feels the tug of home. This unsettled attitude is registered in 'Glengormley', the title referring to the Belfast suburb where he grew up: 'By/ Necessity, if not choice, I live here too' (*CP* 14). He juxtaposes the contemporary suburban order – 'the terrier-taming, garden-watering days' – with the mythological Ulster past. The tone throughout is ambivalent, implying mixed feelings about both the so-called heroic past and the so-called civilised present. Another poem, 'The Spring Vacation', was originally entitled 'In Belfast', the change of title

---

3   John Brown, *In the Chair: Interviews with Poets from the North of Ireland* (Cliffs of Moher, Salmon Publishing, 2002) p. 109.

marking a significant shift of emphasis from the idea of homecoming to that of tourism. The speaker is 'walking among my own ... between shower and shower' (*CP* 13). Though back in Belfast, he admits that he is unable to feel any strong identification with his own people. The poem keeps its distance from the human dramas to which it vaguely alludes:

> One part of my mind must learn to know its place.
> The things that happen in the kitchen houses
> And echoing back-streets of this desperate city
> Should engage more than my casual interest,
> Exact more interest than my casual pity.   (*CP* 13)

Only 'one part' of his mind need concern itself with knowing 'its place': on one level, the place is Belfast, on another, knowing his place is knowing what is expected of him in society. Either way, he is careful about how much of himself he is prepared to mortgage to 'place' poetry. 'Should' at the beginning of the penultimate line again qualifies his involvement, while the pun on 'interest' and the intricate parallel construction of the last two lines suggest a greater investment in the pleasure of linguistic ingenuity than genuine feeling for his home place.

Homecoming always leaves him feeling dissatisfied, estranged. He is one of the 'unreconciled' ('Glengormley', *CP* 14). When he returns home it is not out of a sense of belonging or allegiance, but of obligation, or a desire for self-knowledge. Many of his poems are crossings, exchanges between different places, cultures and states of being. 'Going Home' (dedicated to the doyen of Ulster regionalism, John Hewitt) is structured on a contrast between English and Irish landscape, similar to that which we find in MacNeice's 'Woods'. Mahon begins in England, where he might 'Become a home for birds,/ A shelter for the nymphs/ And gaze out over the downs/ As if I belonged there too' (*CP* 95), but acknowledges that this is not his natural environment. Yet neither does he feel at home in the harsh Irish landscape, with its 'last stubborn growth' rooted 'On the edge of everything/ Like a burnt-out angel/ Raising petitionary hands': Ireland is a terminal place of 'anguish and despair' (*CP* 96).

'Afterlives' describes a night-crossing: he is 'going home by sea/ For the first time in years'. If, as the poet says in 'In Belfast'/'The Spring Vacation', 'One part of my mind must learn to know its place', in 'Afterlives' his home place is scarcely recognizable:

> And I step ashore in a fine rain
> To a city so changed
> By five years of war
> I scarcely recognize
> The places I grew up in,
> The faces that try to explain.
>
> But the hills are still the same
> Grey-blue above Belfast.
> Perhaps if I'd stayed behind
> And lived it bomb by bomb

> I might have grown up at last
> And learnt what is meant by home.   (*CP* 59)

'Should ... Perhaps ... might have': Mahon's is a poetry of hypothetical scenarios, alternative states, virtual realities, afterlives, roads not taken, imagined futures.

Such is 'The Last of the Fire Kings' where the speaker/poet experiments with a plurality of identities, traverses a variety of landscapes. The use of an unencumbered, mobile three-line stanza, and a hard, bare diction produces an effect of dream-like fluency. He wants to be like 'the man who descends/ At two milk churns/ .../ and vanishes/ Where the lane turns,/ Or the man/ Who drops at night/ From a moving train' and 'strikes out over the fields' into the unknown, 'not knowing a word of the language' (*CP* 64) – an itinerant, an outsider confident in the sufficiency of his own language, a tourist in his own country. Where Heaney, driving through the man-killing parishes of Jutland, 'Watching the pointing hands/ Of country people,/ Not knowing their tongue', feels 'lost, unhappy/ and at home',[4] Mahon welcomes the experience of separation and isolation, the possibility of escape from history. His desired persona is elusive, unable to be pinned down or categorised, a marginal figure without origins or destination, the 'Or' at the beginning of the third stanza indicating his adeptness at choosing an identity rather than having one imposed upon him. Moving imaginatively through a range of symbolic personae – American hobo, pagan king, Yeatsian aesthete, social realist – he maintains a tentative, questioning tone, ending up much less confident of the possibility of freedom ('die their creature and be thankful') than when he started out ('I want to be ...'). He wants to be 'Through with history', but his tribe, 'the fire-loving/ People, rightly perhaps', demand 'that I inhabit,/ Like them, a world of/ Sirens, bin-lids/ And bricked-up windows' (*CP* 64). 'Rightly perhaps' acknowledges the impossibility of ever completely erasing the claims of public pressure or social conscience. The speaker, though resisting socially-imposed identities, is not the infinitely dispersed subject of 'Lives'.

For Oscar Wilde, 'The real life is the life we do not lead':[5] Mahon wishes to give a voice to the multiple lost 'lives we might have led' ('Leaves', *CP* 60), those virtual, placeless lives of pure imagination which exist outside definition, as unfulfilled desire, to which the poet refers in the polyvalent term (and poem) 'Leaves'. The unitary, imperial self is always haunted by 'an infinite/ Rustling and sighing' of the 'dead leaves' (*CP* 60) of other selves, other lives which clamour for recognition. In his best-known poem, 'A Disused Shed in Co. Wexford', the lost, the forgotten, the casualties of history represented by the mushrooms, are longing either for transcendence in the protectorate of the poet's art or for re-integration, recognition and fulfilment in history:

> Lost people of Treblinka and Pompeii!
> 'Save us, save us,' they seem to say,
> 'Let the god not abandon us

---

4   Seamus Heaney, 'Tollund Man', in *Opened Ground*, p. 64.
5   Quoted in Rodney Shewan, *Oscar Wilde: Art and Egotism* (London, 1977) p. 193.

Who have come so far in darkness and in pain.
We too had our lives to live'. (*CP* 90)

Wexford, Treblinka and Pompeii merge in what is a characteristic Mahonian approach to place: 'Tithonus' juxtaposes Golgotha, Krakatoa, Thermopylae, Peking, Dresden, Hiroshima and Ethiopia; the eponymous lighthouse in Maine 'might be anywhere –/ Hokkaido, Mayo, Maine;/ But it is in Maine';[6] while the eponymous garage in Co. Cork 'might be anywhere – in the Dordogne,/ Iquitos, Bethlehem' (*HBN* 56). Mahon's poems are full of place names which, as Eamonn Hughes remarks, 'suggests a form of anxiety rather than any settled or possessive relationship to place'.[7] Mahon wants us to recognise the specificity of his places, their 'weird haecceity',[8] but his descriptions always serve a larger purpose – what we might call Mahon's existential vision. Place tends to be treated conceptually or analogically or parabolically, rather than in any kind of geographical or topographical detail, or in the affective terms of 'sense of place', or as a *flâneur* might experience it. Both 'A Garage in Co. Cork' and its companion poem, 'A Disused Shed in Co. Wexford', are studies of displacement, closely reflecting Mahon's particular personal and cultural perspective. They also illustrate his self-consciously intertextual construction of place, 'A Disused Shed' explicitly acknowledging its debt to J.G. Farrell's big house novel *Troubles* (1970), and 'A Garage in Co. Cork', as Paul Muldoon has shown, playing off Elizabeth Bishop's 'Filling Station' (from her 1965 collection *Questions of Travel*): 'his "mound of never used cement" echoing her "cement porch behind the pumps", her "pumps" echoed in his image of "a god ... changing to petrol pumps an old man and his wife"'.[9] Both 'A Garage in Co. Cork' and 'Filling Station' are meditations on the meaning of home by poets who themselves seemed to be continually on the move and could never truly feel at home anywhere. Bishop emphasises the humanising effect of a feminine, aesthetic influence which bespeaks the desire to be at home even within the dirty, greasy, emphatically masculine space of the filling station: 'Why the extraneous plant?/ Why the taboret?/ Why, oh why, the doily?/ (Embroidered in daisy stitch ...)'.[10] Mahon, by contrast, moves to a much darker, didactic conclusion:

> We might be anywhere but are in one place only
> One of the milestones of earth-residence
> Unique in each particular, the thinly
> Peopled hinterland serenely tense –
> Not in the hope of a resplendent future
> But with a sure sense of its intrinsic nature. (*CP* 131)

---

6   Derek Mahon, 'A Lighthouse in Maine', in *The Hunt By Night* (Oxford, Oxford University Press, 1982) p. 44. Hereafter abbreviated to *HBN* and page references incorporated into the text.
7   Eamonn Hughes, '"Weird/ Haecceity": Place in Derek Mahon's Poetry', in Elmer Kennedy-Andrews (ed.), *The Poetry of Derek Mahon* (Gerrards Cross, Colin Smythe, 2002) p. 98.
8   Derek Mahon, 'The Sea in Winter', version in *Selected Poems* (Loughcrew, The Gallery Press, 1991) p. 117.
9   Paul Muldoon, *The End of the Poem: Oxford Lectures on Poetry* (London, Faber, 2006) p. 11.
10 Elizabeth Bishop, *Complete Poems* (London, Chatto & Windus, 1984) p. 127.

This final stanza represents a sudden, shocking contradiction of all that has gone before, a demoralised repudiation of the play of imagination which had sought to invent a narrative to 'place' the garage and those who lived there. Since all places are the same and interchangeable there is no point in looking beyond the local; change and progress are an illusion; everywhere is exile.

Nevertheless, yearning for some kind of re-connection, wholeness or 'at-homeness' pervades and animates Mahon's oeuvre. In 'Nostalgias', the longing of the objects to cohere into wholeness is expressive of his longing to belong to a larger community. The series of fragmented images listed in a displaced, de-politicised locale heightens the sense of isolation. 'Nostalgias' is a poem of yearning for a return to origins in which the poet speaks, with near-religious pathos, out of a Protestant sense of loss and abandonment: 'In a tiny stone church/ On the desolate headland/ A lost tribe is singing "Abide With Me"' (*CP* 75). But the very idea of a return to origins is ridiculed as well as intensified by the juxtaposition of human yearning with that of chair, kettle and soap: 'The chair squeaks in a high wind,/ Rain falls from its branches,/ The kettle yearns for the/ Mountain, the soap for the sea' (*CP* 75). 'The Studio' resembles 'Nostalgias' in beginning with the hypothetical longing of inanimate objects in a room. The speaker imagines these objects – 'deal table', 'ranged crockery', 'frail oilcloth' – as desperate to break out of their isolation and enter the public arena of history outside the window:

> You would think with so much going on outside
> The deal table would make for the window,
> The ranged crockery freak and wail
> Remembering its dark origins ... .
> > > But it
> Never happens like that. Instead
> There is this quivering silence
> In which, day by day, the play of light and shadow (shadow mostly)
> Repeats itself, though never exactly. (*CP* 36)

The poem rehearses the familiar tensions: between imagination ('You would think ...') and reality ('But it/ Never happens like that ...'), interior and exterior, subject and object, poetry and history. These failed connections are dramatised in Mahon's broken, enjambed phrasal units and irregular rhyming, and imaged in the reference to the light bulb filament which never quite touches but derives its generative power from this very condition of incompleteness.

The poet's displacement from origins, from place, family and community, also involves displacement into the linguistic, discursive and ideological systems in which he is inscribed. 'Love Poem'/'Preface to a Love Poem' expresses awareness that language is not transparent, allowing direct access to meaning. There is no possibility, even for the autobiographical poem, of finding some pure and origi-nary point of consciousness which pre-exists the symbolic order of codes and discourses. An ineradicable gap exists between subject and object. The earlier title indicates the partial and provisional nature of the poem, unsettling any notion of poetic authority. The poem is, the poet goes on to say, 'a circling of itself and you', 'A form of words, compact and compromise', 'a blind with sunlight filtering through', 'at one remove, a substitute' (*CP* 18) – a play of signifiers that constantly elude any single centre, essence or meaning. Obsessed with the condition of loss, difference and absence out of which any poetry is written, the speaker longs for silence, for a return to a pre-verbal pre-history of 'mute phenomena'. History is always a construct, a text. 'Tithonus' declares the inevitable selectivity of historical narratives: 'I forget nothing/ But if I told/ Everything in detail –/ …/ I would need,/ Another eternity,/ Perish the thought'.[11] But if it is impossible to recover or know the past, the poet, as 'Lives' illustrates, can delight in the variety of modes he can use to recover it, and play with reality in the very act of constituting it.

*

Where Montague is circling to return home, and Heaney keeps harking back to the 'untoppled omphalos',[12] Mahon recognises what Larkin called 'the importance of elsewhere' (the title of a Larkin poem). Through allusion, intertextuality, translation and Lowellesque 'imitations', Mahon enters into dialogical relationship with works of art from other times and places, and seeks to locate the local and personal within a wider cultural world. 'The Snow Party' draws a parallel between contemporary Ulster and seventeenth-century Japan.[13] In this poem, the ritual of tea ceremony and snow-viewing is a distraction from the public upheaval taking place outside the frame of the poem, the violence that is described more readily suggesting European rather than Japanese historical events: 'Elsewhere they are burning/ Witches and heretics/ In the boiling squares' (*CP* 63). The aesthetic composure of the snow-party, which is mimicked by the poem's own formal rigour, contrasts with the violence occurring 'elsewhere'. Perhaps Mahon is thinking of himself and the other Ulster poets indulging their Stevensian rage for order in the face of the contemporary Troubles. Mahon raises questions of art's responsibilities in time of war and disturbance, and answers them by offering the poem's elegance, stillness and control as ironic commentary on art's claims to autonomy.

In 'Courtyards in Delft', the speaker recognises in the world of seventeenth-century Dutch painting an image of his own Ulster Protestant childhood: 'I lived there as a boy …' (*CP* 105). De Hooch's painting is an image of 'trim composure' and 'chaste/ Perfection'. The speaker senses a troubling absence or suppression: 'No spinet-playing emblematic of/ The harmonies and disharmonies of love,/ No lewd fish, no fruit, no wide-eyed bird/ About to fly its cage'; 'we miss the dirty dog/ The fiery gin'. As in 'The Snow Party', the appearance of calm is undercut by intimations of violence. Mahon emphasises the larger historical and political contexts in which the decorous iconography of the painting must be understood:

> I must be lying low in a room there,
> A strange child with a taste for verse,

---

11 Derek Mahon, 'Tithonus', in *Selected Poems* (Harmondsworth, Penguin Books, 1991), 169–70.
12 Seamus Heaney, 'The Toome Road', *Opened Ground*, p. 150.
13 See also Michael Longley's *The Weather in Japan* and Ciaran Carson's *The Twelfth of Never* which also draw on Japanese culture in their quest for new perspectives on home.

> While my hard-nosed companions dream of fire
> And sword upon parched veldt and fields of rain-swept gorse.
>
> (*CP* 105)

'Lying low' suggests a poetic situation which, as Edna Longley comments, is 'well placed to subvert'.[14] It represents a marginal, oblique point of view in relation to dominant social, familial, communal values and expectations. And it is that displaced angle of vision which conditions the speaker's response to the world of the painting. The tone of the poem is a finely modulated combination of admiring identification and critical detachment. In the occasional fifth stanza (omitted from both the *Collected Poems* and *Selected Poems*), that balance is lost and detachment shifts to outright repudiation: the poet fantasies about an apocalyptic eruption of dark, pagan female energy in the form of the Maenads, to overthrow the oppressive, patriarchal Protestant order that he acknowledges as part of his own heritage.

Similarly, in 'Girls on the Bridge', based on a series of paintings by the Norwegian artist Edvard Munch, Mahon once again finds himself contemplating an image of people – the young girls on the bridge at twilight – as if frozen in time. But the picture of the contented, laughing girls on the bridge is no more immune from history than those of de Hooch's courtyards in Delft or the Japanese snow party: 'Grave daughters/ Of time, you lightly toss/ Your hair as the long shadows grow/ And night begins to fall' (*CP* 152). Falling under Mahon's penetrating gaze, the cold dream of a place out of time, with its images of apparent permanence, transcendence and peace, is made to yield up its hidden alienating and disruptive content.

Another aspect of Mahon's interest in internationalising his aesthetic is his recurrent identification with an international band of famous exiles and artists who typify existential isolation – Brecht, Camus, Corbière, Hamsun, Van Gogh, Villon. In 'A Kensington Notebook', he recreates the ferment among the metropolitan artistic community in 1920s London, at the centre of which was the expatriate Ezra Pound, who lived at No. 10 Church Walk between 1908 and 1920. Conscious of the incompatibility of artistic culture and an advancing modernisation, Pound, like many American artists in the early twentieth century, moved to Europe, because here, they believed, was the home of a redeeming civilisation. A self-confessed 'out and out traditionalist'[15] such as Mahon was unlikely to be stirred by Pound's technical and stylistic experiment (though he shares Pound's interest in the Image and the haiku): what the deracinated American primarily represented for Mahon was the figure of the artist-exile in the modern world. There are obvious affinities between the two poets. Both disdained their roots, fled provincialism and identified with bohemianism. Both are self-appointed spokesmen for a kind of intellectual and spiritual aristocracy, and have denounced the philistine gehenna of contemporary society. Like Pound, Mahon espouses a disciplined aestheticism and traverses cultures and languages, like the thoroughgoing cosmopolitan he is. Following in the footsteps of the medi-

---

[14] Edna Longley, 'Derek Mahon: Extreme Religion of Art', in Michael Kenneally (ed.), *Poetry in Contemporary Irish Literature* (Gerrards Cross, Colin Smythe, 1995) pp. 280–303, 287.

[15] John Brown, *In the Chair*, p. 117.

evalising and classicising 'Ezra Pound, M.A.', Mahon is a prodigious summoner of imagined elsewheres through his 'adaptations' of sources, from Sophocles to Pasolini, Juvenal to Brecht, the *trobairitz*, Nerval, Valéry, Baudelaire, Pasternak, Rilke and Ní Dhomhnaill.[16] Pound's *Lustra* (1916) contains 'Provincia Deserta', a poem inspired by his walking tour in troubadour Provence, in which he laments the decline of one of the great provinces of medieval France: Mahon adapts Pound's title for one of the sections of *The Yellow Book*, 'America Deserta', which is an excoriation of society's addiction to 'post-modern kitsch' and an elegy for 'an older America of the abrasive spirit,/ *film noir*, real jazz and grown-up literate wit' (*CP* 255–6). Section II of 'A Kensington Notebook' offers an impressionistic sketch of the lone reactionary modernist, exponent of Imagism and Vorticism, obsessive translator and confirmed aesthete who sought to renew a debased and venal present by invoking the cultural resources of past civilisations – the troubadours and Guido Cavalcanti, Sophocles and Sextus Propertius, the Japanese Noh and the Confucian *Ta Hsiao*:

> The operantics of
> Provence and Languedoc
> Shook the Gaudier marbles
> At No. 10 Church Walk
>
> Where 'Ezra Pound, M.A.,
> Author of *Personae*',
> Sniffed out the image with
> Whiskery antennae.   (*CP* 144)

The verse mimics Pound's modernist bareness, suppleness and delicacy, his laconic decorum, his colloquial eloquence. John Goodby identifies the element of parody: '"A Kensington Notebook" cleverly pastiches the metrical conservatism of Pound's Mauberley poems – one of the few formal points of entry for Mahon.'[17] Mahon hails Pound's invocation of 'The Spirit of Romance' (*CP* 145) (the title of Pound's 1910 prose study of the medieval troubadours) in a dark age, though in mock-heroic vein. He recalls, too, Pound's cultivation of the young sculptor, Gaudier-Brzeska, whom he met in London in 1913 and helped to re-direct away from the tradition of Rodin towards the principles of the emergent Vorticist movement. The author of *Lives* could identify with the 'Author of *Personae*', both poets recognising the multiplicity of the poetic self, both exercised by the tension between the claims of social conscience and those of artistic freedom. Pound's poetry is much more archival and 'intellectual' than Mahon's, but both poets represent a cultural elitism, or, more bluntly, snobbery, which characterises their stance of principled exile in the midst of a cultural and spiritual wasteland. Mahon, for example, complains:

> (Not Dowland, not Purcell
> 'The age demanded',

---

16   See Derek Mahon, *Adaptations* (Loughcrew, The Gallery Press, 2006).
17   John Goodby, '"The Soul of Silence": Derek Mahon's Masculinities', in Elmer Kennedy-Andrews (ed.), *The Poetry of Derek Mahon*, p. 217.

But the banalities
Of the *Evening Standard*)   (*CP* 144)

Here, Mahon reflects on lines from 'Hugh Selwyn Mauberley' (1920), Pound's 'farewell to London', which took the form of a savage critique of England in the years surrounding World War I:

The age demanded an image
Of its accelerated grimace,
Something for the modern stage,
Not, at any rate, an Attic grace;

Not, not certainly, the obscure reveries
Of the inward gaze;
Better mendacities
Than the classics in paraphrase![18]

Throughout 'A Kensington Notebook', Mahon is mindful of where Pound's aestheticism led him, and follows the trajectory of the American's career from his Kensington period to the time when 'He drawls "treason" into/ A Roman microphone' – a reference to Pound's wartime Rome radio broadcasts propagandising on behalf of Mussolini. Pound's belief in a perfect aesthetic realm propelled him towards fascism as an exemplary political system that gave 'Kulchur' and the artist the central position in society he deemed so necessary. While sharing Pound's despair at the contemporary world, Mahon distances himself from the Poundian project of resistance, as indicated by the wryly humorous, ironic tone that he maintains throughout 'A Kensington Notebook'. Adopting the Poundian repertoire of sarcastic epigram and casual disdain, Mahon turns it against Pound as well as society. Where Pound tended toward an affirmation of centralised control, absolute efficiency, ideological imperialism, a politics of the artist who must lead society to political perfection and historical greatness, Mahon self-consciously retreats from this authoritarian role, aligning himself with the Decadents and Symbolists as an antidote to the prescriptive ideologies of power poetry and power politics. 'A Kensington Notebook' ends with a querulous image implying the uncertainty of the Poundian legacy:

Un rameur, finally,
Sur le fleuve des morts,
Poling his profile toward
What farther shore?   (*CP* 147)

The note of exile is more plangently sounded in Mahon's recreation of Ovid. In giving voice to Ovid's feelings of isolation in the barbarian wasteland of Tomis, in 'Ovid in Tomis', he articulates his own sense of exile in his native Ulster: 'The Muse is somewhere/ Else, not here/ By this frozen lake –/ Or, if here, then I am/ Not poet enough/ To make the connection' (*CP* 157). Mahon's Ovid makes it clear that the exile of which he speaks is no mere political and cultural displacement, but a fundamental spiritual and ontological deracination: 'Pan is

---

[18]   Ezra Pound, 'Hugh Selwyn Mauberley', II, lines 1–8, in *Selected Poems 1908–1959* (London, Faber, 1984) pp. 98–9.

dead, and already/ I feel an ancient/ Unity eave the earth' (*CP* 157). In 'Brecht in Svendborg', he identifies with Brecht who in 1933 fled Germany with his family to Zurich, and then to Svendborg in Denmark, where he worked on his poetry collection *Svenderborger Gedichte*, fragments of which Mahon re-works in his poem. Using Brecht's situation, Mahon alludes to the greatest challenge facing the exile – establishing 'a home from home': 'This could be home from home/ If things were otherwise' (*HBN* 17). Despite work and family, Brecht cannot establish a home from home because he is continually aware of the encroaching 'War-games of the Reich'. Not even exile permits an exit from history. Returning to the idea of the 'home from home' in 'The Globe in North Carolina', Mahon, with his apocalyptic sense of history, opts for the 'theoptic view', the deterritori-alised perspective not located in any particular place, but in 'the glory-hole/ Of space, a home from home' (*CP* 141).

The later American poems in 'The Hudson Letter' mark a notable closing of the distance between self and world. In 'The Hudson Letter', Mahon describes himself as 'an amateur immigrant' (*CP* 190), a 'resident alien' (*CP* 190). The earlier anguished sense of displacement gives way to a more accepting attitude, a new cosmopolitan confidence, a fascination with the multiple fusions of the global village where he seeks to improvise a sense of self from his heteroge-neous experience. Here he meditates on the migrant condition, discovering the diasporic notion of place and home, not only in terms of the Irish immigrant experience, but also that of others – African-American, Chinese, Jewish, Haitian, Hispanic. The tendency in the sequence is to normalise exile, to aestheticise homelessness. In doing so, Mahon continues to make his own belated contribu-tion to the modernist mythology of the 'artist in exile' who is never at home, always existentially alone, and shocked by the experience of displacement into significant new insights and forms. Mahon is a follower of Malcolm Cowley's 'lost generation' of the 1920s, except that where educated, middle-class young men such as Pound, Crane, Hemingway and Fitzgerald moved from America to Europe, Mahon develops his exilic aesthetics in the American metropolis. Central to Malcolm Bradbury's classic study of literary modernism is the trope of exile:

> For Modernism is a metropolitan art, which is to say it is group art, a specialist art, an intellectual art, an art for one's aesthetic peers: it recalls, with whatever ironies and paradoxes, the imperium of civilization. Not simply metropolitan, indeed, but cosmopolitan: one city leads to another in the distinctive aesthetic voyage into the metamorphosis of form. The writer may hold on to locality, as Joyce held on to Dublin, Hemingway to the Michigan woods; but he perceives from the distance of an expatriate perspective of aesthetic internationalism ... Thus frequently it is emigration or exile that makes for membership of the modern country of the arts ... The writer himself becomes a member of a wandering, culturally inquisitive group – by enforced exile (like Nabokov's after the Russian revolution) or by design and desire. The place of art's very making can become an ideal distant city, where the creator counts, or the chaos is fruitful, the *Weltgeist* flows.[19]

---

[19] Malcolm Bradbury, 'The Cities of Modernism', in Bradbury and James McFarlane (eds.), *Modernism: 1890–1930* (Pelican Guide to European Literature, 1976) p. 101.

Displacement, whether voluntary or enforced, is the defining feature of modernist sensibility. In George Steiner's words, the modernist writer is 'extraterritorial' or 'unhoused'. Harry Levin, in his influential essay, 'Literature and Exile', views the modern era as a 'deracinated culture', marked by the 'metic condition, the polyglot understanding of our time'.[20] The writer may be always 'looking homeward, bearing it continually in mind', but he remains estranged from collective identity and historical experience: 'Detachment of the one from the many ... is the necessary precondition of all original thought.'[21][20] The flight from national or provincial origins and their besetting political and social conflicts into the cosmopolitan and polyglot city that underscores most late twentieth-century ideologies of modernism is reproduced in Mahon's transatlanticism.

Mahon's modernist exile poetics struggle to deal with postmodernity's challenges to those modernist values and forms of culture. The disruptions of master narratives that postmodernism implies include questioning of the modernist concept of the autonomous, transcendent art object. Deriving from the Horatian verse epistle and the Juvenalian verse satire, Mahon's 'Hudson Letter', with its irregularly rhyming, loosely iambic pentameters, ghosted by the eighteenth-century rhyming couplet, maintains its connection with the aestheticised criteria of modernism. Yet the poetry is marked by a notable shift away from modernist discourses of transcendence and towards the unstable ground of the postmodern metropolis. With the emphasis on local, micro, or regional cultural elements, and on images of multiplicity, fragmentation and difference, Mahon absorbs the world around him – billboard advertisements, newspaper headlines, graffiti, snippets of conversations and monologues, literary translations and imitations. The poems include a wide range of geographical, cultural, historical, linguistic and literary references. As well as allusions to writers who are outsiders and exiles (Ovid, Camus, MacNeice, Auden, Wilde, Lorca), there is an unprecedented embracement of popular culture, with references to Woody Allen, Noel Coward, Satchmo, Eartha Kitt, *King Kong, The Exterminator*, Batman, Guns 'n' Roses. Traditional borders and cultures are deconstructed and dissolved into new ones. 'Chinatown', both place and poem, is a paradigmatic site of cultural fusion and confident cosmopolitanism. No longer situating himself in bleak, barren terminal landscapes but in the heart of the multicultural metropolis, in his 'rented "studio apartment" in New York' (*CP* 186), he develops a new looser, confessional and conversational style to accommodate this pluralistic, diverse world.

Mahon attempts to give depth and texture to his 'letter' by entering into intertextual dialogue with others who have likewise sought to record the Manhattan experience. Two other signatories of particular moment are Hart Crane and Frank O'Hara. On occasion, Mahon's America seems even more dead and depressed than it was in Crane's day: 'a fog-horn echoes in deserted sheds/ known to Hart Crane, and in our vigilant beds./ No liners now, nothing but ice and sleet' (*CP* 190). In Crane's 'Proem: To Brooklyn Bridge', the speaker identifies with the seagull, but there is uncertainty about the freedom which it represents (the seagull being both 'inviolate' and 'apparitional'):

---

[20] Harry Levin, 'Literature and Exile', in *Refractions: Essays in Comparative Literature* (New York, Oxford University Press, 1966) p. 65.

[21] Ibid., p. 81.

How many dawns, chill from his rippling rest,
The seagull's wings shall dip and pivot him,
Shedding white rings of tumult, building high
Over the chained bay waters Liberty –

Then, with inviolate curve, forsake our eyes
As apparitional as sails that cross
Some page of figures to be filed away;
– Till elevators drop us from our day … [22]

Similarly, Crane's eponymous bridge represents only a brittle faith in industrial man. Just as Crane struggles to find sources of vitality for the modern world, so too Mahon is divided between confidence and despair. The confidence is reinforced by the example of Frank O'Hara. Mahon is attracted by the debonaire O'Hara's light, insouciant style and bright vulgarity. With O'Hara to lead him, Mahon gives free rein to his childlike excitement in the metropolis, allowing himself to be seduced by consumerism and popular culture, and striking up a chummy, camp rapport with the reader:

I go nightshopping like Frank O'Hara I go bopping
up Bleeker for juice, croissants, Perrier, ice-cream
and Gitane filters, pick up the laundry, get back
to five (5!) messages on the answering machine
from Mary K. and Eliza, Louis, Barry and Jack …   (*CP* 211)

'The Hudson Letter', that is, expresses Mahon's dual sense of the (post)modern. At times he seems at home with homelessness, at other times the note of exile prevails. Crane's seagull reappears in Section VI, in the form of two escaped seabirds, an Inca tern and Andean gull, figures of the artist. The seabirds, exhilarated and frightened in their new surroundings of downtown New York, 'stare/ at the alien corn of Radio City, Broadway and Times Square' (*CP* 196). Mahon links the birds with both F. Scott Fitzgerald and Keats: 'Like Daisy's Cunard nightingale, they belong in another life'. They symbolise the plight of the romantic in an unromantic world. With no fixed points of reference, and unprepared for new conditions, they have little chance of survival in the fight 'on the city street/ with urban gulls, crows, and other toughs of the air'. Modernist tropes of displacement are inscribed within the urban and social space of postmodernism.

Two sections explore specifically Irish exilic experience. Section V, 'To Mrs Moore at Inishannon', takes the form of a pastiche letter of Bridget Moore, a nineteenth-century domestic in service in New York whose horizons are still bounded by her native Co. Cork. The poem ridicules the girl's naïve and sentimental attachment to her native place ('as if Earth's centre lay in Central Park/ when we both know it runs thro' Co Cork', *CP* 195) especially since the pull of homeland loses out so decisively in the end to material considerations (she stays because 'the money's good' in America). In 'Imbolc: JBY' Mahon identifies with John Butler Yeats, the accomplished portrait painter and prodigal father of the

---

[22] *The Complete Poems of Hart Crane*, edited by Waldo Frank (New York, Doubleday Anchor Books, 1958) p. 3.

great poet, William B., and artist son, Jack B. Originally from Co. Down, John was a restless spirit, graduating in law from Mahon's old Alma Mater, Trinity College Dublin, then pursuing a career as a painter. He moved back and forth between England and Ireland before emigrating in 1907 at the age of sixty-eight to New York, where he lived for fourteen years until his death in 1922. The image of John Yeats, the figure of perpetual migrancy, 'negotiating the ice-fields of Eighth Avenue/ … past the Blarney Stone and the White Rose,/ to die on West 29th of the Asian "flu"' (*CP* 218), places him in unstable terrain, negotiating the shifting markers of a globalised modernity. Mahon concentrates on John Yeats's sensitivity to the suffering of the poor and the outcast, recalling his concern for another kind of exile whom the painter met in New York: 'a young woman with a sick child she tried to hide/ … / soft-spoken, "from Donnybrook", amid the alien corn'. This suggestion of the perennial female persona of Ireland, the visionary Cathleen Ni Houlihan, and the references to the biblical story of Ruth and Keats's 'Ode to a Nightingale' help to generalise the condition of homelessness. Exile extends beyond modernist aestheticised displacement (John Yeats), social prejudice (the nameless young mother) and colonial dispossession (as in the political aisling) to become the sign of an existential condition, a condition of the soul, regardless of the facts of material life. We are all exiles now, the last four lines would seem to say:

> Now, to 'Yeats, Artist and Writer', may we add
> that you were at home here and in human nature?
> – But also, in your own words, lived and died
> like all of us, then as now, 'an exile and a stranger'? (*CP* 219)

Unlike earlier poetry, and despite the plea in the last line of the last section – 'We have been too long in the cold. – Take us in! Take us in!' ('The Small Rain', *CP* 222), which contains its own delightful pun – the overall tone is not so much one of anguish as acceptance of homelessness. The old binaries of exile and homeland are complicated and blurred as the poet, so unlike Bridget Moore, moves through a wide range of geographical and cultural spaces, and towards a multiple sense of home. In the earlier poetry, a sense of placelessness predominates, but with 'The Hudson Letter' the migrant condition leads to a closer engagement with the people who make up the shifting, postmodern world in which he lives. Collapsing the notoriously elitist postures of modernism, he identifies with the plight of the dispossessed.

The title of Section XII, 'Alien Nation', refers to several things: first, Mahon's America; second, a general existential condition of exile deriving from his own expatriate situation; and third, the alienated subculture within the American nation – the outsiders who haunt the margins of society. For the first time in his work, he examines the plight of the poor and homeless, and explicitly identifies with them. His vernacular speech and conversational tone reinforce his sense of solidarity: 'I know you and you me, you wretched buggers,/ and I've no problem calling you my brothers/ for I too have been homeless and in detox/ with BAAAD niggaz 'n' crack hoes on the rocks' (*CP* 207–8). Embarrassing as Mahon's attempt at black street rap may be, his style is nothing if not heterogenous. This section takes as its epigraph a piece of journalistic reportage on the homeless, proceeds with a collage of advertisements, then shifts to a more conventionally formal and literary style:

> RX ROTHAM DRUG GAY CRUISES SONY LIQUORS MARLBORO
> ADULT VIDEO XXX BELSHAZZAR FIND THE CURE
> IGLESIA ADVENTISTA DEL 7MO. DIA ...
> ... We come upon them in the restless dark
> in the moon-shadow of the World Trade Centre
> with Liberty's torch glimmering over the water,
> glued to a re-run of *The Exterminator* ... (*CP* 207)

The basic verse line remains the iambic pentameter stiffened by persistent if irregular rhyme. For all the poet's going out into the 'real world' of history and people, he invariably retreats into a closeted aesthetic world of high culture. As John Goodby remarks: 'The poems (in *The Hudson Letter* and *The Yellow Book*) often begin with a New York scene but appeal, in seeking fit closure, to the likes of Glenn Gould, George Herbert, Confucius and Racine. The irony is all at the expense of the present.'[23] The pervasive and corrosive postmodern scepticism concerning subjectivity, identity and representation does not erase from the poetry a central core or structure of meaning; nor does it cancel the possibility of renewal and redemption, which *The Hudson Letter* attempts to affirm in an exquisite lyric close. By necessity, if not choice, he inhabits an 'alien nation', and the poignant yearning for connection that is sounded in 'In Belfast'/'The Spring Vacation', 'Nostalgias' and 'A Disused Shed' continues to animate a poetic quest for home and wholeness.

The Yellow Book evinces a noticeable hardening of attitude to the decadence of contemporary life. Ensconced in his own attic room in Dublin, he knows the intellectual isolation of those exemplary artists described by Edward Wilson in *Axel's Castle*. In section II, 'Axel's Castle', he contrasts his current abode in Fitzwilliam Square with Coole Park, and the Dublin of Yeats and Wilde with the present commercialised, hi-tech metropolis:

> The fountain's flute is silent though time spares
> the old beech trees with their echoes of Coole demesne;
> foreign investment conspires against old decency,
> computer talks to computer, machine to answering machine.
>
> (*CP*, 227)

The 'high' culture which he values – '*Fanny Hill, A Rebours, The Picture of Dorian Gray* –/ the pleasures of the text, periphrasis and paradox,/ some languorous prose at odds with phone and fax' (*CP* 226) – is irrelevant to a materialistic, utilitarian society of commuters and businessmen. Mahon is 'a decadent who lived to tell the story' (*CP* 239).

Section X, 'The Idiocy of Human Aspirations', is a version of Juvenal's *Satire X*, a powerfully depressing and pessimistic castigation of the corruption and degeneracy of everyday life in Imperial Rome. Following Dr Johnson (in 'The Vanity of Human Wishes') and Robert Lowell (in *Near the Ocean*), Mahon

---

23 John Goodby, 'The Soul of Silence', p. 223.

uses Juvenal's masterpiece of fierce moral invective and vivid portraiture as an expressive model for framing his own savage criticisms of contemporary life: 'all anyone does now is fuck and shit;/ instant gratification, infotainment, celebrity' (*CP* 244). In section XI, 'At the Chelsea Arts Club', contemporary art is damned for its lack of intellectual and formal rigour, its elevation of popular culture and sensationalism: 'the body art, snuff sculpture, trash aesthetics/ the video nasties and shock computer graphics' (*CP* 245). The new freedoms produce worse art than the old repressions: 'our chains gone/ that bound with form the psycho-sexual turbulence/ .../ at home now with the ersatz, the pop, the phony' (*CP* 231). For Mahon, we are no longer capable of responding to the 'sublime' or the tragic sense of life, no longer appreciative of 'creative tension': 'Bring on ivy and goatskin, pipe and drum,/ for Dionysus son of Semele is come/ to release us from our servitude to the sublime,/ no further resistance offered by the medium,/ the whole history of creative tension a waste of time' (*CP* 242). Section IV ('Shiver in your Tenement') recreates the atmosphere and personalities of literary Dublin in the 1960s, in 'the days before tourism and economic growth,/ before decon-struction and the death of the author' (*CP* 230), and, like a latter-day Matthew Arnold bemoaning the retreat of the Sea of Faith, he laments the loss of 'patience, courage, artistry', qualities that have disappeared from 'the pastiche paradise of the post-modern' (*CP* 231). In an age of global, homogenised culture he feels like 'an alien among aliens .../ spying for the old world in the new' (*CP* 255). He is pessimistic about the future of literary culture in a mass technological age: 'real books will be rarities in techno-culture,/ a forest of intertextuality like this' (*CP* 240). The pervasive intertextuality in the form of allusions, quotations and epigraphs serves to emphasise the poet's commitment to the increasingly arcane and disprized practices of literary culture, his elaborate literariness functioning as an act of defiance in an age which no longer values the pleasures of the text. Many of the references are to Decadent literature (Baudelaire, Huysmans, Wilde), which Mahon invokes as a parallel to his own aesthetic. His heroes, mentioned by name, include Austin Clarke (IV) who represents artistic personality in an age which proclaimed the death of the author, freedom of thought in a time of reli-gious conservatism, and authentic artistry in a postmodern age when anything goes; Eugene Lambe (VI), the courteous bohemian; and Elizabeth Bowen (III), a figure of displacement and liminality for whom the Shelbourne Hotel 'is home really, a place of warmth and light,/ a house of artifice neither here nor there/ between the patrician past and the egalitarian future' (*CP* 229).

The new turn in Mahon's career represented by the looser, long-lined, conver-sational poems in *The Hudson Letter* and *The Yellow Book* were not to the taste of all erstwhile Mahon fans. Patrick Crotty writes of 'the sometimes banal truth of the discursive verse' in *The Hudson Letter*, finding some sections 'slack in conception' and many 'slacker again in execution'.[24] The writing, Crotty says, is at times little more than 'loosely versified whining and opining', characterised by 'irritatingly journalistic phrasing',[25] and amounting to 'a species of nostalgic populism so unexamined as to deserve the customary epithet "mindless"'.[26] Peter

---

[24] Kennedy-Andrews, p. 280.
[25] Ibid.
[26] Ibid., p. 292.

McDonald complains of Mahon's 'conflating style with personality',[27] and criticises the 'apparent casualness of the poetry's content' and the 'loose form ... with its often lazy rhyming and rhythmic slackness'. In McDonald's view, 'Mahon's former alertness and searching irony with regard to language has rotted into an indiscriminate impatience and intolerance ... an uninspired gruffness'. The poet, McDonald concludes, is too caught up in the quarrel with others to make his own self-interrogation interesting.

Mahon himself, let it be said, is not unaware of his tendency towards curmudgeonliness and self-indulgence, though his occasional gestures of self-criticism ('Maybe I'm finally turning into an old fart/ but I do prefer the traditional kinds of art,/ respect for materials, draughtsmanship and so on –' (*CP* 245)) are hardly enough to fend off the debilitating effects of so much easy generalisation and opinion, lack of rhythmic enactment and strident rhetoric. By aligning *The Yellow Book* with the famous literary magazine of the same name that was published between 1894 and 1897 and associated with Aubrey Beardsley, Oscar Wilde and the Decadent and Aestheticist movements, Mahon would seem to be signalling two things: first, the idea that the twentieth-century *fin de siècle* mirrors the decadence of the nineteenth-century *fin de siècle*, both periods being characterised by rampant vulgarisation, philistinism and alienation, loss of certainty in knowledge, morality, society, science and technology, and a sense of exhaustion and entropy; and, second, his own 'decadent' aesthetic belief that art and morality are distinct realms, that art has an autonomous existence and is in fact a refuge from reality, a counterbalance to the materialism and utilitarianism of the contemporary world. In his essay 'Decadence in Later Nineteenth Century England', R.K.R. Thompson sets out the dilemma faced by the decadent subject:

> [T]he Decadent is a man caught between two opposite and apparently incompatible pulls: on the one hand he is drawn by the world, its necessities, and the attractive impression he receives from it, while on the other hand he yearns towards the eternal, the ideal, and the unworldly. The play between these two poles forms the typical Decadent subject matter and is at the root of much of the period's manner ... [T]he incompatibility of the two poles gives rise to the characteristic decadent notes of disillusion, frustration, and lassitude at the same time as the equally characteristic self-mockery.[28]

'Disillusion, frustration and lassitude' would seem to sum up fairly accurately much of Mahon's feeling in *The Yellow Book*. Taking his epigraph from Cyril Connolly's 'The Unquiet Grave' – 'To live in a decadence need not make us despair; it is but one technical problem the more which a writer has to solve'[29] – Mahon attempted to develop a new style that would be expressive of the characteristic 'decadent' tension between being a part *of*, and the desire to be apart *from*, the psycho-social condition which he is exploring. The stridencies of *The Yellow Book* testify to the difficulty of resolving this besetting tension.

---

[27]   Peter McDonald, 'Incurable Ache', *Poetry Ireland Review*, 56 (Spring 1998) pp. 117–19.
[28]   Quoted in Ian Fletcher (ed.), *Decadence and the 1890s* (New York, Holmes & Meier, 1980) p. 26.
[29]   Derek Mahon, *The Yellow Book* (Loughcrew, The Gallery Press, 1997), npn.

Appearing after a virtual thirteen-year silence, *The Hudson Letter* and, four years later, *The Yellow Book*, together represent a remarkable attempt at self-reinvention. One aspect of these new directions is the poet's re-insertion of himself as representative figure into the historical process. Another is his drive beyond the apocalyptic rhetoric of earlier work towards affirmation of an ecocentric vision of hopeful new beginnings. The last section of *The Yellow Book*, 'Christmas in Kinsale', juxtaposes the conflicting narratives of apocalyptic doom and millennial hope, the title evoking the memory of racial defeat and subjugation at the Battle of Kinsale in 1601, but also thoughts of new beginnings as told by the Christian story of the Nativity. Mahon imagines people congregating at the great sites of history, waiting for revelation: 'The young are slouching into Bethlehem/ as zealots turn out for the millennium/ on Sinai and Everest, Patmos and Ararat' (*CP* 264). More emphatically than in his earlier speculations on post-apocalyptic new beginnings (in such poems as 'The Apotheosis of Tins' or 'Thamuz'), the new millennium provokes visions of a hopeful future, a restoration of the broken bond between the human and the natural, a return to primitive animal and vegetable origins:

> The harsh will dies here among snails and peonies,
> its grave an iridescence in the sea-breeze,
> a bucket of water where the rainbow ends.
> Elsewhere the cutting edge, the tough cities,
> the nuclear wind from Windscale, derelict zones;
> here the triumph of carnival, rinds and skins,
> mud-wrestling organisms in post-historical phase
> and the fuzzy vegetable glow of origins.
> A cock crows good-morning from an oil-drum
> like a peacock on a rain-barrel in Byzantium;
> soap-bubbles foam in a drainpipe and life begins.
> I dreamed last night of a blue Cycladic dawn,
> Again the white islands shouting, 'Come on; come on!' ...   (*CP* 265)

Here, Mahon insists upon what in 'The Sea in Winter' he calls nature's 'weird/ facticity' (*CP* 117). Nature is anterior to, more fundamental than, any belief in social constructedness: it is an irrefutable actual presence which affects us, and which we can affect, perhaps fatally, if we mistreat it. The lines above emphasise ecocentric values of close observation and appreciation of the miracle of the ordinary, collective ecological responsibility, and the claims of the natural world beyond ourselves. They re-affirm the assurance that emerges in Section XVII ('The World of J.G. Farrell') where the poet's elegiac meditation on the end of empire inspired by the novels of his friend, J.G. Farrell, concludes with succinct reference to the teachings of the Taoist philosopher Chuang Tzu, who 'knew our vital unity with the rest of nature' (*CP* 259).

One of the tutelary spirits hovering over Mahon's latest collection, *Harbour Lights*, is Rachel Carson, whose book about the catastrophic effects of industrial pollution, *Silent Spring* (1962), is one of the foundational texts of modern environmentalism. The title of that book provides another intertextual source of Mahon's pervasive bird imagery, the 'silent spring' being an allusion to the absence of birdsong in Keats's 'La Belle Dame', and, more generally, to the obliteration of the pastoral myth of peace and harmony by environmental apocalypse. Mahon's title poem, 'Harbour Lights' is prefaced by a Carson quotation – '*And I … a mere newcomer whose ancestors had inhabited the earth so briefly that my presence was almost anachronistic*'[30] – which Mahon uses to establish the vast ecocentric perspectives within which the human struggle should be understood. The quotation is from an earlier Carson work, *The Edge of the Sea* (1955), in which the Pennsylvanian marine biologist wrote about the wonders of ocean life, celebrated the diversity and beauty of nature and warned against the senseless destruction of the environment by a society blinded by technological progress. Echoing Chuang Tzu, Carson remarks: 'In each of my books I have tried to say that all the life of the planet is inter-related, that each species has its own ties to others, and that all are related to the earth.' Such a pronouncement represents a significant re-orientation away from the postures of alienation which characterised Mahon's earlier work.

Inter-relatedness becomes Mahon's central theme and major compositional principle. He quotes from Eliot's *The Dry Salvages* (intertextuality itself being a way of demonstrating inter-relatedness): '*Lady, whose shrine stands on the promontory*' (*HL* 64). Like Eliot, Mahon compares modern secular society to an endless voyage with no apparent destination, and prays for guidance and protection to the Holy Virgin who, in 'Harbour Lights', is pictured 'gazing out over the transatlantic cable/ with a chipped eye towards Galicia and the Azores' (*HL* 64). The poem is set in Kinsale, but, like the statue, gazes out in all directions. Kinsale is a multiple, transnational, transethnic, transhistorical terrain, a place out of time: 'I could be living here in another age.' The dreamy woods are 'straight out of Chekhov' (*HL* 61), the gardens are 'made for 19th-century love' (*HL* 61); 'trans-national, the skies are Indian skies,/ the harbour lights Chinese or Japanese' (*HL* 61); young people chatter 'as in a Russian novel' (*HL* 62); the strand is 'where Cuchulainn fought the waves' (*HL* 63); the speaker walks 'in the loud, work-glow of a Roumanian freighter' (*HL* 63). Old ideas of bounded community, organic culture, regionalism, nationalism, can no longer account for transnational circuits of culture and people. The poem emphasises links between diverse locations and people, bridging and deconstructing essentialist constructions of home. 'Will the long voyage end here among friends?' Mahon asks, suggesting that homecoming may be an impossibility, that he is forever a migrant subject-in-transit.

Home is ultimately the whole interconnected world, 'each thing distinct but in oblique relation' (*HL* 63). The mind that has been exiled from nature is ecologically reintegrated. 'Swimming with a loved one from white strands/ the sea loud in our veins' (*HL* 67), he identifies with a swarming, fecund underground life, leaguing himself with dark, mysterious, poetic forces and 'secret cultures': 'Dim souls wriggle in seething chaos, body/ Language and new thought forming there already/ In hidden depths'. Dislodging essentialist identities in favour of creative,

---

[30] Derek Mahon, 'Harbour Lights', in *Harbour Lights* (Loughcrew, The Gallery Press, 2005) p. 61. Hereafter abbreviated to *HL* and page references incorporated into the text.

relational acts of identification, the poem concludes by connecting Kinsale and the Galapagos:

> No, this is Galapagos and the old life-force
> rides Daz and Exxon to the blinding surface.
> Down there a drenching of the wilful sperm,
> congenital sea-fight of the shrimp and worm
> with somewhere the soft impulse of a lover,
> the millions swarming into pond and river
> to find the right place, find it and live for ever …? (*HL* 67)

The language and imagery, reminiscent of Yeats's 'mackerel-crowded seas', return us to the Carson epigraph. Opting for a biological metaphor of the poem/home, 'Harbour Lights', ending with ellipses and a question mark, refuses to offer guarantees of the future, but, equally, rejects the apocalyptic rhetoric of 'The-End-of-Nature' narrative.

The opening poem, 'Resistance Days', sets the tone of the rest of the collection, mobilising a poetics of social protest against unhappy trends which the poet discerns in modern life – postmodern barbarism, the homogenisation and commodification of culture, the death of the author and the rejection of originality. 'Resistance Days' speaks for a 'fugitive' art, 'creative anarchy' (*HL* 17); the poet's own resolution is 'to study weather, clouds and their formation' (*HL* 17). Clouds drift through the entire collection, which invokes Lucretius, Bonnefoy, Brecht and Aristophanes on clouds. Clouds are thoughts, fleeting and indeterminate, 'from whose precipitations images gather/ as in the opacity of a developing-bath' ('The Cloud Ceiling', *HL* 29). It is to the empyrean realm of the clouds that the poet belongs: 'even at sixty I can still walk on air' ('During the War', *HL* 31), he says, playfully aligning himself with Heaneyesque notions of art's magical powers. Amid the arid wastelands of (post)modernity, 'Lucretius on Clouds' affirms the life-giving process of distillation, poetic as well as meteorological: 'As for the rain clouds, how they come to grow/ and fall as rain on the drinking earth below –/ a multitude of life-germs, water semen …' (*HL* 21). Clouds are the wispy, insubstantial, ever-changing symbols of a world beyond the 'mud and junk' of 'earthly intercourse' ('During the War', *HL* 31); 'I toy with cloud thoughts as an alternative/ to the global shit-storm that we know and love' ('Harbour Lights', *HL* 66). Mahon's 'cloud cinema', part of a new, insistently elemental aesthetic of earth, air and water ('two worlds, earth and air;/ water, the best of both', 'Shorelines', *HL* 48), opposes itself to fixed views of the world: the formal rigour of earlier 'hard-wired' work becomes more flexible and fluid, more directly confessional and sentimental:

> I who, though soft-hearted, always admired
> Granite and blackthorn and the verse hard-wired,
> Tingle and flow like January thaw-water
> In contemplation of this rosy daughter.
>
> ('The Cloud Ceiling', *HL* 30)

Clouds, like the earlier imagery of water – the 'unstructurable sea', rivers, shorelines – the flight of birds, refractions of light, represent the unpredictability and mutability of the natural world which both defies and provokes the human urge towards equilibrium and order.

Distancing himself from the new cultural orthodoxies, he continues to identify with the dislocated, the itinerant and the homeless, as in 'Jean Rhys in Kettner's' and the very fine 'Calypso'. He is drawn to the figure of Jean Rhys, the West Indian white Creole writer, self-destructive and alcoholic, whose life was divided between England and the Caribbean, and whose theme in works such as *Wide Sargasso Sea* was that of the helpless female, the outsider, victimised by her dependence on male support and protection: 'bewitched, bewildered, in at least two minds,/ we found no true home in our chosen west' (*HL* 37). Using the strict order of the sonnet form, Mahon dramatises the speaker's experience of 'fighting to keep sane/ in a new age', living out 'two lives/ between the water and the *vie en rose*' (*HL* 38). The significance of this liminal space between land and sea – a recurrent Mahonian setting – is explained by another exacerbated female figure, the widow of Kinsale (in the poem of that name). The 'strand' is where the widow is brought to contemplation of the elemental facts of life, the claims of primitive nature:

> The best place is the strand,
> Its primitive life-forms
> When the last light warms
> Islands of shining sand
> And the ebb-tide withdraws
> With a chuckle of bony claws. (*HL* 43)

In 'Calypso', Ulysses is the man who allows himself to be seduced from his 'chief design', who turns his back on wife, home, family and nation, and explores 'alternatives to war and power' (*HL*, 57). These alternatives lie in Thoreau-like withdrawal from society 'to live in peace with violent nature', and appreciation of 'the redemptive power of women' (which apparently does not include Penelope). Viewed as an ecofeminist poem, 'Calypso' repudiates an androcentric value system which privileges culture, reason and mind, and exalts femininity, nature, irrationality, emotion and the body. In this respect, Mahon's Ulysses is very different from Tennyson's Victorian image of the indomitable superman, the undefeated will, the macho hero who (in Tennyson's own words) exemplifies 'the need for going forward, and braving the struggle of life'.[31] Mahon's Ulysses, having escaped the known, staid world of 'home' and social responsibilities, remains in thrall to Calypso's 'shape-shifting witcheries', an unregenerate outsider to the end: 'Homer was wrong, she never "ceased to please"' (*HL* 57).

*

Harbour Lights marks not only a return to nature but, as McDonald punningly opines, a 'triumphant return to form'.[32] Yeats is a pervasive presence. In the title poem, Mahon quotes from 'Lapis Lazuli' – 'All things fall and are built again' (*HL* 64) – bringing into focus Yeats's insistence on both tragic acceptance of

---

31   See Project Gutenberg's 'Ulysses', in *The Early Poems of Alfred Lord Tennyson*, etext 8601.
32   Peter McDonald, p. 117.

loss and catastrophe, and the pleasure of continual recreation. Mahon has his own 'Lapis Lazuli' poem, written, like Yeats's, in five rhymed verse paragraphs. Yeats's poem, written in 1936, the year of the outbreak of the Spanish Civil War and Hitler's invasion of the Rhineland, meditates on the role of art in time of disturbance. Mahon's view of his world is no less apocalyptic: 'While plains that consume deserts of gasoline/ darken the sun in another rapacious war' (*HL* 25). Yeats's response to catastrophe was to affirm the kind of 'tragic joy' – 'Gaiety transfiguring all that dread'[33] – that he believed was best demonstrated in Shake-spearean tragedy. Mahon is rather more questioning, his aestheticism tempered by a renewed humanism:

> Do we die laughing or are we among those
> For whom a spectre, some discredited ghost
> Still haunts the misty windows of old hopes?   (*HL* 25)

Mahon's lines juxtapose Yeatsian 'gaiety' with the 'hope' that lies in literary culture, the continuance of which is dependent on both a discriminating reader-ship, represented by the 'young woman' reading in a train, 'skipping the obvious for the rich and rare', and exemplary (and notably French) artists and intellec-tuals such as the 'twinkling sages in the Deux Magots' (*HL* 25), who are Mahon's version of the Chinese ascetic and pupil climbing the mountain carved on Yeats's lapis lazuli.

Mahon's final resting-place, as he makes clear in the book's concluding poem, 'The Seaside Cemetery', a brilliant translation of Paul Valéry's famous poem 'Le Cimitière Marin', is in the deterritorialised, paradoxically shifting, symbolic space of the poem itself. The poem marks a move away from the prosaic, discursive attitudinising of *The Hudson Letter* and *The Yellow Book*, and a reaffirmation of Symbolist principles. Valéry in fact claimed to be the originator of the term 'pure poetry', and to be the author of 'fabrications' that were 'absolutely devoid of ideas'. At the beginning of 'The Seaside Cemetery', the sun and sea cast their spell, and the speaker identifies with what seems pure, tranquil, silent, remote, non-human, an aestheticised reality where

> … light freezes above the gulf,
> A gem revolving in its radiant gleam
> Such many-faceted and glittering foam
> That a great peace seems to extend itself,
> Those clear-cut artefacts of the continuum,
> Time and knowledge, take the shape of a dream.   (*HL* 71)

But, as in 'The Last of the Fire Kings' or 'Courtyards in Delft', he is finally forced to concede the claims of life. At the end of 'The Seaside Cemetery', life, like the unruly Maenads, bursts in, reasserting the Heraclitean flux over the demoralising philosophy of Zeno, which would seem to forestall any possibility of change or progress:

---

[33] *W.B. Yeats: Selected Poetry*, ed. A. Norman Jeffers (London, Pan Books, 1974) p. 182.

> Zeno, harsh theorist of conceptual zero,
> have you transfixed me with your winged arrow
> which quivers, flies, yet doesn't fly at all?
> ...
> The wind rises; it's time to start. A vast breeze
> Opens and shuts the notebook on my knees
> And powdery waves explode among the rocks
> Flashing; fly off, then, my sun-dazzled pages
> And break, waves, break up with ecstatic surges
> This shifting surface where the spinnaker flocks!   (*HL* 75)

Mahon's 'break, waves, break up with ecstatic surges' sounds like Whitman, but is also partly a reference to that other doorkeeper of the palace of art, Tennyson, as in 'Break, break, break,/ On thy cold gray stones, O Sea'.[34] Valéry/Mahon, high-priests of the religion of art, in the end admit the shapelessness and wildness of ecological life. A wind rises to blow away the deadly languor of the beginning. The 'thought' which in the first stanza held the speaker rooted is finally routed. From brooding on mind, the speaker in the end accepts the claims of the body. Reference to the poet's 'sun-dazzled pages' (*HL* 75) intimates his choice of life over death. The poem moves from exhaustion to renewal, from meditative stasis to the climactic flurry of creativity. But the brightening world of the ending complements rather than cancels out the moribund world we begin with. This is the significance of the Hydra image in the penultimate stanza. The Hydra eats its own tail 'in a perpetual, silent-seeming turmoil' (*HL* 75). Mahon's poem, through its shifting, deliquescent language, enacts a perpetual turmoil of signification, like the bodies losing and changing shape in their graves. Recycled words and phrases are like leitmotifs in music, heard the second time round with a difference, registering tonal shifts, amplifying meaning. The poem balances out the physical and the cerebral; the claims of self-expression and referentiality merge with the impersonal concerns of structure and musicality. Life flows into death, death into life; the taste of the fruit reaches greatest intensity 'where its form dies' (*HL* 72). Preserving Valéry's strict decasyllabic six-line stanza and subtle rhyming pattern, Mahon holds the urge towards freedom and wildness within rigorous formal constraints. The poet recognises that he too is part of the same flux: 'everything flows, ourselves the most' (*HL* 74). Not even his poem will survive, as 'Heraclitus on Rivers' insists: 'The very language in which the poem/ Was written, and the idea of language,/ All these things will pass away in time' (*CP* 114). The earlier 'The Sea in Winter', which 'The Seaside Cemetery' echoes in some important respects, indicates the great challenge for the poet: surrounded by 'a strange poetry of decay', his task is to 'Effect mutations of dead things/ Into a form that nearly sings'.[35] 'The Seaside Cemetery', Mahon's last poem in his last collection, also recalls 'In Carrowdore Churchyard', his first poem in his first collection, *Twelve Poems* (and retained as the first poem in his *Selected Poems*): in both, the poet from his vantage point on 'high ground' (*CP* 17) or 'high point'

---

34 Alfred, Lord Tennyson, 'Break, Break, Break' (1842).
35 Derek Mahon, *Poems 1962–1978* (Oxford, Oxford University Press, 1979) pp. 110 and 113. The couplet on p. 113 does not appear in the version of this poem in *Collected Poems*.

(*HL* 71) contemplates the graves, drawing together the opposites which make up human existence: life and death, time and eternity, earth and sea, flux and order. Reconstituted through poetic form, meaning is never fixed or static but contained in the perpetually shifting balance of opposites, and enacted in the constantly metamorphosing play of language: 'The ironical, loving crush of roses against snow,/ Each fragile, solving ambiguity' (*CP* 17).

Chapter 8

TOM PAULIN: DWELLING WITHOUT ROOTS

In the course of his essay, 'Dwelling without Roots', on the famously home-less and geographically displaced American poet Elizabeth Bishop, Tom Paulin makes clear his deep distrust of those views of place which see it as a constant, the source of authentic value and identity. For Paulin, ideas of home rooted in history, land, language, tribe, ancestry and race memory harbour a dangerous essentialism. Such ideas conjure up for him the figure of Martin Heidegger and Heidegger's image of the peasant cottage in the Black Forest that has long been dwelt in and embodies 'the forces stemming from earth and blood'. In Paulin's view, Heidegger dwells on the apparently natural and traditional in order to naturalise a violent politics: 'How easily Romantic ideas of authenticity, rooted-ness, traditional crafts, folklore, take on the stink of power politics and genocide'.[1] Instead, Paulin feels drawn towards those poets such as Elizabeth Bishop who use their poems to 'erect a makeshift building nowhere' (*M* 191). This 'rooted'-'makeshift' axis is used to structure his long poem 'The Caravans on Luneberg Heath'. Here, Heidegger's idea of authentic dwelling is summarily dismissed: 'Go chew acorns/ Mr Heidegger/ you went with the Nazis'.[2] Central to the poem are two images which are set in opposition to the philosophy of Heideggerean rootedness: first, the eponymous caravans on Luneberg Heath (symbols of transit and transience) in which the dream of world domination was laid to rest with the signing of the German surrender at the end of World War I; and, second, the 'pumpkin hut' in which an informal Köningsberg literary society (the 'Cucumber Lodge') led by Simon Dach (1605–59) met during the period of the Thirty Years War: 'sangar blockhouse lookout poet OP/ you made a garden in its place' (*F* 56). The contrast is drawn between the Heideggerean idea of home which led to the Holocaust, and the 'Musical "Pumpkin Hut" and the Little Garden', with its connotations of congenial society, and natural and artistic fruitfulness. John Kerrigan suggests that with the 'Cucumber Lodge' Paulin had something much closer to home in mind – the Irish Orange Lodge, especially in its original self-proclaimed role of protector of civil and religious liberties. The references to the non-sectarian activity of the 'Cucumber Lodge' at a time when Europe was

---

[1] Tom Paulin, 'Dwelling without Roots: Elizabeth Bishop', in *Minotaur: Poetry and the Nation State* (London, Faber, 1991) p. 190. Hereafter abbreviated to *M* and page references incorporated into the text.

[2] Tom Paulin, *Fivemiletown* (London, Faber, 1987) p. 62. Hereafter abbreviated to F and page references incorporated into the text.

convulsed by war between Protestant and Catholic was, Kerrigan argues, part of Paulin's larger concern to retrieve 'the Enlightenment origins of a masonic and Orange Lodge tradition'.[3] In contrast, Paulin's Heidegger, 'digging trenches on the Rhine' (*F* 59), parodies the poet of 'Digging', and the whole idea of roots in the soil, the spirit of nation:

> this red Rhine clay
> lignite and gravel
> Grund
> I stood on the wet
> ontic particles
> my boots bogged
> in muddy water   (*F* 59)

The grounding of German historical dwelling and identity in the conjunction of land and language echoes Heaney's *dinnseanchas* – 'the black O/ in Broagh', 'Anahorish, soft gradient/ of consonants, vowel-meadow', 'the tawny guttural water/ spells itself ... / bedding the locale/ in the utterance'. The problem with attempting to dig down to mystic *Volk* or Gaelic origins under the layers of history and colonialism is that you end up 'bogged/ in muddy water' – thus, Heaney's eventual recognition that 'the wet centre is bottomless'.[4]

Paulin's distrust of invocations of atavism and the autochthonous is made explicit in another poem which again glances sideways at Heaney. In 'At Maas' (a Co. Donegal town) Paulin re-writes those Heaney poems which listen in to 'all the realms of whisper' and the ghostly voices of the ancestral dead: 'Put your ear to the ground/ and you'll catch the *chthon-chthon*/ that spells *must*',[5] says Paulin. But the message he receives is very different from that which Heaney hears from the tribal voices whispering by the shore or the Viking longships' swimming tongue:

> The Adam form
> through the trees
> says, "Take up your pen,
> make a new barm
> and try the whole thing again.
> No more talk about stock
> or the joining sea,
> just plant your big foot, love,
> hard down on the bedrock
> and give a last shove."   (*LT* 63)

'The Adam form' at first sight might seem to continue the idea of autochthonous or aboriginal knowledge, but turns out to be that of the eighteenth-century Scottish Enlightenment architect Robert Adam whose neoclassical Georgian mansion

---

3   John Kerrigan, 'Earth Writing: Seamus Heaney and Ciaran Carson', *Essays in Criticism*, 48, 2 (1998) pp. 144–68.

4   Seamus Heaney, 'Bogland', in *Opened Ground: Poems 1966–1996* (London, Faber, 1998) p. 41.

5   Tom Paulin, *Liberty Tree* (London, Faber, 1983) p. 63. Hereafter abbreviated to *LT* and page references incorporated into the text.

house style inaugurated a new Golden Age of civilised urban living in Ireland and throughout the world. 'The Adam form/ through the trees' recalls the 'Adam house' in the earlier 'Going in the Rain':

> An Adam house among tall trees
> Whose glaucous shadows make the lawn
> A still pool; bracken on the screes
> Wedged above a lichened bawn ...[6]

Here, the 'Adam house' is the symbol of a decayed and irrelevant Yeatsian Ascendancy cultural ideal:

> Georgian architects, ironic
> Deists, crossed over from the mainland
> To build a culture brick by brick,
> And graft their reason to a state
> The rain is washing out of shape.   (*SM* 21)

In 'At Maas', however, the 'Adam form', though speaking out of a condition of cultural exhaustion, calls for renewed commitment to an original Enlightenment reason and *civilitas*. The 'Adam form' counsels, not passivity or the backward look, but *doing* ('take up', 'make', 'try', 'just plant', 'give a last shove'), a strenuous effort toward rational, pragmatic, forward- and outward-looking re-construction. Ultimately, the poem expresses Paulin's endorsement of the 'fierce impulse towards modernity and immediacy' (*M* 12). That this is an essentially Protestant impulse is signalled by the word 'barm' (yeast), which recalls the image of new bread rising in 'Presbyterian Study' a few pages earlier: 'It is a room without song/ That believes in flint, salt,/ And new bread rising/ Like a people who share/ A dream of grace and reason' (*LT* 49). The 'new bread rising', with its connotations of agency, insurgency and change, as well as its literal meaning of food for survival, is the product of 'grace and reason', a phrase which alludes both to a central tenet of Protestantism – the doctrine of divine grace – and to belief in Enlightenment rationalism. This 'dream of grace and reason' is 'new' because it represents an alternative to both the exhausted Yeatsian dream of Protestant Ascendancy and the nativist Heaneyesque dream of return to an originary, authenticating place.

Mainstream Irish nationalists have traditionally prioritised the concept of an Irish 'nation' over that of an Irish state, which the 'nation' has long predated. The problem with the resultant essentialist myths of an originary, long-oppresssed Irish nation seeking its own sovereign state is that they can produce a parochial, violent, ethnic nationalism that fails to provide a home for a modernising, heterogeneous society. Thus, Paulin shifts the emphasis from the nation to the notion of a rationally ordered and just state. As Eamonn Hughes remarks: 'the primary place in Paulin's poetry is not the nation (nor its attenuated analogues: home, parish, townland, region) but that ultimate institution the state'.[7] For Paulin,

---

6   Tom Paulin, *The Strange Museum* (London, Faber, 1980) p. 21. Hereafter abbreviated to *SM* and page references incorporated into the text.

7   Eamonn Hughes, '"Could anyone write it?" Place in Tom Paulin's Poetry', in Colin Graham and

the concept of 'a state of justice' derives from a specific strand of Protestant and Enlightenment social and political thinking associated with eighteenth- and nineteenth-century European republicanism. Much of his prose writing is in fact devoted to relating the Ulster dissenting tradition, with its stress on individual conscience and religious freedom, its championing of free thought and the defence of individual rights, to this larger context of liberal and radical thought. Of particular interest to Paulin is the example of William Hazlitt,[8] the Whig radical and republican, whose life and writing were dominated by the French Revolution. Hazlitt's desire for change, his reputation as 'day-star of liberty', his northern Irish background, his relation to the radical dissenting tradition, his ambiguous Puritanism, his internationalism, his optimism, all recommend him to Paulin as an important precursor.

The priority for Paulin is a social democratic Irish republic, founded on equality of citizenship and the civic institutions of the just state, and capable of transcending inherited colonial and religious divisions:

> My own critical position is eclectic and is founded on an idea which has as yet no formal or institutional existence. It assumes the existence of a non-sectarian, republican state which comprises the whole island of Ireland. It also holds to the idea of sanctuary and to the concept of 'the fifth province'. This other, invisible province offers a platonic challenge to the nationalistic image of the four green fields.[9]

Just as Yeats had his imaginary Ireland, so Paulin has his 'platonic' republic founded on a myth of Protestant radicalism deriving from a highly selective historical memory which centres on the rebellion of the United Irishmen in 1798. The 1798 rebellion occupies a central place in Paulin's imagination, representing for him the possibility of a union between Ulster Presbyterian and Irish Catholic who, placing rational ideals of political independence and self-determination above considerations of religious denomination, fought side by side for the republican cause. In 'Presbyterian Study', Paulin recognises that such a union no longer has currency: 'for they live,/ Those linen saints, lithe radicals,/ In the bottled light/ Of this limewashed shrine' (*LT* 49). Current Protestant culture is drained of the activist dynamic of earlier times: 'We wait on nature,/ Our jackets a dungy pattern/ Of mud and snapped leaves,/ Our state a jacked corpse/ Committed to the deep' (*LT* 50). 'Desertmartin' emphasises the negative connotations of 'lime', as both defilement and ensnarement:

> It's a limed nest, this place. I see a plain
> Presbyterian grace sour, then harden,
> As a free strenuous spirit changes
> To a servile defiance that whines and shrieks
> For the bondage of the letter: it shouts
> For the Big Man to lead his wee people
> To a clean white prison, their scorched tomorrow. (*LT* 16)

Richard Kirkland (eds.), *Ireland and Cultural Theory: The Mechanics of Authenticity* (Houndmills, Macmillan, 1999) p. 179.

8   See Tom Paulin, *The Day-Star of Liberty: William Hazlitt's Radical Style* (London, Faber, 1998).

9   Tom Paulin, *Ireland and the English Crisis* (Newcastle-upon-Tyne, Bloodaxe Books, 1984).

Paisley's authoritarian, self-righteous theology is linked with the fanaticism of 'Masculine Islam, the rule of the Just' (*LT* 17). Both these arid, inflexible ideologies have suppressed the living word, reducing it to fixed meaning.

> And now in Desertmartin's sandy light,
> I see a culture of twigs and bird-shit
> Waving a gaudy flag it loves and curses.   (*LT* 17)

Given this debasement of the Protestant dissenting spirit and the unlikelihood of his social and political vision ever finding formal or institutional existence, Paulin settles for an ideal of '*civilitas*', which he believes exists in England but not nearly as strongly in Ireland. He describes his ideal state in the early 'A New Society', where he 'want[s] to believe in some undoctrinaire/ Statement of what should be. A factual idealism// ... an order that's unaggressively civilian,/ ... / Where the Law is glimpsed on occasional traffic duties/ And the streets are friendly'.[10]

The society presented in the early poems is very different. The Protestant Unionist state is a 'cadaver politic', Ulster a 'lost province'. Images of congealment, fixity, stasis and entrapment predominate. 'Under the Eyes' describes a completely regulated, homogenised, dehumanised society. Everything is measured, known: 'All the machinery of state/ Is a set of scales that squeezes out blood./ Memory is just, too. A complete system/ Nothing can surprise'. Even the violence seems to belong to a vicious cycle: 'Its retributions work like clockwork/ Along murdering miles of terrace-houses' (*SJ* 9). Motifs of surveillance, determinism and regulation recur in 'Surveillances': 'In the winter dusk/ You see the prison camp/ With its blank watchtowers;/ It is as inevitable/ As the movement of equipment/ ... / You know this is one/ Of the places you belong in,/ And that its public uniform/ Has claimed your service' (*SM* 6). 'A Partial State' presents the uneasy 'stillness' of life under a repressive regime. Just beneath the pretence of order is a frightening, irrepressible energy. Repression cannot contain the spirit of revolt:

> The chosen, having broken
> Their enemies, scattered them
> In backstreets and tight estates ...
>
> Stillness, without history;
> Until leviathan spouts,
> Bursting through manhole covers
>
> Special constables train their
> Machine guns on council flats;
> Water-cannons, fire, darkness.

Ironising the idea of a Protestant elect, a 'chosen' people, the poem ends: '*What the wrong gods established/ no army can ever save*'. The 'stillness, without history' is the subject of 'Before History':

---

10 Tom Paulin, *A State of Justice* (London, Faber, 1977) p. 19. Hereafter, abbreviated to *SJ* and page references incorporated into the text.

> This is the lulled pause
> Before history happens,
> When the spirit hungers for form ...   (*SM* 1)

The poem brings us to the brink of cataclysm, to the point where history can be blinked no longer. Poetry becomes a subversive act, a defiance of a discursive order designed for the ideological suppression of potentially rebellious impulses. It is a gesture of spontaneity in an increasingly manipulated world, a search for new 'form'.

Surveying the importance of Protestantism to Paulin's aesthetic, Peter McDonald wonders whether the poet is 'attempting to redeem or destroy his subject, and whether he is addressing himself to this dissociated culture, or is holding it up to an outside audience for easy ridicule'.[11] In a 1981 interview, Paulin stressed the negative. Alluding to 'how fundamentally ridiculous and contradictory' he believed it now was to be an Ulster Protestant, he confessed: 'I pretty well despise official Protestant culture, and can't now understand how people can simultaneously wave the Union Jack and yet hate the English, as many Protestants do.'[12] These criticisms are followed by even more vehement denunciation in the prologue to *The Hillsborough Script*, which castigates 'that servile, demoralized, parasitic crowd, the Unionist middle class', 'wee provincial philistines in their Orange Free State'.[13] In this play, as in the poem, 'The Defenestration of Hillsborough', he pictures Ulster Protestants driven to the edge by the course of events, forced on to a window-ledge. The image, a reference to the 1618 Defenestration of Prague which plunged Europe into a Thirty Years War between Protestants and Catholics, was used, Paulin tells us, by a loyalist leader at the time of the signing of the Anglo-Irish Agreement on 15 November 1985 to describe the sudden shock of being marginalised, forced out of the British nation. The poem ends with the words: 'This means we have a choice;/ either to jump or get pushed' (*F* 54). To jump will be an act of defiance, the seizing of an opportunity to escape old attitudes.

Returning to the loyalist plight in 'An Ulster Unionist Walks the Streets of London', he adopts the persona of Harold McCusker, the then deputy leader of the Official Unionist Party, whose impassioned speech to Parliament following the signing of the Anglo-Irish Agreement (included in Paulin's section on 'Northern Irish Oratory' in *The Field Day Anthology of Irish Writing*) is re-worked in the poem. The Agreement, which was designed to give the southern Republic an unprecedented say in the affairs of Northern Ireland, was concluded without consultation with the Unionist parties. The poem records the Unionist sense of betrayal ('I waited outside the gate-lodge/ waited like a dog/ in my own province'), and projects movingly the alienation of the speaker who feels an outsider both among the 'London Irish' and at Westminster, at the very centre of the state to which his allegiance has been pledged. Ulster Unionists are the 'lost tribe', bereft of their identity, disoriented and unsure of where they belong. In poems

---

[11]   Peter McDonald, *Mistaken Identities: Poetry and Northern Ireland* (Oxford, Oxford University Press, 1997) p. 104.

[12]   John Haffenden, *Viewpoints: Poets in Conversation with John Haffenden* (London, Faber, 1981) p. 159.

[13]   Tom Paulin, *The Hillsborough Script: A Dramatic Satire* (London, Faber, 1987) p. ii.

such as 'The Defenestration of Hillsborough' and 'An Ulster Unionist Walks the Streets of London', Paulin identifies with the deracinated, homeless condition of the Ulster Protestant who, as Peter McDonald puts it, comes to recognise 'an impossible imperative of "belonging" to something which, under scrutiny, might cease to exist'.[14] It is a condition of profound ontological insecurity, and Paulin describes it poignantly in the Introduction to *Minotaur*:

> ... what it feels like to belong to a people – a tribe like the Ulster Protestants – but a people that is not a nation. To adapt Benedict Anderson's famous phrase, there is an underground 'imagined community' ... This community is not internationally accepted: it is "kept under" and has no leader or prophet, no place where it can feel secure to worship its God. To have no place to worship is like a version of penal times. (*M* 16–17)

What counters the feeling of determinism or dead-endedness is a sense of the constructedness of history: 'Can you *describe* history I'd like to know?/ Isn't it a fiction that pretends to be fact/ like *A Journal of the Plague Year*?' ('Martello', *LT* 55–6). Like Heaney and Muldoon, Paulin is conscious of walking a line between poetry as private craft and poetry as public utterance. In 'Song for February', he sneers at frivolous verse: 'Light verse is now the norm/ and academic fellows/ File limericks by the score' (*SM* 3); and in 'Surveillances', distances himself from 'a culture, of bungalows/ And light verse' (*SM* 6). The 'well-made poem' comes under fire in 'A Lyric Afterwards'. 'Trotsky in Finland' contrasts the 'minor art' of the sonneteer with the project envisioned by Trotsky, 'plunging from stillness into history' (*SM* 30). In 'The Garden of Self-Delight' he writes against 'art ... for art's sake' which 'prays to mirrors in the sand,/ its own mirrors of burnt sand./ where the smooth forms look pure' (*SM* 40–1). But he is also opposed to propagandist art. 'Where Art is a Midwife' mocks totalitarian attitudes and the bureaucrats engaged in turning art into a function of the state. His ambivalence about the proper function of art is dramatised in the long poem 'The Other Voice'. The first section is autobiographical, describing the moment of departure from the securities of tradition. The second section is also autobiographical, recalling youthful commitment to Trostkyism, which gets confused with '60s student flower-power. In the third section, the choice is between the poetic life conducted in an ahistorical English vacuum – 'Life, my dear, is a fixed order/ And your verse should flow/ With a touching sweetness' – or condemning oneself to 'the level emptiness/ Of pulp culture' in the Ulster maelstrom. No sooner is 'the process of history' invoked than all the unfortunate consequences of commitment come clamouring to the fore: 'I see a regiment of clones/ Waving their arms and shouting:/ A glossy brutalism dances/ To a parody of song'. In looking for endorsement of the Stevensian idea that the poem 'serves only the pure circle of itself', the speaker thinks of Mandelstam who died in the Gulag rather than renounce his personal vision. The poem ends with Mandelstam's proclamation of the lyric faith: 'In the great dome of art/ (It was this we longed for/ In our Petropolis)/ I am free of history./ Beyond dust and rhetoric,/ In the meadows of the spirit/ I kiss the Word'. Oscillating between one and 'the other voice', Paulin

---

14   McDonald, p. 94.

himself is unable to find the means whereby he can speak with stereophonic authority.

In other poems, too, Paulin turns to the example of the Russian and East European poets to help him explore the tension between political obligation and imaginative freedom. As 'The Book of Juniper' pushes toward its climactic vision of reconciliation, Paulin invokes the figure of Mandelstam: 'Exiled in Voronezh/ the leavening priest of the Word/ receives the Host on his tongue' (*LT* 25) – a figure of the artist as celebrant of both creative freedom and social responsibility. 'Voronezh' is a free translation of a poem by Akhmatova, written in 1936, about her friend Mandelstam's exile. Akhmatova's description of the frozen town of Voronezeh is reminiscent of many of Paulin's 'theoretical locations' ('The Hyberboreans', *SJ* 22) which are similarly defined by images of surveillance, darkness, confinement, tense oppressiveness, and the struggle of 'the Word' to survive in difficult conditions. In 'Black Bread', a poem dedicated to Pasternak's niece, he joins in communion with the Russians who have endured persecution for their refusal to toe the party line:

> It's a lump of northern peat, itself alone,
> and kin to the black earth, to shaggy speech;
> I'll taste it on my tongue next year in the holy,
> freed city of gold and parchment. (*LT* 35)

Paulin has a whole essay on 'shaggy speech' in *Crusoe's Secret: The Aesthetics of Dissent*, where 'shagginess' is associated with 'integrity, and the refusal of a servile conformity',[15] and exemplified by such writers as the primitive peasant poet John Clare, and others who had already made an appearance in Paulin's anthology *The Faber Book of Vernacular Verse* (1995). Such deliberate 'roughening [of] the conventional lyric image', Paulin asserts, serves to 'code a republican politics' (*CS* 214). In comparing the black bread to 'shaggy speech', he confirms Mandelstam's faith in the transubstantiative power of the word: 'I'll taste it next year in the holy,/ freed city of gold and parchment'. To indicate the extreme conditions in which writers like Mandelstam and Pasternak lived, Paulin includes reference to Mandelstam's famous epigram (which can be found in Paulin's *Faber Book of Political Verse*) criticising Stalin, and for which he was arrested in 1934. Paulin recreates the scene where Stalin was supposed to have made a phone call inquiring of Pasternak if he had been present when Mandelstam read his epigram: 'Claudius is on the phone, hear that hard/ accent scraping its boots on the threshold,/ his thick acid voice in your uncle's conscience,/ *I'd have known better how to defend my friend*' (*LT* 35). Stalin is Claudius, the murderous enforcer determined to suppress dissent in the state; Pasternak is the equivocating Hamlet of the 'antic disposition'. In Pasternak's poem, 'Hamlet in Russia, A Soliloquy' (1946), the stage-fright of the actor playing Hamlet is secret code for the terror in the Stalinist state. The poem ends with the actor/poet's re-affirmation of his commitment to his personal vision, whatever the hardships and risks involved: 'The sequence of scenes was well thought out;/ the last bow is in the cards, or

---

[15] Tom Paulin, *Crusoe's Secret: The Aesthetics of Dissent* (London, Faber, 2005) p. 217. Hereafter, abbreviated to *CS* and page references incorporated into the text.

the stars −/ but I am alone, and there is none …/ All's drowned in the sperm and spittle of the Pharisee −/ To live a life is not to cross a field'.[16] *Hamlet* was one of several Shakespeare plays Pasternak translated during the 1930s and '40s when he was unable to publish his own poetry. It was seeing the Russian film of the play, scripted by Pasternak, in Belfast in the mid-1960s, Paulin says, that marked his first sense of *Hamlet* as 'a twentieth-century political drama' (*M* 213), adding, somewhat exorbitantly: 'In the − with hindsight − unreal quiet of that city, the film threw the spectre of Stalin's terror across the screen' (*M* 213).

This conflation of history, whereby Stalinist Russia is superimposed on Unionist Ulster, is as controversial as Heaney's diagnosis of the diseased psycho-pathology of the Ulster Catholic community in terms of the Vikings and Iron Age Bog People. Is Paulin seriously asking the reader to accept an equivalence between the conditions under which the poet operates in Unionist Ulster and those which sent Russian poets to the Gulag? His dubious historical sense is evident in other ways too. Edna Longley accuses him of 'writ[ing] Northern Protestants out of history unless prepared to go back and start again in 1798'.[17] Too readily adopting the stereotypes and myths on which identity-politics rely, he generally tends to view Ulster Protestants from outside, at a distance, as speci-mens in 'a strange museum'. Capable only of momentary imaginative identifica-tion, his attitude to the Ulster Protestant community, it would appear, is deeply ambivalent.

He is drawn to the Russians, he explains in his Introduction to *The Faber Book of Political Verse*, by their 'supremely unillusioned quietism', which is neither cynical nor apathetic, but 'the wisest of passivities' (*FBPV* 51). Produced in a closed world, Russian poetry, says Paulin, is 'without hope but with an obsti-nate integrity which simultaneously negates as it creates'. The poets are 'like prisoners tapping out messages along the heating pipes in a cell block, they speak to us in a cipher from an underground culture that we in the West have difficulty comprehending' (*FBPV* 51). Russian poetry is not 'anti-political', but rather 'the most advanced type of political verse … a form of anti-poetry or survivor's art. It proffers a basic ration of the Word, like a piece of bread and chocolate in wartime' (*FBPV* 52). Paulin could be writing about himself (and in a sense he is), for his own style of literary engagement is marked more by what he calls 'general historical awareness' than 'a specific attitude to state affairs',[18] and by a commitment (however partially realised) to the living, organic Word rather than to ideologically forced single meanings. Russian and East European poetry provides a model for his increasingly oblique and hermetic style which itself becomes a subversive form of engagement, a declaration of dissent from dominant discursive structures. He favours the subversive role of underground man, the persona described in Tadeus Rosewicz's 'Poem of Pathos', which Paulin quotes in *The Faber Book of Political Verse*:

---

16 Boris Pasternak, 'Hamlet in Russia: A Soliloquy', trans. Robert Lowell, in Tom Paulin (ed.), *The Faber Book of Political Verse* (London, Faber, 1986), p. 399. Hereafter abbreviated to *FBPV* and page references incorporated into the text.
17 Edna Longley, *Poetry in the Wars* (Newcastle-upon-Tyne, Bloodaxe, 1986) p. 192.
18 Tom Paulin, *Writing to the Moment* (London, Faber, 1996) pp. 104–5. Hereafter abbreviated to *WM* and page references incorporated into the text.

> A poet buried alive
> is like a subterranean river
> he preserves within
> faces names
> hope
> and homeland   (*FBPV* 51)

This is precisely Paulin's position in 'Under Creon', where Creon stands for the hegemonic power of the state, in this case the Ulster Unionist establishment. Like Sophocles's Antigone who disobeys Creon's order not to bury her brother Polynices, Paulin pursues his desire, invisibly, secretly, to preserve the past and the dead by commemorating the forgotten heroes of that strain of radical Presbyterianism which, as Paulin put it in a 1981 interview, 'more or less went underground after 1798':

> A neapish hour, I searched out gaps
> In that imperial shrub: a free voice sang
> Dissenting green, and syllables spoke
> Holm oaks by a salt shore, their dark tangs
> Glistening like Nisus in a night attack.
>
> The daylight gods were never in this place
> And I had pressed beyond my usual dusk
> To find a cadence for the dead: McCracken,
> Hope, the northern starlight, a death mask
> And the levelled grave that Biggar traced.   (*LT* 13)

The 'free voice' of northern republicanism equates with the song of the earth.

Another poem, 'A Nation, Yet Again' is a version of an 1818 Pushkin poem, 'To Chaadayev'. The title of Paulin's poem alludes to the Republican mantra 'A Nation Once Again', but disrupts it with a comma, and replaces 'Once' with 'Yet', which introduces the suggestion of alternative possibility, or at least hesitation about traditional concepts of 'nation'. In his poem, Paulin says he is looking for 'a secular mode of voicing the word *nation*', 'a delicate, a tough, new style/ that draws the language to the light/ and purifies its tribal rites'. He ends by affirming:

> There's a classic form
> That's in our minds, that makes me warm
> To better, raise, build up, refine
> Whatever gabbles without discipline:
> See, it takes me now, these hands stir
> To bind the northern to the southern stars.

There is an ironic echo here of the colonialist Miranda's speech to the monstrous Caliban: ('When thou didst not, savage,/ Know thine own meaning, but wouldst gabble like/ A thing most brutish, I endowed thy purposes/ With words that made them known'[19]), and an equally ironic recall of Heaney's voice, 'A voice

---

[19] William Shakespeare, *The Tempest*, Act 1 scene ii, lines 358–61.

caught back off slug-horn and slow chanter/ That might continue, hold, dispel, appease' ('Clearances' II), a folk-voice seeking re-absorption into the old 'tribal rites'. Paulin's lines, in decorous rhyming or half-rhyming couplets, yet never far away from colloquial speech, also reflect on Pushkin's great project which was to create Russian anew as a literary language, employing classical verse forms in combination with the spoken language of the people. Like Pushkin, Paulin wants to elevate the vernacular to enable it to articulate serious matters, progrsssive thinking – nothing less than a new vision of the future. Paulin aligns himself with Pushkin, the 'poet of freedom' as he was known in Russia, continually under suspicion from the bureaucrats, friend to the Decembrists, whose 1825 revolt against Imperial Russia represented the beginnings of a revolutionary move-ment in Russia, and supporter of Pyotr Chaadayev (1794–1856), the Western-ising Russian philosopher whose radical critique of Russian institutions such as autocracy, the Church and serfdom resulted in Nicholas I denouncing him as insane.

While much of Paulin's early poetry emphasises the repressiveness of the state, the answer does not lie with some concept of free Rousseauesque individualism: he freely acknowledges the value of civic life and stable polity, the need for law and order in both society and poetry. The revolutionary strand in his writing which privileges the Protestant belief in the supremacy of the individual conscience and the tradition of dissent is tempered by a Hobbesian recognition of the need for some kind of state power to curb the forces of anarchic individualism. Paulin's commentary on Auden's poetry is revealing. Auden, he says, 'becomes Hobbe-sian in his political thinking. Reluctantly Hobbesian it's true ... but nevertheless firmly on the side of law and order', and, Paulin adds approvingly, 'For anyone who sees a culture and a community, however imperfect, threatened by violent louts, Auden's poetry, with the valuation it places on civic life, sounds crucially right.'[20] Taking his cue from this remark, John Haffenden, in his 1981 interview with Paulin, asked: 'Am I right to infer from your own writings that you person-ally are anti-Romantic, and reluctantly Hobbesian, and that while you affirm a sense of *civilitas*, you also allow for the possibility of dissenting voices?' Paulin replied, 'I think Hobbes's view of life is tremendously dispiriting and I don't *want* to believe in it', going on to admit that his own attitude towards politics and society was 'a having-it-both-ways view'.[21]

This tension is present from his earliest work. 'States', the first poem in his first collection, pictures a troop-ship going up Belfast Lough. The vessel is 'a metal convenience' (*SJ* 7), a pragmatic requirement if order is to be maintained in the state, especially a state built on a Hobbesian 'nature' of 'blackness' and 'a dark zero/ Waste' (*SJ* 7). There is a price in terms of lives and freedom, and the speaker seems resigned to paying it in the interests of ensuring 'safety' and 'security': 'their security/ Threatened but bodied in steel/ Polities that clock us safely/ Over this dark; freighting us' (*SJ* 7). The balance of values is formally embodied in terms of the regularity of the poem's containing stanza structure, yet tensions persist: 'clock us' has reassuring connotations of measure and metre,

---

[20] Tom Paulin, '*Letters from Iceland*: Going North', in John Lucas (ed.), *The 1930s: A Challenge to Orthodoxy* (Sussex, Harvester Press, 1978) pp. 59–77, 67.
[21] Haffenden, pp. 163–4.

but also of inexorable mechanistic control; 'freighting us' is both stabilising and provisioning but also carries suggestions of being weighed down, and isn't far from 'frightening us'. The intense orality of the phrasing and the forceful defiance of normative metre threaten security, but the appearance of regularity which Paulin affords the eye-reader evinces a concern to smooth out possible threats and difficulties, so that we can be transported safely across choppy waters.

What the early poems stress are the dangers of state authority turning into a congealed totalitarian reality. Fearing stasis and fixity, Paulin recognises a place for the subjective, anarchic, revolutionary energies in self and society. As he put it in his Haffenden interview: 'Although my ambition is to be responsible in a way, to give a sense of history and of society, what I really want to do is to punch holes in history – tunnel through it – in order to get out into a kind of freedom which is contemplation and vision.'[22] The remark indicates the streak of murderous violence in his aesthetic, his interest in the spontaneous, the irrational and the fragmented, the desire to write to the moment. This disruptive, individualistic aesthetic inevitably comes into conflict with a responsible, rational politics. One of the reasons why Hazlitt is of special interest is because Paulin discerns in the eighteenth-century writer the same tensions that haunt his own work – tensions between the individual and the state, the aesthetic and the political, between the imperious demands of the imagination which is 'a very anti-levelling principle', and the understanding which is a 'levelling' or 'equalizing' 'republican faculty' (*CS* 175). If Paulin's work, as Patricia Horton argues, is 'a striving towards that seemingly paradoxical entity, the republican imagination',[23] his prolonged dialogue with Hazlitt may be read as a concealed investigation of this struggle.

An important aspect of Paulin's aesthetic project is the development of a kind of poetic speech calculated to disturb official, institutionalised and authoritarian language. His models, invoked in the Introduction to *The Faber Book of Vernacular Verse*, are Burns, Clough, Clare, Whitman, Twain, Rossetti, Hopkins, Hughes, and Walcott, but his most important source is Ulster dialect: 'From an early age', he tells us, 'I became immersed in the wild dash and wit and loving playfulness of Northern Irish speech.'[24] Resistant to the idea of linguistic purity and historical determinism, the 'savage vernacular energies', Paulin insists, 'are essentially democratic and Protestant' (*FBVV* xii). Making free with Ulster speech and other dialectal forms, coinages, slang, jargon, nonsense, onomatopoeic and foreign usages, and disrupting standard grammar, syntax, punctuation and typography, he experiments in his own verse with a poetic language designed to roughen Standard English and create a radical, inclusive, accessible, democratic language capable of speaking for 'an alternative community that is mostly powerless and invisible' (*FBVV* x). What that community might be, in an Irish/Ulster context, remains unspecified. He is more interested in elaborating aesthetics than exploring ethics.

Vernacular language is for Paulin a means of 'writing to the moment' (his

22 Ibid., p. 168.
23 Patricia Horton, 'A "Theological Cast of Mind": Politics, Protestantism and the Poetic Imagination in the Poetry of Tom Paulin', *Literature & Theology*, 16, 3 (August 2002) p. 312.
24 Tom Paulin (ed.), *The Faber Book of Vernacular Verse* (London, Faber, 1990) p. xxi. Hereafter abbreviated to *FBVV* and page references incorporated into the text.

Introduction to *The Faber Book of Vernacular Verse* is included in the collection of essays entitled *Writing to the Moment*), and both, as he repeatedly seeks to emphasise, are expressions of the revolutionary imagination of Protestant dissent. 'Writing to the moment', he explains, represents an 'eager, volatile, intense form of consciousness', which 'appear[s] to be one of the legacies of the Reformation' (*WM* xi). In '51 Sans Souci Park', he expresses his attraction to this provisional, off-hand, risky poetics:

> And a voice threshing in the wilderness
> An unstill enormous voice
> Is offering me this wisdom
> *Action's a solid bash*
> *Narrative a straight line*
> *Try writing to the moment*
> *As it wimples like a burn*
> *Baby it's NOW!*[25]

He wants a poetry with a passionate, impromptu spoken texture. Rather than aesthetic distance, he aspires to the condition of the action painter 'working furiously within, not outwith a canvas' (*WM* 221). Jackson Pollock has himself stressed the importance of this kind of immediacy: 'On the floor I feel more at ease. I feel nearer, more a part of the painting, since that way I can walk around it, work the four sides and literally be *in* the painting.' Writing about D.H. Lawrence, Paulin quotes Pollock: 'I don't paint nature, I am nature' (*CS* 290). 'I Am Nature' is Paulin's 'homage' to Pollock: it is a poem which dispenses with linear narrative or consecutive logical development in order to convey 'the almost unbearable intensity of the moment', 'the now of consciousness' (*WM* 222):

> just banging on
>   like a bee in a tin
>   like the burning bush
>
> cracking dipping and dancing
>   like I'm the last
>   real Hurrican Higgin
>   critter and Cruthin
>   scouther and skitter
>   witness witness
>   WITNESS TREE!   (*F* 33–4)

Paulin's claim to a puritan anti-aesthetic of unmediated, artless naturalness and authenticity should not be allowed to obscure the poem's artfulness. The poem mimics Pollock's practice of dancing deliriously over canvases spread out on the floor, lost in his patternings, pouring paint rather than using brushes and palette, bearing direct witness to his interior vision. Paulin lets this free individual conscience loose in an intensely dramatic manner, turning the poem into a crescendo of theatrical Presbyterian self-presentation (Pollock was of Scots-Irish

---

25 Tom Paulin, *Walking a Line* (London, Faber, 1994), pp. 33–4. Hereafter abbreviated to *WL* and page references incorporated into the text.

Presbyterian stock), an image of 'bad boy' Protestant radicalism confounding institutional ways of thinking. The identification with 'Hurrican Higgin' alludes to the devastatingly effective Ulster snooker player, Alex 'Hurricane' Higgins, from the Protestant Sandy Row area of Belfast, twice world champion, who was also known for his wild and violent behaviour. In the poem's tangled shrubbery of Presbyterian burning bush, republican juniper tree and Frostian witness tree there lurk darkly sinister intimations of self-destructive violence ('Hurrican Higgin'), reactionary Protestant nationalism (in the reference to Ian Adamson's 'Cruthin' who were supposed to be the original pre-Gaelic, Pictish inhabitants of Ireland from whom Ulster Protestants could claim ancestry) and uncontrolled subjectivity (signified by the promiscuous, heavily-accented, rhyming and half-rhyming acoustic mix of Scots, Irish and American vernacular forms) – though, ironically, all this disturbance is undermined by the idea that it may be no more than a storm in a teacup, 'just banging on/ like a bee in a tin'.

The title of Paulin's collection, *Walking a Line*, encodes the tension at the heart of his poetry. 'Walking a line' could refer to the kind of poetry that follows a given ideological or literary line, and thus tends to speak to a preordained agenda; or, to use Paul Klee's words which form the opening line of Paulin's 'What's Natural', it could mean 'taking a line out for a walk' (*WL* 55) and seeing where it might lead. This would be to allow for the serendipitous, the unknown, the delights and excitements of new discovery. It is the same tension that pervades Heaney's work, and which Heaney indicates in his similarly punning title *The Government of the Tongue*: the tongue may be governed by orthodoxy, system or ideology, or 'the tongue, governed for so long in the social sphere by considerations of tact and fidelity, by nice obeisances to one's origin within the minority or the majority, this tongue is suddenly ungoverned. It gains access to a condition that is unconstrained ...'.[26] Heaney's words are echoed at the end of Paulin's 'L':

> This tongue thing's a supple instrument
> Kinda decent and hardworking
> And often more welcome than the penis
> – too many poems speak for that member
> maybe it's time I unbuttoned my tongue? (*WL* 20)

'L' is a celebration of the tongue, that 'supple instrument' of immediate, personal, vernacular speech which, freed from history, from censorship, from official controls, can 'enter small apertures', probe secret places and private lyric spaces, to reach those parts that conventional print culture is unable to reach. The sustained cunnilingual metaphor turns the act of love into a revolutionary act against convention and decorum, a relishing of the delights of barbarism – of living beyond the pale. In developing an erotics of vernacular speech, Paulin contrasts its 'more welcome' activity with the authoritarian and more invasive interventions of a phallogocentric print language. As he insists in one of his essays: 'Orality – the vernacular imagination – can be a means of resisting the dominance of the nation state' (*M* 89).

However, taking a line out for a walk is never an ideologically-free project:

---

[26] Seamus Heaney, *The Government of the Tongue* (London, Faber, 1988) p. xxii.

'Taking a line out for a walk/ ought to seem – well/ second nature/ like the way you laugh or talk/ – though both speech and laughter/ have to be learned/ inside a culture' ('What's Natural', *WL* 44). Lines are always conditioned by culture – but nature has a habit of breaking in and disrupting or blurring the received boundary lines. The 'little yolky sun' with its connotations of fertility and femininity, wishes it could 'chuck itself – splittery/ splattery/ all over the scrake/ – the wheeze and piss/ of dawn' (*WL* 55). The irregularity of these lines, and the vernacular departure from a standard lexicon suggest the disruption of the usual 'horizon' of meanings. The absence of punctuation or any full-stop signals the refusal of definitive meaning: we don't ever come to the end of the line, we can't ever confidently draw a line under anything.

An anti-aesthetic intended to accommodate 'the moment' cannot be more than a 'provisional architecture' (*WM* 224) such as that imaged in 'History of the Tin Tent':

> these halfsubmerged sheds
> have a throwaway permanence
> a never newpainted
> sense of duration
> that exists anywhere
> and belongs nowhere
> – ribbed basic
> set fast in pocked concrete
> they're almost like texts
> no one wants to read
> – texts prefabs caves
> a whole aesthetic in reverse   (*WL* 4)

Like the caravans on Luneberg Heath, the tin tent is an image of a temporary, flexible, adaptable dwelling which is both ontological and writerly symbol. In contrast to the rootedness of Heaney, Montague or Hewitt's aesthetic, Paulin emphasises improvisation, the need to assemble an aesthetic, an identity, a culture, a language, out of diverse bits and pieces: 'every sentence/ builds itself/ on a kind of clearance/ builds itself on risk/ and an ignorance/ of what's been hacked down/ or packed up' ('The New Year', *WL* 9). 'The Lonely Tower' takes as its epigraph a wanted ad. – 'WANTED – *coastal farm, site, derelict house, period house, stable yard, outhouse, lodge, Martello. Must be on sea. Immediate cash settlement. Box Z0490*' (*WL* 11) – and, in contrast to the solidity and permanence symbolised by Yeats's Thoor Ballylee, proceeds to celebrate the enterprising spirit that is wide open to new possibilities, receptive to whatever is available:

> most any building
> in this squally clahan
> could quicken into newness
> – you can write them out in a verse
> or jump in a lorry
> rammed with cement and timber
> then *bash bash bash* till the day
> when you paint *Wavecrest* on the gatepost   (*WL 12*)

Paulin finds a heroic image for these powers of adaptation and improvisation in the figure of Paul Klee who presides over this collection. Klee spent his time in an air-force depot during World War I painting camouflage on airplanes and making art out of squares of canvas from the wings and fuselage of crashed planes: 'surviving barely/ using whatever scraps came to hand/you still found the time/ to sit back and jeer/ at the Kaiser's sleek airplanes' ('A Last Gesture', WL, 78). Klee exemplifies the kind of improvisatory spirit that, for Paulin, is key to 'writing to the moment':

> Like someone repairing a tractor engine in a hurry, or like an artist making a cento, a collage, a sculpture out of bits and pieces – a few quotations, scraps of paper, some nuts, bolts, lengths of piping – these writers work very fast, very intensely. They adapt and recycle what's given or lies to hand. Hence the adrenalin, all-in-a-rush excitement of the process. And all to produce something that's gone the next day, lie a Navaho sand painting. (*WM* xiv)

This essentially optimistic outlook pervades the collection. The opening poem, 'Klee/Clover' sets the tone of what's to come:

> He wrote home to Lily
> *It's nice this spring weather*
> *And now we've laid out a garden*
> *between the second and third runways*
> *The airfield's becoming*
> *More and more beautiful*   (*WL* 1)

Writing home to his wife, Klee makes clear a sense of values which places importance not on war and history, but on the transformative power of art. 'Klee' means clover, and in 'Basta', Paulin, after imagining the routing of the armies and the destruction of the 'punishment block', affirms a delirious return to the fecund world of nature associated with the artist:

> So we waded right into
> That watery plain
> That blue blue ocean
> And started diving and lepping
> Like true whales in clover.   (*WL* 103)

'Almost There', as the title suggests, is about the 'speechjolt' that is on the brink of articulation, the poem that is self-reflexively 'almost there'. 'Thereness' is grounded in speech and text, not place. Although 'there's a kind of glitch/ in what you're saying', the poem's pivotal 'but' initiates a counter-movement that promises ignition ('wet spark') or conception ('travelling through darkness and moisture') of new meaning, that may indeed be dependent on the disruptive effect of the 'glitch' and the exposed and temporary condition of the speaker's dwelling:

> as it is
> there's a kind of glitch
> in what you're saying

> that tar and felt shack on the headland
> is windy with our belonging
> but the speechjolt
> its wet spark
> is travelling still
> travelling through darkness and moisture   (*WL* 21)

The tendency in this collection is to break down the notion of a fixed, stable world, to deconstruct the sense of place and identity, and to insist instead on a fictional reality, the illusoriness of the world. 'That's It', the last poem in the volume, begins with clear lines and spaces, but place – a studio flooded with marine light – quickly loses definition. The chest of drawers is only meaningful as 'a proposition', a 'big bold drawing', or 'as a novel/ as a complete fiction'. Similarly, the man on the mattress becomes suddenly aware of his own insubstantiality and contingency: 'all of which says only/ that though I may be lying on a mattress/ really I'm afloat/ on a pool of light and illusion/ yes light/ and yes illusion' (*WL* 105). This balancing of 'light' against 'illusion' is reminiscent of the Heaney of *Seeing Things*: in 'The Settle Bed', for instance, Heaney allows for the power of imagination to break down the 'givenness' of the world, to dissolve its heavy materiality and turn heavy things into light, but, like Paulin, he acknowledges finally that these transformations may be no more than make-believe.

Paulin's concern with his own poetics continues to loom large in *The Wind Dog*. In the punningly entitled 'Stile', he takes a quotation from Hardy as epigraph, and links the image of the threshing-machine in *Tess* – the 'red tyrant' which makes a 'despotic demand' upon the women who 'serve' it – with a formal, official language which similarly enforces suppression of natural or native energies. Paulin champions an alternative, anti-canonical language that shows scant respect for Yeats and Donne:

> because most critics they're vexed
> by what's clumsy or naïf
> it must never happen
> that something other than platonic form
> or hammered gold or pure gold leaf
> – that gold to airy thinness bate
> should touch us or should warm
> the playful serious wondering great
> mischeevious child in most of us[27]

'Bate' and 'mischeevious', two words drawn from Ulster dialect, signal Paulin's commitment to a vernacular aesthetic which may involve 'sentences gawky or a tad misshapen/ – spelt wrong or babu even/ tend to provoke laughter'. Picking up the image of the 'glitch' in 'Almost There', he describes his line in 'My Skelf' as having a 'kink': it 'doesn't pour out fine/ and handy/ like a length of cord/ all loose and easy/ and with never a knot' (*WD* 74). Using the image of a fishing line, he explores the idea of an anti-rational, anti-teleological anti-poetic where

---

27 Tom Paulin, *The Wind Dog* (London, Faber, 1999) p. 2. Hereafter abbreviated to *WD* and page references incorporated into the text.

'the mind/ needn't go A to Bwards/ or bind all the time/ as if the only direction is towards/ some naff goal/ as if there must be a link/ from this to that/ with no room ever to tinker/ soodle or dander' (*WD* 74). This is a poetry which is both statement and enactment of its own Frostian commitment to the fugitive, the random, the serendipitous, the incidental pleasures of sound and digression. The 'skelf' is the 'crick', the 'grig', the 'thorny wee tick' that disrupts the smooth discursive surfaces and straight lines of official language. It is the break with orthodoxy, the deliberate seeking out of controversy. It is what stimulates sudden, unexpected new insights, questions and associations: '- it's the way you might bait a fish hook/ with a little lump of curd/ and ask why ever was I born?/ why did I go into that cellar ...' (*WD* 75). The situation is similar to that identified by translator Brian Massumi who argues that when unfamiliar language violates our usual horizon of meaning 'a crack has opened in habit, a "zone of indeterminacy" is glimpsed in the hyphen between the stimulus and the response. Thought exists in widening that gap, filling it further and further with potential responses.'[28]

'?Chesterfield' approaches the same ideas with a similar playful inventiveness. Here, Paulin's central image is Chesterfield's Anglican church spire which is 'buckled', 'oddly angled', 'dinged' (*WD* 82). Like the skelf, the broken spire is 'another breach in nature', an opening into free lyric space. Paulin's vigorous dialectal usages to describe the spire – 'a skreeky rhythm that keeps/ trying to sort itself out' (*WD* 82), 'perpetual scringe' (*WD* 83), 'a dropped stitch/ haitch/ missing rhyme or tune' (*WD* 83) – mark an anti-poetic grounded in the 'homey dissonance' (*WD* 84) of a (would-be) authentic vernacular. The broken spire figures an originally transcendent aspirational vision pointing toward 'Eden or heaven' that has become 'twisted' into comic scepsis: 'its bingdring/ turns into a grin'. The poem places a question mark against, but does not erase, the traditional certitudes of faith, place and community.

While poems such as 'My Skelf' and '?Chesterfield' emphasise dislocation and fragmentation, 'Cuas' recognises the need for order and form. The word 'cuas' means 'a space between rocks; a cavity, a recess; a hollow', ideas which Paulin transfers to the Heaneyesque image of a gaping leather bag. The leather bag 'has to be tamed strapped/ otherwise it sags/ has neither form nor pattern' (*WD* 42). Yet the poem, which is unpunctuated free verse without end-stops or closure, resists being too severely 'tamed' or 'strapped'.

Paulin's deconstructive, presentist aesthetic puts conventional poetic structures under very great strain, and the question of how much disorder the necessarily ordering protocols of art can be expected to sustain is nowhere more acute than in relation to his title-poem 'The Wind Dog'. In the Introduction to his collection of essays, *Crusoe's Secret*, he explains that he 'found again and again that it's an individual sound ... or a word or a cadence that has acted as the *donnée* for an essay' (*CS* xix): this is the case in 'The Wind Dog'. The oral nature of the poem is underscored by the fact that it was originally commissioned as a radio poem in celebration of the fiftieth anniversary of Radio Three in 1996.

---

[28] Brian Massumi, *A User's Guide to Capitalism and Schizophrenia: Deviations from Deleuze and Guattari* (Cambridge, Mass., MIT Press, 1993) p. 99.

Paulin recalls the genesis of the poem six years earlier, in the Introduction to *The Faber Book of Vernacular Verse*:

> When I consider ... the way in which print-culture overrides local differences of speech and vocabulary – I recall a moment when that imagination spoke directly to me. I was out in a boat, lazily fishing for mackerel with a man I was fond of, an old merchant seaman from Islandmagee in Co. Antrim. He nodded up at the rainwashed, blue sky and said, 'D'you see thon wind-dog?' I looked up and saw a broken bit of rainbow and thought how rare and new 'wind-dog' seemed, how dull and beaten thin 'rainbow' was. (*FBVV* xxi)

A 'wind dog', he reiterates in the poem, is 'a wee broken bitta rainbow' (*WD* 30), his explanation now also providing an image of the poem's radically fragmented textuality. The substance of the poem consists in its attempt to improvise a Belfast childhood from relished memories of the past – people, places, books, but especially remembered sounds and speech. Knowing that, as he puts it in the early 'What is Fixed to Happen', 'the eye is such a cunning despot/ We believe its wordless travelogues/ And call them *History* or *Let it Happen*' (*SM* 34), Paulin opts for the defamiliarising and revivifying methodologies of the auditory memory and imagination, and a vernacular aesthetic devoted to the speech-sounds of the living voice. Through words and sounds he seeks to make his way back into childhood and its 'lingo-jingo of beginnings'. The poem is a sensitive recording instrument of 'the microclimates of pronounciation'[29] in Belfast to which he was exposed as a child (a schoolgirl's way of saying 'tar' as 'tarr', a friend's '*thee dee*', his mother's Ulster-Scots '*modrun novel*' and 'fanatic'), Ulster, Scots and English dialectal usages ('*hinny*', 'jum', 'sheugh', 'brangle', 'skift', 'crack'), placenames ('*Gweebarra*', 'Ormeau Avenoo', 'Elsinore') and snatches of Belfast street-songs, all of which suggests a complex, hybrid cultural formation. Then there are the simple onomatopoeic words ('crump', 'clishclash', 'slickslock', 'bock') which are sometimes self-consciously literary (like the allusion to Muldoon's 'quoof') through which childhood is mediated, and a further layer of words and sounds supplied by the books the poet read as a child. Later there are the sounds of the Troubles, and his adult reading. Much of 'The Wind Dog' consists of scraps from Frost, MacNeice, Joyce, Shakespeare, Clare, Marvell, Kipling, Masefield, the Ulster poets, Van Morrison, so that the poem appears as a species of 'found' or 'appropriated' poetry, a melding or patchwork of sounds and words from diverse sources, a meeting-place of heterogeneous people and voices. Out of this mélange, Paulin constructs an anti-epic or counter-epic, specifically rejecting the Virgilian 'arma virumque cano' which opens the *Aeneid*, concerning himself with the man but not the arms, not the public, imperial theme of classical epic.

As a speech act, the poem, issuing from the natural anarchism of oral tradition, deliberately breaks with and subverts official forms. Dispensing with punctuation and formal grammar and syntax, Paulin aims for an oral style of writing that circumvents the 'bondage of the letter' and challenges the posture of mastery and control in conventional printed text:

---

[29]   John Brown, *In the Chair: Interviews with Poets from the North of Ireland* (Cliffs of Moher, Salmon Publishing, 2002) p. 154.

so let me trawl and list
a couple or three sounds in my archive
– not the images
not the pictures
there must – because the ear
the ear is the only true reader –
there must be nothing seen or sighted
no moral message neither
no imperative
because out of the ocean of all sound
one little drop
two little drop
three little drop
shall come forth and fall back   (*WD* 24)

Through these lines, Paulin intimates his desire to evade any suggestion of institutional fixity, completeness or stability. As he said of D.H. Lawrence: 'This is the unrestful, ungraspable poetry of the sheer present, poetry whose very permanency lies in its wind-like transit' (*CS* 274). All is motion and fluidity, definition and closure continually deferred.

Paulin's refusal of authorial authority echoes Mark Twain's 'Notice' at the beginning of *The Adventures of Huckleberry Finn*. In this prefatory announcement, Twain makes a joke out of the possibility that this (highly moralistic) novel might have meaning and morality:

> Persons attempting to find a motive in this narrative will be prosecuted; persons attempting to find a moral in it will be banished; persons attempting to find a plot in it will be shot.
> By Order of the Author
> Per G.G., Chief of Ordnance.[30]

Twain's assertion of authorial freedom from narrative convention is backed up by an absurdly authoritarian voice, which is simultaneously undercut with comic irony. Thus, the 'Notice' introduces the novel's central concern with different voices and discourses all contending for authority, and alerts us to the fact that there will be no pure, single voice, and no plain, straightforward message in this novel. From the outset, Twain signals openness and playfulness. *Huckleberry Finn* is an exemplary text for Paulin because it goes against the genteel, hierarchical conventions governing literary composition in nineteenth-century America by handing the narrative over to the vernacular or folk voice of an ill-educated child, whom Twain proceeds to use to dialogise a whole range of other folk voices. In the 'Explanatory' paragraph which follows the 'Notice', Twain lists the various dialects which are to be heard in the novel and insists on the care he has taken to reproduce them faithfully in their finest shadings, while in the novel itself the classics of the English canon are held up to ridicule through the antics of the king and the duke. 'The Wind Dog' begins with the reworking of a passage from *Huck Finn* that is evidently an old favourite of Paulin's for he discusses it

---

[30] Mark Twain, *The Adventures of Huckleberry Finn* (Harmondsworth, Penguin, 1978) p. 48.

in the Introduction to *The Faber Book of Vernacular Verse*. When Paulin refers to the 'visionary actuality' (*FBVV* ix) of Twain's writing, its 'vernacular authority that bonds the reader in an immediate, personal manner' (*FBVV* x), we can understand exactly what he is aiming for in his own poem. In particular, Paulin notices the way 'Huck's limber prose is a spoken prose, carefully worked to make it sound as natural and informal as the impromptu conversation he hears and reports' (*FBVV* ix). That is, Twain's skill in dialogising Huck's voice with the various political, religious and moral discourses and voices in the novel is what especially attracts Paulin's appreciative attention. Like Twain, Paulin incorporates a multiplicity of social voices all dialogised by a central speaker. Though he intends the poem to tell the story of 'my life', as the closing line has it, the lyric subject tends to evaporate in the poem's subordination of narrative, character and situation to the play of language and sound. The impression created, far from being that of the traditional well-wrought urn, is more of an endlessly reverberating echo-chamber or demented tower of babel. No sufficiently defined central voice – such as Huck's – is present to control the text's unruly polyphony with the result that 'The Wind Dog' is never as dramatically exciting a confabulation as *Huck Finn*.

It is, however, another American who is Paulin's major sponsoring authority – 'Farmer Frost' – with his celebrated doctrine of 'sentence sound' and 'the sound of sense' (*WD* 22). Frost takes his place in Paulin's pantheon of 'Protestant' poets, that is, those who have sought to escape the 'bondage of the letter', break with the past, and destroy 'the aesthetic'. For Paulin, Frost's concern with language as a living, dramatic medium is exemplary. The American's many pronouncements are well-known: 'Words exist in the mouth not in books. You can't fix them and you don't want to fix them. You want to adapt their sounds to persons and places and times. You want them to change and be different.'[31] Sound is the crucial element of Frost's imagination: 'Sound is an element of poetry, one but for which the imagination would become reason.'[32] In his poem, 'Sentence Sound', Paulin quotes Frost: 'the ear/ is the only true reader/ the only true writer' (*WD* 11), and in his own writing practice follows Frost's privileging the ear over the eye:

> but to start with sound
> the plumque sound of sense
> the bite and kick of it
> – green chilli
> kerali
> white mooli radish
> all crisp and pepper definite
> – so my vegetable love did grow
> vaster than pumpkins and more slow
> for the sound of sense
> is what the pretend farmer
> – Farmer Frost that is
> used call sentence sound

---

31 Robert Frost, letter to Sidney Cox, 19 January 1914, Beaconsfield. Lawrance Thompson (ed.), *Selected Letters of Robert Frost* (New York, Holt, Rhinehart & Winston, 1964) p. 25.
32 Ibid., p. 25.

> because a sentence he said
> was a sound in itself
> on which other sounds called words may be strung   (*WD* 22)

With the help of Frost and Marvell, Paulin would seem to be laying claim to an organicist aesthetic which, in another poem, 'Sarum's Prize', he links with 'English Gothic': 'so Gothic's a style like frett-/ y chervil – that is organic/ like a salad' (*WD* 54). But in stressing the importance of a language with 'bite and kick', Paulin contrives an exotic Synge-song of sounds and images, a concentrated language as fully flavoured as a nut or apple – but quite unlike the natural speech tones of Frost's vernacular. Frost's 'sound of sense' is an essentially undoctored language that manages to give a sense of eavesdropping: Paulin merely replaces one conventionalised poetic language with another that is equally artificial and literary, a far cry from the living language that men do use. It is, in fact, a species of poetic language to which Frost would heartily object, as this comment would suggest:

> There are two kinds of language: the spoken language and the written language – our every day speech which we call the vernacular; and a more literary, sophisticated, artificial, elegant language that belongs to books. We object to anybody's talking in this literary, artificial English; we don't object to anybody's writing in it; we rather expect people to write in a literary, somewhat artificial style. I, myself, could get along without this bookish language altogether.[33]

Where Frost's is a rooted vernacular, expressive of rural New England, Paulin's is a poetry of dislocated voices which do not belong convincingly to any particular place.

Seeking to de-territorialise the imagination and counter the reactionary, standardising tendencies in both nationalist and unionist identity-politics, Paulin aims to free the notion of dwelling from reference to landscape and the Romantic sense of place, and relocate it within a concept of 'the vernacular city'.[34] His addiction to the recycling of the work of others in his centos and 'Translations, Versions, Imitations' in *The Road to Inver* (2004), and his commitment to an aesthetic of speech-sounds are all aspects of a lifelong project to recover revitalising cultural energies that have been submerged or obliterated by exclusionary and exclusivist histories. In his essay, 'A New Look at the Language Question', he advocates the institutionalisation of a 'federal concept of Irish English', believing that 'a language that lives lithely on the tongue ought to be capable of becoming the flexible written instrument of a complete cultural idea' (*WM* 65). His actual practice, however, can only be adjudged a partial fulfilment of this grand project. The 'vernacular energy' to which he aspires is dissipated in a highly literary and academic poetic expression. His 'Wind Dog' is shaggy and awkward, which is how he believes any free and vital poetry must be, but its words and references are bookish and intellectual, and his obsessive ringing the changes upon

---

[33] Robert Frost, 'A Visit in Franconia', in Edward Connery Lathem (ed.), *Interviews with Robert Frost* (New York, Holt, Rhinehart & Winston, 1966) p. 13.

[34] See Tom Paulin, 'The Vernacular City', in Nicholas Allen and Aaron Kelly (eds.), *The Cities of Belfast* (Dublin, Four Courts Press, 2003) pp. 233–42.

the sounds of words goes beyond most readers' patience. The poetry of private reference slips into exclusionary zones that are not accessible to the reader, and the irrational becomes merely modish rather than metaphysical.

Something of the contradiction at the heart of his aesthetic is evidenced in his recent essay 'The Vernacular City':

> That speech is built, ironically, out of English, Irish and Ulster Scots, and it is essential to recognize that culture which the politicians of all political parties are now engaged in extending and consolidating is one which cherishes all the languages of the province, and which looks beyond them and draws on every possible language.[35]

On one hand, there is the desire for the authentic sound of a specific people, place and historical experience, a vernacular language that comes lithely off the tongue as the expression of an organicist conception of culture. Such a poetics inevitably approximates a Heideggerean language of dwelling, and demonstrates a totalising cultural concern that finds expression in Paulin's advocacy of *A Dictionary of Irish English*.[36] On the other hand, Paulin wants to 'look beyond' the given languages, to 'draw on every possible language'. His own poetic practice, full of glitches and skelfs, is such a writing against the grain. Constantly, he is engaged in a deliberate effort to estrange and disrupt, to turn the poem into a vehicle of defamiliarisation, scandal and permanent critique. The question that has haunted him from the beginning remains unresolved: how to give expression to the radical, anti-authoritarian impulse which privileges the spoken word as the medium of the vernacular and the voice of minority cultures without falling into the void of subjectivism, irrationality and excess. The concept of the 'vernacular city' and the notion of 'dwelling without roots' would, in the end, appear to be a contradiction in terms.

---

[35] Tom Paulin, 'The Vernacular City', *Cities of Belfast*, p. 240.
[36] See 'A New Look at the Language Question', in *Writing to the Moment*, pp. 51–67.

Chapter 9

CIARAN CARSON: THE NEW URBAN POETICS

Heaney's statement in his essay 'The Sense of Place' that it is to 'the stable element, the land itself, that we must look for continuity'[1] suggests a basic opposition: the land as timeless constant, the image of the past, the place of traditional ways, of all that is human and natural, the organic society; and the city as flux and change, the engine of progress and modernisation, the route to the future. Referring to the city, Raymond Williams draws attention to how 'within the new kind of open, complex and mobile society, small groups in any form of divergence or dissent could find some kind of foothold, in ways that would not have been possible if the artists and thinkers composing them had been scattered in more traditional, closed societies'.[2] City-life complicates traditional monolithic nationalisms, whether Irish or unionist, because it gives a foothold to other forms of struggle – class or gender, for example – which cut across the traditional divisions and oppositions. Drawn to the 'stable element', Heaney, we can agree with Eamonn Hughes,[3] has difficulty engaging directly with the metropolis, for what is notable about Heaney's treatment of the city is his tendency to mythologise or allegorise it, as seen from the iconic portraiture of the early 'Docker' to the construction of Belfast as the city of plague in 'A Northern Hoard' in *Wintering Out* (1972). Through a series of hallucinatory images, Belfast is pictured as a diseased and blood-soaked city, 'Out there ... / Where the fault is opening again'. It is 'old Gomorrah', 'No man's land', 'No sanctuary'. 'What do I say if they wheel out their dead?'[4] he asks himself. His answer is to withdraw from the city, back to the Co. Derry farm for most of the rest of the poems in this volume and, in Part I of his next collection, *North* (1975), away from Belfast and the contemporary massacre into Scandinavian and Viking myth. Carson, in his well-known review of *North*, '"Escaped from the Massacre"?', registers his objections: 'Heaney seems to have moved from being a writer with the gift of precision, to become the laureate of violence – a myth-maker, an anthropologist of ritual killing, an apologist for "the situation", in the

---

[1] Seamus Heaney, *Preoccupations: Selected Prose 1968–1978* (London, Faber and Faber, 1980) p. 149.
[2] Raymond Williams, *The Politics of Modernism: Against the New Conformists*, ed. Tony Pinckney (London, 1989) pp. 44–5.
[3] Eamonn Hughes, '"What itch of Contradiction?" Belfast in Poetry', in Nicholas Allen and Aaron Kelly (eds.), *The Cities of Belfast* (Dublin, Four Courts Press, 2003) pp. 101–116, 112.
[4] Seamus Heaney, 'A Northern Hoard', *Wintering Out* (London, Faber and Faber, 1972) pp. 39–44.

last resort, a mystifier.' Carson objects to the attempt to impose a trans-historical, totalising framework within which the contemporary violence is to be understood and ultimately transposed into 'the realm of inevitability'.[5]

In contrast to Heaney's 'untoppled omphalos',[6] Carson's exploded view of the city's secret places reveals a brutally unromantic viscera of 'cables, sewers, a snarl of Portakabins,/ Soft-porn shops and carry-outs'.[7] Carson's Belfast, viewed as a debased, crudely improvised commodity culture, is the antithesis of Heaney's grounding rural home. Heaney's is a predominantly commemorative poetics, born of a sacral sense of place, and honouring the communal calendar customs and the traditional craft work of digging, ploughing, fishing and thatching, all of which are presented as analogues of the poet's craft rather than expressions of a commercial or economic view of life. Carson's city is a site of alienation, confusion and violence, an unstable conceptual or virtual arena as well as an equally unstable physical space. But there is also in his poetry a humane and affirmative vision that refuses to surrender to either irony or pathos. Compulsively, he keeps returning to his native Belfast, providing affectionate portraits of its sites and citizenry (from Horse Boyle in 'Dresden' to the two winos in the poem of that name), and enunciating a sense of the city as a place of new opportunities, where questions of identity and nationality have to be re-addressed. 'Clearance' describes the kind of 'collapse' which takes place 'under the breaker's/ pendulum' (*BHMSB* 24) rather than as a result of the urban guerilla's bomb. Urban development is both liberating and estranging, allowing for fresh, new perceptions of the city. Through his direct, dramatic address, Carson gives his observations epiphanic force: 'A breeze springs up from nowhere –/ There, through a gap in the rubble, a greengrocer's shop/ I'd never noticed until now … Everything –/ Yellow, green and purple – is fresh as paint. Rain glistens on the aubergines/ And peppers; even from this distance, the potatoes smell of earth'. If the potatoes still smelling of earth suggest that Belfast people are never far away from their rural origins, the peppers and aubergines intimate the city's implication in wider international currents of exchange. Carson's title recalls Heaney's sequence 'Clearances', in which the poet's quest for an 'omphalos' leads to the space which is 'utterly empty, utterly a source'.[8] Where Heaney concentrates on the moment of transition from the physical world to the 'bright nowhere', the 'placeless heaven' of textual plenitude, Carson's 'Clearance' remains rooted in the physical world which, even in the midst of destruction, is still able to provoke rhapsodic catalogues of urban variousness, hymns to fruitful serendipity.

In Carson's challenge to Heaney, Neil Corcoran reads 'the ground of a Northern Irish poetry of the postmodern beginning to prepare itself'.[9] Carson's own poetry, Corcoran continues, is a search for a way of registering 'the full

5   Ciaran Carson, '"Escaped from the Massacre"?' in *The Honest Ulsterman*, 50 (Winter 1975) pp. 183–6.
6   Seamus Heaney, 'The Toome Road', *Opened Ground*, 150.
7   Ciaran Carson, 'Night Patrol', in *The Ballad of HMS Belfast* (Loughcrew, The Gallery Press, 1999) p. 26. Hereafter abbreviated to *BHMSB* and page references incorporated into the text.
8   Seamus Heaney, 'Clearances' VIII, *Opened Ground*, p. 314.
9   Neil Corcoran, '"One Step Forward, Two Steps Back": Ciaran Carson's *The Irish for No*', in Neil Corcoran (ed), *The Chosen Ground: Essays on the Contemporary Poetry of Northern Ireland* (Bridgend, Seren Books, 1992) pp. 213–237, p. 215.

shock of the challenge to recognised modes and forms represented by the realities of post-1968 Northern Ireland, and more particularly post-1968 Belfast'.[10] Carson's work exemplifies the ways in which 'open' or discontinuous or broken forms function to represent epistemological attitudes. His gapped, elliptical poems whose parts refuse to combine into unified wholes, constitute a distinctive view of the world, one originating from within a society in the throes of violent breakdown. A broken style reflects a fractured society. As many of the poems demonstrate, discontinuity can place considerable demands on the reader who is left to arrange the elements more or less as he sees fit. Incompleteness and indeterminacy in the poem reflect the incompleteness and indeterminacy, and even the necessity of such incompleteness and indeterminacy, of our knowledge of reality. Whatever knowledge is available takes the form of disjointed facts or observations with no comprehensive explanations to connect them. Rationalistic metaphysics, and the form in which it is usually presented, are rejected because they give a misleadingly coherent picture of our knowledge of reality.

The first line of 'Night Patrol' – 'Jerking his head spasmodically as he is penetrated by invisible gunfire' (*BHMSB* 26) – presents an image of what one might expect from the title. But then, it would seem, this is all metaphor and the soldier is actually in bed dreaming or, possibly, masturbating to 'pull-outs from *Contact* and *Men Only*', death on the streets from a sniper's bullet linked with the 'little death' of orgasm. The soldier is in 'a room that is a room knocked into other rooms', just as the poem itself moves uninterruptedly from the soldier's bedroom to remembered rooms 'in Balkan Street and Hooker Street' to the entire Grand Central Hotel (an hotel that was actually 'knocked into' an army barracks), to the streets of the city generally. The image of 'a room that is a room knocked into other rooms' might stand for Carson's poetic methodology which is always challenging arbitrarily imposed demarcations and notions of discrete identity. The objects of the phenomenal world, rather than being distinct, are seen as actually shading into or merging with one another or joining together in a process of promiscuous hybridisation. As he puts it in another poem, 'Jawbox', 'one image warps into another, like the double helix/ Of the DNA code' (*BHMSB* 83). Thus, the masturbatory motif in 'Night Patrol' is extended to the entire city, which is revealed in a state of vulgar dishevelment: 'the whole Victorian creamy façade has been tossed off'. 'Telstar', the name of the communications satellite, is 'knocked into' the name of a taxi firm ('Telstar Taxis'), whose depot is 'a hole' that has, quite literally, been 'knocked into' 'a breeze-block wall' in the material fabric of the city. These multiple conjugations find their lexical enactment in the proliferation of words that have been 'knocked into' each other to form hyphenated compounds. The poem ends with reference to 'a wire grille and a voice-box uttering gobbledygook'. Whose disembodied voice is this? What is this 'gobbledegook' – merely nonsense, or a soldier's coded message? The discontinuous form of the poem reflects indeterminacy and incomplete knowledge, denying us the possibility of a unified and definitive picture of the world.

'Queen's Gambit' is another example of a poem which doesn't simply tell us about discontinuity; it *is* that discontinuity. Through episodic fragmentation of

---

[10]   Ibid., p. 216.

the narrative, the absence of causal explanations, the disjointing of chronology, Carson achieves a radical discontinuity, which is a function of 'content'. The poem sets up several narrative lines which begin to unfold in different time frames but which fail to cohere into any reliable meaning. The final italicised section offers some putative order when a barber, while giving the speaker a haircut, tells his version of events. But the barber's story leaves much unexplained. Littered with tags such as 'It seems …', and 'If you ask me …', it acknowledges its own provisional, partial and unreliable status: 'It looks to me, it was a set-up job, though who exactly/ Was set up, God only knows …/ … If you ask me,/ With these confidential telephones, you never know who's doing who, or why' (*BHMSB* 71). Poetic form is a field of possibilities, like the 'stoolie-pigeon spool', which, when replayed, 'Its querulous troughs and peaks map out a different curve of possibility' (*BHMSB* 70). In the continually mutating world of the poem – 'It's all go, here, changing something into something else' (*BHMSB* 68) – even the speaker at the end, shorn of hair and beard, feels 'like a new man'. Re-entering the outside world, he leaves the barber 'to a row of empty mirrors' (*BHMSB* 72). Peter Barry wants to rescue Carson from postmodern 'new narrativism', claiming that the postmodern label 'does some disservice to the starkness and impact of many of these pieces, which lack the disembodied, ludic, but perhaps ultimately rather pointless complexities of this mode of writing'. In the typical Carson poem, according to Barry, the 'chronotope is always clear, its viewpoint consistent, and all the apparently random details are clicked into place at the end'.[11] The radical instability of 'Queen's Gambit' might be invoked to refute the validity of this description. In 'Queen's Gambit', details *are* left 'teasingly untied' rather than 'pushed relentlessly home', ludic *jouissance is* a marked feature of the writing, questions of meaning *are* left unresolved. But the resulting poem is not one of 'pointless complexity': the poem questions the possibility of a true narrative, but doesn't discount the possibility of *some* truth. By playing with narrative in various ways, Carson challenges ontological and epistemological certainty, but he does this in order to demonstrate the difficulty of constructing a reliable history, not to invalidate the humanist quest for truth and moral value.

'Belfast Confetti' suggests, in its 'stuttering' but powerfully energetic way, a connection between history and poetry, civil disturbance and textual disturbance, the city and the language in which it is (de-)constructed:

> Suddenly as the riot squad moved in, it was raining exclamation marks,
> Nuts, bolts, nails, car-keys. A fount of broken type. And the explosion
> Itself – an asterisk on the map. This hyphenated line, a burst of rapid fire …
> I was trying to complete a sentence in my head, but it kept stuttering,
> All the alleyways and side-streets blocked with stops and colons. (*BHMS* 23)

No longer able to maintain conventional structure, the poem consists of disjointed lists of things presented without subordination, giving the impression of a discourse unmediated by an ordering rational mind, responding directly to the exigencies of the moment. Relying on an accumulating power of perception,

---

11 Peter Barry, *Contemporary British Poetry and the City* (Manchester University Press, 2000) p. 228.

the poem, proceeding through a series of alternating staccato bursts and arrests, speaks emphatically of the here-and-now. The suggestive image of confetti (lifted from Padraic Fiacc's poem, 'The British Connection'[12]), with its ironic connotations of union and celebration, refers to the missiles hurled by the rioting mob, the disrupted text of the poem, and the confusion of the poet's own shredded thoughts. Against this backdrop of violent disturbance, questions of identity ('What is/My name?'), origins ('Where am I coming from?') and purpose ('Where am I going?') are thrown into confusion. We can't even be sure who's asking the questions. Is the poet questioning himself? Or has he been stopped by the police or the army? Or is this a similar situation to that described in 'Question Time',[13] where he is watched and followed and then interrogated by local Falls Road vigilantes? Where Heaney's place-names (Anahorish, Broagh, Derrygarve) provide the reassuring co-ordinates of home, Carson's mark out an alienating imperial past: 'I know this labyrinth so well – Balaclava, Raglan, Inkerman, Odessa Street –/ Why can't I escape?' The speaker, though assimilated to the city, cannot dominate the situation but, instead, begins to lose his initial, complacent 'self' in a process which opens the self to the battering assault of otherness and contingency. Carson replaces the rational, abstract, ahistorical, unified subject with a de-centred consciousness. The subject that emerges is a provisional, historical figure, composed through its interaction with the 'other', through remaining 'in play', in movement, a harried *flâneur*. Without a sense of centre, the abstract binaries – subject/object, self/city, inner/outer – which have formed the basis of knowledge and certainty – dissolve into each other, and the subject as autonomous agent is relocated within the networks of historical process, deprived of the distance that would enable him to produce a 'grand narrative' that is without gaps or elisions, without stops or stuttering. As if in response to Nietzsche's words – 'It was out of this pathos of distance that they assumed the right to create values, to coin the names of values'[14] – Carson's poem proclaims the primacy of lived, historical contingencies over metaphysical abstraction, being over truth. Caught up in the complexity – the dangers and excitement – of the city, Carson's persona is rather different from the Baudelairean or Benjaminian *flâneur* who was a detached observer who found refuge in aesthetic contemplation. Carson's *flâneur* galvanises poetic discourse into a performative or expressionist moral act conveying with a strict immediacy all the menace, tension and confusion in a situation which threatens to overcome him.

The *flâneur* is the pedestrian observer of the metropolis, the 'gentleman

---

12 And youths with real bows and arrows
  And coppers and marbles good as bullets
  And oldtime thrupenny bits and stones
  Screws, bolts, nuts (Belfast confetti)

  Padraic Fiacc, 'The British Connection', in *Ruined Pages: Selected Poems* (Belfast, Blackstaff Press, 1994) p. 110. The conceit does not originate with Fiacc but is in fact a long-established shipyard term for anything lying around that could be used as a weapon to throw at or drop on somebody who wasn't liked.
13 Ciaran Carson, *Belfast Confetti* (Loughcrew, The Gallery Press, 1989) pp. 57–73. Hereafter abbreviated to *BC* and page references incorporated into the text.
14 Friedrich Nietzsche, *On the Genealogy of Morals*, quoted in R.J. Hollingdale (ed.), *A Nietzsche Reader* (Harmondsworth, Penguin, 1977) p. 109.

stroller of city streets', the 'botanist of the sidewalk', first identified by Charles Baudelaire. Since adopted by Walter Benjamin in his accounts of urban life in 'A Berlin Chronicle' (1932) and the unfinished *Arcades Project* on which he worked throughout the 1930s up to his death in 1940, the *flâneur* has come to typify the subjective experience of urban space. More recently, he illustrates forms of practice and perception which are characteristically found in the contexts of postmodernism, media and consumer culture, virtual environments and cyber-space. The *flâneur*, as reader of the city, transforms the city into a text. Being part of the crowd as well as watcher of the world go by, the *flâneur* enjoys no neutral, privileged vantage-point. His readings of the semiotic city are inevitably momentary and fragmentary. Restricted temporally and physically, he is unable to produce any overarching vision of the modern city as a totality, only glimpses of its parts. The continual shifting of perspective creates a montage of moving images, fleetingly and impressionistically registered. In this respect, the *flâneur* indicates a transformation of perception in the new metropolitan milieu, and it is this perspective of situatedness, historicity and fragmentariness that forms the basis of Carson's new urban poetics. For though Benjamin's *flâneur* oper-ated in the streets and arcades of nineteenth-century Paris, the type is imme-diately recognisable in the Carsonian persona, for whom the city of Belfast is also a space of reading, a semiological environment bound up in individual and cultural memory.

Carson's image of the city as labyrinth is a familiar Benjaminian trope, as in this passage taken from 'A Berlin Chronicle':

> Not to find one's way in a city may well be uninteresting and banal. It requires ignorance – nothing more. But to lose oneself in a city – as one loses oneself in a forest – that calls for quite a different schooling. Then, sign-boards and street names, passers-by, roofs, kiosks, or bars must speak to the wanderer like a cracking twig under his feet in the forest.[15]

In this passage, the city labyrinth is as much of an enchanted and mysterious place as the forest in Heaney's 'The Plantation', where 'You had to come back/ To learn how to lose yourself,/ To be pilot and stray – witch/ Hansel and Gretel in one'.[16] Both Heaney's walker in the forest and Carson's *flâneur* follow Benjamin in suggesting the subversive and productive power of poetic lostness. In the laby-rinth of the city, self-location and self-affirmation become a struggle. Mastery – intellectual and psychological – is unsettled. Losing one's way results in a de-territorialisation of knowledge. Poetic wandering denies the authority of the offi-cial maps and resists the systematisation of the world. But such disorientation can lead to awakening, the discovery of new meaning, and this recuperative dimension of lostness distinguishes Heaney's Romantic wandering from both Carson's postmodern *flânerie* and Mahon's modernist narrative of perpetual *unheimlich* exile. Like Benjamin, Carson surrenders to the spell of the labyrin-thine city, attempting to read and decode the meaning of urban space from clues,

---

15 Walter Benjamin, 'A Berlin Chronicle', in P. Demetz (ed.), *Reflections: Essays, Aphorisms, Autobio-graphical Writings* (New York, Schocken, 1986 [1932]) pp. 3–60, 8–9.
16 Seamus Heaney, 'The Plantation', *Door into the Dark* (London, Faber, 1969), p. 50.

traces, fragments that present themselves in what often threatens to become an unbearable sensory overload. The resulting poetry is a profusion of instantaneous, partially registered, swiftly moving images which reflect the key modern experiences, not only of the urban voyeur observing the collapsing city, but also, as the proliferation of commodity brand names in Carson's poetry would suggest, of the Benjaminian customer and consumer.

Benjamin collected thousands of seemingly trivial items of nineteenth-century Parisian bourgeois industrial culture, which were published posthumously as a montage of found materials interspersed with occasional comment. The Arcades Project takes its name from a nineteenth-century architectural form. Arcades were covered passageways through blocks of buildings with lines of shops on either side. A whole building was made up of connected parts. Similarly, Benjamin's literary form is a structure of fragments. He valued collections as a form of historiography because their fragmentary arrangements resisted the degree of order and control implied by a 'grand narrative'. In the crowded, bustling arcades, historical time is broken up into a glorious, phantasmagoric array of diverse commodities, and in attempting to grasp reality in terms of scattered and apparently banal objects and artefacts, Benjamin sought to explore from his Marxist standpoint the lost spaces and histories underlying the ideological mask of modern consumer society:

> [I]t was not the great men and celebrated events of traditional historiography but rather the 'refuse' and 'detritus' of history, the half-concealed, variegated traces of the daily life of 'the collective', that was to be the object of study, with the aids of methods more akin – above all, in their dependence on chance – to the methods of the nineteenth-century collector of antiquities and curiosities, or indeed to the methods of the nineteenth-century ragpicker, than to those of the modern historian.[17]

Another kind of 'detritus' which absorbed Benjamin's attention was the ruin. Since the Parisian arcades dated back to the 1820s, many had fallen into ruin by the time Benjamin began his researches. For Benjamin, it was the ruins of a great building, or the historical epoch the building represents, which could awaken in us a true sense of history. Benjamin interprets ruin as the opposite of the urban spectacle. Ruin enables us to see history not as a smooth chain of events in linear time, expressive of the glory of civilisation, but as the sign of death and collapse. The modern city, epitome of industrial culture, hides behind the allure of commodity. Historical consciousness is shrouded in the mists of fetishism and phantasmagoria. But the city as ruin can be excavated to reveal nightmarish experiences of alienation and displacement, the latent anxiety of death and catastrophe, the metropolitan uncanny which places the homely, the domestic and the ordered under threat. As James Donald puts it, 'this modern uncanny always returns as the labyrinth to haunt the City of Light'.[18]

So, Carson, idling in the spaces of the city, presents a kind of dream world

---

[17] Walter Benjamin, *The Arcades Project*, trans. Howard Eiland and Kevin McLaughlin (Cambridge, Mass., Belknap Press, 1999) p. ix.
[18] James Donald, *Imagining the Modern City* (Minneapolis, University of Minnesota Press, 1999) p. 73.

in which the human subject, entranced by the phantasmagoria of commodity fetishism, street violence and the technologies of state control, finds itself petrified, disorientated, divested of agency, placed under surveillance – in a word – commodified. Even language and text are part of a wholesale process of objectification, as in 'Belfast Confetti', where exclamation marks and broken type are rioters' missiles, an asterisk is an explosion, a hyphenated line is gun-fire, and alleyways and side-streets are blocked with stops and colons (*BHMSB* 23). Wandering through the ruins of the chiasmal arcades of Smithfield Market – a microcosm of the city – the poet reflects the sense of life as a myriad of disconnected impressions. 'Smithfield Market' is something of a rag-picker's random collection of material, a series of vivid, intense, disjointed yet fluid images. Like Benjamin, Carson seeks to discover half-hidden energies of history that are slumbering in the depths of the city that might provide clues for finding a way out of the labyrinth:

> Sidelong to the arcade, the glassed-in April cloud – fleeting, pewter-edged –
> Gets lost in shadowed aisles and inlets, branching into passages, into
>   cul-de-sacs,
> Stalls, compartments, alcoves. Everything unstitched, unravelled – mouldy
>   fabric,
> Rusted heaps of nuts and bolts, electrical spare parts ...
>
> Since everything went up in smoke, no entrances, no exits.
> But as the charred beams hissed and flickered, I glimpsed a map of Belfast
> In the ruins: obliterated streets, the faint impression of a key.
> Something, many-toothed, elaborate, stirred briefly in the
>   labyrinth.   (*BHMSB* 28)

Ending on this ambiguous note, the poem awaits an unknown future. Trapped in the labyrinth, the Thesean *flâneur* comes into possession of the key, or at least 'the faint impression of a key', that may unlock the meaning of Belfast – or take him further into darkness and danger. The poet stirs up repressed communal, historical or revolutionary remembrance within the alienated city spaces, alert to both the disruptive traces of the unconscious and the possibility of recouping neglected, half-buried collective experience. Lost among the discarded, unpromising material of the everyday, he is ready to undertake the hazardous task of opening up a space for alternative histories, myths and memories in the city's broken labyrinth.

This idea of a spatial practice of resistance to the official city is taken up by Michel de Certeau in *The Practice of Everyday Life*. De Certeau writes of the private, artful manoeuvres of the pedestrian, who thereby denies the power of the planner or strategist to determine the pedestrian's movements. In de Certeau's analysis, walking in the city can be an assertion of the individual's freedom from governmental, scientific or architectural ordering of space. By making use of mental maps of spaces and routes that defy official or communal grids, the individual is no longer merely a consumer of space nor its compliant subject. For de Certeau, walking in the city is more than just the marginal activity of the *flâneur*: the pedestrian is viewed, somewhat exorbitantly, as a clandestine urban hero engaged in continual acts of transgression and resistance against the strategic controls of the city. Naturally, such resistance will be even more remarkable in a (para)militarised and heavily policed environment such as Belfast, with its curfews, cameras, check-points, barriers, barricades and 'no-go' areas, a city where the possibilities for creative movement are severely curtailed. Repeatedly, the Carson persona is drawn into the public realm as a site for creative misbehaviour or subversion of the controlling desires of civic government, cartography or surveillance agencies. 'Last Orders', for example, has the speaker seeking entry to the ambiguous space of a late-night drinking-club. We wonder to which paramilitary group the club is linked, and from which religious background the speaker comes. The poet is deliberately unforthcoming in providing us with reliable co-ordinates: 'I, for instance could be anybody. Though I'm told/ Taig's written on my face. See me, would *I* trust appearances?' (*BHMSB* 73). He could never be just 'anybody' in Northern Ireland's reductive sectarian calculus of 'us' and 'them', though the 'Taig' attribution is as quickly undermined as it is suggested. In the world of this poem 'you never know for sure who's who'. What is palpable is the ever-present suggestion of violence: the speaker squeezes the buzzer 'like a trigger', but it's 'someone else' who has him in 'their sights'. Once inside, he orders *Harp* which 'seems safe enough, everybody drinks it', though the brand-name is decidedly Irish nationalist. He notices that an unidentified 'someone' 'looks daggers at us' in 'the *Bushmills* mirror', the brand name this time linked with the staunchly loyalist north Antrim town where the whiskey is made. The play with pronouns and perspectives leads to complete confusion of self and other, the speaker ultimately identifying simultaneously with both bombers and victims:

> how simple it would be for someone
> Like ourselves to walk in and blow the whole place, and
> ourselves, to Kingdom Come.

'Last Orders' challenges the normative patterns that structure the logic of the public realm, and elaborates an unauthorised version of reality which defies both the panoptic controls of the city's ubiquitous surveillance technologies and the public gaze of a divided society. Out of the experience of disorientation, de-familiarisation and transgression, the speaker articulates the possibility of rupture within the abstract spaces of the sectored city. In seeking to subvert the logic of the system, Carson questions dominant teleological modes of knowledge and being, and implicitly demonstrates an alternative, heuristic register for experiencing the world that values subjective experience of place over more conventionalised means of spatial inscription. With the intrusion of the interloper into the strictly managed environment of the pub, all certainty vanishes: here, 'last orders' might refer to the last drinks of the night, or the last, fatal command given to the bombers. The speaker can only remain alert, suspended in a state of transitional flux and speculative unease.

The linguistic and textual application of his theory is not lost on de Certeau, who draws an explicit parallel between the tactics of the pedestrian in the rational city and those of the poet writing his poem:

Unrecognised producers, poets of their own affairs, trailblazers in the jungle of functionalist rationality, consumers produce something resembling the *'lignes d'erre'* described by Deligny. They trace 'indeterminate trajectories' that are apparently meaningless, since they do not cohere with the constructed, written, and prefabricated space through which they move. They are sentences that remain unpredictable within the space ordered by the organising techniques of systems. Although they use as their material the vocabularies of established languages (those of television, newspapers, the supermarket or city planning), although they remain within the framework of prescribed syntaxes (the temporal modes of schedules, paradigmatic organizations of places, etc.), these 'traverses' remain heterogeneous to the systems they infiltrate and in which they sketch out the guileful ruses of different interests and desires. They circulate, come and go, overflow and drift over an imposed terrain like the snowy waves of the sea slipping in among the rocks and defiles of an established order.[19]

Like the pedestrian, the poet has to use the given grids or structures but can do so in unpredictable and in an almost infinite number of ways. Place, identity, subjectivity, meaning are thus continually being reconstituted and performed within conditions which, though given, yet provide endless opportunities for creative social practice. This transgressive urban impulse is clearly exemplified in the eccentricities of Carson's writing practice. 'Linear B' features an eccentric pedestrian 'threading rapidly between crowds in Royal Avenue', while writing in a black notebook:

> ... peering through
> A cracked lens fixed with Sellotape, his *rendez-vous* is not quite *vous.*
> But from years of watching, I know the zig-zag circle:
> He has been the same place many times, never standing still.
>
> One day I clicked with his staccato walk, and glimpsed the open notebook:
> Squiggles, dashes, question-marks, dense as the Rosetta stone.
> His good eye glittered at me: it was either nonsense, or a formula – for
> Perpetual motion, the scaffolding of shopping lists, or the collapsing
>   city.   ('Linear B', *BHMSB* 25)

Carson 'clicks' with this odd character who, with his glittering eye, seems to be as anxious as Coleridge's ancient mariner to disburden himself of some kind of secret, troubling knowledge. That knowledge is encoded in what Carson describes, with wry humour, as a form of 'Linear B' – a script that was used for writing Mycenaean, the earliest known form of Greek, dating back to 1,500 BC. In his own poetic mapping of the city, Carson playfully suggests, he too opts for zig-zag circles and cracked lenses, refusing simple linear progression, and approximating instead this ancient, esoteric language which for centuries defied decipherment.

Carson is the kind of consumer of rational spaces described by de Certeau. The 'tactics' of the consumer – pedestrian or poet – indicate the impossibility of total 'strategic' control. In de Certeau's analysis, 'strategy' is the practice of power which can produce or impose 'proper' spaces, while 'tactics' refers to the pedes-

---

19 Michel de Certeau, *The Practice of Everyday Life* (Berkeley, University of California Press, 1984) p. 34.

trian practice of using, manipulating and opposing these spaces. Thought, too, is 'strategic' or 'tactical'. 'Strategic' thought derives from Enlightenment rationality invested in the spaces and institutions of power, while 'tactical' thought is represented by the poet's wayward logic, which opposes the totalising discipline of official thought and puts the hegemonic discourses under constant threat and disruption.

Maps are usually taken to be scientific, objective, impersonal, authoritative, seemingly able to provide firm ground on which to stand, a sense of security for those who like to know where they are. Maps figure importantly in Carson's work but, like other texts (including Carson's own), their meanings are shown to be neither fixed nor singular. It is impossible to write Belfast: 'No, don't trust maps, for they avoid the moment: ramps, barricades, diversions, Peace Lines' (*BC*, 58). The recitation of street names in poems such as 'Belfast Confetti' suggest the poet's own desire to map the city, to try and hold it together, even while it is collapsing around him. This is why, in 'The Exile's Club', he can identify so readily with the Irish-Australians, the emigrants of the 1950s and '60s who meet every Thursday in the Wollongong Bar to reconstruct from memory and the latest news reports the Falls Road they have left. The poem is delicately poised between acknowledgement of the human desire to fix reality and recognition of the ever-changing, teeming complexity of that reality. No map, no form of representation, can accommodate the flux of life, particularly the life of a city in a constant process of destruction and re-construction. Maps contradict the peculiarly human qualities of the urban landscapes that they reference. They can never capture truly the reality inherent in a city's historical memory or its convoluted array of cultures, stories, languages and experiences. The city disrupts traditional ideas of single, homogenous truth and promotes the view of truth as deriving from our being-in-the-world, from our continual becoming in the languages in which we are inscribed. The past survives not as traces of a unique tradition, but as elements of different histories that can be continually reconfigured. Carson maps a world where nothing stands still, where there are no absolute fixed points, where boundaries are always porous, and where it is always possible to envisage the possibility of change. 'Turn Again' concentrates on the unreliability of maps and texts, the poem informed by the postmodern understanding of the inevitable mis-match between reality and its representation. In this poem, 'The linen backing is falling apart' (*BHMSB*, 53) – an image which subtly links textual collapse with historic disintegration resulting from the decline of Belfast's linen industry. But the immediately preceding poem, 'Patchwork', offers an emblem of stitching and mending – the grandmother's patchwork quilt that she made for a wedding that never took place. Though time has unravelled the family, there remain connective traces, evidenced most particularly in the patchwork ('*your father's stitched into that quilt,/ Your uncles and your aunts*'), which has passed down to 'some one of us' (*BHMSB 48–52*). The poem itself is a patchwork made out of fragments of memory and speech, that is, something new made out of old bits and pieces. The city can be caught, as Carson's poems acknowledge, only in fragments, in the economy of disorder. His postmodern fragmentation does not imply an original unity that has been lost: it is rather a form of dissemination, a scattering of origins, centre, identity, presence and belonging.

Formalists see the work of art as possessing a symmetry, a completeness that life lacks. As Henry James put it in *The Art of the Novel*: 'Really universally, relations stop nowhere, and the exquisite problem of the artist is eternally but to draw by a geometry of his own, the circle which they shall happily *appear* to do so. Where, for the complete expression of one's subject, does a particular relation stop – giving way to some other not concerned in that expression?'[20] The parts earn their place in the whole according to the nature of their contribution to the truth toward which the work is pointing. A form that is orderly rather than digressive is founded upon the principle of relevance to the truth. But if there is no central truth to be presented, the rationale for seeing the work of art as a closed circle collapses. Unable to impose a transcendent perspective, the poet is unable to control his material by subordinating the parts to such a perspective. His only hope is to include everything. But art cannot do that. Seeking to capture the truth of reality, but unable to know the truth, the poet can only digress. Digressiveness, then, is the embodiment of an epistemological dilemma, and Carson's whole *oeuvre* reads like a fabric of digressions, ranging from apparently arbitrary details to long interpolated narratives. Things are continually seen from more than one point of view. No detail seems to be irrelevant; each is worthy of elaboration. The poet refuses to allow himself to be recruited to any one version of reality, preferring to 'walk between the story lines'. 'Dresden' is a longish, meandering, apparently pointless poem made up of a series of narratives that disrupt and intersect each other. The poem begins by introducing Horse Boyle, his brother Mule, and the caravan they live in:

> Horse Boyle was called Horse Boyle because of his brother Mule;
> Though why Mule was called Mule is anybody's guess. I stayed there once,
> Or rather, I nearly stayed there once. But that's another story.
> At any rate they lived in this decrepit caravan, not two miles out of
>   Carrick.   (*BHMSB* 13)

Identities are uncertain, a Saussurian matter of establishing relationships among signs without there being any absolute terms. We listen to the speaker working with his materials, initiating narrative, then retracting and qualifying it, then dismissing it altogether – but eventually returning to it at the end of the poem where, for a second time, the story of why he didn't stay the night is abruptly rejected: 'there's no time/ To go back to that now; I could hardly, at any rate, pick up the thread' (18). The caravan, associated with itineracy, temporariness and provisionality, symbolises an aesthetic as well as a life-style – the unsettled, serial mode of the whole poem. The caravan reminds the speaker of an old-fashioned shop, then, as Muldoon would say, 'of something else, then something else again'.[21] Questions about the daughter of the shop-owner lead back to Horse who not only knew all the local news but was a great storyteller. One of his stories is about 'young Flynn', an IRA man in the 1920s whose recollection of the scraping sound he made when digging a reclaimed tip of 'delph and crockery ware' reminds him of chalk squeaking on a blackboard, which reminds him of

---

20 Henry James, *The Art of the Novel* (New York, Scribners, 1934) p. 5.
21 Paul Muldoon, 'Something Else', in *Poems 1968–1998* (London, Faber, 2001) p. 173.

Master McGinty, who came from Narrow Quarter, a place which Horse knew well. Only at this point does the poem pick up its 'major', titular narrative, the story of Horse as a rear gunner in the RAF: 'Of all the missions, Dresden broke his heart. It reminded him of china' (*BHMSB* 17). As a memento of that awful experience, Horse has kept a china milkmaid from his childhood. The poem ends with Mule's 'careful drunken weaving/ Through the tin-stacks' as he makes his way to the caravan, while the speaker, unable to pick up the thread of the 'Mule' story, leaves the caravan home and 'wandered out through the steeples of rust, the gate that was a broken bed' (*BHMSB* 18). All is contingency. We can't be sure that the end is indeed what the rest of the poem was leading towards. This is 'open' poetry, poetry which eschews resolution or even definition. But, as 'Dresden' powerfully demonstrates, it is also a warmly humanistic poetry that scrutinises individual lives with compassionate understanding.

Underlying Carson's fragmented, temporally and spatially mobile, digressive poetics is his intuition of centrelessness. He radically undermines the idea of a centre capable of providing discursive unity and fixity, and the claims of any culture to possess a pure and homogeneous body of values. 'Snow' begins with recollection of playing ping-pong as a child. Despite the speaker's efforts to recreate the actuality of the past as clearly and accurately as he can, he is forced to recognise the emptiness at the heart of experience: 'I broke open the husk so many times/ And always found it empty; the pith was a wordless bubble' (*BHMSB*, 58). In Heaney, emptiness is transformed, by the power of imagination, into wordless plenitude, as the poet discovers a space which is 'utterly empty, utterly a source'. Contrastingly, in Carson, 'Though there's nothing in the thing itself, bits of it come back unbidden'. Heaney's poetry allows him to affirm transcendent wholeness: Carson makes do with postmodern patchwork. Carson, like Wallace Stevens' poet in 'The Snowman', is trying to make something out of nothing, relying on the prompts provided by ordinary everyday objects and experience. One such prompt is 'this thirties scuffed leather sofa', which the speaker finds particularly redolent of childhood. Carson is no doubt thinking of Heaney's 'A Sofa in the Forties'. In Heaney's poem, the sofa is transmogrified into 'ghost train' and 'death-gondola'.[22] A transformative dynamic is at work, the 'engine' of imagination capable of turning what is 'earthbound, for sure' into the 'potentially heavenbound'. In Carson, however, the sofa remains itself, the poet insistent that 'anything's too much when you have nothing'. Rather than a transformative, otherworldly aesthetic, Carson's is 'earthbound, for sure', childhood memory leading finally to the scene of a wake and the unavoidable fact of human mortality. The closing line is ambiguous: 'Roses are brought in, and suddenly, white confetti seethes against the window'. The whole poem – but this line especially – recalls MacNeice's 'Snow', which begins: 'The room was suddenly rich and the great bay-window was/ Spawning snow and pink roses against it/ Soundlessly collateral and incompatible:/ World is suddener than we fancy it'.[23] Like MacNeice's 'spawning snow', the image of seething white confetti, synthesising 'incompatible' ideas of life and death, wedding and wake, heat and coldness,

---

22 Seamus Heaney, 'A Sofa in the Forties', in *Opened Ground*, p. 397.
23 Louis MacNeice, 'Snow', in *Collected Poems*, p. 30.

anger and celebration, connotes ferocious organic process, incorrigible plurality, 'the drunkenness of things being various'. The great task facing the poet is to find an ordering structure that nevertheless won't violate 'plurality' or unduly confine 'drunkenness'. Both Mahon, in his elegy on MacNeice, 'In Carrowdore Churchyard', and Muldoon, in 'History', refer to MacNeice's 'Snow', but, as Edna Longley has pointed out, Mahon departs from MacNeice and Muldoon, and we might add from Carson, in the way he 'goes on to claim that poetry can in some sense "solve" or at least sieve the "inrush" of phenomena and history'.

> This, you implied, is how we ought to live –
>
> The ironical, loving crush of roses against snow,
> Each fragile, solving ambiguity. So
> From the pneumonia of the ditch, from the ague
> Of the blind poet and the bombed-out town you bring
> The all-clear to the empty holes of spring;
> Rinsing the choked mud, keeping the colours new.

As Longley concludes, 'Rhythmically and rhetorically it (the above stanza) moves beyond "ambiguity"'.[24] Contrast Mahon's teleologism and Heaney's transcendentalism with MacNeice's, Muldoon's and Carson's desire to remain open to the flux of consciousness and history.

The 'spawning' 'seething' snow is also present in Carson's 'Loaf', the poem immediately preceding 'Snow'. The speaker is 'muffled by forgotten drifts/ Of flour', the white dough reminds him of snow, he and his workmate write their names 'on the snowed-up panes' (*BHMSB* 56). Like the bread which is being baked, 'Loaf' rises from the yeasty ferment of the poet's memories of a summer job in McWatters' bakery, the poem repeatedly suggesting a connection between writing and the work in the bakery: empty flour-sacks are 'cloudy caesurae', bread is like blotting-paper, the speaker and his mate write on the floury windows. The young worker has to submit to the discipline of the factory but still finds plenty of time for skiving, talking, writing, making up stories, just as the poet, within the general structures of his poem, finds room for all kinds of digressive and transgressive textual play. Much of this playfulness is generated by the attempt to 'pin down' an elusive reality. There is a constant awareness that words are not up to the job of capturing or encoding a 'spawning', 'seething' world: 'the nib keeps skidding off. Or the ink won't take' (*BHMSB* 54). Reality refuses to let itself be written. It cannot be contained within the given structures and discourses and ready-made formulae, but overspills or eludes the received categories. As MacNeice put it, 'World is suddener than we fancy it./ World is crazier and more of it than we think'. 'Loaf' reiterates Carson's 'in-between' subject position, his sense of identity, meaning, imaginative power as lying between, rather than in, things:

> Blue-black
> *Quink* is what I used then. I liked the in-between-ness of it, neither

---

24 Edna Longley, 'The Room Where Macneice Wrote "Snow"', in *The Living Stream* (Newcastle-upon-Tyne, Bloodaxe Books, 1994) p. 259.

One thing nor the other. A *Conway Stewart* fountain-pen, blue-ish green
Mock tortoiseshell ...   (*BHMSB* 54)

'Snowball' breaks down the difference between significant and trivial, high
and low, central and peripheral, to consider 'All the signs' (*BHMSB* 34). These
signs are never fully explained; they are suggestive rather than definitive. Specifi-
city promises precise meaning ('An Audi Quattro sidles up in first gear past
the loading-bay of Tomb Street/ GPO – a litter of white plastic cord, a broken
whiskey bottle –') but doesn't deliver, and simply 'revs away'. Desired connec-
tions don't get made, unions fail to materialise, the parts don't add up, though
everything is potentially connected to everything else. 'All the signs' accumu-
late with accelerating rapidity, snowballing. But the thing about snowballs is
that they melt. In the words of the poem, 'Like a fish-net stocking, everything
is full of holes'. The fragments remain disconnected and unconnectable. The
poem authorises multiple combinations but, since we can never be sure how the
elements ought to be arranged, none of the possible interpretations is validated
or sustainable.

The difficulty of holding together a coherent narrative is repeatedly empha-
sised in Carson's poetry:

As someone spills a cup of tea on a discarded *Irish News*

A minor item bleeds through from another page, blurring the main story.
It's difficult to pick up without the whole thing coming apart in your hands ...
                                          ('Queen's Gambit', *BHMSB* 69)

Minor items not only blur but threaten to displace the main story, so that the
difference between 'major' and 'minor' dissolves. Narrative is always palimpsestic:
'Like the names on a school desk, carved into one another till they're indeci-
pherable'; '... the sketch that's taking shape on the Army HQ blackboard, chalky
ghosts/ Behind the present, showing what was contemplated and rubbed out,
Plan A/ Becoming X or Y; interlocked, curved arrows of the mortgaged future'
('Queen's Gambit'). If narrative cannot escape the past, neither should it close
itself off to the future, but remain open to change and revision, to chance and
the unpredictable:

What comes next is next, and no one knows the *che sera* of it, but must allow
The *Tipp-Ex* present at the fingertips. Listen now: an angel
    whispers of the here-and-now.

The future looms into the mouth incessantly, gulped-at and unspoken;
Its guardian is intangible, but gives you hints and winks and
    nudges as its broken token.   ('Second Language', *BHMSB* 98)

Given a world of flux and contingency, the great challenge is to 'pin down' the
uniqueness of experience, the precise nature of the 'here-and-now': 'Aromas,
sounds, the texture of the roads, the heaviness or lightness of the air –/ All
these contribute to the sense of place. These things are what we are,/ Though
mitigated by ourselves' ('Two to Tango'[25]).

---

[25] Ciaran Carson, *First Language* (Loughcrew, The Gallery Press, 1993) p. 18.

Carson's aesthetic requires a return to concrete particulars as the basis of knowledge. The question is how to give structure to the array of particulars without violating their particularity. With Carson, systematic arrangements, whether those of individual poems or 'chapters' of prose, serve merely to undermine themselves, to reveal their affinity with the artificial arrangements of dictionaries. The alphabetical format used in *Opera Et Cetera*[26] gives primacy to the parts at the expense of the whole. Encyclopaedic form signifies a turn away from unity and universals. According to John Locke, parts rather than wholes conform more closely to external reality and are therefore to be prized more highly:

> General and universal belong not to the real existence of things, but are the inventions and creatures of the understanding, made by it for its own use, and concern only signs, whether words or ideas. Words are general ... when used for signs of general ideas, and so are applicable indifferently to many particular things: but universality belongs not to things themselves, which are all of them particular in their existence ... When therefore we quit particulars, the generals that rest are only creatures of our own making: their general nature being nothing but the capacity they are put into, by the understanding, of signifying or representing many particulars.[27]

But while this may be so, there is still value in establishing connections between parts. This faith is attested to by Carson's compulsive cross-referencing, echoing and pattern-making. Thus, for example, the alphabetical format of the opening section of *Opera Et Cetera*, 'Letters from the Alphabet', is repeated in the distorting mirrors of the closing section, 'Opera', which is based on the radio operator's alphabetical code. The alphabetical arrangement itself is an image of the stubborn particularity of things, while the 'careful drunken weaving' of connections within and among poems represents a countervailing impulse towards unification. Carson's aesthetic is poised between anti-essentialism and organisation. His encyclopaedic form, with its discontinuous, apparently arbitrary arrangement of particulars and its artificial patternings, at once proclaims the unity of the whole and undermines that unity. The resulting narrative is historical *and* fragmentary, structured *and* open, continuous *and* discontinuous.

He takes fragmentariness even further in his most recent collection *Breaking News*, the first part of which is remarkable for his abandoning the long line for an extremely short-lined, broken format which owes a good deal to William Carlos Williams. The title works on several levels. It alludes to the continuous stream of reportage that brings the most up-to-date news of what is happening around the world, but also refers to the convulsions of war in the poet's home place and around the world, and to the breaking up of conventional poetic form under pressure of violent events. The collection title is broken across two poems which appear on facing pages. The first, 'Breaking', contains the image of a car

---

26 Ciaran Carson, *Opera Et Cetera* (Loughcrew, The Gallery Press, 1996).
27 John Locke, *Essay Concerning Human Understanding*, ed. John W. Yolton (rev. ed. London, Everyman, 1964), bk 3, chap. 3, section 11.

'about to disintegrate'[28] in an eerily silent street. The second, 'News', concerns the aftermath of the car-bomb. The actual explosion falls into the gap between the two poems, unrepresented and unrepresentable. In 'News', the sign above the *Belfast Telegraph* shop now reads '*fast rap*' (*BN* 17), reminiscent of the situation described in the earlier 'Gate', where a boutique called 'Terminus' has lost its T and r as a result of a bomb, leaving '*e minus*'. Writing, like maps, is never adequate, especially in times of rapid, violent change:

> Difficult to keep track:
> Everything's a bit askew ...   ('Gate', *BC* 45);

> It's that frottage effect again: the paper that you're scribbling on is
>   grained
> And blackened, till the pencil-lead snaps off, in a valley of the
>   broken alphabet ...   ('Queen's Gambit', *BHMSB* 67)

The collection opens with 'Belfast', a poem gesturing towards Williams' rhythms of speech and living, in which Belfast is enveloped in an unreal silence – except for the whistling of a blackbird. Carson's poem, with a similar painterly vividness and concrete precision as one finds in Williams' 'The Red Wheelbarrow', emphasises patterns of colour, the relationship of the parts of the picture to each other. No one thing stands for something else; it is uniquely itself: 'No ideas but in things'.

> east
>
> beyond the yellow
> shipyard cranes
>
> a blackbird whistles
> in a whin bush
>
> west
>
> beside the motorway
> a black taxi
>
> rusts in a field
> of blue thistles   (*BN* 11)

Here, William Carlos Williams and American Imagism meet early Irish Gaelic nature poetry. Carson's poem, written with haiku-like precision and clarity, exhibits the kind of freshness and directness, the kind of watchfulness towards nature, that we associate with early Irish nature poems. Indeed, 'Belfast' closely echoes the well-known 'The Blackbird of Belfast Lough', written by a seventh-century Irish monk in the margins of an illuminated manuscript.

Heaney mentions this poem specifically in 'The God in the Tree', his essay on early Irish nature poetry, where he uses Wordsworth's phrase 'surprised by joy' to describe the way this art, combining 'suddenness and richness', 'precision and

---

[28] Ciaran Carson, *Breaking News* (Loughcrew, The Gallery Press, 2003), p. 16. Hereafter abbreviated to *BN* and page references incorporated into the text.

suggestiveness', gives us 'the tang and clarity of a pristine world'.[29] Something of this archaic apprehension of the natural world is found in Carson's compact concrete lines, for the powers of the Celtic god in the tree, manifest in black-bird and thistle, continue to hover over the modern metropolis with its motor-ways, black taxis and shipyard cranes. 'Belfast' presents a curious social ecology, a heterogeneous discursive field of fluctuating languages and contexts in which the imagery of an exhausted metropolis gives way to the semiotics of nature, suggestive of a wider frame for re-thinking and re-presenting the city. The yellow shipyard cranes and black taxi may now be redundant, but the blue thistles and blackbird's whistles (picked out by the poem's only rhyme), are testimony to nature's irrepressible vitality in the midst of desolation.

The blackbird is heard again in 'Wake', another poem about the immediate aftermath of a bomb going off. In 'the lull' after the explosion, 'a blackbird/ whistled in/ a chink/ of light/ between that world/ and this' (*BN* 53). Of crucial importance in this collection are the breaks, lulls, gaps, moments of suspension, in-between states that Carson repeatedly homes in on. The constant sound of the army helicopters over the poet's home in north Belfast is the subject of two short revs of poems, 'Spin Cycle' and 'Spin Cycle 2'. In the first, the sound of the helicopter is like the whir of a washing-machine is like the spin cycle of the poem itself. Michael McAteer suggests that Carson alludes to Vorticism,[30] Pound's notion of the poem as 'a VORTEX, from which, and through which, and into which, ideas are constantly rushing'.[31] The vortex or 'spin cycle' of the poem comes to an end when the speaker 'put in/ the ear-plugs' and 'every-thing went/ centrifugal' (*BN* 39). In the companion poem, 'Spin Cycle 2', the lyric 'I' has disappeared completely, obliterated by or assimilated into a world of objects: 'gun-gun/ ear-plugs in/ blank-blank' (*BN* 40). In its simplistically pared down economy, the poem gives us stimulus, response and outcome in rapid succession. Political violence is metonymically reduced to the childish 'gun-gun', human response to mechanical reflex – 'ear plugs in', while 'Blank-blank' not only suggests the muffled sound of gunfire or the blanking out of the victim's life, but also the Beckettian blank of 'nothing to express'. Signifier and signified, word and world, become one. Language, unable to gesture beyond itself, is just another object. Together, these two poems would seem to declare the death of the author. However, another poem which keeps the Beckettian connection alive in its title – 'Breath' – describes how once the noise of the helicopter overhead stops, 'I feel/ rinsed/ clean', as 'when the/ washing-machine/ stops/ shuddering' (*BN* 23). Here, the poem opens onto a moment of visionary calm, of self-presence and compo-sure, a Heaneyesque 'clearance' – which could also be the moment of death. A similar defamiliarising effect is recorded in 'Minus' where the sudden silence of the helicopter seems to galvanise the speaker into perceiving the world in a fresh new William Carlos Williamsian way, with preternatural vividness, though (as

[29] Seamus Heaney, 'The God in the Tree', in *Preoccupations*, p. 181.
[30] See Michael McAteer, 'The Word as Object: Commodification in the Poetry of Ciaran Carson', in Elmer Kennedy-Andrews (ed.), *Ciaran Carson: A Collection of Critical Essays* (Dublin: Four Courts Press), forthcoming.
[31] Ezra Pound, 'Vorticism', in *Gaudier-Brzeska: A Memoir* (New York, New Directions, 1970) pp. 81–94, 90.

the title would suggest) not an unambiguously positive one: 'I raise/ the blind/ on/ a moon/ so bright/ it hurts/ and oh/ so cold/ my breath/ sounds/ like frost' (*BN* 46). In 'Home', the poet, 'hurtling' down the airport road, stops to look down over Belfast, as if reading a map: 'motionless/ at last/ I see everything' (*BN* 12). Once again, clearance or distance is momentarily achieved. The spectacle of the orderly laid out city below, with its reassuring landmarks, offers a sense of security, a contrast to the disorder of the 'fields of scrap/ and thistle/ farmyards' he has passed. All of these short, minimalist poems, shorn of punctuation and using flexible line lengths, line breaks and line spacing as a kind of musical notation to suggest pauses and breaks, embody with particular acuity and precision the tensions between sound and silence, motion and motionlessness, order and disorder, presence and absence, life and death that characterise the disjunctive and unsettling conditions of the metropolitan terrain.

If the danger in a localist or particularist focus is that poems might become a series of isolated fragments unable to speak beyond their own moment, it is through the sheer intensity of the poet's concentration and the degree of imaginative responsiveness that he brings to bear, that his detailed vignettes of particular incidents or scenes assume universal dimensions. Small, apparently insignificant details disclose far-reaching insights, parts contain wholes, fragments tell a bigger story. 'Fragment' refers to a bit of a Tupperware lunchbox from which 'they could tell/ the bombmaker wore/ *Marigold* gloves' (*BN* 37), the single word '*Marigold*' suggesting a whole conspectus of orders – natural, domestic and religious – that the bombmaker has violated.

Belfast itself becomes a site of transit, an intersection, part of a wider story. As the last and title poem of *The Ballad of HMS Belfast* emphasises, Belfast, set loose from her moorings, begins to drift, to enter other places, other stories The city does not stand for a firm and rational referent, but becomes a floating signifier, moving through diverse interpretations and narratives, its usual binary demographic re-configured, in a spirit of Joycean plurability, into 'Catestants and Protholics' (*BHMSB* 113). Whether caught in the modes of hallucinatory fantasy, as in 'The Ballad of HMS Belfast', or in the mythical half-light of imagined foreign battlefields, as in *Breaking News*, Belfast, in Carson's account, is a more open and extensive place than the one we have been accustomed to inhabiting. *Breaking News* testifies to the centrality of the battlefield in the figural economy of Carson's Belfast. Poems about Belfast and the Troubles are interspersed with poems about the Russian Revolution, the Indian Mutiny and the Crimean War, the depiction of scenes of different wars reverberating against each other. Diverse histories intersect and open up the space of an encounter, a dialogue, in which neither history is reduced to the other. Narrowly focused snapshots of battle scenes and their immediate aftermath convey the de-humanisation of entire societies. Such is 'Waste Not', a macabre close-up of a Crimean battlefield where the women are 'harvesting' (*BN* 34) gold buttons shorn from dead soldiers' uniforms. 'Harvest' is the bitterly ironic title of another poem where wounded soldiers crawl through the harvest fields 'like mutilated bees' (*BN* 41), an image of a terrible metaphysical bleakness. 'Some Uses of a Dead Horse' dramatises a cold and inhuman aestheticism. The poetic voice is withdrawn in its meticulous calm. Observation, even of the horrific, is unemotive and the tone undeclamatory, avoiding the public modes of historical generalisation or moral comment. It might seem, as Lionel Trilling said of the short stories of Isaac Babel (to whom Carson dedicates his poem 'Russia') that Carson's poetry is itself 'touched with cruelty'. Carson deals with extreme violence and destruction, yet describes it, as Trilling believed Babel did, 'with a striking elegance and precision of objectivity, and also with a kind of lyric joy, so that the reader cannot be sure how the author is responding to the brutality he records'.[32] While conceding that Carson's poetry is a relentless detailing of mutilation, desecration and destruction, the reader experiences the predictable human feelings of shock, horror and moral outrage all the more powerfully precisely because of the poet's cool postmodern style – its ironic detachment and objectivity, its apparent indifference to 'depth', 'meanings' and 'values', its refusal of explicit human sympathy.

The collection concludes with a sequence of poems based, sometimes verbatim, on dispatches from the Crimean War sent back by the Anglo-Irish journalist William Howard Russell. Carson's versions of Russell's versions of nineteenth-century Gallipoli, Varna, Dvno, Balaklava, Kertch, Tchernaya and Sedan reflect on his native city which, as he repeatedly emphasises, is closely linked with Britain's imperial heyday, particularly the Crimean adventure. In 'Exile' he walks 'the smouldering/ dark streets/ Sevastopol/ Crimea/ Inkerman/ Odessa/ Balkan/ Lucknow' (*BHMSB* 23). Belfast, as Carson goes on to say in the same poem, 'is many/ places'. The 'War Correspondent' sequence returns to many of his favourite themes, in particular that of nature's fragile beauty, continuance and promise. 'Tchernaya' echoes 'Belfast' with its description of the birdsong and the colourful flowers enlivening degraded surroundings: 'Strange to hear them sing about the bushes/ in the lulls between the thud of the bombs,/ or to see between the cannon-flashes/ the whole peninsula ignite with blooms' (*BN* 68). 'Sedan', the last poem in the sequence, ends with a final affirmation of both nature and art. The speaker, making his way through the 'debris' of 'a ruined empire', as the poet made his way through the ruined streets of Belfast in 'Smithfield Market', comes upon the tokens of hope for the future:

> even the bomb-shelters
> ransacked, though in one dug-out
> I found a music-book
>
> With a woman's name
> In it, and a canary bird,
> And a vase of wild flowers.   (*BN* 72)

Suffering has not extinguished music and song. Though it foretells danger, the canary bird with its bright splash of yellow stands out more prominently against dark surroundings than the blackbird of 'Belfast'. Wild flowers are still found in the midst of the rubble. Where the battlefield flowers in 'Tchernaya', like Keith Douglas's 'desert flowers' or Isaac Rosenberg's poppies in Flanders fields, represent the pathos of nature's enduring innocence and piercing beauty amidst the collapse of civilisation, Carson's vase of flowers, retrieved and preserved by human hand, signifies faith in the *human* potential to transform a violent and debased present. 'Sedan' merges images of the battle of Sedan (1870) fought during the

---

[32]   Lionel Trilling, 'Introduction', in *Isaac Babel: Collected Stories* (London, Penguin, 1961) p. 10.

Franco-Prussian War with scenes of the siege of Sevastopol (1854) which took place during the Crimean War, and places in the midst of these bloody encounters the vase of flowers which, like Wallace Stevens' jar in Tennessee, symbolises the aesthetic sense, our only guarantee of the future.

What all of these poems have in common is their privileging of the fragmented detail, the specific event, the body, the voice, with the inevitable consequence of dispersing unified identity, universal subjectivity and continuous narrative. The variousness of our being-in-the-world is given precedence over positivist, universalist or hermetic modes of discourse. In rewriting the grammar of urban historiography in terms of discontinuity and centrelessness, Carson isn't simply writing in the margins of dominant discourses. By moving from a poetics of margins to a poetics of differences, he dissolves the relationship between power and knowledge on which our understanding of what is central and what is marginal has traditionally been founded. By doing away with the centre, the authorising principle, he does away with those binary oppositions in which one term is always privileged over the other. Instead, he wants to open us to considerations beyond ourselves, beyond the usual hegemonic structures of understanding and representation, to what exists only as trace or echo or shadow. Heidegger alerts us to the significance of the shadow as ghostly portent of 'otherness':

> Everyday opinion sees in the shadow only the lack of light, if not light's complete denial. In truth, however, the shadow is a manifest, though impenetrable, testimony to the concealed emitting of light. In keeping with this concept of shadow, we experience the incalculable as that which, withdrawn from representation, is nevertheless manifest in whatever is, pointing to Being, which remains concealed.[33]

Thus, Carson's 'Edward Hopper: *Early Sunday Morning, 1939*' concentrates on the concrete details of the street scene, including the long shadow which falls across the picture: 'another shadow/ falls/ from what/ we cannot see/ to what/ we cannot see/ dawn/ before the War' (*BN* 54). The picture/poem occupies the interstitial space between the twin mysteries of origins and destiny which lie forever outside the bounds of what is known and representable.

Similarly, 'Last Effect' asks us to consider a bullet-dented watch-case, its hands arrested at the exact moment the owner was saved from death, yet curiously pointing to the 'incalculable', that which remains 'withdrawn from representation': 'O what is time/ my friend/ when faced with/ eternity' (*BN* 48). 'Detail' describes a similar incident and frames it in a similar way: a war veteran opens his Bible to reveal the way the bullet 'stopped at Revelation' (*BN* 33).

The Carson poem is typically gapped or holed – an excess without a centre – yet indicates redemptive potential. In its breaks and lulls, it registers its sometimes stunned awareness that there are other stories, languages and identities. Categories leak and spill; they cast shadows over one another; they interpenetrate each other. Identity is always open, never finite nor resolved. This new urban poetics implies a very different sense of 'home' from that which we find

---

[33] Martin Heidegger, 'The Age of the World Picture', in Martin Heidegger, *The Question Concerning Technology and Other Essays* (New York, Harper & Row, 1977) p. 154.

in the older generation of Heaney or Mahon. Carson's 'home' is neither fixed nor closed, but mobile, mutable, constructed in the movement of language that constitutes the sense of place, belonging and identity. Dwelling is sustained, not by roots but by dialogue with other histories, other places, other people. The sense of place that is constructed is always contingent, in transit, with neither origin nor end.

Chapter 10

MEDBH McGUCKIAN:
THE LYRIC OF GENDERED SPACE

The Postmodern

Medbh McGuckian has devoted her entire career not only to re-imagining women's relation to the female body, to the domestic environment, and to the wider world of society, politics, religion and culture, but to re-constituting the very basis of female subjectivity and self-expression. She explains the demoralising state of affairs that prompts such a revolutionary enterprise:

> I know being a woman for me for a long time was being less, being excluded, being somehow cheap, being inferior, being sub. I associated being a woman with being a Catholic and being Irish with being from the North, and all of these things being not what you wanted to be. If you were a woman, it would have been better to be a man; if you were Catholic, it would have been a lot easier to be Protestant; if you were from the North, it was much easier to be from the South; if you were Irish, it was much easier to be English. So it was like everything that I was was wrong; everything that I was was hard, difficult, and a punishment.[1]

McGuckian's confession of feelings of comprehensive lack – an ironic revision of the 'hierarchy of values' that Hewitt delineated in his attempt at an assertion of confident (male) Protestant identity – may be understood in Lacanian psychoanalytic terms. According to Lacan, and also to psychoanalytic French feminist thought, personal, social and cultural identity is acquired within a network of social and symbolic discourses organised in and through language. In a phallocentric culture, masculinity is the decisive signifier of status, power and authority. Identity is constructed in and through language that takes masculinity as its norm. Women can occupy the position of a masculine subject, that is, one with status, power and authority, but women will always be marked as different and inferior. The feminine position (which, in McGuckian's case, can include such associated 'inferior' categories as 'Catholic', 'Irish' and 'Northerner') is designated as lacking, 'other'. Since subjectivity is constituted through one's position(s) within the symbolic order of culture, then finding oneself in an alien

---

[1]   Danielle Sered, '"By Escaping and [Leaving] a Mark": Authority and the Writing Subject of the Poetry of Medbh McGuckian', in *Irish University Review*, 32, 2 (Autumn/Winter 2002) pp. 273–85, 283.

space produces a sense of non-meaning and non-identity – a sense of homelessness – such as McGuckian describes.[2] Where Heaney's or Montague's poetry is largely an act of attempted recovery of a lost time and place, McGuckian, with no prior state of ideal femininity to refer to, is more properly to be seen as engaged in a process of (self-)*dis*covery. It is a mark of the ambition and audacity of the poet that, setting herself in adversarial relationship with the hegemonic discourses, she should undertake a project of no less moment than that of re-inventing the world.

McGuckian has devoted her entire poetic career to exploring the relationship between gendered identity and the spatial, social and symbolic orders in and through which masculinist power and feminist resistance operate. Her poetry mobilises the deconstructive forces of resistance brought to bear on the spatial and symbolic strategies of patriarchy and colonialism, grounded in the physical spaces of home, landscape, city, prison, nation, earth, and in the symbolic orders of language, politics and religion. In this sense, her poetry may be seen to continue the project central to much feminist and postcolonial work of displacing the hegemonic discourses with a disruptive poetical re-configuration of the meanings given to femininity, Ireland and spirituality. This project involves a radical refurbishment of the forms of representation through which subject and space are discursively understood. As Clair Wills explains:

> Rather than attempting to change public or national forms of representation by 'including' feminine narratives, McGuckian's work suggests instead the impossibility of separating domestic and national histories to begin with. The drive towards the increased representation of women's narratives is in danger of ignoring the politics inherent in the use of the traditional lyric form, focusing instead on the content of the feminine experience (both personal and communal) which must be introduced into the literary institution.[3]

McGuckian doesn't seek simply to include women's voice and experience within the existing hegemonic discourses, but to undertake a radical re-writing of the very categories of subject and space. Specifically, as Wills points out, she dissolves the traditional binary opposition of private and public worlds. Women's issues – the female body, sexuality, maternity, self-vindication – are viewed not only as personal matters occurring within subjective or domestic space but as part of the larger social, political and religious discourse. Moreover, McGuckian's disturbance of traditional lyric form, since it entails a fundamental revision of the 'public or national forms of representation', gives her work an inherently political function.

Much has already been written about the radical displacements of McGuckian's poetic psychodrama, about its indeterminacy and obscurity, its surrealism and secret symbolism, its hidden messages and buried allusions. Place – physical or social setting – tends to be vague, unstable, deliquescent. The 'action' of the poem is difficult to make out: 'Every poem I've written', McGuckian confided to

---

2   See Jacques Lacan, 'The Mirror Phase', *New Left Review*, 51 (1968) pp. 71–7; Hélène Cixous, 'Laugh of the Medusa', *Signs*, 1, 4 (Summer 1976) p. 879.

3   Clair Wills, *Improprieties: Politics and Sexuality in Northern Irish Poetry* (Oxford, Oxford University Press, 1993) p. 75.

Catherine Byron, 'is about something that's happened to me ... but I've coded it.'[4] Without McGuckian's gloss on 'The Soil-Map',[5] for example, the reader would miss much of the poem's relation to a particular concrete milieu, for McGuckian's use of ordinary, everyday images such as those of houses or rooms is, to say the least, extraordinary. 'The Soil-Map', she tells us, refers to the time when she was moving from a Catholic to a Protestant area of Belfast, and to a house that was previously owned by a Protestant family. Descriptive detailing of the house is concrete but cryptic. The references to its 'two-leafed door' and 'petalled steps',[6] McGuckian explains, are meant to suggest the grandeur of the house, though it is a 'decayed richness'. Even more abstruse are the references to the 'hump of water', the 'discolouring' and 'saddling derangement' which are meant to relate to the dissension in the North. The second stanza, she says, links house and female body, and suggests a parallel between the new occupant's 'going in' and the rape of a woman, which may explain the male gendering of the speaker in the first stanza. The poem delineates place not only in terms of the physical house, but also in terms of environing political and historical forces. The title, which refers to the kind of map which shows the distribution of different qualities of soil in a particular area, introduces the idea of geographical difference which also has historical ramifications: good soil has traditionally been occupied by the Protestant colonist, while the native Catholic population was relegated to areas of poorer soil. However, in saying 'I will not/ Take you in hardness' (*FM* 37), the speaker refuses to continue operating on the basis of old animosities, though she cannot deny who she is or where she comes from. She proceeds to try and remember the actual women who lived in these Protestant houses: 'Annsgift or Mavisbank,/ Mount Juliet or Bettysgrove: they should not/ lie with the gloom of disputes to interrupt them/ every other year'. She concludes by raising a toast to these women: 'I drink to you as Hymenstown', the reference connoting boundary-crossing, marriage, celebration of the society of women as an alternative to the public, male world of disputes, violence and rape. Meanwhile, she awaits her 'power as a bride', the word 'power' emphasising what this poem has been about all along – the poet's self-realisation as a gendered and political being located on the uncertain and polluted ('soiled') ground of the shifting, variegated Ulster soil. 'Even after twenty years', McGuckian's interviewer records, 'she still hates this house. She says she and the house have never gotten along, and she feels weird and strange within it.'

Geographers distinguish between three interwoven elements of place: 'locale', the settings in which social relations are constituted; 'location', the effects upon locales of the wide sweep of social and economic forces; and 'sense of place', the local 'structure of feeling', to use Raymond Williams's phrase.[7] One or more of these elements may predominate in a particular poem. 'The Soil-Map' may

4   Medbh McGuckian, interview with Catherine Byron, 'A House of One's Own: Three Contemporary Women Poets', *Women's Review*, 19 (May, 1987) p. 33.
5   See http://faculty.vassar.edu/mijoyce/Clodagh Web/roomshou/troubles.html
6   Medbh McGuckian, 'The Soil-Map', in *The Flower Master* (Loughcrew, The Gallery Press, 1993) p. 36. Hereafter abbreviated to *FM* and page references incorporated into the text.
7   See John Agnew, 'Representing Space: Space, Scale and Culture in Social Science', in James Duncan and David Levy (eds.), *Place/Culture/Representation* (London, Routledge,1993) pp. 251–71, p. 263.

(just about) be seen to represent place on all three levels, but this is rarely the case in McGuckian's work. Typically, there is less recognisable 'sense of place' to reinforce a social-spatial definition of place from inside, as it were, or to provide the ground of subjective identity. Often, the objective local social world of place, and the subjective territorial identity of 'sense of place' are virtually dissolved, and it is the macro-order of social and historical process operating at wider scales which locates the poem. The representation of locale and 'sense of place' requires a degree of cohesiveness that McGuckian's poetry usually does not possess. Hers is a poetry which seems to reject all the usual lyric norms: there's no clearly identifiable lyric centre, no controlling voice to order the images and shape the poem, no coherent narrative or development, no unity, no closure, no single or reliable meaning, no adherence to grammatical rules. Images proliferate wildly, shifting and drifting like clouds or smoke. Her ambition, it would seem, is to abolish the lyric 'I' and let the poem write itself: 'A poem dreams of being written/ Without the pronoun "I"' ('Harem Trousers'[8]) where, notably, the subject of the verb is not 'I' but 'A poem'. Elsewhere, she indicates a Whitmanian multiple or aggregate 'I' – 'Another I who is everybody' ('Reverse Cinderella'[9]). 'The Appropriate Moment' speaks of a diffused or dispersed 'I': 'They say that I am not I,/ but some kind of we, that I do not know/ where I end' (*CL* 22–3) where, again, the 'I' (despite being repeated four times) is not the subject of the sentence. 'The Invalid's Echo' refers to 'my name, that comes/ From nowhere, and is ownerless'.[10] 'Smoke', the first poem in the *Selected*,[11] uses the image of burning whins to broach questions of identity, control and definition: 'They seem so sure what they can do./ I am unable even/ To contain myself, I run/ Till the fawn smoke settles on the earth' (*FM* 11). 'Slips' is about the way words and images slip and slide into each other in a process of compulsive imaginative fluidity and free association. Like Muldoon who thinks of 'something else, then something else again', and exploits the poetic potential of 'errata'. McGuckian confesses: 'But I forget names, remembering them wrongly/ where they touch upon another name,/ a town in France like a woman's Christian name' (*FM* 21). This text is not to be trusted for it is the site of slippages between names, places, languages, countries, cultures. Dependent on misprisions and 'tricks', the poem is at once vividly precise and dreamily indeterminate. The title of another poem, 'What Does "Early" Mean?', indicates the poet's stance of questioning uncertainty, her refusal of authority. The usual markers of time – 'early', 'six o'clock or seven' – have lost their meaning and are no longer able to give structure to the flux of life. The poem avoids definitive or fixed meanings of any kind. Meaning is always shifting and elusive, always in progress, as indicated by the proliferation of metaphors, trailing rhythms, extensile grammatical structure and frequent enjambment:

---

[8] Medbh McGuckian, *On Ballycastle Beach* (Oxford, Oxford University Press, 1988) p. 43. Hereafter abbreviated to *OBB* and page references incorporated into the text.
[9] Medbh McGuckian, *Captain Lavender* (Loughcrew, The Gallery Press, 1994) p. 54. Hereafter abbreviated to *CL* and page references incorporated into the text.
[10] Medbh McGuckian, *Marconi's Cottage* (Loughcrew, The Gallery Press, 1991) p. 13. Hereafter abbreviated to *MC* and page references incorporated into the text.
[11] Medbh McGuckian, *Selected Poems* (Loughcrew, The Gallery Press, 2001).

None of my doors has slammed
Like that. Every sentence is the same
Old workshop sentence, ending
Rightly or wrongly in the ruins
Of an evening spent in puzzling
Over the meaning of six o'clock or seven:

Or why the house across the road
Has such a moist-day sort of name,
Evoking ships and their wind-blown ways.   (*OBB* 11)

'None of my doors has slammed/ Like that' would seem to be a metaphor-ical reference to McGuckian's sentences which resist decisiveness and closure. 'Every sentence is the same/ old workshop sentence' suggests endless crafting of the same familiar materials, a process which always inevitably disintegrates into puzzlement and aporia. Puzzling over the time leads not to resolution but a shift to puzzling over the name of a house. Names confer identity and fix meaning, but the name of the house in McGuckian's poem is a matter of conno-tation not straightforward denotation. Rather than directly give us the fixity of a name, the speaker concentrates on what the name evokes: 'Ships and their wind-blown ways' – a line which comments tellingly on the poem's own erratic and unpredictable movement, and ironically upsets the usual symbolism of a house being a secure place. Even while gesturing towards homing and naming, the poem withdraws from or diffuses any tendency towards fixed location or definition. It moves back and forth between a real house ('the house across the road') and metaphorical houses ('a retina of new roofs', 'None of my doors has slammed', 'old workshop sentence'), conflating outer and inner, reality and imagination, place and poetry. Thomas Docherty answers the poem's title-ques-tion by saying that to be 'early' is to be 'untimely', concluding that McGuckian's writing is 'equally "untimely"': 'To be early is to be out of place as well as out of time: it is to be "flitting", to be on the nomadic move, between situations'.[12] By the time we get to the end of the poem the original question has been lost, just as by the time we get to the end of a chain of McGuckian metaphors the original referent no longer matters.

Docherty constructs his de-constructivist reading of McGuckian within the parameters of the postmodern critical and theoretical paradigm:

> The verse often reads as if the language itself, a language devoid of a consciousness, were directing it ... Often it is difficult to locate any single position from which the poem can be spoken ... the relation between the speaking Subject or 'I' and the Object of its intention is mobile and fluid. It reads as if the space afforded the 'I' is vacant: instead of a stable 'persona', all we have is a potential of personality, a voice which cannot be identified.[13]

Under these conditions, it would seem unlikely that McGuckian would have much to say about home as it is commonly understood. Indeed, this is one of

---

[12]   Thomas Docherty, 'Postmodern McGuckian', in Neil Corcoran (ed.), *The Chosen Ground: Essays on the Contemporary Poetry of Northern Ireland* (Bridgend, Seren Books, 1992) p. 203.
[13]   Ibid., p.192.

Docherty's central assertions: 'I argue for a postmodern McGuckian. She offers the availability of a poetry which is not defined by its relation to a tradition or place; rather, her writing offers a way of breaking away from the "place-logic" which is central to the formulation of a national culture, tradition or lineage.'[14] On the assumption that 'she questions the modern belief in the availability of identity', Docherty concludes: 'the arrangement of matter may appear stable, but it is invisible ... by extension, of course, "North" would also have no intrinsic meaning, nor would "Ireland", nor would "McGuckian" and so on'.[15]

Docherty's claims need to be examined closely. Cautionary notes have already been entered by Danielle Sered and Shane Alcobia-Murphy. The former argues that 'if, as McGuckian posits, "beauty lives/ by escaping and leaves a mark", then both that escape and that mark it leaves must be understood as essential. It is this double capacity of beauty – that of escape and imprint – that is at risk if meaning and authorship are too thoroughly eradicated.'[16] The latter, objecting to Docherty's 'overemphasis on the postmodern fractured self', suggests that while 'the voice may be "unidentified", ... this does not void it of "identity"; and although the "I" may be multiple in the poem, he (Docherty) is incorrect to consider this as nullifying its actuality'.[17] It is Murphy's view that 'instead of signifying the death of the author or the crisis of identity', McGuckian's highly intertextualised poetry 'express[es] the idea that the Muse is external to the poet's personality',[18] and represents a restatement of T.S. Eliot's doctrine concerning the poet and tradition.

Following these critics, I would argue that McGuckian cannot be located solely within the cultural context of the postmodern, but that her poetry provides a discursive space for a negotiation of the postmodern with both post-feminism and post-colonialism. Linda Hutcheon has articulated the positive view of post-modernism, considering it not simply in terms of nihilism and scepticism but as referring to a process, an open and flexible mode of representation which can renew an exhausted tradition.[19] Certainly, deconstruction and post-structuralism have played a major role in helping define the position of the (feminine and colonial) marginalised subject while drawing attention to the limitations of all human positions and discourse. Fragmentation, dislocation, fluidity, mobility, multiplicity: these recognisably postmodern characteristics of McGuckian's work need not necessarily signify the ultimate dissolution of reality and meaning, but lay the ground of a possible reconstitution of space/place, identity, authenticity and authority. Her disruptive poetics, her refusal to produce concrete meaning or come to the point, her mobilisation of the Derridean techniques of dissemination, deferral and undecidability, are a deliberate means of creating resisting spaces, unwriting existing discourses, and affirming openness, otherness and strangeness. Her obscurity and stylistic difficulty are themselves significant statement,

---

14 Ibid.
15 Ibid., p. 206.
16 Sered, p. 283.
17 Shane Murphy, '"You Took Away My Biography": The Poetry of Medbh McGuckian', *Irish University Review*, 28, 1 (Spring/Summer 1998) pp. 110–32, 112.
18 Ibid.
19 See Linda Hutcheon, *A Poetics of Postmodernism: History, Theory, Fiction* (London and New York, Routledge, 1988) p. 27.

part and parcel of her thought. Critics tend to assert either that McGuckian's style is fundamentally communicative or that it is fundamentally uncommunicative. This is to overlook the central paradox of her work – that it is both. The poet presents herself as an authentically individual female subject by speaking through the interstices of the alien male symbolic order. As the blurb on the jacket of *Drawing Ballerinas* has it: 'Her dreamlike poems underscore the notion that one finds clarity by repeatedly stepping outside one's usual frame of reference.'[20] By undoing what appears harmonious and comprehensible she discovers what is opaque or alienating. Her language, freed from denotation and mimesis, is opposed to fixity, stability, system: it is made to perceive or suggest what it doesn't want, or is unable, to say, to refresh the usual formulations of love, hate, revolt, reconciliation, faith and negation. In reply to Docherty's contention that McGuckian's poetry is not defined by its relation to a tradition or place, I see the poet's work as in fact concerned with reordering the ways in which such terms as subject, place and tradition are understood. This project is not simply a matter of critique: resistance works through a renovation of resources in the poet's peculiar heritage that have been oppressed and repressed.

The Feminine

Julia Kristeva provides a helpful theoretical framework for an understanding of McGuckian's post-feminist writing. Kristeva distinguishes between the function of the semiotic and symbolic in language. The symbolic is the patriarchal sexual and social order, the domain of structure and grammar. The semiotic is not yet language but can be discerned in language, in tone, rhythm, and the bodily and material qualities of language. It belongs to the pre-Oedipal stage when the child is closely connected to the mother's body, and is thus associated with femininity and with repression, for in entering the symbolic order the child must repress the semiotic. Terry Eagleton's description of the semiotic applies directly to McGuckian:

> The semiotic is fluid and plural, a kind of pleasurable creative excess over precise meaning, and it takes sadistic delight in destroying or negating such signs. It is opposed to all fixed, transcendental significations; and since the ideologies of modern male-dominated class-society rely on such fixed signs for their power (God, father, state, order, property and so on), such literature becomes a kind of equivalent in the realm of language to revolution in the sphere of politics. The reader of such texts is equally disrupted or 'decentred' by this linguistic force, thrown into contradiction, unable to take up any one, simple 'subject-position' in relation to these polymorphous works.[21]

Like Kristeva, McGuckian lays claim to an unrepressed flow of 'feminine' and maternal energy, representing the Body-of-the-Mother and resisting the Name-of-the-Father. Kristeva doesn't privilege the semiotic (indeed most of her exam-

---

[20] Medbh McGuckian, *Drawing Ballerinas* (Loughcrew, The Gallery Press, 2001). Hereafter abbreviated to *DB* and page references incorporated into the text.
[21] Terry Eagleton, *Literary Theory* (Oxford, Blackwell, 1996) pp. 163–4.

ples of 'revolutionary' writing are male), but sees it as a process within language, which questions and transgresses its limits. Similarly, McGuckian, while drawing from the tradition of the (male, English) symbolic 'other', works upon it to release the semiotic from within the symbolic, so to produce her own distinctive, highly individualistic (feminine, Irish) poetics.

Her poetry thus represents a re-configuration of the lyric in a gesture of female self-restoration and self-redefinition:

> An acorn of a blind, denuded, unbegun,
> unsheltered and unfinished, draws across a floor
> on the mortal side of language,
>
> a leaf detaching itself
> from the narrative 'tree'
> attempts to seal its meaning.
>
> Then the voice that supplied the story
> Will be a character rounded-off outside it,
> Writing itself into those fumbling breaks
> Through which desire is completely trained:
> Bound in the bed like an account book.
>
> ('Dante's Own Day', *CL* 34)

'Blind, denuded, unbegun,/ unsheltered and unfinished' is an awkward-sounding list of words that may be supposed to describe the McGuckian 'sentence', though no noun is included for these adjectives to qualify. Both 'unbegun' and 'unfinished', the would-be sentence goes nowhere. There is no conventional progression from A to B. McGuckian plays with our readerly expectations, blatantly defying our attempts to construct meaning. The acorn doesn't grow into anything, but is abruptly replaced by a new subject, 'A leaf'. 'Meaning' is (quite literally) achieved only by the leaf detaching itself from the tree: only by the poet detaching herself from the established master narratives. The 'slips' in the earlier poem, we see now, are also horticultural: cuttings taken from the parent plant for grafting or re-planting. The final stanza speaks of the voice converting itself to text, but occupying an interstitial position between available discourses, operating tentatively and experimentally in the 'fumbling breaks'. The last two lines hint ominously at the dangers of semiotic desire losing its wildness, being 'trained' into a return to postures of fixity and conformity.

Looking back at 'Slips' in the light of McGuckian's feminist agenda, we might note that slips are not just mistakes but female undergarments: that is, a language of slippage and 'tricks' is identified with femininity. The opening references to moon and milk likewise ground the poem in femininity:

> The studied poverty of a moon roof,
> the earthenware of dairies cooled by apple trees,
> the apple tree that makes the whitest wash ...   (*FM* 21)

The poem registers the elusiveness of female subjectivity – it slips and changes like the moon. But the imagery of earth, dairies and trees suggest that women's creativity is also 'grounded' in place and in the body. As Clair Wills reminds us, women writers, as a consequence of maternity, have had less opportunity to experiment with travel or exile than their male counterparts.[22] While the female poet happily reflects on the fact that she is occupying the shell of another tradition ('My favourite fairy tales the shells/ Leased by the hermit crab'), the last stanza refers to slips from the patriarchal rules of propriety.

> I see my grandmother's death as a piece of ice,
> My mother's slimness restored to her,
> My own key slotted in your door –
>
> Tricks you might guess from this unfastened button,
> A pen mislaid, a word misread,
> My hair coming down in the middle of a conversation. (*FM* 21)

The 'conversation' – language, the word of the father, the symbolic order – is disrupted by the sensual, the female body, the semiotic. Against Docherty's conclusion that in McGuckian's poetry 'Reality ... constantly slips away',[23] we might point to the way 'Slips' foregrounds the techniques of female presencing, and, as the references to 'grandmother' and 'mother' would suggest, lays the ground of a feminist genealogy.

Looking more closely at 'Harem Trousers' and McGuckian's apparent abolition of the lyric 'I', we should also note that authorial control does not disappear as thoroughly as Docherty suggests. Rather than a poem about 'the postmodern questioning of the real',[24] 'Harem Trousers' may be more appropriately read as a feminist questioning of the poet's relation to patriarchy. If titles such as 'Harem Trousers' and 'Scenes from a Brothel' indicate a poetic locus of male pleasure involving the exploitation of the female, in these poems the female writes back in a bid to take over these traditionally male spaces. 'Harem Trousers' begins by situating the speaker in the physical world and then displacing this scenario by introducing the possibility of a poem that is not dependent on the existence of any controlling consciousness: 'Asleep on the coast I dream of the city./ A poem dreams of being written/ Without the pronoun I' (*OBB* 43). There follows an example of such writing without an 'I', but the poet's clinging to a concept of rational control is marked by the eventual return of the 'I':

> As I run to fetch water
> In my mouse-coloured sweater,
> Unkempt, hysterical, from
> The river that lives outside me,
> The bed whose dishevelment
> Does not enchant me. (*OBB* 43)

The dishevelled bed of poetic tradition does not enchant because it is the patriarchal bed that has historically proved inhospitable to the female poet. It is 'the river that lives outside me', but from which she must nevertheless 'fetch water'. The final stanza reflects the anxiety of the female poet in her negotiations with

---

[22] See Wills, pp. 170–1.
[23] Docherty, p. 209.
[24] Ibid., p. 194.

the masculine discourses imaged in the phallogocentric terms of 'A stem, a verb, a rhyme'. Not only does she run the risk that she 'may be expelled at any time', but in trying to conform, to 'control a dream', she may find that she 'Puts the just-completed light to rest' (*OBB* 43). 'Harem Trousers' both enacts and displaces the notion of the lyric 'I'. McGuckian's 'I' cannot find in language any authentication, any reassuring identity or ancestry, but she doesn't disown it: she chooses to traverse it with her own outlandish idiom, experimenting with a Kristevan female polylogical discourse. In 'The Novel as Polylogue', Kristeva indicates a kind of writing which reactivates the instinctual rhythms of erotic desire, a lost body, maternal origins. This is the experience of the subject in process which discovers the possibility of regaining unity within the symbolic order but in a way that exceeds the law-giving paternal language and disrupts homogeneity. The 'I' returns, but 'language is affected by it, the concept is twisted'.[25] In elaborating a poetics based on such a synthesis of the unconscious and the conscious, 'Harem Trousers' is closer to Kristeva than to Marina Tsvetaeva, the Russian poet whose influence, in terms even of language as well as ideas, Alcobia-Murphy has identified as playing a crucial role in McGuckian's poem:

> According to Tsvetaeva, the poet's identity is made up of distinct selves, one irrational, the other conscious, expressed through language: 'The poet's self is a dream-self and a language-self; it is the "I" of a dreamer awakened by inspired speech and realised only in speech.' Here Tsvetaeva's thoughts on poetic conception are in harmony with those of McGuckian.[26]

However, as Alcobia-Murphy notes, McGuckian goes on to distance herself from a notion of poetry as pure dreamwork. In the end, she shows closer affinity with Kristeva's recognition of the need to find some form of verbal embodiment for the unpredictable rhythms and images of the unconscious.

This use of other writers' work has proved one of the most controversial elements of McGuckian's poetic procedures. Her borrowings, often stitched together with little modification, go unacknowledged, left to the critics to find them out. It was Clair Wills' pioneering exploration of McGuckian's debt to Osip Mandelstam in 'The Dream Language of Fergus'[27] that set Shane Murphy off on the hunt to track down other borrowings[28] – from such diverse sources as Nadezhda and Osip Mandelstam, Winifred Gérin's biography of Emily Bronte, Tatyana Tolstoy's biography of her father, Rebecca West's study of William Joyce, Gerry Conlon's *Proved Innocent*, Carlo Ferdinando Russo's study of Aristophanes, Angela Bourke's *The Burning of Bridget Cleary*, Tim Pat Coogan's biography of Michael Collins. My purpose here is not to join the hunt, merely to consider briefly the implications and effects of McGuckian's borrowings. Certainly, there is a consonance between McGuckian's poetic practice and Kristeva's theory of

---

25 Julia Kristeva, 'The Novel as Polylogue', in *Desire in Language: A Semiotioc Approach to Literature and Art* (London, Blackwell, 1989), p. 164.

26 Shane Alcobia-Murphy, *Sympathetic Ink: Intertextual Relations in Northern Irish Poetry* (Liverpool University Press, 2006) p. 234.

27 See Wills, pp. 172–82 where she traces McGuckian's use of excerpts from Osip Mandelstam's essays, 'Conversation about Dante', 'About the Nature of the Word' and 'Notes About Poetry'.

28 See *Sympathetic Ink: Intertextual Relations in Northern Irish Poetry*.

intertextuality – the idea that all literature is constantly in conversation with all other literature, undetachable, as a single unit, from the textual mass. Kristeva's ideas provide a rationale for liquidating metalanguages, obliterating the subject as a determined and determinate identity, and erasing the poet as an authoritative, 'essentialising' voice speaking for some cause. Working from these theoretical principles, critics such as Alcobia-Murphy and Wills find in McGuckian's intertextualism evidence of a complex subjectivity, a desire to subvert a social or patriarchal belief in universal truth, and to assume multiple personae, inhabit diverse situations and contexts. By appropriating foreign texts, she is taken to destabilise the traditional Irish poetics of home, overthrow the influence of English models, internationalise a traditionally insular poetics, deterritorialise the English language, and repudiate her own anglicisation. Her intertextual allusions to prior female authors is a way of acknowledging female literary tradition and inscribing within her own poem the troubled process of female literary authorship. By re-citing foreign *male* writers she is further credited with demonstrating how the female writer can adapt male precursors to her own purposes, thus creating a doubled speaking self and securing a way of inserting the female poet into the (male) poetic tradition. Other readers are less kindly disposed towards what they consider the poet's apparent abdication of her role as creative artist and communicator. If the purpose of McGuckian's intertextuality is to execute an innovative perversion of the (male) canon and re-activate lost or submerged elements in the tradition, this essentially dialogic process crucially depends on the reader's familiarity with the prior texts that are being worked upon. It is possible to regard the poetry as a multi-layered texture of echoes, a Kristevan politicised female polylogical writing, which makes differences communicate, only if these echoes and differences are made apparent. Since McGuckian's favoured prior texts are out-of-the-way essays and biography which are not at all part of the common cultural currency the reader may well feel some resentment at being excluded from what is in effect a private language.

Traditionally, male writers have figured femininity in terms of place, land, nature, nation, with the result that the actuality of women's lives have been turned into ideological abstraction and stereotype, and women have been consigned to historical silence, passivity and marginality. In a provocative countermove, McGuckian writes the female body back into the text, in an Irish version of French '*écriture féminine*'. Probing the depths of unconscious erotic desire with a mixture of self-defensiveness, seduction and aggression, she flirts with the reader ('I see my audience very much as male'[29]), teasing the reader's desire for clarity, refusing to produce fixed and reliable references, and taking protective colouring in obliquity. As opposed to the reassuring images of maternity found in the traditional discourses of Irish womanhood, she emphasises the female body as a site of trauma, and the mother as a figure of loss and wildness. The mother tongue is torn away, 'vanquished' ('The Dream-Language of Fergus', *OBB 57*); the home is always insecure and invaded. Where Catholicism and nationalism attempted to appropriate the female body to confirm a sense of national integrity, McGuckian identifies the forces of disruption and alienation inherent within

---

[29] Wills, p. 161.

maternity, the home, family, motherland and language. 'The Hollywood Bed' strips away the romance and presents a 'narrowing' of the marital relationship:

> We narrow into the house, the room, the bed,
> Where sleep begins its shunting. You adopt
> Your mask, your intellectual cradling of the head,
> Neat as notepaper in your creaseless
> Envelope of clothes, while I lie crosswise,
> Imperial as a favoured only child,
> Calmed by sagas of how we lay like spoons
> In a drawer, till you blew open
> My tightened bud, my fully-buttoned housecoat,
> Like some Columbus mastering
> The saw-toothed waves, the rows of letter *ms*.   (*FM* 24)

The title suggests unreality and make-believe, ideas that are reinforced by the later reference to 'mask' and 'sagas', and the pun on 'lie'. Sleep unromantically 'shunts' the couple apart into separate, private worlds. The poem emphasises sexual difference in describing their contrasting sleeping patterns. 'Crosswise' is a key term: the poem works not so much by way of antitheses (male–female, order–disorder, dominance–subjection, reason–nature, symbolic language–semiotic language), as by way of a 'crossing' of differences. Their former closeness, it would seem, has been disrupted by pregnancy, which is described in terms of male violation of female youth, innocence and sense of romance ('you blew open/ My tightened bud'). The speaker's resentment is registered in her tone and in her adoption of the clichéd image of a deflowering. 'Columbus mastering/ The saw-toothed waves' conjures up the oft-repeated McGuckian image of the storm, a dangerous orgasmic wildness that subsides in the soft murmurings of 'rows of letter *ms*'. 'Saw-toothed' is morphed into the more rounded, feminine shape of the 'rows of letter *ms*'. In relating the use of sound in poetry to primary sexual impulses, Kristeva points to how the opposition between 'Mama' and 'Papa' sets nasal 'm' against plosive 'p', the 'm', according to Kristeva, transmitting maternal 'orality'.[30] While in her analysis of the semiotic in Mallarmé's poetry, she traces the poet's use of sounds which resemble children's murmurs.[31] In 'The Hollywood Bed', the act of sex marks a transference of power from female ('imperial') to male ('Columbus mastering'). Yet, the speaker is 'calmed' by memory of previous dangerous moments on the high seas of passion. To the end, the relationship remains deeply ambiguous. In the last stanza she contemplates 'The outline that, if you were gone,/ Would find me in your place': does this mean that if he were gone she would still need him and have to try and play the role that he has played, or that she doesn't need him and if he were gone she would be free to be her own mistress?

The maternal body offers a way of understanding the relationship with both language and politics. In the early, prize-winning 'The Flitting', McGuckian elabo-

---

[30] See Maggie Humm, *Contemporary Feminist Literary Criticism* (Hemel Hempstead, Harvester Wheatsheaf, 1994) p. 101.

[31] See Raman Selden, Peter Widdowson and Peter Brooker, *A Reader's Guide to Contemporary Literary Theory* (Harlow, Prentice Hall, 1997) p. 168.

rates a metaphorical association between poetry, the house, the female body and the North of Ireland. The poem was, she has said, 'prophetic in a sense because I wrote it before I ever got pregnant and I had no idea what this changing shape meant – and this was a metaphor for the change in the country':[32]

> 'You wouldn't believe all this house has cost me –
> In body-language terms, it has turned me upside down.'
> I've been carried from one structure to the other ...   (*FM* 54)

'Body-language' establishes the essential connection in this, and other poems, between female body and poem. Deterritorialisation, dislocation and separation are the preconditions of creativity. The speaker covers the 'bumps and cuts' of the house/body with Vermeer paintings. These pictures of 'dreamy' girls 'making lace' or holding a mandolin present figures of the female artist, products of the dominant, patriarchal, capitalist, bourgeois ethos of seventeenth-century Dutch culture. The girls exude silence, order, self-absorption, and they are complicit with darkness:

> She seems a garden escape in her unconscious
> Solidarity with darkness, ...
> Her narrative secretes its own values, as mine might
> If I painted the half of me that welcomes death.   (*FM* 54)

Poetry is associated with the unconscious, death, perhaps post-natal depression, the subversive currents of the feminine. The speaker stands on the brink of what Kristeva calls the 'abject', which threatens annihilation of the self. Flitting across the border of the symbolic, the subject enters the 'semiotic chora', the realm of drives and primary processes that both precede and transcend language, the source of dangerous anarchic pleasures. Poetry, in Kristeva's view, is a 'privileged site' because it opens itself to the basic impulses of desire and fear which operate outside the 'rational' systems. In the last stanza, McGuckian's speaker retreats from these dark zones of abjection: 'I postpone my immortality for my children' (*FM* 54). This is poetry nourished by a subterranean tension between order and anarchy, time and timelessness, law and desire, the claims of responsibility and the lure of transgression.

'Venus and the Sun' takes up the characteristic McGuckian tropes of doubles and mirror-images which she uses to dramatise deep psychic conflict. The struggle for 'authority' between 'Venus' and the 'sun' is based on an opposition drawn from Kristeva's mythological configuration of the relationship between the (male) symbolic order and the (feminine) semiotic order:

Sun: agency of language since it is the 'crown' of rhythmic thrust, limiting structure, paternal law abrading rhythm, destroying it to a large degree, but also bringing it to light, out of its earthy revolutions, to enunciate itself. ... Thus, there is no choice but to struggle eternally against the sun; the 'I' is successively the sun and its opponent, language and its rhythm, never one without the other, and poetic formulation will continue as long as the struggle does. The essential point to note

---

32   Interview with Michaela Schrage-Früh, *Contemporary Literature*, 46, 1 (2005) pp. 1–17, 11.

is that there would be no struggle but for the sun's agency ... Only by vying with the agency of limiting and structuring language does rhythm become a contestant – formulating and transforming.[33]

The other term in Kristeva's linguistic cosmology is 'the feminine figure, all-powerful mother or forbidden virgin' present 'within and against the system of language':

> Here, pagan mythology is probably nothing more than rhythm substantive: this *other* of the linguistic and/or social contract, this ultimate and primordial leash holding the body close to the mother before it can become a social speaking subject.[34]

Thus, in McGuckian's poem, authority shifts back and forth between 'Venus' and 'the sun':

> The scented flames of the sun throw me,
> Telling me how to move – I tell them
> How to bend the light of the shifting stars:
> I order their curved wash ...
>
> I am the sun's toy – because I go against
> The grain I feel the brush of my authority.[35]

Venus, restricted by its solar orbit, enviously contemplates the stars 'at large', able to 'fly apart/ From each other to a more soulful beginning'. The stars are emblems of undecidability and deferral at the other extreme from the constant sun which 'holds good'. Through this astronomical imagery of refraction/reflection, heliocentrism and planetary motion, McGuckian explores the 'choice', and the limits of choice, facing the female struggling to find a point of balance between dependence and independence, between following her own path and orbiting or reflecting other beings.

Like 'The Flitting' and the two 'Venus' poems, 'The Rising Out' is also structured on an opposition, a conflict between the poet/speaker and the 'dream sister', who, it is suggested, is the baby she is carrying or the poet's 'dream-self'. The dream-sister is potentially destructive of the poet's muse, yet the speaker would not be without her, for the dream-sister, however much she may inhibit the poet's freedom, is also the 'seed' of creativity, the means whereby the poet/speaker can rise out of depression and silence. The closing lines suggest the power of the dream-sister to raise and transform:

> If she had died suddenly I would have heard
> Blood stretched on the frame, though her dream

33 Julia Kristeva, *Desire in Language: A Semiotic Approach to Literature and Art*, ed. Leon S. Roudiez, trans. Thomas Gora, Alice Jardine and Leon S. Roudiez (Oxford, Blackwell, 1980). In David Lodge (ed.), *Modern Criticism and Theory : A Reader* (London, Longman, 1988) p. 235.
34 Lodge, p. 235.
35 Medbh McGuckian, *Venus and the Rain* (Loughcrew, The Gallery Press, 1994) p. 11. Hereafter abbreviated to *VR* and page references incorporated into the text.

> Is the same seed that lifted me out of my clothes
> And carried me till it saw itself as fruit. (*VR* 36)

The title links the poet's 'rising' with the political events of Easter 1916, the last stanza perhaps recalling Pearse's rhetoric of blood-sacrifice and the redemptive power of martyrdom. 'Rising out', McGuckian further informs us, is a translation of the Irish *éirí amach*, a term referring to the peasant marriage tradition in which the father and men of the bride's family ceremonially transport her to the family or tribe of her husband. In light of this information, the poem becomes, in McGuckian's words, 'very ambiguous … in that the woman never had a moment of herself. She either belonged to this man or belonged to that man. She never had a rising to herself'.[36] Moved from one house, one family, one place, one man, to another, the Irish woman is unable to represent an independent, 'risen', unified motherland, as the traditional patriarchal linkage of femininity and nationhood would insist upon.

Just as the maternal body is always negotiating with the other within, so the female poet is always negotiating with those undifferentiated, primordial semiotic forces within the official symbolic systems. As the title of 'No Streets, No Numbers' suggests, the poem is not situated in any particular place; it is written in a language without an address or addressee. On one level, it is a poem about miscarriage: 'the simple/ Double knock of the stains of birth and death' (*MC* 39). Miscarriage refers to the failure to produce both child and poem:

> That dream
> Of a too early body undamaged
> And beautiful, head smashed to pulp,
> Still grown in my breakfast cup. (*MC* 40)

The speaker, adrift in the world, is anxious about how to recover fertility, re-discover her poetic voice:

> And how am I to break into
> This other life, this small eyebrow,
> Six inches off mine, which has been
> Blown from my life like the most aerial
> Of birds? (*MC* 41)

The closing lines fuse biological and poetic creativity and look forward to the future when she is at last able to locate herself once again in the world:

> Our first summer-time
> Night, we will sit out drinking
> On the pavement of Bird Street,
> Where we kissed in the snow, as the day
> After a dream in which one really was
> In love, teases out the voice reserved for children. (*MC* 41)

The voice reserved for children is the semiotic voice rescued from abjection.

---

[36] Schrage-Früh, p. 10.

The 'most aerial/ Of birds', symbol of freedom, song, life itself, is finally given an address, inscribed in both language and place ('Bird Street').

The Postcolonial

'I forfeit the world outside/ For the sake of my own inwardness', McGuckian writes in 'Sky-Writing' (*MC* 79): but with her fifth collection, *Captain Lavender*, she moves towards a more explicit historical and political engagement, though not towards any more determinate meaning. In the epigraph to *Captain Lavender* she quotes Picasso: '*I have not painted the war ... but I have no doubt that the war is in ... these paintings I have done*'. The book cover, Jack Yeats's painting 'Communicating with the Prisoners' (1924), illustrates her new, more explicitly political direction, and foregrounds the human, personal and figurative basis of her politics. She announces her commitment to a new kind of poetry in 'The Albert Chain':

> I am going back into war, like a house
> I knew when I was young ...
> I am learning my country all over again,
> How every inch of soil has been paid for
> By the life of a man, the funerals of the poor.   (*CL* 68)

Where before she had concentrated on refurbishing the category of 'woman', now she aims to do the same for those of 'Catholic', 'Irish' and 'Northerner'. In this process, she re-orients herself away from open, fluid structurings of subjectivity and space, and towards a concept of a re-tribalised and re-territorialised identity, as the emphasis on 'house', 'my country' and 'soil' would suggest. Where in the earlier poems 'going back into ... a house' meant going into private space, the female body, the domestic realm, in order to open up uncharted spaces of the feminine, in the political poems 'going into the house' means a return to the known world of childhood, birthright, family, tribe and nation. Her discontinuous, hermetic verses must now accommodate the desire to express continuity and attachment, appreciation of male self-sacrifice and heroism in devotion to the Republican cause. She recognises that she must develop yet another new kind of language to deal with the legacy of British imperialism and the political realities of the H-Block, hunger strikes, ceasefires and emergent Peace Process:

> I could escape
> from any other prison but my own
> unjust pursuit of justice
> that turns one sort of poetry into another.   (*CL* 69)

This change of emphasis, McGuckian explains, was due partly to changed social conditions ('It was basically just slightly safer to be clear where you stood'[37]), partly to the experience of holding a series of creative writing workshops for pris-

---

37 Sawnie Morris, 'Under the North Window: An Interview with Medbh McGuckian', *Kenyon Review*, 23, 3/4 (Summer/Fall 2001) pp. 64–74, 72.

oners in the Maze in 1993. Her father had died the year before, and, McGuckian tells us, in her imagination the death of her father was associated with the 'living death' of the prisoners.[38] 'The Albert Chain' symbolises these linkages. The poem, she says, was written for a particular prisoner who was a poet and who was serving a life-sentence for something which she believed he did not do. She also tells us that her father's middle name was Albert, that the prisoners often bought Albert chains for their wives, and that she had been given one of these chains at this time.[39] In this, as in other poems about the prisoners, McGuckian's writing tends towards hero-worship and hagiography. The first stanza offers a disparate and apparently arbitrary series of images that suggest torture and life wasted for an ideal: 'the fruit hangs/ from the end of a dead stem', 'the wild cat ... half-stripped of its skin', 'a squirrel stoned to death' (*CL* 68). In the second stanza, the poet identifies with both prisoner and dead father, viewed as through a Judas window, figures of disintegration: 'I was born in little pieces, like specks of dust,/ only an eye that looks in all directions can see me'. Keen to mitigate the prisoner's actions, she emphasises how desperation drove him to violence, and heightens the sense of pathos by merging the figure of the prisoner with that of the father. Identifying the prisoner with her father's corpse in its coffin, she performs an act of homage which turns the prisoner into an object of erotic desire, a pagan god of nature: 'I uncovered your feet as a small refuge,/ damp as winter kisses in the street,/ or frost-voluptuous cider over/ a fire of cuttings from the vine'. The poem ends with the poet's recognition of her own imprisonment, the nature of which she described in her interview with Rand Brandes: 'I disguise myself as the real prisoner and as dead as him, more dead because I continue to believe in the law which has betrayed him. And do not let my poetry become political rather than personal.'[40]

Written for the prison writing group in general (*CL* 68), 'Flirting with Saviours' offers a strongly empathetic glimpse of the lives of the prisoners, though not without irony. The title, McGuckian insists, 'meant I was toying with the idea of going along with their notion of themselves as sacrificial victims for the extent of the poem, and also in a playful sense'.[41] With the help of McGuckian's interview gloss of the poem, it is possible to construct a fairly coherent picture. The first stanza describes the setting of the Maze prison, an unreal place, hidden away, surrounded by 'rebellious sea', protected by helicopters. As the imagery of the second stanza suggests ('Folded world', 'eye-catching kisses', 'basin/ of enlaced hands', 'fettered to the undecaying moon'), the men are feminised by their close confinement, their enslavement to time, their repression of feeling, their longing for a voice. The third stanza describes the poetry sessions, how peaceful the men ironically were, uneasily suspended outside time. The poet's ambivalence emerges most strongly in the closing lines: 'outbreak of history better than no catastrophe ever./ Stored statelessness, hereafter glimpses,/ surfaces to which gold could be applied, worse than saints –/ men utterly outside themselves, with the

---

38 Rand Brandes, 'A Dialogue with Medbh McGuckian', in *Studies in the Literary Imagination*, 30, 2 (Fall 1997) pp. 37–61, 42.
39 Ibid.
40 Ibid.
41 Ibid.

taint of women' (*CL* 53). As McGuckian comments: 'They are either a symptom of disease or a cure. They are icons, bearing the brunt of the weight of things. Reduced or raised to femininity'.[42]

Shelmalier introduces another set of ambiguous heroes, the rebels of 1798. Shelmalier, the poet explains, is a barony in Co. Wexford where some of the fiercest fighting took place, the placename being 'an Anglicization of the Irish phrase "Siol Malure", which is the seed, the people, the race, the tribe'.[43] The actuality of place, however, remains as insubstantial and generalised in this volume as in her previous collections, whose titles – *On Ballycastle Beach, Marconi's Cottage* – somewhat ironically hinted at a recognisably rooted, place-based poetry. In the Author's Note, the poet presents *Shelmalier* as an act of retrieval of a history that her education had denied her. The historical narrative recalls a time 'when, unbelievably, hope and history did in fact rhyme', but reading about 1798 also evoked 'the experienced despair of a noble struggle brutally quenched' and the knowledge of 'figures of an integrity I had never learned to be proud of'.[44] As with the Maze prisoners, the weight of the poet's feeling lies in identification with, rather than interrogation of, these ghosts of the past. In the title poem, history returns as bodily symptom that is also poetic form – the aisling. Reversing the traditional aisling roles, McGuckian has a male revenant, a victim of 1798, appear to the female poet in her sleep. She sees herself as inheritor of past violence: 'It is I who am only just left in flight, exiled/ into an outline of time' (*S* 75). The ghostly figure's 'great estrangement has the destination of a rhyme', which recalls the illusory moment in the past when hope and history appeared to rhyme before foundering into despair. Perhaps we are to understand that 'the destination of a rhyme' will only be reached in the present moment. Yet, the vision is not encouraging. The apparition is no more than an icon of 'grief', the eyes unable to look beyond the exacerbated present: 'promising avenues, they keep their kingdom'. Far from opening up new possibilities for the future, 'Shelmalier' constructs contemporary Irish politics within fixed structures and archaic generic possibilities. Unable to epitomise *différence* or disruption, the undead continue to haunt the living: 'like a century about to be over, a river trying/ to film itself, detaching its voice from itself/ he qualified the air of his own dying' (*S* 75). The return of the repressed leads not to renewal and re-integration, merely marks bodily possession, unconscious repetition, transformation of the site of maternal origin into the place of death.

In the *Shelmalier* poems, McGuckian is drawn to the Romantic idea of identity as something 'real' that has been buried or repressed by the Law of the Father (Jameson's 'political unconscious'), and to a poetic role as spokesperson for those excluded by the official history emanating from the English colonial centre. The contemporary model for such a poetics of historical excavation is Seamus Heaney and his idea of poetry as 'divination, poetry as revelation of the self to the self, as restoration of the culture to itself; poems as elements of

---

42 Ibid.
43 Ibid., p. 65.
44 Medbh McGuckian, *Shelmalier* (Loughcrew, The Gallery Books, 1998) p. 13. Hereafter abbreviated to *S* and page references incorporated into the text

continuity, with the aura and authenticity of archaeological finds'.[45] The extreme demand for identification with the nation that nationalism imposes upon the writer is particularly problematic for the women writer. 'The tendency to fuse the national and the feminine', says Eavan Boland, 'to make the image of the woman the pretext of a romantic nationalism – these have been weaknesses in Irish poetry'.[46] A predominantly male Irish literary tradition, in identifying women and nation, effectively rendered women invisible and robbed them of their actual, physical womanhood. Referring to her own 'particular darkness as an Irish poet',[47] Boland has described the challenge of retrieving from the darkness of Irish literary tradition her female self and bringing it into the light. McGuckian, it would seem, plunges women underground again. Her poem, 'Stone with Potent Figure', re-cycles the old male trope of the nation as a woman, the woman as national muse, as Dark Rosaleen or Cathleen Ni Houlihan, as Heaney's bog-queen waiting for the 'rising', symbol of dormant nationhood. In McGuckian's poem she is the undead country asleep and forgotten in the ground after the failure of the Rebellion in the summer of 1798:

> That she herself was buried
> weaponless in her coffin
> in that summertime I know
> from the flowering head of yarrow
> laid with care by her right knee –
> carpenter's or soldier's wort, a cure for possession.   (*S* 81)

She is waiting to come into 'possession' of herself; 'possession' also casts her as a mad woman, and, echoing Yeats's 'delirium of the brave',[48] highlights McGuckian's ambivalent attitude to political violence. As in the male poetics described by Boland, McGuckian's female figure is 'passive, decorative, raised to emblematic status',[49] deprived of the actuality of her life, become an element of style rather than an aspect of truth. McGuckian's nationalism cuts across both her feminism and her postmodernism. Referring to the early poetry, Clair Wills proposes that 'though "grounded", McGuckian's allegorical female has no resemblance to purist representations of the integrity of the community or its traditions. Like the maternal relation itself, the national community is built upon loss and separation.'[50] Yet, it is precisely the sense of historical continuity and 'grounded' national identity – the myth of origins – that the excavatory aesthetic expresses. The McGuckian imagination, in revivalist mode, seeks to lose itself in nostalgic celebration of a submerged history of 'united Irishmen'.

In her next volume, *Drawing Ballerinas* (2001), she plays with various versions of the mythic feminine figure. The image of the eternal female victim, wracked

45 Seamus Heaney, *Preoccupations: Selected Prose 1968–1978* (London, Faber, 1980) p. 41.
46 Eavan Boland, *Object Lessons: The Life of the Woman and the Poet in Our Time* (Manchester, Carcanet, 1995) p. 151.
47 Ibid., 151.
48 W.B. Yeats, 'September 1913', *Selected Poetry*, ed. A Norman Jeffers (London, Macmillan, 1962) p. 56.
49 Boland, p. 134.
50 Wills, p. 192.

and wrenched in 'Stone with Potent Figure' ('Her head to the west,/ her legs to the east,/ her black-stained left arm bent', *S* 81), reappears in the title poem:

> The body turns in, restless, on itself,
> in a womb of sleep, an image of isolated sleep.
> It turns over, reveals opposing versions of itself,
> one arm broken abruptly at elbow and wrist,
> the other wrenched downwards by the force of the turning.

(*DB* 14)

While ostensibly describing one of Henri Matisse's ballerinas, McGuckian presents the dancing girl as a bomb victim. The footnote explains: 'This poem was written to commemorate Ann Frances Owens, schoolfellow and neighbour, who lost her life in the Abercorn Café explosion, 1972. The painter, Matisse, when asked how he managed to survive the war artistically, replied that he spent the worst years "drawing ballerinas"'(*DB* 15). Pathos vies with irony in a poem which asks the same question as Shakespeare posed in *Timon of Athens*: 'How with this rage shall beauty hold a plea/ Whose action is no stronger than a flower?' McGuckian looks to the feminine, not only to express nationhood but, like Matisse, to locate the source of grace, beauty, art and civilisation, and the solace they can offer, at a time when the public world is convulsed by violence. Viewed from the outside, Ann Frances Owens is transferred from memory to allegory, turned into an 'object lesson', an essentialised image of suffering nation/womanhood.

'Hazel Lavery, The Green Coat, 1926' is about the female figure who was used as the image of Ireland on the currency of the new Irish Republic, though the painting 'Hazel Lavery, The Green Coat, 1926' is not the portrait which appeared on the banknotes, as McGuckian mistakenly seems to think. 'Hazel Lavery, The Green Coat, 1926' is a virtuoso full-length portrait in oils of Hazel Lavery in formal modern dress, and it hangs in the Ulster Museum. Irish banknotes between 1928 and 1975 bore the imprint of another painting of Hazel Lavery by her husband, in which she appears as a green-shawled rural peasant Cathleen Ni Houlihan. Hazel Lavery was an American beauty, married to the Belfast Catholic painter, Sir John Lavery, who had made his way into the British and European artistic establishment and was in fact rewarded with a knighthood for his services to the Crown as a war-artist. Hazel Lavery was also rumoured to have been Michael Collins' mistress, and is reputed to have influenced Collins to accept the compromise 1922 Treaty which left Northern Catholics feeling abandoned and betrayed. To McGuckian, Hazel Lavery was a 'travesty' of the dream of Irish unity and nationhood.[51] Significantly, McGuckian's indignation is directed at the inappropriateness of the chosen public national image of femininity not at the continued objectification and co-option of women for political ends.

The 'real story' of Irish women is again submerged in 'Disinterment', a poem written against the background of the unfolding Northern Ireland Peace Process and signing of the Good Friday Agreement in 1998. In contrast to the traditional warlike nationalist symbol of Cathleen Ni Houlihan or Mother Ireland calling upon her lovers/sons to avenge her colonial despoliation, McGuckian drops the territorialised symbolism of Irish femininity to take up the ancient and equally reductive image of the female as the personification of Peace: 'Deep-quivering Muse, army-dissolver,/ you who have driven war away,/ dance with me, anoint/ my warlike eyes with peace' (*DB* 53). Emptied of subjective life and stripped of realism, the female figure is hailed as a cloud-like symbol of change and fluidity, a floating signifier, a new *spéirbhean* or 'sky-woman' which, the last stanza suggests, recreates the archaic and sustaining myth of motherhood: 'Come here or, rather, come into the sky:/ where any movement of Peace's head/ that cloud-woman, island-woman,/ will introduce the aerial, invisible/ failed clouds pulling on her ropes' (*DB* 54). The traditional allegorical identification of Ireland with a woman historically trapped women and the whole Irish race in a debilitating stereotype. McGuckian frees women from this particular disabling association with nature, the land, the nation that must be rescued and re-possessed, but only to re-constitute her as another kind of revered abstraction rather than as a 'real' speaking subject.[52] This is a surprising turn, both regressive and reactionary, for a poet who throughout her career has fought to release the feminine from categorical confinement, even from notions of fixed and stable identity. The subversive energy and daring of McGuckian's early poetry are replaced by postures of obeisance and supplication.

The Spiritual

However, it is possible to see in her attempts to re-write her childhood Catholicism a continuation of her concern to find ways of refusing conformity, of liberating the multiply colonised female subject. While embracing nativism and tribal solidarity, she rejects the restrictions of Catholicism:

> My name, Medbh, is quite important, because I am repudiating the anglicization of myself. And some part of me is desperately seeking a spiritual reunion with my native, Irish-speaking, peasant, repressed and destroyed, ancestors and ancestresses. If to be Irish is to be Catholic, at the same time as you're trying to get away from the anglicization of yourself, you are trying to get away from the colonization of your soul by Roman Catholicism. I can't accept that kind of restriction. I'm trying to re-christianize myself, to get back to whatever true Christianity is.[53]

Recent poems are concerned with constructing a New Age feminine maternal spirituality that is unconfined by the laws of Church or language. The poem which closes *The Face of the Earth*, 'She is in the Past, She has this Grace' is about her mother, and locates God in the maternal body:

> and within a space which is doubled
> one of us has passed through the other,
> though one must count oneself three,

---

52 See Elizabeth Butler Cullingford, '"Thinking of Her ... as ... Ireland": Yeats, Pearse, and Heaney', *Textual Practice*, 4, 1 (Spring 1990).

53 Gillean Somerville-Arjat and Rebecca E. Wilson (eds.), *Sleeping with Monsters: Conversations with Scottish and Irish Women Poets* (Edinburgh, Polygon, 1990) pp. 1–7, 6.

> to figure out which of us
> has let herself be traversed.[54]

Working with a powerful, innovative visionary idiom, the poet transforms the traditional domestic character of feminine reality into the realm of religious mysticism, thereby affirming 'the presence of her absence' (the Heaneyesque title of another poem in this collection):

> who will be there,
> at that moment, beside her,
> when time becomes sacred,
> and her voice becomes an opera,
> and the solitude is removed
> from the body, as if my hand
> had been held in some invisible place?   (*FE* 82)

These intimations of the transcendent contrast with the tenor of an earlier poem, 'Woman with Blue-Ringed Bowl', also written on the death of the poet's mother. That poem ended with :

> A gust of wind, and colour flies to the door
> that cannot be kept so narrow, my notebook lies
> useless as a womb on my knees. The blue ensnared
> is a careful, sad, a Marie-Louise blue,
> and she has remained both woman and flaxen page:
> but, when I saw the picture again, the sun had gone.   (*OBB* 58)

Those lines emphasised change, loss and mortality, the defeat of creativity (symbolised by the useless womb and notebook) by death. In the later poem, the poet discovers in a new discourse of feminist spirituality 'A word which appeases the menace/ of time in us' (*FE* 81).

'She is in the Past, She has this Grace' is McGuckian's 'Stabat Mater', her version of the medieval hymn on the suffering of the Holy Mother at Christ's crucifixion, which has been set to music by many composers. The 'Stabat Mater' represents a controversial idealisation of intimate feminine emotion and the female body (which subsequent composers have felt compelled either to play up or play down), an image of the female as focus for identification and supplication. Femininity is associated with compassion, devotion, perseverance in the face of catastrophe. Moving beyond the restrictions of her Irish female Catholic identity, McGuckian reclaims maternity, music and the 'semiotic' for a new discourse of feminist spirituality, much as Kristeva seeks to do in her essay also entitled 'Stabat Mater'. Responding to Pergolesi's setting of the 'Stabat Mater', Kristeva calls for a new discourse of maternity, and envisions a 'herethics' based on qualities she associates with the maternal, 'that which in life makes bonds, thoughts, and therefore the thought of death, bearable: herethics is undeath, love'.[55] Kris-

---

[54] Medbh McGuckian, *The Face of the Earth* (Loughcrew, The Gallery Press, 2002) p. 81. Hereafter abbreviated to *FE* and page references incorporated into the text.

[55] Julia Kristeva, 'Stabat Mater', in *Tales of Love*, trans. Leon S. Roudiez (New York, Columbia University Press, 1987) p. 263.

teva, notes how, faced with his own mortality, Pergolesi invoked the mother as a figure of enduring love: 'the young Pergolesi ... was dying of tuberculosis when he wrote his immortal *Stabat Mater* ... Man overcomes the unthinkable of death by postulating maternal love in its place'.[56] His music belongs to 'the subtle gamut of sound, touch, and visual traces' through which mothers communicate, 'older than language and newly worked out'.[57] The *Stabat Mater*, that is, exemplifies the 'semiotic', which is associated with poetic language, with 'the extralinguistic regions of the unnamable ... the tremendous territory on this and that side of the parenthesis of language'.[58] McGuckian's image of the maternal body in 'She is in the Past, She has this Grace' – 'within a space which has doubled' – suggests the idea of the two-in-one or other within which Kristeva elaborates in her essay as a model for all subjective relations. Like the maternal body, we are all subjects-in-process negotiating the other within, never completely the subjects of our own experience. McGuckian's poetry clearly represents an enactment of Kristeva's idea of the subject-in-process as an alternative to traditional notions of an autonomous, unified (male) subject. The poet's linguistic derangements allow the music of the feminine to swell forth to take the reader/listener, wordlessly, timelessly, in the hand of the mother, 'in some invisible place'.

In her essay, Kristeva is also concerned to show that maternity is the place where multiple boundaries blur – those between nature and culture, inside and outside, the semiotic and the symbolic, self and other.[59] McGuckian adopts a similar 'maternal' model of female creativity, one which refuses to choose identity over difference or vice versa, and instead emphasises indeterminacy and liminality. In *The Book of the Angel*, the poet's developing spirituality is invested not only in mythic femininity but also in Christian mysticism, personified by a genderless or hermaphrodite angel-Muse, taken from the Old Irish eighth-century *Liber Angeli*, the 'Book of the Angel', in which Saint Patrick is granted the ecclesiastical see of Armagh through colloquy with an angel. Working within a generally Christian metaphysical scheme, the poet receives the angel-Muse like the sacramental host, 'taking his lifetime/ into my mouth as a word/ to make a world'.[60] The angel-Muse is a recognisably McGuckian figure of transition and undecidability, both powerfully and frighteningly 'other' and touchingly human and 'inward'. In 'Saint Faith' the poet, meditating on the stirrings of the angel-Muse, confounds the usual distinctions between 'him' and 'her', self and other, the mundane and the divine:

> Summer stood nude, as alone as the rain,
> her family smile absent, as many sleepless
> eyes on her body as she has feathers.
>
> I heard a roar of wings, a darker flesh,
> and started walking, lest the mountain
> should soar right out of the book,

---

56 Ibid., p. 252.
57 Ibid., p. 253.
58 Ibid., p. 250.
59 Ibid., p. 182.
60 Medbh McGuckian, *The Book of the Angel* (Loughcrew, The Gallery Press, 2004) p. 11. Hereafter abbreviated to *BA* and page references incorporated into the text.

> then kneel down inwardly
> over a holy organ such as a feather.   ('Saint Faith', *BA* 38)

The usual categories of perception and understanding are collapsed, as the angel-Muse mutates from 'Summer' to monumental nude figure, to bird, to mountain, to prayerful supplicant. The ambiguity of this elusive and mysterious figure is summed up in the last words of the last poem in the book, 'Poem Rhyming in "J"': 'Words remain on the shore, but when the angel/ falls in love, with his different prayer movements,/ he is the perfect human' (*BA* 85), where 'perfect' could refer either to an essential humanity or a perfect state beyond the human.

Other poems tend towards ecofeminist celebration of the close relationship between women and nature in terms of body, spirituality, fertility and female reproduction:

> I fold nature into
> my gently bewildered body
> as a girl leaves her hair
> open to be enjoyed
> by the moon's fine touch.[61]

By simply privileging the previously denigrated terms in the male/female, mind/body, culture/nature dualism, ecofeminism threatens to leave these oppositions in place. However, McGuckian's fluid, unstable and provisional language suggests the constructed nature of meaning, and represents a non-essentialist feminist approach to ideas of identity, landscape, place and nature which is potentially liberating and empowering. Judith Butler argues that effective power remains in the hands of the symbolic through whose linguistic order the semiotic, which ostensibly undermines it, is understood: 'The law that is said to repress the semiotic may well be the governing principle of the semiotic itself, with the result that what passes as "maternal instinct" may well be a culturally constructed desire which is interpreted through a naturalistic vocabulary'.[62] McGuckian refuses to cede power to either the male symbolic law or the feminine semiotic to the point where she obliterates the terms of the debate. Rather than surrender to an unavoidable male superiority or elaborate an idealised, all-powerful femininity, she mediates between the situated and the sublime, between the demands of rational communication and the flux of female, maternal feeling and self-expression.

---

[61] Medbh McGuckian, 'Mappa Mundi', in *The Currach Requires No Harbour* (Loughcrew, The Gallery Press, 2006) p. 16.

[62] Judith Butler, *Gender Trouble: Feminism and the Subversion of Identity* (New York, Routledge, 1990) p. 116.

Chapter 11

NEW VOICES:
Peter McDonald, Sinéad Morrissey,
Alan Gillis, Leontia Flynn

The 'Northern Renaissance' – that journalistically touted efflorescence of creative talent and activity that corresponded more or less with the outbreak of the Troubles in 1969 – began with those poets born in the late 1920s and '30s who came to prominence in the early years of the Troubles (Montague, Heaney, Mahon, Longley). They were succeeded by a second generation born in the 1940s and 1950s who have also secured international reputations (Muldoon, Carson, McGuckian). Now we have a third wave, young poets born in the 1960s and '70s who grew up during the Troubles and who made their mark in the 1990s or early 2000s and are continuing to do so – Peter McDonald, Sinéad Morrissey, Alan Gillis, Leontia Flynn. While these new young poets may not represent anything as clear-cut as a definite break with the older generations, new directions and emphases may nevertheless be discerned in their work. Received identities and concepts of home continue to be interrogated as these new young poets seek out the fault-lines in familiar terrain, question the official maps, cross borders, break up consecrated ground, take roads less travelled by. Frequently, the desire to belong is in open conflict with the urge to flight. Attention is no longer focused on 'one dear perpetual place', but on multiple other places. Traversing internal, national and international frontiers, the younger poets are most at home occupying in-between places or inner spaces, zones between dream and reality, this world and the otherworld. The home place is viewed from foreign perspectives: the poet can be in several places at one time. These new poets, we could say, represent the first genuinely post-national generation, less preoccupied with the binary opposition of England and Ireland than their predecessors, as evidenced by their lack of interest in the old colonial theme – even to deconstruct it – as Muldoon or Carson have done. Though they grew up during the Troubles and still refer to them, they are more outward looking, more open to outside influences, without succumbing to bland cosmopolitanism. Not only nationalism, but other traditional themes – Irish ruralism, Ulster regionalism, exile-and-return – have had less compelling power. Only if identity can be construed as expansive and fluid is it useful to poetry. For these poets belong and respond to a rapidly changing (post)modern world, one in which the myth of the centre has come under increasing pressure and the binary opposition of centre and periphery is disintegrating. Now, the poet tends to see him/herself as a transitional being, his/

her life defined by more than one identity or culture. In an age of unprecedented global interchange, cultural perception is relativised, all values are revalued. The Western concept of the universal self no longer holds, and ideas of national integrity or coherence seem increasingly illusory. Northern Irish poetry, more than ever before, is marked by openness and difference, by multiplicity (of cultures, of centres, of truths), uncertainty, exchange, synthesis, hybridisation, ambivalence. While tribal or ancestral atavisms may still exert a palpable pressure, and the effects of violence have still not been forgotten, the Troubles are not as pressing a matter as they used to be. The poetry devotes itself to a great diversity of things, to something else, then something else again.

Peter McDonald: Pastoral Perspectives

Peter McDonald was born in Belfast in 1962 and attended Methodist College Belfast, before proceeding to University College, Oxford. Most of his adult life has been spent in England, where he has taught at the universities of Cambridge, Bristol and, currently, Oxford. As well as teacher and poet, he is a distinguished critic of modern and contemporary British and Irish poetry. This critical work provides useful indicators of his interests and preoccupations as a poet. Indifferent to the strictures of Peter Porter, Stan Smith and other critics who have complained about the Northern Irish poets' addiction to formalism in a time of crisis,[1] McDonald in his book, *Mistaken Identities: Poetry and Northern Ireland*, spells out a poetics for Northern Irish poetry based on a refurbished formalism as the route to 'progressive' new seeing and understanding. Returning to the formalist credo that form *is* content, form, McDonald argues, has a moral, epistemological and political force. Far from sealing poetry into an irresponsible hermeticism, formalism is a means to engage with the public world. Denouncing the totalising ambitions of identity-politics, he shows how Northern Irish poetry, by making an issue of poetic form, subverts political analogies in terms of 'identity'. An advocate of 'close reading', McDonald argues 'for the significance and value of poems as discrete achievements ... things which possess, so to speak,

---

[1] Peter Porter (*Observer*, 19 December 1992), for example, describes Irish poets (he mentions Mahon and Heaney specifically) as 'marooned outside time': 'Reading it (Mahon's *The Hunt by Night*) feels like time-travelling, even if the poetry is full of details from our own age. It is this that separates Irish poets like Mahon and Heaney from an audacious formalist like Auden, who for all his crustiness and Anglican high jinks is firmly lodged in the twentieth century. The Irishmen seem outside time, to be playing up to some committee preparing a Pantheon. "Irish poets learn your trade,/ Sing whatever is well made", wrote Yeats. They have learned it too well, they are banishing from their verse whatever parts of experience and necessity pose a problem to the shaping spirit'. Stan Smith, in *Inviolable Voice: History and 20th Century Poetry* (Dublin, Gill and Macmillan, 1982) accuses Northern Protestant poets of retreating from the public world into a privileged, but panicked, middle-class privacy which finds expression in the complacencies of the 'well-made poem': 'In accents familiar from "The Movement" such a poetry performs its civic duties equitably, by reflecting, in an abstracted kind of way, on violence, but its hands are indubitably clean. It speaks, at times, with the tone of a shell-shocked Georgianism that could easily be mistaken for indifference before the ugly realities of life, and death, in Ulster' (p. 189).

identities of their own'.[2] Muldoon, in McDonald's view, is the kind of poet whose complex ironies sabotage received certainties, defined identities and allegiances. Muldoon's concern with form, McDonald shows, promotes a post-nationalist poetry freed from 'identity':

> To praise a poem … in terms of a perceived fidelity to some notion of shared iden-
> tity is really to recruit the writing itself to a project in which the identity in ques-
> tion is propagated and strengthened. In Northern Ireland, such an activity is no
> contribution to 'progress' … but part of the deeper, obstinately rooted problem.
>
> (*MI* 17)

In McDonald's view, Muldoon's poetry, with its developing concern with form, does not represent a disavowal of life or 'content', but an attempt to deconstruct the received notions of identity (whether personal, local, or national), in order to 'achieve something new, unexpected, and unprepared-for' – an originality which is 'far from simple or comforting' (*MI* 187). More recently, in *Serious Poetry: Form and Authority from Yeats to Hill*, he continues the argument for a concept of 'serious poetry' (as opposed to media-processed poetry and populist literary values) based on the authority of poetic form: 'the unique property of a real poem is its capacity to work against the grain of opinion, or in complex and guarded relation to it, so as to create an original order in which language overpowers the "weight of judgement or opinion" through an individual (and essentially unrepeatable) form'.[3]

Following his own polemical prescription, McDonald's poetry, eschewing preconceived notions of identity and place already mapped out in cultural and historical terms, is expressive of personal discovery rather than recovery of a communal reality (Northern) Irish or English. More valuable to him than the reiteration of known truth, is the exploration of the unpredictable strangeness of the 'here and now' of the poem itself as a formal construct. In the controlled and understated 'Sunday in Great Tew' in his first collection, *Biting the Wax*, the Northern Irish home place is viewed obliquely, from English perspectives. On the same day as the Remembrance Sunday bombing in Enniskillen (8 November 1987) in which eleven people died, the poet finds himself in the Oxfordshire village of Great Tew – in the heart of England and English heritage. The picture of the poet in conversation with his friends in the famous Oxfordshire pub, 'The Falkland Arms', contains an implicit allusion to the Great Tew Circle (whose members included Ben Jonson, Thomas Hobbes and Edward Hyde) of pre-Civil War times, which met to discuss philosophical and literary matters on the Great Tew Estate of Lucius Cary, Second Viscount Falkland. The Great Tew Circle, standing by a commitment to the rule of law and the principles of reason and tolerance, represented a latitudinarian alternative to the absolutist tendencies of Archbishop Laud and the Puritans alike. In McDonald's poem, these resonances of English history are juxtaposed with the shock-waves of another civil war, all the more urgent for emanating from the poet's home ground, and all the more

---

[2] Peter McDonald, *Mistaken Identities: Poetry and Northern Ireland* (Oxford, Clarendon Press, 1997) p. 6. Hereafter abbreviated to *MI* and page reference incorporated into the text.
[3] Peter McDonald, *Serious Poetry: Form and Authority from Yeats to Hill* (Oxford, Clarendon Press, 2006) p. 4.

distressing for surfacing in the peaceful setting of the famous Oxfordshire pub. England seems unreal: the village is 'a replica of some England,/ an idea on show', 'some pretend backwater with picture-postcard views'.[4] The pub, 'the Falkland Arms', is itself an act of remembrance. Conversation seems removed from actuality: 'we're discussing/ far-off acts of war, the real thing, here in the Falkland Arms'. The sounds of English voices – 'conversation jumping from one silence to another/ in ripe Oxonian vowels' – make the poet feel 'alien', and prompt a guilty recall of the more familiar accents of home. In the context of the pressing circumstances of Northern Ireland, the poet registers his wariness of moving too far from 'the real thing'.

In 'Victory Weekend. May 1945/ May 1995', he is again situated within an English cultural history, but proceeds by unsettling any comfortable sense of belonging. The poem begins in London with a night at Covent Garden (*King Arthur. Or the British Worthy*, music by Purcell, lyrics by Dryden), then moves to a fly-past of World War II aircraft, then on to memories of how 'the last War went into storybooks'[5] and vague feelings of disquiet at the present efforts to commemorate past events and affirm national identity ('All fantasy: their fantasies; my own;/ the show an exercise in make-believe/ disguised as memory; all the overblown/ music and glitter of a coarse, naïve/ history-carnival'); then escape from the VE Day celebrations and a walk through the London streets of Milton and Blake; then the train journey back to his English pastoral retreat ('away from the weekend, away from London,// and landed before long in our attic space/ that looked straight into clouds over the Downs,/ where we and the great elms sat face to face'). But the public world cannot be so easily escaped. His West Country idyll is suffused with intimations of war and noise: birds are 'strafed with light', the sun is 'blanket fire', seagulls form 'raiding-parties' and sound an 'all-clear'; the poet's thoughts turn to memories of a Belfast childhood. The remembered Troubles represent 'a burst map of the past', 'abstracted history cracked up' – harsh refutation of the grand narratives of history and patriotism which the Victory celebrations were intended to confirm. Two decades on, however, the poet succumbs to the utopian power of pastoral's emotive claim on the real:

> The burn of sunset now, two decades on
>   lit miles of sky in coral and louder red:
> I was safe; the past was over; the sun shone
>   pitilessly on me and all the dead,
>
> for this was pastoral; I could almost see
> the dead together in a wall of light,
> closing their hearts, climbing away from me,
> into a ghost-glare early in the night,
>
> in march-past, in a simple, strict parade ...   (*P* 26)

---

4   Peter McDonald, *Biting the Wax* (Newcastle-upon-Tyne, Bloodaxe, 1989) p. 58.
5   Peter McDonald, *Pastorals* (Manchester, Carcanet, 2004) p. 22. Hereafter abbreviated to *P* and page references incorporated into the text.

But the idealised pastoral vision of social relations, the fantasy of an archaic whole and healed 'British' space or communal memory lasts only 'until the fireworks split up in the dark' – 'the rush and rustle, click and smack and boom/ of lights as they sprayed and scattered everywhere'. Referring to the fireworks display, the poet says 'we both sat it out' (*P* 26), a phrase recalling an earlier restricted time when, a schoolboy in Belfast in the '70s, he had to sit out the disruption that was caused by the bombs, 'not moving, locked on the Stranmillis Road,/ on the Malone and Lisburn Roads, stacked down/ to Shaftesbury Square' (*P* 26).

Raymond Williams has provided the standard critique of the ideology of the pastoral mode:

> The idea of the country is the idea of childhood: not only of local memories, or the ideally shared communal memory, but the feel of childhood: of delighted absorption in our own world ... Great confusion is caused if the real childhood memory is projected, unqualified as history. Yet what we have finally to say is that we live in a world in which the dominant mode of production and social relationships teaches, impresses, offers to make normal and even rigid, modes of detached, separated, external perception and action: modes of using and consuming rather than accepting and enjoying people and things.[6]

Heaney, writing from deep down in his rural environment and community, remembers his childhood in the 1940s in terms of 'local memories', an 'ideally shared communal memory', 'the feel of childhood' and 'a delighted absorption in the world'. Conjuring this imagined past, he has been accused of the very thing that Williams warns against – projecting the pastoral dream as history. McDonald, whose background is urban, and who grew up at the height of the Troubles in Belfast in the 1970s, does not have Heaney's purchase on an Irish pastoral tradition. McDonald's childhood memories are filled with images of the Troubles; his *locus amoenus*, at least in 'Victory Weekend', is sought (though never really found) in the English countryside. In comparison with Heaney, his handling of pastoral is more self-conscious. His pastoral looks from the city to the country but also uses his imagined country to look back at the city: it faces two ways at the same time.

His third collection, entitled *Pastorals*, takes its epigraph from the little-known Greek poet, Satyrus:

> An echo is when sound comes back late, and misses itself,
> with no tongue to call its own: in deep pasture-land
> birdsong is repeating when the birds themselves have flown
> out of earshot – have flown straight into the daylight
> of broad fields, echoless, where voices get lost in the wind.   (*P* 6)

McDonald seeks to recapture these echoes of birdsong in the formal structures of his art. The conventionality of pastoral conventions is itself an important part of his subject. Theocritus is credited with inaugurating the pastoral tradition in the third century BC, and McDonald's version of Theocritus's first idyll offers

---

6   Raymond Williams, *The Country and the City* (New York, Oxford University Press, 1973) pp. 297–8.

an emblem of the cult of artifice that informs his collection, and characterises the whole pastoral convention. 'The Cup', like 'Ode on a Grecian Urn', freezes vignettes of real life in timeless detail. In another poem, 'The Long Look', the 'painted figures' on an ancient tomb are more compelling to the poet than the 'real birds on the wing' which look 'sidelong, and different, and not right' (*P* 37). Pastoral images express the longing for a lost Golden Age of simplicity, inno-cence, closeness to nature, sensuous pleasure, freedom from struggle and death. They highlight poignant alternatives to the public world, encoding imaginative possibilities that have been forced out of the hegemonic calculus of the 'real'. Formalism and pastoralism are both modes which register a desire to transform the world; both represent strategies of resistance; both are attempts to change how we understand and define history. 'The Trees', for example, which McDonald strategically places at the beginning of his collection, re-works Spenser's alle-gory of Fraelissa and Fradubio in *The Faerie Queene*. The speaker, like Redcrosse Knight in the Wandering Wood, comes upon two trees, 'stood off from one another' – 'the stuck souls of Fraelissa and Fradubio/ confirmed in bark and moss, always to grow/ apart in separately wordless pain' (*P* 9) – a desolating symbol of Northern Ireland's divided society. 'The Stand-Off' pictures two oppo-nents who 'stare each other out like basilisk/ and gorgon': 'Ready to take each other to their knees,/ they stand on motionless by the made bed/ with faces set, guests of the thief Procrustes' (*P* 56). The subtext is again the situation in the North. 'Eclogue', an imitation of Virgil's first eclogue, is a more personal use of classical models. In Virgil's poem two shepherds discuss the pains and gains of 'exile'/ 'freedom' in the city. McDonald uses this debate as a basis for articulating his own ambivalence about his native place. There are two voices in his poem: the voice of going affirms the importance of family connections in Northern Ireland, but declares: 'I'm lost to home, as home is lost/ to me, and there's no going back –/ just visiting' (*P* 62–3); while the voice of staying articulates the sense of attachment to place and responsibility to the dead: 'these hills and roads, the people here,/ or here no longer, the thin ghosts:/ I keep on looking out for them/ or listening for their voices in mine' (*P* 63). At the end, the two voices merge. Jettisoning fundamentalist versions of identity politics, the speaker chooses the symbolic space between home and exile.

McDonald's Ulster pastoral is composed of memories centred on the local hills and roads and people – the 'thin ghosts' of family members, especially his mother and father – who lived in the townlands or suburbs around Belfast. 'Two Memorials at Gilnahirk' demonstrates his concern to maintain the bonds with past generations of his family. Reaching back two generations, the speaker attempts to improvise two memorials to his grandmother's two husbands, the first lost in the Great War, the second, the poet's grandfather, who also died early. 'At Castlereagh Church', another fine poem of familial piety, is an act of imaginative recollection with a luminous, emblematic force which yet avoids any tendency towards abstract mythologizing. The sonnet's decorous formality perfectly embodies the poet's ceremonial, affectionate regard for his parents whom he pictures, years ago in the days of their courtship, walking the country roads around Castlereagh church. With considerable delicacy, the poem deline-ates the shadows that darken bucolic bliss, the sense of the fragility of life, the vulnerability of the two lovers: his father is 'in his travelling clothes' (*P* 13), his mother 'in her summer coat'; 'they feel the chill'; the clematis is not yet ready to 'risk a flower'.

The pervasive presence in *Pastorals* is the poet's father, to whose memory the book is dedicated. One of the most moving tributes is 'The Blood-Bruise'. The poet's sight of his own arms 'scrabbed and scarred' (*P* 45) from working in the garden brings to mind – with a sickening jolt – the image of the blood-bruise on his father's arm 'where they unhooked/ and undid you, when all of their work was done'. The description of nature's wild profusion in the first stanza hints proleptically at death and mortality: 'those deathly-delicate/ *trompettes*, and their lime-white/ mouths that opened up, and opened again'. The poet's futile fight to control wild nature, ironically conveyed in a punctiliously rhyming regular stanza, mirrors the father's final struggle against the forces of nature so prosaically, yet all the more movingly, figured in the last stanza. Dark pastoral indeed.

His latest volume, *The House of Clay*, contains 'Three Rivers', dedicated to his daughter Louisa. The poem, in three parts – 'Isis', 'Lagan' and 'Jordan' – offers three versions of pastoral, based on three key places in the poet's life. The title of the first section locates the poem in the Oxfordshire countryside. The poet recalls driving his new-born daughter home through the rain; then, his impressions of the Oxfordshire locale when he himself 'crash-landed'[7] there for the first time twenty years before. 'Isis' constructs an idyllically idealised world, bright and full of love and rich promise. The repeated references to rain connote life and creativity, as does the title reference to the Egyptian goddess worshipped as the feminine archetype for fertility and motherhood. Intoxicated by the wonderland in which he finds himself, the poet quotes from Thomas Traherne's poem 'Wonder', 'How like an angel came I down', a line which has also been used as a title by Bronson Alcott, Louisa May Alcott's father who, incurable romantic that he was, believed in the innate divinity of children and cast his teachings in the form of a book of conversations with children on the Gospels.

In the second poem, 'Lagan', the poet recalls helping his father along the Lagan towpath; then, thinks of a future in which he, an old man, is helped along the same path by his daughter, as he had helped his father, to visit the place where his father used to live. Moving from the sense of plenitude, energy and new beginnings symbolised by the gushing, spilling Isis in the first poem, 'Lagan' has a quieter movement, a sad, autumnal feel, with its images of bodily decline and springtime that has long gone as surely as his father's river cottage. What matters to the poet are family bonds, a sense of continuity, the generational cycle. In the third poem, 'Jordan', place loses geographical actuality, dissolves in images of shadows and reflections, transformed into a visionary state:

> the quickened surface and deep calm below
> were imaged in each other, we in them,
> two bodies made of frail and heavy earth,
> one bending up to scoop the busy water
> into a bottle held firm in the light –
> your mother, who moves with you, step by step,

---

7 Peter McDonald, *The House of Clay* (Manchester, Carcanet, 2007).

> across the sky from one bank to the other
> on a well-worn, inevitable path
> that goes waist-high and waist-deep in the river.

Crossing Jordan is a key image in the biblical salvation narrative, associated with the Israelites' crossing from bondage in Egypt into the freedom of the Promised Land and, more generally, the Christian's crossing from life into Paradise. Playing on the biblical and symbolic significance long associated with the river Jordan, McDonald seems in the end less concerned with lost pastoral landscapes than with an imagined paradise where the tensions between subject and object, the ideal and the real are magically resolved in the self-contained, transcendent poetic symbol.

Sinéad Morrissey: The Migrant Muse

Sinéad Morrissey was born in Portadown, County Armagh, in 1972. She spent her first six years living on working-class republican housing estates, before moving to Belfast, where she attended Belfast High School. After taking a degree in English and German at Trinity College Dublin, she lived and worked in Japan (where she met and married her American husband) and New Zealand, before returning to Northern Ireland where she now lives. She speaks with wry self-consciousness of her dislocation from the usual coordinates of identity in Northern Ireland:

> Society in Northern Ireland is rigidly divided between the Nationalist and Loyalist communities. Coming from a Communist household, militantly atheist, was just one factor that contributed to a sense of dislocation, of belonging to neither community. Both my brother and I were given Irish names, attended Protestant schools, lived in Catholic areas, knew neither the 'Hail Mary' nor the words of 'The Sash', were terrified by agonised Catholic statues and felt totally excluded from the 12th July celebrations.[8]

Her poem, 'Thoughts in a Black Taxi', immediately establishes her mobile, in-between situation. Circulating through the streets of the city in the black taxi, she registers her fascination with the preparations being made for the 12th July bonfires and the other tribal rituals yet is acutely aware of her alienation from either community, and fearful of the threat posed by both communities because of her assumed allegiance to the enemy. 'To be nothing', she has said, '– neither Catholic nor Protestant – was too removed from the dominant frame of reference to be believed':[9]

> I always walked with my heart constricting,
> Half-expecting bottles, in sudden shards

---

8 'Sinéad Morrissey in Malta: Workshops and Public readings 22–30 Nov. 2003' http://www.geocities.com/inizjamedmalta/sinead_morrissey_in_malta.htm?2006100.
9 Ibid.

Of West Belfast sunshine,
To dance about my head.[10]

But apart from a strong sense of dislocation, Morrissey's unorthodox Northern Ireland childhood also left her with a great sense of freedom. The 'Mercury' sequence, she tells us, is a poetic account of the period in her life when her parents divorced and the family home in Belfast was sold. Taking a year out from her studies at Trinity, she moved to Flensburg in Germany, 'to try and control the ensuing sense of disorientation'.[11] The sequence, she says, records her fascination with 'the fragile reality of places and the role that memory plays in building homes'. 'Bottom Drawer', the first poem in the series, presents an image of a settled, introverted existence: a woman preserves a comprehensive record – diaries, letters, photographs – of everything that has happened to her. The archival trope, which in Hewitt, Montague or Heaney is grandly historicised and politicised, is in Morrissey's poem closely and subtly worked to dramatise the pathos of an ordinary individual's life. 'Leaving Flensburg' both reiterates the role that memory plays in building homes and suggests the fragile reality of places: 'Memory built the way/ In which you recognised the place, decided how much your going/ Would cost: a few confused days in the next stop-over, or dreamscape for a year' (*FV* 37). Presiding over the sequence, we should keep in mind, is the figure of Mercury, messenger of the gods, patron of travellers and also of rogues, vagabonds and thieves. 'Nomad', another poem in the sequence, begins:

It's this leaving of villages,
One after the other –
The repeated conclusion
It's not here either –
Beauty, home, whatever –
That leaves you where you are,
Where you always are –
Side-stepping yourself, side-
Stepping the days you find no sense in ...   (*FV* 34)

The broken syntax and halting rhythms, the recursive and repetitive structures, enact a kind of 'side-stepping', the frustration the speaker feels at not ever being able to find 'Beauty, home, whatever' – she's not sure even what she's looking for. The title, 'Nomad', hits on a key term of contemporary cultural theory. Historically, nomadic existence entailed endless migration, the rejection of territorial or national roots, and defiance of boundaries of land and governance. In the age of globalisation, nomadism has, for theorists such as Deleuze, Guattari and Rosi Braidotti, become a useful postmodern epistemological category. In Deleuze and Guattari's theory, nomadism is a revolutionary alternative to the power of the State. It is a way of always being in the middle or between points:

---

[10] Sinéad Morrissey, *There was Fire in Vancouver* (Manchester: Carcanet Press, 1996) p. 20. Hereafter abbreviated to *FV* and page references incorporated into the text.
[11] 'Sinéad Morrissey in Malta'.

> A path is always between two points, but the in-between has taken on all the consistency and enjoys both an autonomy and a direction of its own. The life of the nomad is the intermezzo.[12]

Nomadic existence is characterised by movement and change, unfettered by systems of organisation. The goal of the nomad is to move within the 'intermezzo'. The nomad is the outsider. Nomadic thought is the kind of thought that is opposed to the philosophy of the closed system.

In Morrissey's 'Nomad', the speaker moves in between territories, identities and institutional boundaries. Her nomadism involves leaving habitual domains, fixed social relationships, familiar domestic patterns, psychological conditions and institutional organisation. She is the traveller, connecting with multiple strange experiences, perspectives and ideas, operating on the margins, interstitially, looking for new kinds of representation and meaning. The poem, that is, enacts the nomadic dispersion of desire and subjectivity, the breaking up of the subject of postmodernity. Reflecting the pervasive mobility of postmodern culture, the deterritorialised subject becomes the epitome of a post-identity condition in which the individual is located *across* rather than *in* space and time, and place is no longer a reliable reference point for self-recognition. By subverting the conventions of centred, permanent existence, nomadism promotes experiment with identity that is liminal, shifting, relational, provisional. Identity can no longer be fixed and static but, instead, resolves into constant becoming, formed on the move, always in transit. The nomadic subject, existing within a discontinuous state of being, must continually face the challenge of re-inventing herself, of mutation or adaptation. She is a habituée of 'contact zones'.

From the poet's own autobiographical extra-poetic statement, and from the closing lines of 'Nomad', it would appear that Morrissey's nomadism is at least as much the result of enforced eviction – from home, family-life, the securities of the past – as it is a matter of personal choice. Freedom can be frightening. The feeling in the poem is one of disorientation, of being overwhelmed now that the familiar world has disappeared and the speaker finds herself, like Melville's orphaned Pip, adrift in the wide open spaces. The note of pathos reappears: 'No place to walk through,/ No space to hold. Your books and your spoons/ In a walled up room,/ Somewhere you can't get back to' (*FV* 34).

While 'Nomad' emphasises the anxiety of nomadism, the poem on the facing page, 'Gull Song', balances 'loneliness' against the freedoms of the nomad's life. Another poem, 'Hazel Goodwin Morrissey Brown', casts the mother in the nomadic role, while the poet-speaker takes on a stereotypical maternal attitude ('Out there a psychic/ Explained how, in a previous life, I'd been *your* mother'), expressing not only a mother's anxieties at losing a child ('... when you drove to the airport/ And didn't come back, it was déjà vu. And I had to fight,/ As all mothers do, to let you go'), but also the child's resentment at losing her mother and her childhood home:

---

[12] G. Deleuze and F. Guattari, *A Thousand Plateaus* (Minneapolis, University of Minnesota Press, 1987) p. 380.

> Our lived-in space
> Became a house of cards, and there was nothing left to do but race
> For solid ground. You settled your feathers after the flight
> In a fairytale rainforest. Discovered the freedom of the last resort.
>
> (*FV* 39)

'Fairytale rainforest' implies the illusoriness of the mother's newfound New Zealand freedom, an idea which is reinforced by describing it as 'the freedom of the last resort', for how much freedom can a 'last resort' really offer? In the aftermath of traumatic family break-up (which is compared to the 'French Revolution') the speaker can still recognise the interdependence of mother and daughter. By titling the poem the way she does, listing the mother's several names, including her two different married names, Morrissey highlights the theme of identity, the instability, hybridisation and multiplicity of identity, but the need, nevertheless, to assert its importance. The poem succeeds in fusing an unresolved, unbearably exposed pain and agitation with a remarkable aesthetic energy and control.

In the perspective of Deleuze and Guattari, we are being changed from 'arborescent' beings, rooted in time and space, to 'rhizomatic' nomads who, thanks to globalised communications networks, wander at will across the globe, without necessarily ever moving our bodies at all. Similarly, Rosi Braidotti defines contemporary subjectivity in terms of nomadism:

> Though the image of 'nomadic subjects' is inspired by the experience of peoples or cultures that are literally nomadic, the nomadism in question here refers to the kind of critical consciousness that resists settling into socially coded modes of thought and behaviour. Not all nomads are world travellers; some of the greatest trips can take place without actually moving from one's habitat. It is the subversion of set conventions that defines the nomadic state.[13]

In another poem in the 'Mercury' sequence, Morrissey accepts that nomadism needn't entail actual travel, and that the fabulous 'other' exists right under our noses. The poem is entitled 'No Need to Travel', and in it the poet imagines the tulips nodding their heads in her garden, 'holding court' to 'your stories of Africa –/ The time, the plains, the colours the rain brings':

> And I think how something of the nobility
> Of the wilderness broke ground here also
> In that knack of knowing how to thrust colour skywards,
> Flaunting the unlikely, shocking through bloom. (*FV* 38)

Using a remarkably simple, plain style, Morrissey skews it just enough to release a sense of exciting imaginative 'otherness'. Thinking 'differently' promotes new creative seeing capable of re-vivifying our routine existence. There is no need to travel because 'nobility' and 'colour' are to be found in the ordinary surroundings of one's everyday life. The underestimated quotidian still harbours the wild and

---

[13] R. Braidotti, *Nomadic Subjects: Embodiment and Sexual Difference in Contemporary Feminist Theory* (New York, Columbia University Press, 1994) p. 5.

exotic, the erotic ('flaunting') and the scandalous ('shocking'). The sentiment is similar to that which Patrick Kavanagh immortalised in 'Epic', which ends:

> I inclined
> To lose my faith in Ballyrush and Gortin
> Till Homer's ghost came whispering to my mind
> He said: I made the Iliad from such
> A local row. Gods make their own importance.[14]

Recalling the occasion when, only eighteen years old, she went to Monaghan to receive the Kavanagh Award for poetry and was asked to read a Kavanagh poem, Morrissey reports: 'I read "Epic" (of course)'.[15]

The question of the proper balance between 'home' and 'away' is taken up in another of the 'Mercury' poems, a witty parable based on a literalisation of the cliché that gives the poem its title, 'Finding My Feet'. The poem begins: 'Today I found my feet and vowed/ Not to let them leave again'. One foot, who believed 'the only journeys/ Are inward', has been in danger of dying from lack of oxygen and has had to be dragged into the air; the other foot, 'holidaying in Bangladesh', was 'running out of room to run away in' and had to be flown home (*FV* 36). The poem implies a stance that avoids the fetishisation of else-where, on one hand (or, rather, foot) and, on the other, retreat into solipsism and self-reflection. The book as a whole reflects this balance, combining as it does highly personal poems about the poet's family and people close to her ('My Grandmother through Glass' being a particularly fine example of this kind of poem), as if to affirm connectedness and rootedness, and travel poems in which she explores her experience of foreign places and cultures. The poems tell not only of journeys from place to place, but also of a spiritual journey which takes the poet, in the closing poem of the collection, to ponder a world of 'nothing-ness' which yet seems divinely irradiated:

> It is as though God said
> *Let there be light in this world*
> *Of nothing let it come from*
> *Nothing let it speak nothing*
> *Let it go everywhere.* (*FV* 60)

Jules Smith, in his review of Morrissey's poetry for the British Council, takes the 'modern stained-glass window' on the cover of *There was Fire in Vancouver*, and the 'painting of a girl wearing a Communion dress' on the jacket of her second collection, *Between Here and There* (2002), as evidence of the centrality of 'quasi-religious themes'[16] in Morrissey's poetry. The modern stained-glass window, however, is a purely secular work, a detail from Harry Clarke's 1929 masterpiece, the Geneva Window, which was commissioned by the Irish Free State as a gift to the League of Nations Headquarters in Geneva. Clarke's window

---

14 Patrick Kavanagh, 'Epic', *Collected Poems* (London, Martin Brian & O'Keefe, 1984) p. 136.
15 'Sinéad Morrissey – Interview with Declan Meade', in *The Stinging Fly*, 1, 14. http://www.culturenorthernireland.org/article_t1.asp?county=15&articleID=1970&cul, pp. 1–6, 2.
16 http://www.contemporarywriters.com/authors/?p=authC2D9C28A1129f14F2FmLo24

was a controversial work: eight panels illustrating poems, plays and stories by George Fitzmaurice, Lady Gregory, Sean O'Casey, Liam O'Flaherty, Seamus Kelly, Seumas O'Sullivan, Lennox Robinson, W.B. Yeats, G.B. Shaw and J.M. Synge. In the conservative, puritanical, Ireland of the 1920s, Clarke represented an alternative cultural possibility, in which *fin de siècle* aestheticism is combined with native stories and customs. The Irish Government, following the lead of Dublin's Archbishop McQuade, didn't share Clarke's vision of a liberated, multi-denominational Irish state and returned the window to Clarke's widow. Morrissey's choice of cover may therefore be seen as a declaration of the poet's own subversive intent, her wish to align herself with the Clarkes rather than the clerics, with the movement of progress in Irish society rather than the reactionary forces of Church and State.

Her second book, *Between Here and There*, bears witness to an even more widely travelled intelligence, her diverse poetic worlds encompassing the Orient, the Antipodes, America, as well as Ireland. The collection is prefaced by a short untitled poem:

> My voice slipped overboard and made it ashore
> the day I fished on the Sea of Japan
> within sight of a nuclear reactor.
>
> At first I didn't notice,
> my flexible throat full of a foreign language
> and my attention on the poison of a puffer fish.[17]

The speaker is at sea, on board a boat, the imagery of movement and fluidity emphasising her shifting, unstable subject-position. The opening image of the voice slipping overboard, acquiring an independent, mobile existence separate from the lyric 'I' that controls the poem, recalls Heaney's debates about the proper 'government of the tongue':

> The achievement of the poem is an experience of release ... The tongue, governed for so long in the social sphere by considerations of tact and fidelity, by nice obeisances to one's origin ... This tongue is suddenly ungoverned. It gains access to a condition that is unconstrained.[18]

Morrissey also experiences this sense of freedom and otherness ('my flexible throat full of a foreign language') which is unwilled, occurring when the conscious mind, oblivious to, or disinterested in, the so-called 'important' things ('within sight of a nuclear reactor'), is absorbed by its own concerns ('my attention on the poison of the puffer fish'). The image of the vagrant voice that speaks beyond the control of rational mind contradicts the notion of a single, unified, autonomous self. The voice becomes unmoored, takes on a life of its own, but this occurs naturally ('At first I didn't notice'), and is not a matter of concern or anxiety. Her fragmented, multi-voiced, multifarious identity is actually regarded

---

[17] Sinéad Morrissey, *Between Here and There* (Manchester, Carcanet Press, 2002) p. 9. Hereafter abbreviated to *BHT* and page references incorporated into the text.

[18] Seamus Heaney, 'Nero, Chekhov's Cognac and a Knocker', in *The Government of the Tongue*, p. xxii.

as a source of poetic power and enrichment, capable of 'bringing me everything under the sun'. In saying that the speaker 'pictures' the return of the voice, the poet would seem to imply that the state of wholeness or self-identity exists only in imagination, always in the future. The poem, that is, presents an image of female identity as ungrounded, 'flexible', exiled or displaced from traditional territorial certainties.

The second part of the collection (which the poet tells us she wrote first) is entitled 'Japan'. These poems are based on a two-year sojourn in Japan, which she found to be 'a real spur to writing'.[19] The unsettling of Japan, she said, was a productive dislocation, one which she felt helped her towards a freer, more flexible, more descriptive, more energetic, long-line style. Aware of the dangers of being seen as a facile tourist poet, she tried to avoid this problem by writing, not so much about other places, as about her experience of being there. The sequence emphasises isolation and cultural disorientation, feelings of strangeness which are conveyed through a surrealistic vision and technique. Japan, that is, offered the possibility of undoing her own 'reality', displacing her own voice, position and authority, as in these quiet, mesmeric lines from 'Goldfish', the first poem in the sequence:

> I mistook the black fish for an oriental goldfish the flash of gold
> on its belly meant it carried its message for the element below it
> always one storey down Zen masters attaining one storey down and I,
> falling into you, story by story, coming to rest in the place where
> closing eyes is to see   (*BHT* 43)

By loosening the lines from the syntactic vice and letting them drift free of rational meaning and immediate referents, she gives the impression of going beyond herself, beyond her own language and cultural understanding, thereby challenging the presumed stability of the symbolic order to which she is usually subject. Her eccentric text testifies to the desire to recognise difference without seeking to possess or naturalise or patronise it by bringing it within the domain of 'English' language, knowledge and control. Here difference remains difference, unassimilable to normal perception and language: difference as addition, supplement, an excess that destabilises knowledge and subjectivity. Morrissey's 'Japan' poems propose, not a Baudrillardian end of meaning, but a Barthesian excess of sense. In his writings on Japan, *Empire of Signs* (1993), Barthes discovers in Japanese minimalist expression (such as the haiku) a denial of the Western demand for totality, finality and plenitude of meaning, a kind of writing degree zero, in which meaning remains as only a trace, 'only a flash, a slash of light'.[20] Morrissey reprises this image in her reference to the oriental goldfish's 'flash of gold' that 'carried its message'. She, too, seeks to create that Zen-like utopia, characterised by what Barthes identifies as 'an exemption from meaning',[21] which celebrates language itself. This, as Iain Chambers insists in relation to Barthes,

---

19 Interview with Declan Meade, p. 5.
20 Roland Barthes, *Empire of Signs*, trans. Richard Howard (New York, Hill & Wang, 1993) p. 74.
21 Ibid., p. 73.

'is not to avoid the question of significance but rather supplements, extends and complicates it'.[22]

The volume starts off, however, with 'In Belfast'. She has returned to her home town after an absence of ten years. Part I is an objective, imagistic, conventionalised description of historic Belfast, emphasising weight, oppressiveness, 'gravitas'. Mention of 'Victoria Regina steering the ship of the City Hall', 'Royal Avenue' and 'Albert Bridge' recalls a controversial colonial past, marked by a Unionist bourgeois confidence founded on industrialism and mercantilism in the Victorian era. Another landmark building of very different architectural design – 'the house for the Transport Workers' Union' – defiantly stands for an alternative set of Belfast interests, and marks division within the civic monolith. The references to 'ship' and 'ballast' carry connotations of Belfast's ship-building industry, which was traditionally monopolised by the Protestant working-class. All this history, given such solid, even monumental, material embodiment, is undercut by Part I's closing image, with its intimations of suppressed anger, danger and deceptiveness: 'the river/ is simmering at low tide and sheeted with silt' – a reference to the city's famously unstable foundations, built as it is on 'slobland' reclaimed from Belfast Lough. Part II interpellates the authorial subject:

> I have returned after ten years to a corner
> and tell myself it is as real to sleep here
> as the twenty other corners I have slept in.
> More real, even, with this history's dent and fracture
>
> splitting the atmosphere. And what I have been given
> is a delicate unravelling of wishes
> that leaves the future unspoken and the past
> unencountered and unaccounted for.
>
> This city weaves itself so intimately
> it is hard to see, despite the tenacity of the river
> and the iron sky; and in its downpour and its vapour I am
> as much at home here as I will ever be.   (*BHT* 13)

Returning to Belfast, Morrissey has no strong sense of the place – it's just another corner to sleep in. She recognises the challenge the city offers to any notion of home, nation or identity as homogenous. The city is where our sense of centre is displaced, and our historical, cultural and subjective being is disrupted. Belfast is 'more real' with its 'history's dent and fracture/ splitting the atmospherics'. She seeks to occupy those interstitial spaces so that the idea of home, and the languages, traditions and identities out of which it is composed, is held open to questioning and rewriting. Situated in the gaps, her poetry is an excess that is irreducible to a single centre, origin or meaning. The tear in culture, society and language brought about by a history of sectarian division opens up a space which is the natural home for a poetry eager to explore new stories, languages and identities. As Homi Bhabha puts it:

---

[22] Iain Chambers, *Migrancy Culture Identity* (London, Routledge, 1994) p. 101.

... It is to the city that the minorities come to change the history of the nation ... it is the city which provides the space in which emergent identifications and new social movements of the people are played out. It is there that, in our time, the perplexity of the living is most acutely experienced.[23]

The poet sees herself as the inheritor, not of fixed meanings and identity, but 'a delicate unravelling of wishes'. It is in the unstable, discontinuous city, in its 'downpour and its vapour', that she feels at home, the word 'vapour' suggesting a metaphorical as well as physical manifestation of the legendary Irish mist. The sense of belonging that emerges at the end is resigned and unillusioned, cast about with images of dissolution, disintegration and unreality.

The single, homogenous point of view, epitomised in colonialism, imperialism and rational modernity, implies a totalising vision, mastery of the world. In contrast, Morrissey is absorbed by the incoherence, the estrangement, in modern culture and identity, the gaps opened up by the stranger, the tectonic shifts that displace established meanings and force us to confront the stranger in ourselves. This is the message of the next poem, 'Tourism', which welcomes the upsurge in tourists visiting Northern Ireland in the wake of the ceasefires. In an interview, the poet explains the background to the poem, and speaks revealingly of her own hopes for the future:

> The poem's core is the dissolution of the new Northern Ireland Assembly over the stalled issue of IRA decommissioning. I was furious that this had been allowed to take place, and saw it as a threat to the stability of the peace process. One of the consequences of the peace process is that tourists have started coming here ... I suppose the poem articulates a view of tourism as the great white hope of the future for Northern Ireland in a way. Not so much in the inherent superficiality of much tourism, but in the more basic fact of other people coming here. Northern Ireland is so narrow and parochial – the gene pool is small, nearly everyone is white. I want Northern Ireland to be far more multicultural than it is – to open itself to the broader world and the broader human community. It might put some of our tribal conflict in perspective.[24]

'Our day has come', the poem proclaims, ironically re-citing/re-siting the slogan of the Irish Republican movement, *Tiocfadh ár lá* ('our day will come'): the future lies, not in the fulfilment of national destiny, but in replacement of traditional notions of Irish identity with a new vision of pluralism and multiculturalism. In opposition to the principle of *Sinn Fein* ('ourselves alone'), Morrissey welcomes 'infection' from outside, and calls for a new post-nationalist, European state:

> So come, keep coming here.
> We'll recklessly set chairs in the streets and pray for the sun.
> Diffuse the gene pool, confuse the local kings,
>
> infect us with your radical ideas; be carried here
> on a sea breeze from the European superstate

---

23 Homi Bhabha, *The Location of Culture* (London, Routledge, 1994) pp. 169–70.
24 'Sinéad Morrissey in Malta'.

we long to join; bring us new symbols,
a new national flag, a xylophone. Stay.   (*BHT* 14)

Deliberately countering older notions of place/home as bounded territory, and traditional concepts of identity as racially pure and homogenous, Morrissey welcomes the stranger, and embraces the idea of home as being always contingent, open to new influence, in perpetual transit. We are back with metaphors of journey and nomadism: existence as a continual confabulation, with no fixed identity or final destination. Belfast is a 'splintered city', 'gapped' and 'holed', but out of the fragments a new future may yet be constructed, despite set-back and disappointment. The tours on which the visitors are taken are symbols of the official attempt to create an acceptable post-Troubles narrative out of a place marked by disjunction and disruption. Circulating among the sites of both achievement and failure ('the festering gap in the shipyard/ the Titanic made when it sank./ Our talent for holes that are bigger/ than the things themselves'), the tourists encounter the uncanny truth of ambiguity. The ideas of home, identity and belonging which Morrissey proposes, like the traditional narrative of the nation (Irish or British), involve the construction of an 'imaginary community', but Morrissey's fiction is crucially different from traditional conceptions of community in that it is based on the premise that there is no single language in which 'community' or 'identity' can be incontrovertibly asserted, no single narrative that can claim absolute authority.

In the very fine 'An Anatomy of Smell', place, home and identity are constructed in terms of the intimate language of smell: the smell of her partner's skin ('I would know your skin in the dark: its smooth magnetic film/ would bring me home and cease my being separate'); the smells of other people's hallways; the family smells that children bring to school with them ('slipped giveaways/ of origin'); the smells of poet and partner that constitute their 'identity' and 'home' ('Now we too have an identity –/ the smell of us is through our sheets and wrapped around our home'). Smell 'conquers distance' (*BHT* 34). It is a more intimate and distinctive marker of identity than any of the usual abstract designations such as race or religion: 'any family/ forges something wholly themselves and wholly different/ and marks each child for life with the hidden nature of their generative act'). Though humanly produced, smell is something that exists beyond human will and control, natural, invisible, telltale. In the last stanza the poet refers to the various places from which she and her partner bring smells ('From you, the smell of the Tucson desert:/ copper deposits, animal skulls .../ From me, bog cotton, coal fires, wild garlic, river dirt'), and describes how these smells are mediated and mingled through their bodies, and distilled as 'salt'. The smell of home is made up of many different smells, which are now shared and transformed in the sharing. When she moves house, she is confident that these intimate markers of home and identity will move with them: 'When we move house/ such genealogies as these will follow us'. The poet's concept of home depends not on fixity, boundedness or stability, nor on a sense of belonging to a particular regional, cultural or political tradition. Building on existentialist, not essentialist or metaphysical premises, Morrissey constructs her 'home' experientially, from the intimacies of the personal life, from mobile personal relationships and the fluctuating data of the senses. The poem is a cleverly devised vehicle for its message. Like the smell which 'is through our sheets and wrapped around our home', various co-ordinating textual elements, such as the ghostly presence of rhyme (more strongly evident than is usual in Morrissey's relatively free verse) drifting musically through the sheets of the poem, mimic and fulfil the unifying function which the poet attributes to smell.

Her third collection, *The State of the Prisons* (2005), includes a sequence of nine poems, each written in a different form, chronicling a 21-day journey across China which was sponsored by the British Council. Confined to the train, the poet's experience of the country was severely restricted: 'Windows feature heavily – by necessity I think, as it was through windows that I experienced most of the country – and they are simultaneously windows, walls, and mirrors. I was being denied far more than I was being granted, but the glimpses were tantalising.'[25] Poem 5 registers the frustrations of the constricted 'official' perspective:

> Darkness is gathering itself in. I see a boy and a woman
> lit up by the flare of a crop fire, but can no longer believe in them.
> Windows have turned into mirrors the length of the train.
> Hours pass, and there is only my white face, strained
> in its hopelessness, my failure to catch the day in my hands like a
>   fish
> and have it always.[26]

Travel, as these lines suggest, may always be essentially self-exploration but, shut away from experience, the poet had little opportunity to explore China. As one reviewer remarked of the effects of the enforced distance, 'This is a poem full of lost opportunities.'[27] In the next poem in the sequence, the speaker escapes 'the hold of our hotel' and, led by a local woman, ventures further into the heart of darkness, down a 'rubble-matted' backstreet:

> And stopped me at a doorway
> And pointed down its throat
> I photographed it dumbly
> Lost to what it meant
>
> Her urgency diminished
> I smiled I had to go
> The air was thick between us
> With all I could not know
>
> Day gave without a whimper
> I found myself re-caged
> Staring through the filter
> Of money's privilege   (*SP* 26)

---

25 Sinéad Morrissey in interview with Mark Thwaite http://www.readysteadybook.com/Article.aspx?page=sineadmorrissey

26 Sinéad Morrissey, 'China', in *The State of the Prisons* (Manchester, Carcanet Press, 2005) p. 25. Hereafter abbreviated to *SP* and page references incorporated into the text.

27 'Polly Clark reviews *The State of the Prisons* by Sinead Morrissey. http://www.towerpoetry.org.uk/poetry-matters/july2005/morrissey.html

The Chinese experience is used to highlight the limitations of the perspective of 'privilege', the voyeurism inherent in the tourist's gaze. The poem's self-reflexive encounter with the inscrutable, the unknown, the unspoken, the 'other' side of Western reason, that which denies closure and outruns the poet's language – that for which there's no end-stop – inculcates a humbling sense of the inadequacy of the poet's own language, sign-system and understanding.

In section 8, the poet watches the crowds of Chinese disgorge from the train:

> I stayed to one side, watching
>
> them flow like an out-
> going tide in to the maw of each
> city, ands saw myself
> caught in the pulse of their
> striding, my greenish skin hurled
>
> Under water and hammering *I am*
> *here you are real this*
> *is happening it is*
> *redeemable* – as though touching
> them might be possible.   (*SP* 29–30)

The aquatic references, the adoption of a strange amphibian persona, and the tumble of run-on lines all emphasise ideas of fluidity and mergence, the attempt to dissolve the gap between subject and object. Seeking to overcome her sense of displacement from the Chinese, the poet imagines a kind of touristic sublime beyond the 'English' pale, yet the broken intensity of the language bespeaks irredeemable difference.

An important influence on Morrissey's negotiations with Chinese alterity is W.H. Auden. In *Journey to a War* (1938), Auden and Isherwood's travelogue, combining journalism, poetry and photography, and chronicling their travels across China just at the moment when the Japanese were advancing on Shanghai during the Sino-Japanese war, the authors express their own self-conscious awareness of their privileged, colonialist perspective: 'And we ourselves, though we wear out our shoes walking the slums, though we take notes, though we are genuinely shocked and indignant, belong, inescapably, to the other world. We return, always, to Number One House (the British Ambassador's private villa in Shanghai where they were staying) for lunch.'[28] Included in *Journey to a War* are Auden's twenty-one *Sonnets from China*, comprising a meditation upon the role of the Western subject in China, especially in wartime. In these poems, Auden expresses his sympathy with the Otherness of China, opposes Western cultural hegemonism, questions the possibility of authentic Western readings of the Orient, and explores his own subjectivity as homosexual, British, tourist and colonial insider. Rather than refurbish the usual East/ West binary oppositions, he exploits the discontinuities and slippages in this traditional configuration. It is this orientation of his gaze within the interstices of dominant Western, impe-

---

[28]   W.H. Auden and Christopher Isherwood, *Journey to a War* (London, Faber, 1973).

rialist and Orientalist discourses that makes him a figure of special interest to Morrissey. Her poem, 'The Gobi from Air', alludes to Chapter 10 of *Journey to a War*, where conditions in the Shanghai factories are described:

> His trains all avoided the front.
> The Japanese shielded their eyes
>
> From the sun, and kept on killing.
> He toured warehouses, brothels, remembering,
>
> Out of everything,
> Damp fungus frothing
>
> On the fingertips
> Of the mill girls in Shanghai.   (*SP 31*)

Here Morrissey fixes on the trademark Audenesque strategy of concentrating attention on the minute, apparently insignificant details of life that never make it into the history books. This is the theme of what is probably Auden's best-known poem, 'Musée des Beaux Arts', inspired by Brueghel's 'The Fall of Icarus', and written shortly after the Chinese travelogue. The painting and the poem draw attention to the ordinary life that goes on, oblivious to the drama that takes place all around. Morrissey shares Auden's interest in re-focusing attention on what is forgotten or overlooked. In shifting their gaze from the rhetoric of glory and imperialism, both poets imply a vaster world that goes about its everyday business, its arduous daily cycle, preoccupied with its own unheroic struggle for survival. Just as Auden's version of Bruegel subordinates the image of heroic martyrdom to the worldly indifference of the ploughman, so Morrissey's version of Auden directs attention away from the Japanese aviators who, in *Journey to a War*, are described as falling from the sky (not unlike Icarus) over Hankow during the Sino-Japanese war in 1938, and towards the Shanghai mill girls. In all three works, this juxtaposition of the 'extraordinary' and the 'ordinary' forces a reconsideration of these received categories, encouraging us to see things in a way we normally would not see. Morrissey's title, 'The Gobi from Air', highlights the poem's aerial (Daedalian rather than Icarian) perspective, which, incidentally, it shares with Bruegel's painting. The force of both poem and painting is to move us not only to recognise the indifference to history and suffering inherent in the preoccupation of ongoing life, but also to register shock that it should be so.

If, in Morrissey's 'China' sequence, the 'other' is safely contained beyond the train windows, it cannot always be maintained at a safe distance 'out there', but irrupts into, interrupts, the ordinary routine present, emerging at the centre of daily life. In 'In Praise of Salt', home is invaded by international affairs, news of the war in Iraq. The poet is 'salting an egg in the morning', listening to the radio:

> The radio is documenting
> *The threats we face ...* The cut and lash
> Of voices pitched to shatter glass.
>
> For a second I don't hear the kettle boil
> And wonder: if Iraq mined salt instead of oil?

At Leonardo's table, salvation spilled
As Judas scattered salt. And we're still poised to kill.

In India they made salt and shook an Empire.
Salt makes us what we are, and takes us there.   (*SP* 36)

In an age of global terrorism, no-one is safe any longer. '*The threats we face*'
mutates into 'And we're still poised to kill' (*SP* 36): a vicious circle of violence
and counter-violence on a global scale. Against this depressing scenario, the poet
affirms a radical alternative, an elemental reality represented by the salt the poet
shakes over her morning egg: salt, that 'fifth element' as it is sometimes called, as
necessary to human life as earth, air, fire and water; salt that can never lose its
savour, that is purifying, preserving, sacred; salt that symbolises authentic value:
'Ye are the salt of the earth, but if the salt has lost its savour, wherewith shall it
be salted. It is thenceforth good for nothing but to be cast out and to be trodden
under foot' (Matthew 5. 13). In da Vinci's 'The Last Supper', an overturned salt
cellar lies in front of Judas, signifying bad luck, the breaking of the covenant
of love and friendship. Morrissey links salt to Christ's salvation in the phrase
'salvation spilled', the Latin word for salt embedded in '*sal*vation', just as she links,
syntactically and rhetorically, Judas's act of betrayal to the ominous present-day
stance of an aggressive Occident: '… Judas scattered salt. And we're still poised to
kill.' The last two lines of the poem refer to a speech by Gandhi in 1930 ('With
this salt I am shaking the foundations of the empire'), on the occasion of the 'salt
march' which he led in protest against the imposition of a British tax on Indian
salt. The 'salt march' exemplified Gandhi's tactic of non-violent struggle for self-
rule and self-sufficiency, and marked the beginning of the process which, seven-
teen years later, would end British rule in India. The poet's salting her morning
egg thus becomes a small act of defiance of the consensual Western 'we' ('*the
threats we face*', 'And we're still poised to kill'), a quiet rebuke offered to gung-
ho neo-colonial politicos, an assertion of the body against increasingly abstract
wars. All that apocalyptic, binary-driven rhetoric of the ideologues pouring into
her kitchen is taken, we might say, with a pinch of salt.

Wars fill this collection, but so too does the quietly subversive voice of modern
nomadic subjectivity which re-frames the contemporary world. The dangers of
an oppositional politics is powerfully imaged in 'The Wound Man' where the
events of '9/11' are seen to produce the monstrous Frankenstein-figure of the
American 'wound man' who, scarred and embittered, stalks the globe looking
for vengeance. Rethinking the binary logic that lies behind cultural imperialism
and the centre-figure it tends to employ margins ('First World'–'Second'/'Third
World', 'Christian'–'Islamic'), Morrissey enacts a process of poetic dislocation
and decentering, of imaginative and cultural travelling, suggesting a circulatory
model of culture in which an endless series of exchanges lead to unexpected
mutations, extensions and configurations. Beyond the politics of military coer-
cion, economic imposition and cultural imperialism, Morrissey's poetry proposes
ideas of contamination and hybridity, and reminds us that there is no pure,
absolute truth. 'Zero' tells the story of Alexander the Great bringing back to the
Greeks from his expeditions in the East the concept of zero. In the East, 'zero'
means loss, absence, emptiness, ends; but to the Greeks it is source, origins, foun-
tainhead, plenitude. The point of the poetic parable is that meaning is always a

socially ordained construct, a matter of 'angles' that can easily be come trans-
formed into the illusory truth of transcendent 'angels':

> Sensing where it could lead,
> This number/ no-number that would eat the world,
> The Greeks turned back to Alexander in the advancing shade
> And smiled: for there were still angles, there were still
> Three old angels skipping over heaven carrying harps and
>   signs.   (*SP* 48)

Ideally, the poetics of home must open themselves, and remain open, to other
worlds, experiences, histories, in which the empire writes back to the centre,
and poetic language continually interrogates its relation to hegemonic meaning.
The result is a hybrid poetry that confounds and confuses prior categorisa-
tions, a poetry that defers, disperses and redistributes the processes of authority.
Home continually opens onto another place, the periphery intrudes upon the
centre, like the desert sands engulfing the metropolis in 'The Gobi from Air':
'Ten thousand barrels of sand/ overturned/ on the streets of Beijing in a year./
Some days they fear/ that the earth/ is raining' (*SP* 31). The airborne perspec-
tive informs other poems. 'Forty Lengths' ends by comparing swimming to
flying: 'me up in the sky/ like Lucy, not needing to breathe, or be tired, or be
told, or be older –/ wishboning through the stratosphere' (*SP* 12). The lines not
only invoke Beatles-style acid-tripping ('Lucy in the sky with diamonds') but
bring us back to Kavanagh – the Kavanagh who spoke of being 'airborne', of
the repose that comes from detachment and 'not caring'.[29] Likewise, Morrissey's
airborne perspective is used to articulate a sense of lyric freedom and buoyancy
that offsets her concern with various places and states of imprisonment, as in
the first poem, 'Flight', about the silenced voice of a Royalist woman wearing
a scold's bridle in Cromwell's England, or the long title-poem based on the
life of the eighteenth-century prison reformer, John Howard, with which the
book concludes. One of her poems, actually entitled 'Icarus', is, we are surprised
to find, narrated by Daedalus not Icarus. Icarus is, in fact, marginalised, as in
Bruegel's painting and Auden's poem, reduced to an afterthought, mentioned
only in the last two lines:

> I stayed up for years. Disregarding their expressions.
> Their mud-stranded resignation. In tributaries.
>
> And then my son.
> And what he did to boys. (*SP* 41)

Icarus, as the last two lines imply, has been a baleful influence, instigator of a
dangerous cult of imperialist masculinism, precursor of the Japanese aviators
whom Auden described falling from the skies over the Gobi desert. It is Daeda-
lus's mature and 'buoyant' self-awareness that fills this poem, and it is he, the
Joycean artificer and canny flyer, with whom the poet identifies.

---

[29] Patrick Kavanagh, 'Self-Portrait', in *Collected Pruse* (London, Martin Brian & O'Keefe, 1973)
p. 22.

Alan Gillis: Being In-Between

Reared and schooled in the almost totally Protestant town of Newtownards, Alan Gillis studied English at Trinity College Dublin and then proceeded to postgraduate work at Queen's University Belfast. He taught in the University of Ulster at Coleraine before taking up a position in 2005 in the University of Edinburgh where he is currently teaching. The title of his debut collection *Somebody, Somewhere* is an impassioned cry for an audience and, in his opening poem, 'The Ulster Way', gives immediate notification of a poetics of transit or rambling. Using the metaphor of the ramblers' circular path running all around Northern Ireland, Gillis enunciates an aesthetic grounded in the dynamics of a strict empiricism, a new eco-based 'Ulster Way' of doing poetry:

> For this is not about horizons, or their curving
> limitations. This is not about the rhythm
> of a songline. There are other paths to follow.
> Everything is about you. Now listen.[30]

'Everything is about you': with a playfully punning epigram, Gillis proposes a poetry which dissolves or reconciles the split between self and world, a poetry which is boundless in its boundedness. The world the imagination embraces is both a specific, local one – the 'Ulster Way' – and a personal, individual one. The poems created out of this embrace must bear the stamp of both their locality and their creator, viewed as a representative figure (as the generic 'you' implies). Adopting this attitude as a matter of fundamental identity and vision, the poet establishes the starting-point from which he can aspire to encompassing 'everything'. And yet he refuses to be dogmatic or definitive, but proceeds by outlining a kind of *via negativa*: 'This is not about burns or hedges./ There will be no gorse …' (*SS* 9). This is Gillis's version of 'the road not taken', his poem a mapping out of an 'Ulster Way' that nevertheless leaves plenty of opportunity for digression, exploration, trespass – all kinds of linguistic and rhythmic play.

This concern with elucidating an aesthetic continues in his second collection, *Hawks and Doves*. The title obviously alludes to the dichotomisation of politics, especially American politics in the current time of crisis, into aggressive, gung-ho neo-cons and pacifistic liberals. The intention would seem to be to place the Ulster situation within a larger geopolitical context. 'With *Hawks and Doves*', Gillis says, 'there's hopefully an implicit expansion of the terrain by examining Loyalist themes, WASP culture in general … and masculine aggression and war etc. as part of a complex whole … My gambit with the book is … to imply how hawkish and dovish, good and ill, principles pervade every facet of life … There's always black, and there's always white. It's just never too clear what these things mean.'[31] 'Lagan Weir', one of the poems in *Hawks and Doves*, also uses a topographical feature of the Ulster landscape as poetic metaphor, a weir being a man-made device for controlling the flow of water in a river or canal. Similarly,

---

[30] Alan Gillis, *Somebody, Somewhere* (Loughcrew, The Gallery Press, 2004) p. 9. Hereafter abbreviated to *SS* and page references incorporated into the text.
[31] Gillis, personal correspondence, 4 May 2007.

the poem's regulating devices of metre and stanza-structure come under pressure from the longing for the kind of freedom and unpredictability represented by a flock of starlings reeling and swerving across the sky:

> The way things are going,
>   there'll be no quick fix, no turning
> back the way that flock of starlings
>   skirls back on itself then swerves forward,
> swabbing and scrawling the shell-pink
>   buffed sky, while I stand in two minds …[32]

Paralysed by doubt and uncertainty, the speaker is caught between the promptings of 'a hawk' and 'a dove', symbols of the reductive binary thinking which inhibits the free play of imagination. He feels trapped in time, in rigid teleological systems, in others' expectations, in the language that habitually positions him. The line that begins the poem is also used to end it, emphasising the treadmill circularity of the lives of the 'city dwellers' who 'make their dark way/ homeward, never slowing, not knowing/ the way things are going'. Contrasting with these blind creatures of routine are the starlings, with their swift, aerial geometrics, their virtuoso, self-delighting display of form and style, which symbolises the ideal poetic performance. Hovering over this, as over other Gillis poems, is the presence of one of his favourite poets, Wallace Stevens, who, in 'Earthy Anecdote', described the bucks in Oaklahoma clattering 'in a swift circular line'[33] this way and that, configuring a magnificent, self-limiting, animated pattern, which is the design a poem makes.

More commonly, Gillis's poems feature an urban world, though not the usual 'Troubles' cityscape. Gillis is the laureate of the postmodern, the era of mass communications, rampant commercialisation and popular culture.[34] '12th October, 1994' begins, 'I enter the Twilight Zone' – an amusement arcade which, like countless others, takes its name from the title of the American '60s TV show which specialised in dark, eerie tales of fantasy, science fiction or horror. Since the '60s, the 'Twilight Zone' series has become the inspiration of numerous comic books, television and film revivals, a Disney theme-park ride, songs by Golden Earring, Iron Maiden and The Manhatten Transfer, and a Midway pinball game. With the help of the *OED* we also learn that, originally, the term referred to the line separating the portion of a planet that is illuminated by the sun and that in shadow (that is, the area between day and night), more officially known

---

[32] Alan Gillis, *Hawks and Doves* (Loughcrew, The Gallery Press, 2007) p. 60. Hereafter abbreviated to *HD* and page references incorporated into the text.

[33] Wallace Stevens, 'Earthy Anecdote', in *Selected Poems* (London, Faber, 1976) p. 9.

[34] Though Gillis says that he had no idea that either title of his poetry collections alluded to pop songs, 'Somebody, Somewhere' is a phrase that has been much used in pop songs. It forms the title of a 1950s pop song by American lyricist Frank Loesser, better known for musicals such as *Guys and Dolls*, and is found in a host of other songs, from Rod Stewart's 'Passion' to songs recorded by lesser known artistes such as the Ennis Sisters, Loretta Lynn and Aaron Neville. Similarly, *Hawks and Doves* re-uses the title of Neil Young's 1980 album. While denying that pop culture is a 'big issue' for him, Gillis nevertheless acknowledges its pervasive influence: 'it's just a part of things, and it would be unrealistic not to have it as part of the fabric of the verse' (personal correspondence, 4 May 2007).

as the 'terminator'. Gillis plays on these references and usages, creating his own poetic 'Twilight Zone', that liminal space between fantasy and reality which is also, in Baudrillardian terms, the realm of the simulacrum. In Gillis's poem, the recreational violence of the video games is situated within the context of the actual violence played out every day in the streets of Belfast during the Troubles. 12th October 1994 was the eve of the announcement from the combined Loyalist Military Command (UDA, UVF and the Red Hand Commandos) of a ceasefire dependent on 'the continued cessation of all nationalist/republican violence', and twelve days after the IRA ceasefire. Less than a year before, an IRA bomb on the Shankill Road, Belfast, had killed eleven people and, a week later, the retaliatory gun attack by the UFF on a pub in Greysteel left seven dead. The poem blurs the line between this actual violence and the virtual violence of the electronic games. The poem's narrator interacts with the figures on the screen, not the actual people who come and go, and who, as their cartoon names ('Frankie "Ten Pints" Fraser', 'Johnny "Book Keeper" McFeeter', 'Terry "The Blaster" McMaster', 'Benny "Vindaloo" McVeigh', *SS* 10–11) suggest, themselves assume iconographic identity. Further reinforcing the sense of media-saturation is the meticulously specified sound-track – the catalogue of jukebox hits of the pre-Troubles '60s playing in the background. Despite the narrator's skill at the game, it is he who is controlled by the machine, and integrated into the material process of objec-tification and commodification. Even his language, like the game he plays, is a virtual reality: for all its violent 'self-presencing', it can do no more than gesture towards actualisation while constantly deferring or frustrating it. In the post-modern world of the 'Twilight Zone', signs, surfaces and everyday life have no reliable ontological reality. Surfaces and appearances are deceptive, seductive and mystifying manifestations of an underlying existential reality, which, Gillis seems to be saying, is the alienated condition of contemporary life.

A recurrent poetic scenario involves a central image of private space – kitchen, living-room, bedroom, hotel dining room, car interior – invaded by the global world; and a recurrent persona is that of the individual, located within a network of relations – global, national, local, indigenous, personal – unsettled, disoriented or exhausted by the multiplicity and dynamic simultaneity of these relations. This complication of the link between place and culture is evidenced in 'Saturday Morning'. The poem begins with a picture of a Saturday morning recreated in all its sensuous immediacy:

> The fart and snigger of sausages and free
> range eggs, the beans of a coffee grinder
> and light house music on a Fujifilm CD ...   (*HD* 18)

When the speaker moves to his living-room and 'slabs' (HD 18) on his sofa in front of the TV, he enters another Twilight Zone, zapping from one world to another, his own subjective identity swiftly vanishing in the slipstream of the constant procession of images, 'your face swarming into pixels' (*HD* 20). Refer-ence to the 'mortuary white-/ yellow shake of your hands'(*HD* 18) and the 'slab' of the sofa suggest a kind of death-in-life. For the undifferentiated stream of images levels out the extremes of the banal ('teenage models launching their memoirs') and the truly catastrophic ('where a wave hammer-walled/ through

the coastal village'), producing a feeling of disorientation, a sense of the frag-
mentation of cultural experience, a loss of internal coherence:

> Lie there long enough and you will drown
> In the glut-stream of yourself, or nothing,
> As you dissolve into the screen, its thin lips
> Gaping into such a maw you cannot undo
> Its babbling hoodoo. (*HD* 20)

The older sense of 'home' with which the poem opens is soon undermined as
the impact of the vast contemporary reorganisation of capital, the formation of
a new global space, the use of new technologies of communication makes itself
felt. Place is no longer equated with community, and is therefore no longer able
to provide a stable basis for identity. The poem elaborates a concept of space
which takes the form of simultaneous coexistence of experience at all geograph-
ical scales, from the most local (the intimacy of the kitchen) to the wide space
of transglobal connections, accessed with a 'click' of the remote control:

> Click. A celebrity chef provides fresh ideas
> For sausages. Click. The merlin falls like a brick
> On a bank vole's head. Click. The President.
> Click. The pop star peels down to his gonads.
> Click. 'Oh my God, look at her kitchen!' Click.
> Janjaweed teenagers patrol the road to Chad. (*HD* 19–20)

A particular place – the speaker's living-room – becomes a point of intersection
of vast numbers of social relations stretched out over space. The home place is no
longer singular or bounded, no longer a place of nostalgia. Boundaries between
places are dissolved. The global constitutes the local. Distance becomes mean-
ingless. The identity of both individual and place is multiple, shifting. Doreen
Massey, the social geographer of postmodernism, quotes bell hooks's explanation
of the new concept of home:

> Home is no longer just one place. It is locations. Home is that place which enables
> and promotes varied and everchanging perspectives, a place where one discovers
> new ways of seeing reality, frontiers of difference. One confronts and accepts
> dispersal and fragmentation as part of the constructions of a new world order
> that reveals more fully where we are, who we can become ...[35]

Here, bell hooks gives a positive spin to the contemporary phenomenon of space-
time compression, and the loss of traditional notions of reassuring bounded-
ness. In contrast, Gillis's insistent 'clicking' undermines any stability of meaning,
breaking down conventional boundaries and identities, and producing a subject
who, precariously situated at the intersection of these multiple flows of influence,
is not only reduced to the role of entirely passive consumer, but a notably brittle
one at that. The poem, with its intimation of ideas of speed-up, instantaneous
world-wide communication, constant global flows and spatial interconnected-

---

[35] bell hooks, *Yearning: Race, Gender, and Cultural Politics* (Turnaround, London, 1994) p. 148;
quoted in Doreen Massey, *Space, Place and Gender* (Cambridge: Polity Press, 1994) pp. 171–2.

ness, certainly marks the end of essentialist definitions of home, but it also signals a demoralising homogenisation of culture which not even the poet's vernacular sense of place can hold at bay. Postmodernity facilitates relations with 'absent' others, but these are relations of a very limited and superficial kind; meanwhile, social life characterised by 'presence', by local activity, is displaced, marginalised or obliterated. Gillis raises the spectre of resistance against the flux and disruption of time-space compression, and in doing so re-inserts into the equation the individual human response which the theorists of postmodern geography so often ignore. 'A global sense of place – dynamic and internally contradictory and extra-verted – is surely potentially progressive',[36] declares Doreen Massey. But the global sense of place, as 'Saturday Morning' suggests, can also be unsettling, from both a psychological and a moral point of view: potentially dangerous rather than potentially progressive.

'On a Weekend Break in a Political Vacuum' offers another picture of the condition of postmodernity as experienced by a relatively privileged individual who, significantly, is also figured as an entirely passive isolate. It is more than a merely 'political' vacuum which this young woman occupies: the 'rented back-room' to which she repairs is no haven from the global world, yet paradoxically it is a hermetically sealed space cutting her off from the real-life 'presence' of others. Here, she retreats into subjective space, memory, nostalgia, the dreams of consumer heaven advertised in 'dog eared tourist brochures' and 'high-piled magazines'.

> She's running out of breath,
> chasing windblown leaves that are autumned
> at a touch: flakes of promise bloomfalling
> in a motion of mixed motives, ferris-wheeling
> the nothing of death, the death of nothing.   (*HD* 65)

Larkin, Keats, Stevens, Hopkins all make their ghostly presences felt here. Hopkins provides a model for this kind of heavily alliterated accentual verse, the sprung rhythms, the linguistic energy and innovativeness. But where Hopkins writes about God's grandeur and power, the fecundity of imagination and excited vitality of mind that Gillis displays paradoxically go into the expression of emptiness and frustration. In his solid, irregularly rhyming ten-line stanzas, Gillis evokes the confusion and uncertainty of contemporary consciousness, the vague discontent underlying the glossy surfaces of modern life, the desultoriness of social conscience, the desire for escape from the environing pressures. Gillis's young woman is the daughter of Stevens' troubled young metaphysician in 'Sunday Morning', a poem which, in sound and attitude, 'On a Weekend Break' closely resembles. More Stevensian than Hopkinsian, Gillis's poetry dramatises the tension or opposition between reality and imagination. The corollary of the imagination's freedom is the apprehension of 'the nothing of death, the death of nothing' (Gillis), the 'Nothing that is not there and the nothing that is' (Stevens[37]).

---

[36] Massey, p. 143.
[37] Wallace Stevens, 'The Snow Man', in *Selected Poems*, p. 15.

Central to a number of poems – 'The Lights', 'Wasps', 'There' – is the trope of journey and movement, by car, ferry, airplane, train. 'Putting *Hawks and Doves* together,' Gillis says, 'I realise many of the poems are in transit. By car or by foot, there's a lot of coming and going. Perhaps I should have called it *Neither Here Nor There* ... most of the personae in these poems are in transit, wondering, as a brilliant stockbroker once put it: "Where Do We Come From? What Are We? Where Are We Going?"'[38] 'There', a cover version of Larkin's 'Here', begins by enthusiastically evoking the sensations of movement on the symbolically named Belfast-Dublin 'Enterprise Express' – 'scooshing', 'ratcheting', 'spanging over', 'scudding the dark' (*HD* 27) – but the journey leads away from pastoral 'downs' of 'avocado green' and the 'canopy' of 'elmwood demesnes', and towards the dystopia of the urban and suburban wastelands: 'There you must earn your living:/ locked in food-chains, frigid skylines unforgiving' (*HD* 28). The rhyming couplets figure constant movement as merely another form of entrapment: 'There Way Out signs/ rust quietly'. In this re-working of Sartre's *No Exit*, hell is consumer capitalism. Larkin pushes 'beyond' the cumulative weight of the modern world to discover a 'here' of pure being: 'Here is unfenced existence:/ Facing the sun, untalkative, out of reach'.[39] Heaney notes the way there survives in Larkin 'a repining for a more crystalline reality to which he might give allegiance:[40] but no such consolation beyond the social and historical is available in Gillis's nightmarish vision of contemporary life: No visionary 'main of light' illuminates Gillis's world: his alienated 'there' is where, finally, in a memorably crafted image, 'the lough sluiced pebbles, an ulcered tongue/ slivered over loose teeth' (*HD* 28). In the words Gillis thought of using for the title of his second collection, he is 'Neither Here Nor There'.

To speak less mystically, no reassuring sense of 'home' exists for Gillis. 'I realise many of the poems deal with families, parenthood and responsibility', he says. 'If such things, in all their shifting of significance and nuance for each individual through time, are integrally part of what we call "home", then it's no wonder we're always in transit, in-between, always trying to get there, or away from there. As your mother told you, home is where the heart is.'[41] Driving home, in the poem of that title, brings him, not to rest and peace, but further disquiet and disorientation. On the road, returning from work in his car, he hits and kills a Labrador pup. Like 'There', 'Driving Home' begins with the sounds and images of confident movement ('zipped and vroomed', 'steered and veered', 'hammered headward', *HD* 52), but this assurance is quickly overlaid by guilt and unease, control slips, and he can find no comfort anywhere. Once home, his ultimate homelessness is made poignantly apparent:

> [B]ut it was my turn to take the wee one's
> fire engine, fluffy dog and laser gun
> to bed where we lay below his globed atlas lamp,
> self-timed to fade, rotating projected

38 Gillis, personal correspondence, 4 May 2007.
39 Philip Larkin, 'Here', in *Collected Poems* (London, Faber) p. 137.
40 Seamus Heaney, 'The Main of Light', in *The Government of the Tongue* (London, Faber, 1988) p. 16.
41 Gillis, personal correspondence, 4 May 2007.

> continents on the borderlined walls'
> night-blue planetarium, where we read
> until drift-off into nothing, unmoored
> from the axled turn and low-watt embers
> of the earth's spinning top left long behind.   (*HD* 55)

The childhood home requires the protection of 'fire engine' and 'laser gun'. The 'globed atlas lamp/ self-timed to fade' projects a finite, insubstantial cosmic home. Infiltrating the innocence of the bedroom is the consciousness of death, for contained in that closing image of 'earth's spinning top left long behind' is the memory of the dog which earlier in the poem 'kept spinning/ although left long behind, whirligigging/ in a rear view of my mind' (*HD* 53). Amid the unsettling flux and speed of modernity and under the indifferent sign of an ever-turning world, father and son surrender to the incalculable processes of their own subjectivity, 'unmoored' from their earthly home, drifting into 'nothing'.

In 'Laganside', the home place is again figured as 'shifting terrain' (*HD* 77), and the speaker, 'knowing/ I'll never leave here, or come again' (*HD* 77), occupies a liminal position, 'astray' (*HD* 76) in a world of flux yet at home in homelessness. The river, bearing the mementoes and detritus of the past as well as the inspiriting tokens of nature's enduring beauty and the promise of a re-built city, is an emblem of an ever-changing world which the poem, in its constant metamorphosis of image and meaning, seeks to embody: 'so it's unsurprising I'm a bit bamboozled/ by this crash and build of trees and concrete' (*HD* 76). Repeatedly, the Ulster home is made to yield up its alienating content, and one of the special delights of Gillis's two books is the variety of means that are so skilfully employed to do this, from the vernacular exuberance and delightful comic irony of his Orange marching-poem –

> Marching to the field
> of battle, field of peace, field patrolled by plain
> clothed police; field of Jesus, field of hope, field
> of Bush and fuck the Pope; marching onward into
> heaven to scourge its halls of unwashed brethren;
> then a blue bus home, content with your labours,
> to watch *Countdown* and your favourite, *Neighbours*
>
> ('Carnival', *HD* 38)

– to the confident handling of the sestina form in 'After Arcadia', a witty and irreverent pastiche of Sir Philip Sidney's 'Ye Goatherd Gods'. Gillis's 'gabble-clinkered music' (*HD* 56), with its harsh, consonantal compounds, parallels the cacophonous music of the shepherds ('dreadfull cries of murdred men'[42]) deprived of their beloved shepherdess. Following Sidney, Gillis adopts the double sestina in his manic iteration of despair, each six-line stanza ending with the same six words, although in a different order each time, and the last word in one stanza becoming the last word in the first line of the next stanza. Another kind of repetition also echoes Sidney: Gillis opens two stanzas with 'I used to

---

[42]   Sir Philip Sidney, 'Ye Goatherd Gods', in *The Countess of Pembroke's Arcadia (The Old Arcadia)* (London, Penguin Classics, 1999).

…', corresponding to the two Sidney stanzas beginning 'I that was once …'. Similarly, two Gillis stanzas opening with 'Long since …' correspond to two Sidney stanzas starting with exactly the same words. Two Gillis stanzas beginning 'It seems to me …' echo two corresponding Sidney stanzas beginning 'Meseems I see …'. Each poem ends with a final three-line envoy, which is simple, clear, almost calm, all passion spent. Formally, the poems imitate their content, the despondent music of self-loathing and obsession with loss transforming Arcadia, the pastoral utopia, into nightmare.

Alienation from home and the sources of life is the subject of the punningly titled 'The Mournes', which combines an impression of a day out rambling in the mountains in Co. Down with the idea of 'mourning' for a lost 'authenticity':

> Our heads plunged deep in Blackberries,
> TalkTalk, Anytime, Talk & Text and Flext
> plans, it seems our senses are condemned
> to a life sentence . And so, like Alice
> through the mirror, Humpty-Dumpty men,
> we try to piece ourselves back together again.   (*HD* 11)

The references to 'Blackberries', and later in the poem, 'clamshell phones' and 'honeycomb cones', indicate a technological and commercial appropriation of traditional rural culture: pastoral hijacked by the new gods of the digital age. The natural world is no romantic or reassuring refuge, the last stanza moving towards an unsettling, suddenly darkening, close:

> We look over the Silent Valley, its gorges
> And tors, the Slieves sloping, as ever before,
> Down to the wave-lipped and blue-burst
> Sea of trawlers, yachts, dinghies, and, too far
> Out for us to see, the milk-drops of dolphins,
> Cruisers, carriers, frigates gathering for war.   (*HD* 12)

Nature, for all its vibrant allure, is unable to sustain its reassuring influence. In 'Rabbit Head' it is the source of horror and nightmare, 'a dead place'. In other poems, like 'The Mournes', it is sensed as beautiful but as something fantasised, made up by someone who's elsewhere. 'Killynether' ends:

> It's been years since I walked through Killynether.
> When I wake I wonder if I've been there ever.
> Sometime I must, before I flick the screen
> and set about my business, or pick up the telephone,
> wander over to the big lacquered wardrobe and open
> negotiations with the stranger in the mirror.   (*SS* 59)

'Authentic' nature is no more than a virtual reality, accessed through the Narnian magic wardrobe of the imagination in this poem, or Alice's mirror in 'The Mournes'.

Gillis develops an extensive rhetoric of virtuality: in 'Killynether', a catalogue of experiences of nature which the speaker 'never' had are elaborated in such detail that their imagining takes on a vivid virtual reality:

and it dawns on me I never knew the names

of ladies' smock or orange tips, the meadow
browns and ringlets; I never walked among
the celandine, silverweed, wood sage and clover;
never listened to the stonechats and linnets,
the stocking creepers fluttering over green-winged
orchids, twayblades, samphire, or elder.   (*SS* 58)

Much of 'Driving Home' is in the subjunctive or hypothetical mood: 'I might
have pulled over ...' (*HD* 53), 'I might have looked over the mantilla/ of sheaves
...' (*HD* 54), 'I might have lay below a fluttering of birds ...' (*HD* 54), 'I might
have drifted off ...' (*HD* 54). 'Wasps' details experiences he 'almost' had: 'I almost
found myself in an Escort/ with boom-boom speakers and Johnny/ Darkness
...' (*HD* 31) – charting the music of what *might have* happened. 'Or' is a key
term, destablising the poem's reality, rendering it fluid, optative, insisting on
the constructed nature of the text: 'I saw the jungle or gymnasium/ of cranes,
slips and pulleys', 'I took my blue Picasso or Civic east ...' (*HD* 29). Narratives
unfold within narratives, while a constantly virtuoso display of metaphorical and
metamorphic ingenuity increases the sense of complex, multi-level experience.
The short poem, 'Litter', dramatises the characteristic Gillis tactic of irony and
indirection. The poem, re-cycling Mahon's rubbish theory, voices laziness and
self-absorption, greed and the waste of things, while letting a dim awareness
of something 'big' – historical or ecological, either out there or within – come
through imminently or immanently:

Until that evening, fingering peanuts in my dark
Blue bowl, with nothing on TV, I never heard
The rustle among the shopping mall's debris,
I never saw the plastics refusing to corrode
Among the dockside seaweed, and I lay there,
Coiled against the growls of traffic moaning,
The salt-rasped scouring of an outrageous sea.   (*SS* 29)

The poem's implicit cultural critique calls for change and participation in doing
something about social and ecological problems.

Ecological Gillis is less concerned with 'pastoral retreat' or 'authentic nature'
or 'sense of place' than he is with a social ecological perspective. He moves us
from a poetics of authenticity to a poetics of responsibility. Individual and world
crisis alike are invariably situated in defining environmental contexts. In 'You'll
Never Walk Alone', the worst day in the woman's life was not 'when the dawn
green ocean's heart attack/ churned coastlines into troughs of corpse-stew' but
'the day I broke down and bawled myself blue/ by my front door's graffiti, falling
on the cracked,/ coloured kerb with every bill overdue,/ wishing the ground
would gobble me whole, and/ a neighbour asked if I needed a hand' (*HD* 15).
While in 'Death by Preventable Poverty', the poet's lush pastoral provokes, not
reassuring thoughts of the earthly home, but a radical social ecology which
'rails' (*HD* 68) against the global mismanagement of the earth's resources that
results in the millions of deaths by preventable poverty in those distant places
stricken by drought, famine or war. Both poems emphasise ideas of interrela-

tion, the simultaneous coexistence of social interrelations at all spatial scales, from the most local to the most global. All social relations have a spatial form and a relative spatial location – the debt relations which are spawned in the deprived locales of the inner city, the relations of community which extends a helping hand, the global relations of power politics which condemn millions to death by preventable poverty. The social, Gillis insists, is spatial, environmental and ecological. As he puts it in the poem with which we began, 'Everything is about you'. In poems haunted by awareness of war, Africa, social violence, sexual confusion and ecological crisis, the poet, complicit in the cultural logic of late capitalism, is lying there 'coiled against the growls of traffic moaning' ('Litter', *SS* 29), ambiguously figured, either withdrawn in foetal impotence, or ready to strike out against a vicious modern world. Gillis may be writing at a time when, post-Ceasefire, Northern Ireland was 'normalising' but, he says, 'thought inevitably moves from what's outside the door to what's on-screen: more war, death by poverty, environmental havoc, and so on. As a brilliant insurance man once put it: "The war is only part of a war-like whole." In this light, being in-between is not a cop-out. Simply put, there is no other place to be.'[43] Yet haunting this consciousness of social and ecological threat is a vestigial pastoralism evidenced in the considerable number of poems with a rural Ards setting such as 'Big Blue Sky and Silent River', 'Killynether', 'Thou Hast Enlarged Me', 'When Lying on our Bellies was Brilliant' and 'The Ulster Way'. A conscious, pervasive theme would seem to be the tension between town and country, urban and pastoral. What the poet's liminal position implies for his poetics of home is summed up in this comment which Gillis offers on his work: 'It's all about a constant pull and push between attraction–repulsion, departure-and-return, hate-and-love. I guess that's what Ulster/Belfast mean to me – they're very unsettled phenomena in my head. So there's satire and "realism". And then there's something else.'[44]

Leontia Flynn: The Irrelevance of Place

Leontia Flynn was born in 1974 in Downpatrick, Co. Down. She graduated from Queen's University, Belfast, and proceeded to take her MA at Edinburgh. Returning to Queen's, she completed her PhD on the poetry of Medbh McGuckian in 2004. She was awarded an Eric Gregory award in 2001, which helped her to complete her first collection, *These Days*, for which she won the Forward Prize for Best First Collection and was shortlisted for the Whitbread Prize. In 2006 she was Writer-in-Residence at the Princess Grace Library in Monaco, and is currently Research Fellow in the Seamus Heaney Centre for Poetry at Queen's University.

Her subject matter includes memories of childhood, love, mother and father, friends, student life, but what particularly strikes the reader is her use of mobile images and fluid syntax which unsettle any stable reality, perception or identity, the movement of her verse suggesting transience and refusal of fixed defini-

---

43 Gillis, personal correspondence, 4 May 2007.
44 Gillis, personal correspondence, 4 May 2007.

tions, the impossibility of the idea of home or place as reliable and unchanging. 'Without Me' (the fifth poem in the collection with this title) is about a childhood memory of playing frisbee with the 'plastic lid of an old rat-poison bin'.[45] The poem begins in a specific time ('Once, in the hiatus of a difficult July') and place ('down Eskra's lorryless roads from sweet fuck all'), with unpromising materials (the rat-poison bin lid), but by the end the flat arc described by the pendulum-like frisbee has compassed 'Tyrone's prosy horizon' and the speaker is caught up in a Heaneyesque 'momentum' that carries her out of herself, beyond the here and now:

> And I would have sworn that our throw and catch had such momentum
> that its rhythm might survive, somehow, without me. (*TD* 23)

The poem records what Flynn calls in another poem the 'basic wage take-what-you-can-get epiphany' that becomes suddenly, unexpectedly, available in the midst of an empty landscape, in the 'hiatus' in the usual, the textual connotations of the words 'prosy', 'hiatus', and 'rhythm' turning the experience described in the poem into a metaphor of poetry itself. 'Without Me' is a sharply conceived poem, exquisitely cadenced, with an intricate pattern of rhyme and sound-repetition. If its central idea is a little too echoic of Heaney, other poems, such as 'When I Was Sixteen I Met Seamus Heaney' demonstrate a more playful engagement with Irish tradition: 'I had read *The Poor Mouth* – but who was Seamus Heaney?/ I believe he signed my bus ticket, which I later lost' (*TD* 19).

The wonder of life has nothing to do with the place in which it is lived. In 'It's a Wonderful Life' (the first of two poems with this title) the speaker indicates an ironic 'apotheosis of our lives' in the moment of death:

> They will find us bobbing – like frozen corks – under the eaves
> Of some bridge or other – the Albert? The Ormeau? (*TD* 30)

Their drowning will acquire a tragic and apocalyptic glamour which will render irrelevant the insignificance, or otherwise, of the place and circumstances of their deaths: 'No one, in the end,/ will make jokes about fish – of any size – or about small ponds.' Light, witty, ironic, tonally exact, the poem works its own refreshing transformations on the degraded currency of cliché and stale perception.

The second poem with the title 'It's a Wonderful Life' describes the wonderland created by changes in the weather. The first stanza rhymes (ABCCB) and alludes to the appearance of the sun and its reviving and irradiating effect:

> when, walking through town – the way a dame walks in with a gun
> and a flagging crime plot revives – suddenly from nowhere, the sun
> had thrown her weight behind the afternoon's open spaces.
>
> (*TD* 46)

The surprising, far-fetched comparisons, fluid syntax and synaesthetic effects testify to the difficulty of trying to find words and structures to match feeling and

---

[45] Leontia Flynn, *These Days* (London, Jonathan Cape, 2004) p. 23. Hereafter abbreviated to *TD* and page references incorporated into the text.

perception. The second stanza, which has no end-rhymes, presents the strange feeling in the air left after a storm has passed:

> and the sea – which had been so restless – for now was written in
>   stone.
> Leaving the air flocking and beating around the still wings of gulls,
> leaving the flagstones at my feet, which were beginning to lap and
>   ripple.   (*TD* 46)

Place loses solidity and definition. The usual categories of reality have been disturbed: the air is 'flocking and beating', while the wings of gulls are 'still'; the restless sea is now as if 'written in stone', while solid ground is becoming fluid and unstable. The wonder of life depends not on a sense of rootedness or stability, but the exhilaration of living in a MacNeicean world of flux and metamorphic change. Flynn's flagstones that are 'beginning to lap and ripple' are the source of a very different kind of wonderment from that which is stirred by Heaney's 'untoppled omphalos' or Montague's timeless Knockmany Dolmen. She breaks with the tradition of Irish landscape poetry, and with traditional notions of place as having a vital, even sacred role in the discourse of identity. Refuting this fetishisation of place, she shows very little interest in the specifics of place, its geography, topography, anthropology or history. Her 'wonderful life' is another version of the placeless heaven – not the Heaneyesque recreation in imagination of a personal and racial 'first world', more a MacNeicean appreciation of a drunkenly unstable, various, endlessly and richly surprising present world.

The fact that there are five poems with the title 'Without Me' might be seen as indicative of where the poet's principal concern lies – with questions of self-presence, personal relationships, memory, flux and mutability. In 'Without Me' (3), the speaker describes the end of a three-and-a-half year relationship which has passed 'like fifteen minutes at a bus-stop' (*TD* 15) – the relationship no more than an island in life's constantly moving stream. She recalls the 'casualness' and 'glibness' of the goodbye, and, with another Heaneyesque touch, imagines 'the road receding in the driver's memory' (see Heaney's 'From the Frontier of Writing'). With considerable poignancy, she describes how images of the past stay vividly, pointlessly, fixed in her memory:

> Without me and without you, what's the point
> of the fact that you fried onions like you were harpooning shrimp
> in a wok found in a skip near a flat on Wellesley?   (*TD* 15)

Now, she's surprised to find herself contemplating re-entering the world of flux beyond the bounded experience of her past relationship in the 'flat on Wellesley':

> Suddenly, it's beyond me:
> how I'm turning my thoughts to the bird or two in the bush
> and to all the fish in the intervening sea.   (*TD* 15)

There is a notable contrast between the detailed precision of her memories of the relationship in the past and the vague clichés to which she has recourse in attempting to imagine the unknown future. The 'it's' is finely balanced, pointing both backwards to the moment of parting, and forwards to the speaker's thoughts of life's future possibilities, thus encapsulating the tension in the poem between arrest and flux, between indulging bittersweet memories and submitting to the inexorable stream of life.

'The Furthest Distances I've Travelled' is full of the language of travel, back-packing, foreign place names, airports, tannoys, souvenirs, holidaying and stowa-ways, but ends by emphasising, not the attractions of place and travel, but the inner journey of personal relationships: 'the furthest distances I've travelled/ have been those between people. And what survives of holidaying briefly in their lives' (*TD* 48). As Henry David Thoreau concluded in *Walden*, 'it is easier to sail many thousand miles through cold and storm and cannibals, in a government ship, with five hundred men and boys to assist one, than it is to explore the private sea'.[46] The speaker in Flynn's poem isn't longing for a smooth and settled exist-ence, but shares all the 'restlessness' of the traveller:

> it came clear as over a tannoy
> that in restlessness, in anony
> mity:
> was some kind of destiny.   (*TD* 47)

This acceptance of disjunctiveness is enacted linguistically – in the breaking of the word across the line, the abrupt and ungrammatical disruption enforced by the colon, and the shredding of the conventional rhyming couplet format by the wildly variable line lengths. Later, the speaker again highlights the disrupted nature of her existence by referring to 'routine evictions' and how these only increase the value of her 'souvenirs' of the past – 'alien pants, cinema stubs, the throwaway/ comment – on a Post-It – or a tiny stowaway/ pressed flower'. These are the signifiers of an improvised life, one in which the deterritorialised self depends on neither the anchorage of place nor the adventures of physical travel. Home or away, her holidaying takes place 'briefly' in other people's lives, not in other places.

*

This study has examined the way notions of home, place and identity have been questioned, re-imagined and re-constructed in the work of Northern Irish poets in an era of accelerating migration and globalisation. Older poets, mourning the loss of old traditions, nevertheless understood that in seeking to maintain the mythical bond with the past they were embracing ghosts, that the presumed certainties of cultural identity were never a reality, at best 'well dreams', more cynically, 'pap for the dispossessed'. Challenging the 'closed' notion of a single, coherent place called home, Northern Irish poets have constructed alternative images of place, culture and identity out of the myriad social relations, from intimate personal relations of family, local neighbourhood, street or city, to those

---

[46] Henry David Thoreau, *Walden or, Life in the Woods* (New York, Collier Books, 1962) p. 227.

social relations which are stretched out around the globe. With new communications technologies creating new electronic spaces transcending established territorial boundaries and reconfiguring culture, the concept of a fixed, unitary and bounded culture founded on notions of place, kinship, parish, nation, religious belief and the continuity of tradition, has had to give way to a sense of fluid and permeable cultural identity. Cultural identity is re-imagined in terms of constant interrelation and mixing of cultural influences. Places are porous, more open, products of links with other places rather than exclusive enclosures marked off from the outside world. Against the idea of a closed cultural home, Northern Irish poets have increasingly recognised the experience of diaspora, of boundary crossing, which brings about a sense of the permeability and contingency of cultures, a simultaneous recognition of difference (between places and between cultures) and an essential interconnectedness.

Amidst the flux of contemporary capital, the poet, particularly the poet of the city, often feels all the more acutely the challenge of re-imagining home ground, its distinct heritage, history, style and vernacular forms, to set against the homogenising threat of (post)modernity. For the poets in this study, globalisation and multiple interconnectedness do not mean the end of place. The great task of the contemporary poet has been to map new concepts and images of home in a world of expanding horizons and dissolving boundaries, to propose new relationships between 'flow' and 'place', mobility and coherence, movement and settlement, within the new dynamics of deterritorialisation. A notable feature of this endeavour has been the way the new poets mobilise personal and collective memory, and revalue the indigenous resources of the local, the regional or the national, in pursuit of strategies of resistance against the potentially levelling, homogenising or banalising effects of global 'placelessness'. The poetry is marked by an assertion of difference and particularity as a kind of postmodern re-enchantment of place, while continuing to question systems, theories, the grand narratives of the past. If these poets still reflect the need to be 'at home' in the new and disorientating global space, they also acknowledge that they inhabit a world where there is no place for the absolutism of the pure and innocent. Often, they write about home when they have had the opportunity to leave: it is their mobility rather than their stability in place which is the condition of their writing. Belonging, shadowed now by migrancy, questing, questioning, confusion and homelessness, is no longer orientated toward the bounded state or abstract nation, but a place or places more personally and communally experienced. The virtually prescribed themes and procedures of Irish poetry in the past have been replaced by greater openness, freer imagination, wider horizons. As John Brown says of the twenty-nine 'emerging poets' from the North of Ireland who are featured in his 2006 anthology *Magnetic North*: 'If this collection exerts any magnetic pull whatsoever, it is simply through the whole diverse, unpredictable range and welter of subject matter that crop up when a poet sets to work. ... In fact, the whole strange world of words or language with its infinite patterns, connotations or chaos is the magnetic core of the book.'[47] In recognition of

---

[47] John Brown (ed.), *Magnetic North: The Emerging Poets* (Belfast, Lagan Press, 2006), p. 4.

this remarkable on-going, open-ended process of transformation in the political, social and cultural spheres, it seems appropriate at this point to show restraint in drawing conclusions about the evolving new poetics of place in Northern Irish poetry.

SELECT BIBLIOGRAPHY

Primary Sources

CIARAN CARSON
The Ballad of HMS Belfast (Loughcrew, The Gallery Press, 1999).
Belfast Confetti (Loughcrew, The Gallery Press, 1989).
First Language (Loughcrew, The Gallery Press, 1993).
Opera Et Cetera (Loughcrew, The Gallery Press, 1996).

PADRAIC FIACC
By the Black Stream (Dublin, Dolmen Press, 1969).
Missa Terribilis (Belfast, Blackstaff Press, 1986).
Odour of Blood (Kildare, Goldsmith Press, 1973).
Ruined Pages: Selected Poems of Padraic Fiacc, edited by Gerald Dawe and Aodán MacPóilin
    (Belfast, Blackstaff Press, 1994).
Sea: Sixty Years of Poetry: Padraic Fiacc, edited by Michael McKernon (Belfast, Multimedia
    Heritage Press, 2006).
Semper Vacare (Belfast, Lagan Press, 1999).
(ed.) *The Wearing of the Black: An Anthology of Contemporary Ulster Poetry* (Belfast, Black-
    staff Press, 1974).

LEONTIA FLYNN
These Days (London, Jonathan Cape, 2004).

ALAN GILLIS
Hawks and Doves (Loughcrew, The Gallery Press, 2007).
Somebody, Somewhere (Loughcrew, The Gallery Press, 2004).

SEAMUS HEANEY
Death of a Naturalist (London, Faber, 1966).
District and Circle (London, Faber, 2006).
Door into the Dark (London, Faber, 1969).
The Government of the Tongue (London, Faber, 1988).
The Haw Lantern (London, Faber, 1987).
Homage to Robert Frost, with Joseph Brodsky and Derek Walcott (London, Faber, 1997).
North (London, Faber, 1975).
Opened Ground: Poems 1966–1996 (London, Faber, 1998).
An Open Letter (Field Day Theatre Pamphlets, 1983).
Preoccupations: Selected Prose 1968–1978 (London, Faber, 1980).
The Redress of Poetry: Oxford Lectures (London, Faber, 1995).
Seeing Things (London, Faber, 1991).
The Spirit Level (London, Faber, 1996).
Sweeney Astray (Derry: Field Day Publications, 1983).
Wintering Out (London, Faber, 1972).

Bibliography: Primary Sources

JOHN HEWITT
Ancestral Voices: The Selected Prose of John Hewitt, edited by Tom Clyde (Belfast, Blackstaff Press, 1987).
The Collected Poems of John Hewitt, edited by Frank Ormsby (Belfast, Blackstaff Press, 1991).

MICHAEL LONGLEY
Collected Poems (London, Jonathan Cape, 2006).

PETER McDONALD
Biting the Wax (Newcastle-upon-Tyne, Bloodaxe, 1989).
The House of Clay (Manchester, Carcanet, 2007).
Mistaken Identities: Poetry and Northern Ireland (Oxford University Press, 1996).
Pastorals (Manchester, Carcanet, 2004).

MEDBH McGUCKIAN
The Book of the Angel (Loughcrew, The Gallery Press, 2004).
Captain Lavender (Loughcrew, The Gallery Press, 1994).
The Currach Requires No Harbour (Loughcrew, The Gallery Press, 2006).
Drawing Ballerinas (Loughcrew, The Gallery Press, 2001).
The Face of the Earth (Loughcrew, The Gallery Press, 2002).
The Flower Master (Loughcrew, The Gallery Press, 1982).
Marconi's Cottage (Loughcrew, The Gallery Press, 1991).
On Ballycastle Beach (Oxford, Oxford University Press, 1988).
Selected Poems (Loughcrew, The Gallery Press, 2001).
Shelmalier (Loughcrew, The Gallery Press, 1998)
Venus and the Rain (Loughcrew, The Gallery Press, 1984).

LOUIS MacNEICE
Collected Poems (London, Faber, 1987).
Selected Prose of Louis MacNeice, edited by Alan Heuser (Oxford, Clarendon Press, 1990).
The Strings are False: An Unfinished Autobiography (London, Faber, 1965).

DEREK MAHON
Adaptations (Loughcrew, The Gallery Press, 2006).
Collected Poems (Loughcrew, The Gallery Press, 1999).
Harbour Lights (Loughcrew, The Gallery Press, 2006).
The Hunt By Night (Oxford, Oxford University Press, 1982).
Journalism (Loughcrew, The Gallery Press, 1996).
Selected Poems (Loughcrew, The Gallery Press, 1991; Harmondsworth, Penguin Books, 1991).
(ed.) *The Sphere Book of Contemporary Irish Poetry* (London, Sphere, 1972).
The Yellow Book (Loughcrew, The Gallery Press, 1997).

JOHN MONTAGUE
Born in Brooklyn (Fredonia, NY, White Pine Press, 1991).
Collected Poems (Loughcrew, The Gallery Press, 2003).
Company: A Chosen Life (London, Duckworth, 2001).
Drunken Sailor (Loughcrew, The Gallery Press, 2004).
The Figure in the Cave (Dublin, Lilliput Press, 1989).
Poisoned Lands (Dublin, Dolmen Press, 1977; first published by McGibbon and Kee, 1961).
Smashing the Piano (Loughcrew, The Gallery Press, 1999).

SINEAD MORRISSEY
Between Here and There (Manchester, Carcanet Press, 2002).
The State of the Prisons (Manchester, Carcanet Press, 2005).
There was Fire in Vancouver (Manchester: Carcanet Press, 1996).

PAUL MULDOON
The End of the Poem: Oxford Lectures on Poetry (London, Faber, 2006).
(ed.) *The Faber Book of Contemporary Irish Verse* (London: Faber, 1986).
General Admission (Loughcrew, The Gallery Press, 2006).
Moy Sand and Gravel (London, Faber, 2002).
Poems 1968–1998 (London, Faber, 2001).
The Prince of the Quotidian (Loughcrew, The Gallery Press, 1994).
Shining Brow (London, Faber, 1993).
To Ireland, I (Oxford, Oxford University Press, 2000).

TOM PAULIN
Crusoe's Secret: The Aesthetics of Dissent (London, Faber, 2005).
The Day-Star of Liberty: William Hazlitt's Radical Style (London, Faber, 1998).
(ed.), *The Faber Book of Political Verse* (London, Faber, 1986).
(ed.), *The Faber Book of Vernacular Verse* (London, Faber, 1990).
Fivemiletown (London, Faber, 1987).
The Hillsborough Script: A Dramatic Satire (London: Faber, 1987).
Ireland and the English Crisis (Newcastle-upon-Tyne, Bloodaxe Books, 1984).
Liberty Tree (London, Faber, 1983).
Minotaur: Poetry and the Nation State (London, Faber, 1992).
A State of Justice (London, Faber, 1977).
The Strange Museum (London, Faber, 1980).
Walking a Line (London, Faber, 1994).
The Wind Dog (London, Faber, 1999).
Writing to the Moment (London, Faber, 1996).

JAMES SIMMONS
The Company of Children (Cliffs of Moher, Salmon Publishing, 1999).
Constantly Singing (Belfast, Blackstaff Press, 1980).
Judy Garland and the Cold War (Belfast, Blackstaff Press, 1975).
The Long Summer Still to Come (Belfast, Blackstaff Press, 1973).
Mainstream (Upper Fairhill, Galway, Salmon Publishing, 1995).
Poems 1965–1986 (Loughcrew, The Gallery Press, 1986).

Secondary Sources (books, essays and articles)

Adamson, Ian, *Cruthin: The Ancient Kindred* (Conlig, Nosmada Books, 1974).
Alcobia-Murphy, Shane, *Sympathetic Ink: Intertextual Relations in Northern Irish Poetry* (Liverpool University Press, 2006).
Allen, Donald (ed.), *The New American Poetry 1945–1960* (University of California Press, 1999).
Allen, Nicholas and Aaron Kelly (eds.), *The Cities of Belfast* (Dublin, Four Courts Press, 2003).
Andrews, Elmer (ed.), *Seamus Heaney: A Collection of Critical Essays* (Houndmills, Macmillan, 1992)
—— (ed.), *Contemporary Irish Poetry: A Collection of Critical Essays* (Houndmills, Macmillan, 1992).
Appignanesi, L. (ed.), *Identity. The Real Me: Post-Modernism and the Question of Identity*, ICA Documents, 6 (London, ICA, 1987).

Auden, W.H., and Christopher Isherwood, *Journey to a War* (London, Faber, 1973).

Barry, Peter, *Contemporary British Poetry and the City* (Manchester University Press, 2000).

Barthes, Roland, *Empire of Signs*, trans. Richard Howard (New York, Hill & Wang, 1993).

Bate, Jonathan, *The Song of the Earth* (London, Picador, 2000).

Bayer, Ronald, and Timothy Meagher, *The New York Irish* (Baltimore, Johns Hopkins University Press, 1966).

Bellow, Saul, *Herzog* (Harmondsworth, Penguin, 1985).

Benjamin, Walter, *The Arcades Project*, trans. Howard Eiland and Kevin McLaughlin (Cambridge, MA, Belknap Press, 1999).

Best, Steven, and Douglas Kellner, *Postmodern Theory: Critical Interrogations* (New York, Guilford Press, 1991).

Bhabha, Homi K., *The Location of Culture* (London, Routledge, 1994).

Bishop, Elizabeth, *Complete Poems* (London, Chatto & Windus, 1984).

Boland, Eavan, *Object Lessons: The Life of the Woman and the Poet in Our Time* (Manchester, Carcanet, 1995).

Bowers, Paul, 'John Montague and William Carlos Williams: Nationalism and Poetic Construction', *The Canadian Journal of Irish Studies*, 20, 2 (December 1994) pp. 29–44.

Bradbury, Malcolm, and James McFarlane (eds.), *Modernism: 1890–1930* (Pelican Guide to European Literature, 1976).

Braidotti, R., *Nomadic Subjects: Embodiment and Sexual Difference in Contemporary Feminist Theory* (New York, Columbia University Press, 1994).

Brearton, Fran and Eamonn Hughes (eds.), *Last Before America: Irish and American Writing* (Belfast, Blackstaff Press, 2001).

Brown, John (ed.), *Magnetic North: The Emerging Poets* (Belfast, Lagan Press, 2006)

Brown, Terence, and Alec Reid (eds.), *Time Was Away* (Dublin, Dolmen Press, 1974).

Buxton, Rachel, *Robert Frost and Northern Irish Poetry* (Oxford, Oxford University Press, 2004).

Capra, Fritjof, *The Web of Life: A New Scientific Understanding of Living Systems* (New York, Doubleday, 1996).

Carson, Ciaran, 'Escaped from the Massacre?', *The Honest Ulsterman*, 50 (Winter 1975) pp. 183–6.

Castells, Manuel, *The Informational City* (Oxford, Basil Blackwell, 1989).

Chambers, Iain, *Migrancy, Culture, Identity* (London, Routledge, 1994).

Cixous, Helene, 'Laugh of the Medusa', *Signs*, 1, 4 (Summer 1976) p. 879.

Clifford, James, *Routes: Travel and Translation in the Late Twentieth Century* (Cambridge, MA, Harvard University Press, 1997).

Conquest, Robert (ed.), *New Lines* (London, Macmillan, 1956).

Corcoran, Neil (ed.), *The Chosen Ground: Essays on the Contemporary Poetry of Northern Ireland* (Bridgend, Seren Books, 1992).

Corkery, Daniel, *Synge and Anglo-Irish Literature* (Cork, 1931).

Corner, J., and S. Harvey (eds.), *Enterprise and Heritage: Crosscurrents of National Culture* (London, Routledge, 1991).

Coupe, Laurence (ed.), *The Green Studies Reader* (London, Routledge, 2000).

Cresswell, Tim, *Places* (Oxford, Blackwell, 2004).

Crozier, M. (ed.), *Cultural Traditions in Northern Ireland* (Belfast, Institute of Irish Studies, 1989).

Cullingford, Elizabeth Butler, '"Thinking of Her … as … Ireland": Yeats, Pearse, and Heaney', in *Textual Practice*, 4, 1 (Spring 1990).

Dawe, Gerald, and Edna Longley, *Across a Roaring Hill: The Protestant Imagination in Modern Ireland* (Belfast, Blackstaff Press, 1985).

Dawe, Gerald, and John Wilson Foster (eds.), *The Poet's Place – Ulster Literature and*

Society: Essays in Honour of John Hewitt, 1907–87 (Belfast, Institute of Irish Studies, 1991).

Deane, Seamus (ed.), *Selected Plays of Brian Friel* (London, Faber, 1984).

———, *Celtic Revivals* (London, Faber, 1985).

de Certeau, Michel, *The Practice of Everyday Life* (Berkeley, University of California Press, 1984).

de Lauretis, Teresa (ed.), *Feminist Studies/Critical Studies* (London, Macmillan, 1986).

Deleuze, Gilles and Félix Guattari, *A Thousand Plateaus: Capitalism and Schizophrenia*, trans. Brian Massumi (Minneapolis, University of Minnesota Press, 1987).

Demetz, P. (ed.), *Walter Benjamin Reflections: Essays, Aphorisms, Autobiographical Writings* (New York, Schocken, 1986 [1932]).

Dobson, Andrew (ed.), *The Green Reader* (London, André Deutsch, 1991).

Donald, James, *Imagining the Modern City* (Minneapolis, University of Minnesota Press, 1999).

Duhig, Ian, '"Pictures carried with singing"', *Irish Review*, 12 (Spring–Summer 1992) pp. 165–70.

Duncan, James, and David Levy (eds.), *Place/Culture/Representation* (London, Routledge, 1993).

Duncan, Robert, *The Opening of the Field* (New York, New Directions, 1973).

Dunn, Douglas (ed.), *Two Decades of Irish Writing* (Cheadle Hulme, Carcanet Press, 1975).

Eagleton, Terry, *Literary Theory* (Oxford, Blackwell, 1996).

Eliot, T.S., *The Complete Poems and Plays of TS Eliot* (London, Faber, 1981).

Emerson, Ralph Waldo, *Selected Essays* (London, Penguin Classics, 1982).

Ferguson, Russell, et al. (eds.), *Out There: Marginalization and Contemporary Culture* (Cambridge, MA, MIT Press, 1990).

Ferris, Sarah, *Poet John Hewitt (1907–1987) and Criticism of Northern Irish Protestant Writing* (New York, The Edwin Mellen Press, 2002).

Fiacc, Padraic, 'Violence and the Ulster Poet', *Hibernia* (6 Dec. 1974) p. 19.

Fletcher, Ian (ed.) *Decadence and the 1890s* (New York, Holmes & Meier, 1980).

Foster, Roy, 'Varieties of Irishness', in M. Crozier (ed.), *Cultural Traditions in Northern Ireland* (Belfast, Institute of Irish Studies, 1989) p. 22.

Foucault, Michel, *The Archaeology of Knowledge* (London, Tavistock, 1972).

———, 'Of Other Spaces', *Diacritics* (Spring 1986) pp. 22–7.

———, 'Interview with Michel Foucault on Space, Knowledge and Power', *Skyline* (March 1982) pp. 17–20.

Frank, Waldo (ed.), *The Complete Poems of Hart Crane* (New York, Doubleday Anchor Books, 1958).

Genet, Jacqueline, and Wynne Hellegouarch (eds.), *Studies on Louis MacNeice* (Centre de Publications de l'Université de Caen, 1988).

Gilroy, Paul, *The Black Atlantic: Modernity and Double-Consciousness* (Cambridge, Harvard University Press, 1992).

Goldsmith, Oliver, *Poems and Essays* (London, Groombridge and Sons, 1858).

Goodby, John, *Irish Poetry since 1950: From Stillness into History* (Manchester University Press, 2000).

Graham, Brian (ed.), *In Search of Ireland: A Cultural Geography* (London, Routledge, 1997).

Graham, Colin, and Richard Kirkland (eds.), *Ireland and Cultural Theory: The Mechanics of Authenticity* (Houndmills, Macmillan, 1999).

Hall, Donald (ed.), *A Choice of Whitman's Verse* (London, Faber, 1989).

Hamilton, Ian (ed.), *Frost Robert: Selected Poems* (London, Penguin, 1973).

Hancock, Tim, 'Identity Problems in Paul Muldoon's "The More a Man has the More a Man Wants"', *Honest Ulsterman*, 97 (Spring 1994) pp. 57–64.

Heaney, Seamus, 'The Pre-Natal Mountain: Vision and Irony in Recent Irish Poetry', in

The Place of Writing, Emory Studies in the Humanities (Atlanta, GA, Atlanta Scholars Press, 1989) pp. 36–5.

Heidegger, Martin, *An Introduction to Metaphysics*, trans. Ralph Manheim (Yale University Press, 1959).

———, *Poetry, Language, Thought*, trans. Albert Hofstadter (New York, Harper & Row, 1971).

———, *Basic Writings* (New York, Harper & Row, 1977).

———, *The Question Concerning Technology and Other Essays* (New York, Harper & Row, 1977).

Hewitt, John, *Irish Times*, 4 July 1974.

Hollingdale, R.J. (ed.), *A Nietzsche Reader* (Harmondsworth, Penguin, 1977).

hooks, bell, *Yearning: Race, Gender, and Cultural Politics* (Turnaround, London, 1994).

Horton, Patricia, 'A "Theological Cast of Mind": Politics, Protestantism and the Poetic Imagination in the Poetry of Tom Paulin', *Literature & Theology*, 16, 3 (August 2002), p. 312.

Humm, Maggie, *Contemporary Feminist Literary Criticism* (Hemel Hempstead, Harvester Wheatsheaf, 1994).

Hutcheon, Linda, *A Poetics of Postmodernism: History, Theory, Fiction* (London and New York, Routledge, 1988).

Jacobson, David, *Place and Belonging in America* (Baltimore, Johns Hopkins University Press, 2002).

James, Henry, *The Art of the Novel* (New York, Scribners, 1934).

Jeffares, Norman A. (ed.), *W.B. Yeats: Selected Poetry* (London, Macmillan, 1974).

Johnstone, R., and R. Wilson (eds.), *Troubled Times: Fortnight Magazine and the Troubles in Northern Ireland 1970–1991* (Belfast, Blackstaff Press, 1991).

Kavanagh, Patrick, *Collected Poems* (London, Martin Brian & O'Keefe, 1984).

Kearney, Richard, *Transitions: Narratives in Modern Irish Culture* (Dublin, Wolfhound Press, 1988).

———, *Postnationalist Ireland: Politics, Culture, Philosophy* (London, Routledge, 1997).

Kendall, Tim, and Peter McDonald (eds.), *Paul Muldoon: Critical Essays* (Liverpool University Press, 2004).

Kerrigan, John, 'Earth Writing: Seamus Heaney and Ciaran Carson', *Essays in Criticism*, 48, 2 (1998) pp. 144–68.

Kiberd, Declan, *Inventing Irelands: The Literature of the Modern Nation* (London, Vintage, 1996).

Kinsella, Thomas, 'The Irish Writer', *Eire-Ireland*, 2, 2 (1967) pp. 8–15.

Kristeva, Julia, *Desire in Language: A Semiotic Approach to Literature and Art*, ed. Leon S. Roudiez, trans. Thomas Gora, Alice Jardine and Leon S. Roudiez (Oxford, Blackwell, 1980).

———, *Tales of Love*, trans. Leon S. Roudiez (New York, Columbia University Press, 1987).

Lacan, Jacques, 'The Mirror Phase', *New Left Review*, 51 (1968) pp. 71–7.

Larkin, Philip, *Collected Poems 1938–1983* (London, Faber, 2003).

Lathem, Edward Connery (ed.), *Interviews with Robert Frost* (New York, Holt, Rinehart & Winston, 1966).

Lathem, Edward Connery, and Lawrance Thompson (eds.), *Robert Frost: Poetry and Prose* (New York, 1973).

Levin, Harry, *Refractions: Essays in Comparative Literature* (New York, Oxford University Press, 1966).

Locke, John, *Essay Concerning Human Understanding*, ed. John W. Yolton, rev. ed. (London, Everyman, 1964).

Lodge, David (ed.), *Modern Criticism and Theory: A Reader* (London, Longman, 1988).

Longley, Edna, *Poetry in the Wars* (Newcastle-upon-Tyne, Bloodaxe, 1986).

———, *The Living Stream: Literature and Revisionism in Ireland* (Newcastle-upon-Tyne, Bloodaxe, 1994).

Lucas, John (ed.), *The 1930s: A Challenge to Orthodoxy* (Sussex, Harvester Press, 1978).

McAllister, Daniel, 'The Influence of American Poets on John Montague, Seamus Heaney, Derek Mahon and Paul Muldoon' (unpublished PhD thesis, University of Ulster, 2007).

McDonald, Peter, 'Incurable Ache', *Poetry Ireland Review*, 56 (Spring 1998) pp. 117–19.

McFadden, Roy, 'Review of *Collected Poems* by Louis MacNeice and *The Edge of Being* by Stephen Spender', *Rann*, 7 (Winter 1949–50) p. 11.

McQuade, Donald, et al. (eds.) *The Harper American Literature*, vol. 2 (New York, HarperCollins, 1993).

Massey, Doreen, 'A Global Sense of Place', in *Marxism Today* (June 1991) pp. 24–9.

——, *Space, Place and Gender* (Cambridge: Polity Press, 1994).

Massumi, Brian, *A User's Guide to Capitalism and Schizophrenia: Deviations from Deleuze and Guattari* (Cambridge, MA, MIT Press, 1993).

Moi, Toril (ed.), *A Kristeva Reader* (New York, Columbia University Press, 1986).

Montague, John, 'Tarzan Among the Nightingales', review of Heaney's *Sweeney Astray*, *Fortnight*, 2000 (December 1983) p. 27.

——, 'The Poet's Workshop', *The Guardian*, 27 November 1980, p. 11.

Muldoon, Paul, 'Paul Muldoon writes …', *The Poetry Book Society Bulletin*, 106 (Autumn 1980) p. 1.

——, 'Getting Round: Notes towards an Ars Poetica', *Essays in Criticism*, 48, 2 (April 1998) pp. 107–28.

Murphy, Shane, '"You Took Away My Biography": The Poetry of Medbh McGuckian', in *Irish University Review*, 28, 1 (Spring/Summer 1998) pp. 110–32.

Nisbet, H.B. (ed.), *German Aesthetic and Literary Criticism* (Cambridge, Cambridge University Press, 1985).

Olson, Charles, *Additional Prose* ([California], Bolinas, 1974).

O'Neill, Michael, 'John Montague and Derek Mahon: The American Dimension', *Symbiosis: A Journal of Anglo-American Relations*, 3, 1 (1973) pp. 54–61.

O'Toole, Fintan, *The Ex-Isle of Erin* (Dublin, New Island Books, 1996).

——, *The Lie of the Land: Irish Identities* (London, Verso, 1997).

Peacock, Alan J., and Kathleen Devine (eds.), *The Poetry of Michael Longley* (Gerrards Cross, Colin Smythe, 2000).

Poirier, Richard, *Robert Frost: The Work of Knowing* (New York, Oxford University Press, 1977).

'Polly Clark reviews The State of the Prisons by Sinead Morrissey', http://www.towerpoetry.org.uk/poetry-matters/july2005/morrissey.html

Pound, Ezra, *Selected Poems 1908–59* (London, Faber, 1984).

——, *Gaudier-Brzeska: A Memoir* (New York, New Directions, 1970).

Quinn, Antoinette (ed.), *Patrick Kavanagh: A Poet's Country: Selected Prose* (Dublin, Lilliput, 2003).

Redshaw, Thomas Dillon (ed.), *Well Dreams: Essays on John Montague* (Omaha, Creighton University Press, 2004).

Roethke, Theodore, *Collected Poems* (New York, Anchor Books, 1975).

Rosenthal, M.M., and Sally M. Gall, *The Modern Poetic Sequence: The Genius of Modern Poetry* (New York, Oxford University Press, 1983).

Schott, Webster (ed.), *Imaginations* (New York, New Directions, 1970).

Selden, Raman, Peter Widdowson, Peter Brooker, *A Reader's Guide to Contemporary Literary Theory* (Harlow, Prentice Hall, 1997).

Selected Poetry of Rainer Maria Rilke, trans. Stephen Mitchell (London, Picador, 1987).

Sered, Danielle, '"By Escaping and [Leaving] a Mark": Authority and the Writing Subject of the Poetry of Medbh McGuckian', *Irish University Review*, 32, 2 (Autumn/Winter 2002) pp. 273–85.

Shewan, Rodney, *Oscar Wilde: Art and Egotism* (London, Macmillan, 1977).

Sidney, Sir Philip, *The Countess of Pembroke's Arcadia (Old Arcadia)* (London, Penguin Classics, 1999).

Simmons, James, 'The Man Most Touched', *The Honest Ulsterman*, 46–47 (Nov. 1974 – Feb. 1975) pp. 66–71.

'Sinéad Morrissey in Malta: Workshops and Public Readings 22–30 Nov, 2003', http://www.geocities.com/inizjamedmalta/sinead_morrissey_in_malta.htm?2006100.

Soja, Edward, *Thirdspace: Journeys to Los Angeles and Other Real-and-Imagined Places* (Oxford, Blackwells, 1996).

Stallworthy, John, *Louis MacNeice* (London, Faber, 1996).

Stevens, Wallace, *Selected Poems* (London, Faber, 1976).

Thompson, Lawrance (ed.), *Selected Letters of Robert Frost* (New York, Holt, Rhinehart & Winston, 1964).

Thoreau, Henry David, *Walden or, Life in the Woods* (New York, Collier Books, 1962).

Tuan, Yi-Fu, *Space and Place: The Perspective of Experience* (London, Arnold, 1977).

Twain, Mark, *The Adventures of Huckleberry Finn* (Harmondsworth, Penguin, 1978).

Walder, D. (ed.), *Literature in the Modern World* (Oxford University Press, 1990).

Watson, S., and R. Gibson (eds.), *Postmodern Cities and Spaces* (London, Blackwell, 1994).

Williams, Raymond, *The Country and the City* (New York, Oxford University Press, 1973).

——, *The Politics of Modernism: Against the New Conformists*, ed. Tony Pinkney (London, Verso, 1989).

Williams, William Carlos, *Paterson* (New York, New Directions Books, 1963).

Wills, Clair, *Improprieties: Politics and Sexuality in Northern Irish Poetry* (Oxford, Oxford University Press, 1993).

——, *Reading Paul Muldoon* (Newcastle-upon-Tyne, Bloodaxe, 1998).

Woodward, Kathryn (ed.), *Identity and Difference* (London, Thousand Oaks, and New Delhi, Sage Publications, in association with Open University, 1997).

Wordsworth, William, *The Prelude* (Oxford, Oxford University Press, 1970).

Yaeger, Patricia, *The Geography of Identity* (Ann Arbor, University of Michigan Press, 1996).

Interviews

Brandes, Rand, 'A Dialogue with Medbh McGuckian', *Studies in the Literary Imagination*, 30, 2 (Fall 1997) pp. 64–74.

Brown, John, *In the Chair: Interviews with Poets from the North of Ireland* (Cliffs of Moher, Salmon Publishing, 2002).

Byron, Catherine, interview with Medbh McGuckian, 'A House of One's Own: Three Contemporary Women Poets', *Women's Review*, 19 (May, 1987) p. 33.

Casey, Daniel J., interview with John Hewitt, *Quarto*, 7 (1980–1) p. 38.

Frazier, Adrian, 'Global Regionalism: Interview with John Montague', *The Literary Review*, 22, 2 (Winter 1972) pp. 153–74.

Haffenden, John, *Viewpoints: Poets in Conversation* (London, Faber, 1981).

Healy, Dermot, 'An Interview with Michael Longley', *The Southern Review*, 31 (July 1995) pp. 558–9.

Johnston, Neil, 'Interview with Michael Longley', *Belfast Telegraph*, 30 Jan. 1996.

Keller, Lynn 'An Interview with Paul Muldoon', *Contemporary Literature*, 35, 1 (Spring 1994) pp. 11–12.

McDonald, Peter, 'An Interview with Michael Longley: '"Au Revoir, Oeuvre"', *Thumbscrew*, 12 (Winter 1998/9) p. 2.

'Michael Longley: An Interview with Margaret Mills Harper', *Five Points: A Journal of Literature and Art*, http://www.wbdelsol.com/Five_Points/issues/v8n3/ml.htm

Morris, Sawnie, 'Under the North Window: An Interview with Medbh McGuckian', *Kenyon Review*, 23, 3/4 (Summer/Fall 2001) pp. 64–74.

Morrison, Blake, interview with Seamus Heaney, 'Seamus Famous: Time to be Dazzled', *Independent on Sunday*, 19 May 1991.

Schrage-Früh, Michaela, interview with Medbh McGuckian, *in Contemporary Literature*, 46, 1 (2005) pp. 1–17.

'Sinéad Morrissey – Interview with Declan Meade', *The Stinging Fly*, 1, 14 (Winter 2002–03), http://www.culturenorthernireland.org/article_t1.asp?county=15&articleID=1970&cul

Smith, Kevin, 'Lunch with Paul Muldoon', interview with Paul Muldoon, *Rhinoceros*, 4 (1991) pp. 75–94.

Somerville-Arjat, Gillean, and Rebecca E. Wilson (eds.), *Sleeping with Monsters: Conversations with Scottish and Irish Women Poets* (Edinburgh, Polygon, 1990).

Thwaite, Mark, in interview with Sinéad Morrissey, http://www.readysteadybook.com/Article.aspx?page=sineadmorrissey

Wroe, Nicholas, 'A Sense of Place', interview with Derek Mahon, *Guardian*, 22 July 2006.

INDEX